CW01261761

SOLUTIONS OR SOCIALISM

SOLUTIONS OR SOCIALISM

Creating the Shining City on a Hill
or Becoming Comrades
with Russia, Iran, and China

Ron Mitori

SOLUTIONS OR SOCIALISM
Creating the Shining City on a Hill or Becoming Comrades with Russia, Iran, and China

Copyright © 2024 by Ron Mitori

All Rights Reserved. No part of this book may be reproduced or transmitted in any form by electronic or mechanical means now known or to be invented, including photocopying, recording, or information storage and retrieval systems, without permission in writing from the publisher, except by a reviewer, who may quote brief passages in a review.

ISBNs:
979-8-9914703-0-8 (paperback)
979-8-9914703-1-5 (hardcover)
979-8-9914703-2-2 (eBook)

Library of Congress Control Number: 2024921290

Published by RTM Publishers
Aubrey, Texas USA

Contents

Dedication vii

Introduction 1

Part I: Where the USA Is and Its Two Pathways 13

Chapter 1   How and Why Are We at This Existential Crisis? 15
    How and Why Did We Get There? 15
    Our Founding Principles Corrupted 17

Chapter 2   Corrupt Politics Has Hijacked Our Journey 25
    The Dems and the GOP 26
    The Most Recent Impactful Presidents 49
    Our Journey Continues to Be Hijacked 76

Chapter 3   Socialism and the Alternatives. 79
    Why Is Socialism So Awful? 80
    The Inspirations for US Socialism 87
    Checklist to Build a Socialist Country 93
    Conservatives vs. Regressives 95
    Is Free Market Capitalism Better? 96
    Shining City on a Hill 98

Chapter 4   The China Syndrome Facilitating a USA Collapse . . 101
    The China Syndrome 101
    The Perfect Storm 109
    Comparison to Collapsed Regimes 114

Likely Triggers for the Epic Collapse 122
　　　The Epic Collapse Timing and Result 131
Chapter 5　The Clash of the Titans 135
　　　Chapters 1 through 4 Recap 135
　　　China's Weak Underbelly. 138
　　　The US Off-Ramp Before We Crash. 142
　　　Our Binary Choice Decision 146
　　　The Journey of Another Way Forward. 150

Part II: Creating the Shining City on a Hill. **153**
Chapter 6　Elections **161**
Chapter 7　Government **181**
　　　Executive Branch. 182
　　　Judiciary. 195
　　　Congress. 197
Chapter 8　Crime. **215**
Chapter 9　Immigration. **229**
Chapter 10　Are We Prepared for the China Threat?. **247**
　　　China's Fictional New World Order. 247
　　　China's Unimaginable Journey 250
Chapter 11　Strategic Resources. **281**
　　　Water 282
　　　Energy 308

Part III: The Perilous Path We Followed. **351**
　　　Domestic Authoritarian Markers. 351
　　　Global Authoritarian Markers 362

Conclusion 367
　　　Here's How You Can Make a Big Difference Now. 371
　　　Which Path We Follow Is Up to Us 373

Notes 377

Dedication

This book is dedicated to those astute and often courageous individuals who lived under brutal authoritarian Socialist or Communist regimes and decided to leave everything behind and flee to the imperfect bastion of freedom, the United States of America. They are all deeply concerned that our liberties in the US are being taken away, reminding them of the oppressive countries they left. I have met many of these people, and here are a few highlights from some of their stories.

***

Lore's father had been a successful inventor and businessman who owned a factory that produced household goods during WWII. He was also part of the underground movement that did not support Hitler. Lore had lived with her parents and two sisters in a section of Germany that became East Germany. She wanted to study and become an archaeologist as a child, but war can change your dreams. At the war's end, that area was administered brutally by the East German police, and a wall was built separating East from West Germany. As the oldest, Lore went to live for almost three years with her grandparents because they could get a food ration card if they had a child in the house. One day, her mother had a hunch and packed her husband's suitcases and told him to leave, or the Russians would send him to Siberia. He did and escaped to nearby West Germany.

The next day, the Russians came to their house, kicked the mother and children out, and confiscated the home and the father's factory as theirs. They went to live with a friend while the mother made plans to escape. Months later, her mother gathered up Lore's sisters and dropped them about 20 feet off a bridge into their father's arms below in West Germany. The next day, Lore's mother escaped using another location by the same river. One year later in 1948, at age 12, Lore and a cousin crawled late at night through farmland with patrol and searchlights overhead to escape to the West. Finally, the family was reunited in West Germany. Some years later, the family successfully ran a restaurant and bar, where she met Jerry, who was serving in the US military.

Lore came to the US in 1959, and her immediate family followed afterward. She married Jerry and celebrated many happy years with him before his passing in 2024. As Lore's mom was nearing the end of her life in 2008, she told one of Lore's sisters that she felt sorry for the awful times they would face. Today, Lore recalls her mother's prophetic dying words, as she hardly recognizes the country that used to symbolize freedom to her and her family.

***

Alla left Ukraine when it was part of the Soviet Union. At that time, Jews in major cities like Moscow or Kyiv were not allowed in prestigious higher education unless they were "geniuses." They would have to go to smaller towns for a university education, and similar discrimination occurred in getting good jobs. There was no indoor plumbing in the rural areas away from major population centers, and people used outhouses for toileting. If you could afford to travel, you were often surveilled by the KGB. There was a lower class, an elite upper class, and hardly any middle class.

She recalls looking at people walking down busy streets, not making eye contact with anyone, and having a gloomy countenance on their faces, likely due to their dim outlook for the future. Despite the rich cultural history, including music and literature, this was not a place worth living in and raising a family. In the 1970s, emigration was allowed, and many

Jews left for Israel or the United States. Because she already had family in the US, Alla legally came here with her husband and child. She was pleasantly surprised to see people walking, smiling, and making eye contact. She gladly and proudly waited the required five years to become a US citizen.

She is appalled by the things she sees in textbooks, the replacement of freedoms with totalitarianism, and the re-writing of history, especially the glamorizing of the brutal history of Communism. She is hopeful because many people have woken up to the Socialist fires raging around them and are working hard to reverse that existential threat.

***

Venezuela was the wealthiest country in South America. Pablo was born there, and his father was a very successful lawyer. Pablo's cousin fled from Communist Cuba ruled by Fidel Castro to Venezuela to be near him and his family and escape Communism. One year later in 1999, Hugo Chavez became the leader of Venezuela and began dismantling the capitalism that made the country wealthy with a thriving middle class. That cousin realized he had seen this "movie" before in Cuba and wanted no part in it. He decided to leave after only one year in Venezuela. He convinced Pablo to join him and come to the US, but Pablo's father mistakenly thought his status and wealth would continue, so he remained. Pablo now sends money to him every month to keep him from starving.

***

I recently came across four other stories of immigrants to the US. One is the story of Peter Lumaj, who emigrated from Communist Albania. There are many similarities to the above accounts, and Peter is now a successful US attorney and has political aspirations in Connecticut, where he lives and works. If you search for him on the Internet, you will find the chilling details of his life under Communism.[1] Another is the story of Thomas "Drago" Dzieran, who fled Poland when it was under Soviet control. He came to the US, became a citizen, and retired as an accomplished Navy Seal.[2] The third is the story of Bob Fu, a Chinese pastor who escaped to the US from persecution in China and founded ChinaAid, which monitors Christian persecution in China.[3] The fourth one is of YeonMi Park, who wrote *While Time Remains*, her journey from North Korea to China to South Korea and the US, where she graduated from Columbia University. Her terrible treatment in North Korea and China is a horrifying indictment of the brutality of Communism.[4]

***

These immigrants from repressive Socialist or Communist regimes experienced the heavy hand of their authoritarian societies. They all see the seeds of that in full bloom now in the US and wonder why so many Americans are oblivious or don't understand how deadly the virus of Socialism and Communism is. And that it can soon permanently change the US so quickly.

This book is dedicated to all these clear thinkers, hoping they will continue to speak up and warn complacent Americans that the decay and horrors they see will worsen if we do not change course. We desperately need someone to be a leader and organize this group of immigrants as a voice of experience against Socialism and Communism and spread the message through Social Media and other channels.

This book is also dedicated to those Americans born here who are fully awake and taking action to stop the insanity we are experiencing. Some of them are mentioned in chapters of this book. These two groups of courageous truth tellers will determine whether the Supermassive Black Hole of Socialism will complete its mission to absorb the US. While the odds may be against us, do not underestimate the passion and impact of these brave believers in fixing our country and not destroying it.

You may want to read the book *Putin's Playbook* by Rebekah Koffler for an insight into a Communist dystopia by someone who lived through repression in the Soviet Union.[5] Continuing our authoritarian mandates, losing our freedoms, punishing courageous truth tellers, and absolving destructive intimidators and culture destroyers are recipes for an unhappy ending. Let's heed the warnings of those who fled similar intolerable and oppressive regimes.

Introduction

This book is the product of my deep personal concern for the future of our country. Our destiny to become the Shining City on a Hill has been hijacked. We have already crossed a frightening threshold and now stand on the verge of a New Dark Ages. The ruler of this era will be China, skillfully winning four-dimensional Global Domination Monopoly, while the US has been playing two-dimensional Checkers.

2024's election results have provided a singular opportunity to reverse course and adopt a "Solutionist" approach to realize our destiny. Regardless of political leanings, if you are frustrated by the incompetence of DC to solve long-standing problems and set the tone for a more peaceful and prosperous world than exists today, then this book is written for you. You will stop wondering why problems worsen and see why that is not accidental but intentional.

The original Dark Ages lasted 900 years, from the 5th to 14th centuries. It was enforced by the coalition of the RAGS (religion, academia, government, and science). The dogmas included mandated thinking that the world was flat and later that the sun and planets revolved around the Earth. Those mandates were enforced by public shame, loss of income, incarceration, and even death. That coalition is more powerful and present today (with phony "religion-type causes"), setting us up for a New Dark Ages, mislabeled as the Global Reset or the New World Order.

Within our country, a gigantic Wokesphere has been created by the Democratic-Socialist Uniparty that is home to the RAGS, along with leftist extremists, wokesters, globalists, a large portion of the media and the Deep State, and other destructive elements. This Death Star of the left is powered by unlimited political spending, including large anonymous "dark money" contributions. This corrupt money has become the mother's milk of politics and has allowed many elections to be bought. This was especially evident in the 2020 local and national elections. Fortunately, it failed in 2024.

The Wokesphere is their safe space echo chamber from which they silence different thinking and beliefs. Their tactics include Social Media banning or shadow banning someone's voice, public shaming, name-calling, firing from jobs, costly prosecution for non-crimes, fines, incarceration, and other persecution maneuvers. They should have no issue with challenging their beliefs if they have validity. Because they are unsound, they must resort to tactics used in Socialist, Communist, and terrorist countries, copying the RAGS of the first Dark Ages.

If we continue to sacrifice freedoms for authoritarian mandates, we will complete our transformation into the **USSA (United Socialist States of America)**. A big red carpet will welcome us into the expanding Alliance of Repressive Regimes and usher in the New Dark Ages.

This book will also explain how:
- China affected our 2020 elections.
- One Trump 2021 Cabinet appointment that was not made has resulted in the majority of the domestic and global chaos and strife we have today.
- Some say our deficit is actually $200 trillion more than the $35 trillion officially reported.
- A respected annual survey now ranks the US (the first country to land a man on the moon) 26th in math proficiency.
- Another respected annual survey ranks the US (the first country of significant size not to be governed by a king or other authoritarian tyrant) as 25th in the world for economic freedom.

- The wealthy have spent hundreds of millions to buy elections (over $1 billion just in 2024), and sometimes even receive substantial tax deductions for controversial causes.
- The Democrat-Socialists' "participation trophy" philosophy has produced disasters domestically and globally.
- Our federal government is so bloated with $2 trillion in annual regulation costs that if it were a country, our regulations would be the 8th largest country in the world.

Are you frustrated by the gamesmanship, bureaucracy, cost, and lack of success our government displays? Have you been the victim of the growing crime spree and the Police State some of us are living in? Are you disgusted by all the domestic and foreign media propaganda? Are you concerned about poor election integrity and lack of sane immigration practices? Are you troubled by China's ascendence and intentions and our decline? Do you know our policies risk having an abundant supply of clean water and energy? This book is written to address all these concerns.

Many of us (including me) have acted like frogs in a pot of increasingly warmer water. While we realize the temperature has increased, we either adapt or mistakenly think it will return to a cooler level. Fortunately, a growing number of us have awakened to this dangerous path we are on. Hopefully, we will influence many others before the water hits the boiling point and we are all cooked.

This book is for those feeling the heat and being overwhelmed or not seeing how dire our situation is and for those open-minded to crucial changes. If you are not convinced that much has fallen into place for a potential nightmarish domestic and global transformation, review the third section of this book, "The Perilous Path We Have Followed." You will find a recap from the book of the domestic and global markers we have passed on this journey into dystopia.

We have lost our way by corrupting our Founding Principles (identified in Chapter 1), especially Principle #9, about the citizenry exhibiting strength. Uncorrupt Free Market Capitalism has been largely replaced with Corrupt Capitalism, and corruption has spread throughout government, our institutions, and even our personal lives. Just as the US is polarized internally, so too are the world's countries as they choose who to align with. There is the US, as the #1 superpower with weak, ineffective leadership during 2021-2024 and the primary example of Corrupt Capitalism. While it has had some very positive global impacts, major US societal problems remain unsolved and have actually worsened.

We have created discontentment, polarization, and an opening for other ideas like Socialism—even though its lofty goals are fraudulently propagandized, never realized, and it produces high levels of oppression. That is the other choice for nations to align with – Corrupt Socialism promoted by the #2 superpower, China, with strong leadership and saying all the right things, even though their actions contradict their words. Unfortunately, China is deceptively gaining more alliance partners than the US due to our ineffectiveness and poor leadership.

I decided to research and write this book because I realized neither Corrupt Capitalism nor Corrupt Socialism (and its Communist and terrorist cousins) are good choices. I saw the need for a third choice, the Solutionism process powered by Uncorrupt Free Market Capitalism.

Also. this should not be "liberal vs. conservative" or "Democrats vs. Republicans." Those labels only trigger emotions, but say nothing about holding themselves responsible to create and implement solutions to problems. Most of the Solutionism steps are generally absent from governmental processes. Many successful businesses use some form of it. Its general absence in government causes problems not to be solved, which should have been the focus. Instead, we are bombarded with clever speeches, campaign slogans, laws, and Executive Orders that lack focused priorities, accountability, success measures, and reporting.

My 40-year business career has been primarily as a CFO, finding ways to make operations more efficient and profitable. This often required creative solutions, resulting in financial and operational benefits in different industries. This was the time to combine and adapt that problem-solving methodology with my strong life-long interest in politics and government.

Continuing to be a disgruntled spectator of the chaos and decline happening in the country was no longer an option. And wishing DC to do nothing because they seem to worsen our lives will not work. To stay in power, politicians want to brag about something they "accomplished," so let's make them use a process that holds them accountable to fix problems and report on their progress. My belief is that this is a common sense approach that most of us can embrace.

Solutionism has five steps that are often absent in our governmental processes:

- **Prioritize** the major problems to be addressed.
- **Itemize** key issues and their solution frameworks for each major problem.
- **Compose** the details required to implement each framework.
- **Measure** success with appropriate metrics for each problem and its key issues.
- **Explain** every six months the progress of the metric goals and modify the metrics, goals, or solution frameworks if needed.

Solutionism is supported by a core mindset consisting of the following:

- **Corruption** drainage and minimization.
- **Overwhelm** stoppage and elimination—e.g., illegal immigration.
- **Risk** acceptance for actions taken, **respect** for the lives and property of others, and **restitution** for any damages and harm caused. These are the 3 Rs from the Founding Principle #9 (being a strong citizenry) in Chapter 1.
- **Equal** rights and opportunities and not equal outcomes. This is from the Founding Principle #6 in Chapter 1.

The first two chapters of this book cover how the US has deviated from 12 key Founding Principles and how our politics has been a critical villain in that failure. Chapter 3 exposes how the authoritarian future we have been marching to will make us cousins to the world's repressive regimes. Socialists, Communists, and terrorists head those nations, and they ruthlessly stay in power by using their corrupt media to deceive their citizenry, eliminating their freedoms, and controlling them with mandates from a Police State – does that sound familiar?

Chapter 4 shows how China, a former struggling third-world Communist country, has deviously propelled itself to be the #2 Superpower. It also reveals how our US collapse could happen in this decade of the 2020s and how our path parallels the downfall of other great nations. The 5th chapter identifies the weaknesses of our primary adversary, China, and how to exploit them. That concludes the book's first section, "Where The USA Is Today And Its Two Paths Forward."

Not everyone (including me) is a history buff, but we need to understand our past, the ongoing decay, and the projections by respected authorities of when that implodes. The grounding of the first five chapters is essential. Only then does it make sense to urgently solve our national security problems. That is the book's second section, "Creating The Shining City On A Hill."

There are three chapters on internal national security threats: election integrity (the most urgent threat), government dysfunction, and widespread crime. That is followed by three chapters on external national security threats: immigration, our China threat preparedness, and restoration of an abundant and clean supply of strategic resources (especially water and energy). The major national security problems covered reflect the use of Solutionism to prioritize the major problems that threaten our existence as a freedom-loving constitutional republic.

The structure of these six national security chapters identifies major unsolved and worsening problems jeopardizing our future, their key issues, and solution frameworks for those key issues. The Solutionist methodology for the problems in Chapters 6 to 11 all have the first two steps of Solutionism, and some of the more straightforward problems may have more or all of the last three steps. For more complex issues, the last three steps will generally be better addressed by a collaboration of Solutionist-focused executive and legislative leaders.

Other problems with media, education, culture, infrastructure and the environment, taxation and government spending, senior security, and healthcare are not totally ignored. There is some coverage where they significantly impact national security. While very important, the fuller depth of their key issues and solutions would be too difficult to achieve and maintain without ensuring our national security first. We can still work on these other problems, but national security problems must be given strong priority. Also, including those problems and solutions fully in this book would make it too lengthy. Because each chapter in this book is meant to stand on its own, there is a small amount of repeated information in some chapters due to the relevance of the facts to more than one problem.

The solution frameworks in this book will make the US highly resistant to the increasing corruption, violence, and growing Police State that continues to plague us internally. Those solutions will also strengthen us and allow us to win the economic and political cold war we are clearly in with China. They can be a beacon of hope for those outside the US concerned about the global progression of repressive and bullying regimes. If the US sets a powerful example of success, those bullying regimes will become more fragile and susceptible to positive change. The rest of the world can live more peacefully and adopt the concepts in this book that are appropriate for them.

Most chapters in this book have been the subject of several in-depth 300 to 400-page books. Within that same range of pages, this book covers all 11 topics with enough depth to understand the seriousness of the problems, how they create a toxic mosaic, and the solutions needed. Some readers respond better to words, while others like numbers and data. Those not wanting to digest all the data can gloss over that and feel good that there is an economic foundation to support the narrative.

Don't be overwhelmed by or worry about retaining data. Just absorb the context of where we find ourselves today and the critical need for change. Whether you are a first-time or avid political book reader, this book has a compelling message: We must create our Shining City on a Hill or be the generation that exchanges our democracy for membership in the global New Dark Ages.

Besides all the researched information, the book should also shock you, entertain you with humor and sarcasm, and encourage you that there is a better path if we are courageous and determined to take it. Some of the subjects in this book change almost daily, especially in Chapters 2 and 11, which cover politics and strategic resources. Even if everything was updated when sent to the publisher, there will be new information surfacing, but the positive or negative trends will likely remain.

The format of this book is less traditional than others and often uses a more bulleted approach to make the reading and thought organization easier to follow. For those who like "CliffsNotes," some bolding is used to emphasize or highlight more significant information. There is much more bolding in Chapter 11, because it is the longest chapter and much of the more significant information is new to most of us.

This book is not written in a highly technical style, but how can we discuss financial and other issues without using a few economic terms and numbers? Many politicians run away from or distort numbers and hard facts. They often rely on campaign slogans, clever promises, and lies to get re-elected. This book researched our Founding Principles and strives in Chapters 6 to 11 to simulate the creativity, boldness, and common sense the Founders would use if they were here today to use those principles to deal with the mess we have created.

These solution frameworks do not follow the typical corrupt and phony solutions of "let's throw a few million or billion dollars at our problems" that make us feel good and think that solves our problems. Or "let's pass laws or Executive Orders in response to something," but seldom measure if those actions improve the situation and by how much.

Being a Solutionist should not be confined to one political party. However, the Democrat Party has purified itself and transformed into the Democrat-Socialist (D-S) Party. They have no interest in solving problems but are motivated to worsen them to bring about the one-party authoritarian government they long for. Republican Conservatives must purify and transform their party into one full of Solutionists. They must stop being good talkers of Conservative ideas that lack accountability and progress reporting.

The leftist transformation of the geopolitical landscape to the New World Order of Repressive Regimes that hate democracy and freedom is intensifying. Socialism, Communism, and terrorism are the geopolitical termites of the world. Many democracies are becoming more feeble as they replace their foundations of freedom, economic strength, and moral courage with a more authoritarian approach, cultural decay, and untamed bureaucratic spending (often foolishly chasing unattainable goals with expensive programs). The hungry termite regimes work to make these soft targets even softer, consume their resources, and redefine or eliminate their identity.

This is now happening in Europe with Russia's invasion of Ukraine; in the Middle East with Iran and its proxies terrorizing Israel and the presence of the US and international shipping; in the South China Sea with China's Hong Kong takeover, the bullying of its neighbors like the Philippines and Taiwan, and cultural erasing and war crimes against its minority Uighur, Mongolian, and Tibetan citizens; and globally with China's colonialist One Belt One Road agreements, often with financially struggling countries.

We represent the only viable chance to stop this growing colony of vicious termites from devouring the world's democracies. We must confidently execute our own internal terraforming to usher in a more peaceful planet by using a methodology like Solutionism and draining the corruption out of our institutions. This is the more difficult but more rewarding path.

The easier path is the one we are on. On this trek, many politicians, Deep Staters, institutions, media, extremists, wokesters, and Big Business believe our country is so large that it requires authoritarian control, just like the Socialist, Communist, and terrorist nations have. Those nations are powered by a brutally oppressive, flawed ideology that can only survive in a Police State. If we shift from Corrupt Capitalism to Uncorrupt Capitalism supported by a Solutionist process and return to our Founding

Principles, we won't need an authoritarian Police State to survive and thrive. We will become the Shining City on a Hill and can show the world a new approach that strengthens freedoms, rewards merit, and produces success and peace without the heavy hand of an oppressive government driven by power and control.

By modeling our new success, we can help soft-target nations harden into steel and resist the deceptive allure of repressive phony ideologies. This is the critical geopolitical climate change that must be fixed in the next few years. If not, global democracies will change from being endangered species to extinct ones, and the world will become much more intolerable than from a 1.5 degree rise in temperature. This New Dark Ages will have a much stronger Police State to stay in power indefinitely. Dystopian science fiction will become our reality unless we change our direction, our focus, and our process for succeeding.

These changes won't be easy, and the odds are against us – we must overcome the pervasive sense of inertia and resignation, the entrenched special interests, and the momentum of the degradation and corruption that has grown exponentially in the last few years. But the odds were against us when we successfully fought for our freedom from the superpower British Empire.

This is the time to change the odds for a vibrant, safe, free society and a peaceful world. We all need to be a part of the solution and stop acclimating to the increasingly nasty transformation we have been going through. If we do not laser-focus on solutions, the ugly face of Socialism (that has never worked for the citizens of any country) is only too happy to grab the reins of power to change the US forever into the USSA (United Socialist States of America). China's aggressive actions to take us down are perfectly paired with our inept foreign policy and our internal self-destruction and corruption. If we had not strayed so far from our Founding Principles, that transformation would have seemed unimaginable to most of us.

The awaiting Supermassive Black Hole of Socialism powered by the CCP of China has been gravitationally drawing the world dangerously close to itself, and each of us must decide whether to be a Solutionist or a Socialist. There is no lasting other identity or sitting on the sidelines. We must "wake up and woke down" and act like Solutionists by electing leaders who will be Solutionists accountable for measuring success and reporting results.

The results of our 2024 elections were an excellent first step. That must be followed by sound legislation with goals and regular progress reporting. We must not copy 2017-2020 where we heavily relied on Executive Orders that were reversed in 2021.

***

The prior "Dedication" section had several excerpts from the stories of non-US-born citizens. They came from repressive governments and now see the US becoming what they fled from. These are alien perspectives to most of us, but they are critical to shake us out of our complacency.

PART I

Where the USA Is and Its Two Pathways

Our country was created based on sound principles that governed the group that founded it. Those principles have been corrupted or abandoned, and decay has infected our institutions and the citizenry. Heavily to blame is the corruption of the government that sets a bad example for the rest of the country. Many politicians have forgotten their duty to serve the country's and its citizens' best interests and instead focus on their self-interests for power, prestige, and personal enrichment.

Taking their eyes off the ball of solving big problems has detoured us from becoming the Shining City on a Hill. It has opened the door to Socialism, which never works well for the citizens of a large or superpower country—just ask the Russians and the Chinese (and their persecuted Uighur, Mongolian, and Tibetan minorities). The same is true for the citizenry of lower-tier repressive countries like Iran, North Korea, Cuba, and Venezuela.

Many have glamorized Socialism and Communism, but they have cost the lives of 100–200 million people and minimized the personal freedom of millions more to achieve their dystopia of total government control. That carnage is primarily from Russia and China but also contributed to by every other repressive country.

China has been playing and succeeding at the long game of dethroning the USA. Only now are we waking up to the fact that they are not friendly competitors but an adversary that we have enabled and strengthened over the past 20 years with $6 trillion from our trade deficits with them. That made them a military, technological, and commercial powerhouse superior to us in many ways. They have stolen US tech, spied on us regularly, and worked within the US to create chaos and discontent.

Both the USA and China have serious flaws, and economically, "our emperors have no clothes." Both countries are in severe economic deterioration from massive government spending. Still, they put on a brave face to the rest of the world and, like a magician, use the technique of misdirection to distract everyone to the areas they want them to focus on. In many respects, China is worse than we are, and we need to expose that to win that "economic cold war" that gets hotter every day. China will not be happy just to dethrone the USA and lessen or eliminate our reserve currency status. Their goal is world domination, and they have been playing this game successfully for a long time, but most impressively since their admission into the World Trade Organization in 2001.

Many people realize our internal decay and external adversaries' economic actions against us and are sounding alarm bells and sending out SOSs.

***

These first five chapters expose the critical aspects of our destructive progression. It starts with Chapter 1, which examines the corruption of our Founding Principles and other reasons for the dangerous path we have taken.

CHAPTER 1

How and Why Are We at This Existential Crisis?

We are more than halfway pregnant with Socialism, which has intentionally and somewhat unnoticed crept into our society. Many on the left are now feverishly rushing to give birth to this full-blown Socialist Frankenstein country. They are destroying our culture, borders, language, First and Second Amendment protections, election integrity, and economic well-being with deficits and debt bombs as far as the eye can see.

These fanatics are overwhelming our country with millions of illegal aliens allowed to stay here, excessive crime in blue states that is not counted or prosecuted, and weak foreign policy with our allies and adversaries. Once in place, Socialism is nearly impossible to replace due to the brutal, repressive policies and the elimination or corruption of many rights and freedoms. The exception to that rule might be those few countries that may have Socialist-level taxes but with a culture of a high work ethic, innovation, and Capitalism (and without a brutal internal Police State).

How and Why Did We Get There?

The main reason we are staring into the abyss of the Black Hole of Socialism is that we have not solved our most important problems. Before discussing solutions to our problems in-depth, we need to understand how we got to this awful place.

1. We have not vigorously embraced our Founders' principles. While they were imperfect people, we have corrupted their thoughtful and strong principles. This first chapter covers that corruption.
2. Politicians have played footsies with an ideology that wants to destroy our country as we know it and replace the freedoms and opportunities we are known for with the dystopia of an authoritarian Socialist government. How many politicians today are problem solvers, not just good talkers delivering nice soundbites? More about this misconduct and foolishness is in Chapter 2.
3. This has metastasized and put us on a dangerous path to Socialism and the end of our global leadership position while also placing the entire world in peril. Chapter 3 presents more about the dystopian effects of Socialism and Communism. Our road to implosion is on track with other historic implosions and is laid out in Chapter 4, along with China's singular focus on dethroning the US and creating a New World Order. Absent a strong and free US, the global bullies will overpower the smaller free countries. Chapter 5 examines China's weaknesses and a strategy to exploit them to win this Existential Cold War.
4. We have not understood the inclinations of the individual human spirit, as well as those of their countries and the world collectively, to:
   - Believe in something larger than themselves
   - Be frustrated with significant problems that remain unsolved
   - Become self-absorbed and bored with a comfortable life

That can easily seduce us to the corruption of extreme power, prestige, or personal enrichment. It can also make us highly susceptible to new or trendy alternative philosophies, like Socialism, and elevates constructs like extreme climate activism into the status of a religion with passionate believers. CCP propaganda in TikTok heavily influences our youths' political worldviews, as demonstrated by the campus unrest and takeovers following TikTok's pro-Hamas propaganda after their war crimes and butchery of Jews on October 7, 2023.

The Reboot Foundation published "The TikTok Challenge" in May 2023. **The report discovered that nearly 60% of young adults with the TikTok app would rather surrender their right to vote than give up Social Media—closer to 65% for those in the 13–17 age group. 23% of youth spend more than 4 hours daily on TikTok alone.**[1] **Giving up freedom and civic participation for amusement and anti-US propaganda would be a bad trade.**

5. Because of that ignorance, we have never fleshed out and pursued Ronald Reagan's lofty ideal of what embodies the "Shining City on a Hill." Chapters 6 through 11 transition from the path towards Socialism to the way forward with Solutionism, including problem-solution frameworks for major national security problems to realize that ideal.

Every major civilization that has failed and been replaced has resulted from not solving its problems and living on past glories. At some point, the internal decay of citizens and institutions and the politicians' focus on their power, prestige, personal enrichment, and staying in control creates the environment for the downfall. Internal tyranny is replaced with the external tyranny of a more focused, determined, and stronger country.

Our Founding Principles Corrupted

The courageous men whose "treasonous" actions risked their lives and possessions were uniquely different individuals. Still, they all subscribed to a set of principles as they drafted, agreed, and signed our Declaration of Independence, Constitution, and Bill of Rights. While others cite more than 25 principles, that list has been reduced to the 12 below that are highly connected to our decline, along with our corruption or abandonment of each of them.

1. **We Have Inherent and Inalienable Rights That Are Independent of the Government**
   - The Founding Fathers were religious people who believed in the free expression of whatever religion someone professed. Today, we seldom hear leaders sincerely speak of "God," but only the "good" they claim that the government can do for us if we only obey all the mandates they burden us with. Many believe government can grant or remove our rights to life, liberty, and the pursuit of happiness.
2. **The Right to Govern Derives from the People**
   - The power should rest with the people, but many have ceded their power away and have been brainwashed to believe that power "for their own good" rests with power and profit-hungry institutions, politicians, and big businesses like Social Media, Big Pharma, Mainstream Media, Sports, and Entertainment.
3. **Limited Representative Republican Form of Government**
   - The Founders designed co-equal branches of the federal government with the executive, legislative, and judicial branches, and most governmental powers were reserved for strong state and local governments. We now have a bloated federal bureaucracy that often uses the Executive Branch to push out dictates (like the monarchy we left), backed up with legislative approval or antagonism depending on the party in power.
   - The Supreme Court and lower-level courts are often ideologically politicized in their rulings. The powers of the state and local governments have eroded since our founding and are belittled when in opposition to federal desires. The designed checks and balances have been severely compromised.
   - This is especially concerning with the militarization of federal administrative agencies (Chapter 7), along with the neutering of many local law enforcement organizations and the war on lawful private gun ownership.
4. **A Written Constitution to Be Followed**

- A written constitution that provided protection from the government and that could only be changed by amendments was a key concept. At that time, the most powerful country, England, did not have a constitution. Today, many shortcut "scholars" are creating their interpretations of that document without making the essential effort to amend it as was the original intent. They have no respect for the Constitution or Bill of Rights that blazed a trail for most other democracies.

5. **Private Property Rights and the Rule of Law**
   - The enjoyment of private property rights was fundamental to incentivize citizens and create security for them. The Founders' very lives and liberties were dependent on this concept. How often have we seen people's businesses looted or burned to the ground with little to no consequences for the perpetrators? The degradation of society into the early stages of chaos and anarchy can be seen in many places. We have devolved to live in a real-life version of the dystopian movie *The Purge*.
   - We have witnessed the defunding or abolishing of police, lack of pursuit for those breaking legitimate laws, and the lack of prosecution or minor punishments for those who assault and murder or destroy businesses, public buildings, or other public property. Many look to silence and prosecute those who speak up or defend their fundamental rights. These are all signs of severe decay on the road to chaos and anarchy. That eventually will replace our government with a more authoritarian one.
   - This is an eerie reminder of what the Red Guard youth did in China in 1966. They destroyed culture and history in books, art, and statues and renamed streets that were not "red enough" for Chairman Mao's Socialist/Communist revolution.[2]

6. **All People Are Created Equal, and the Government's Role Is to Protect Their Equal Rights and Not Provide Equal Outcomes**
   - While the stain of slavery brought to the colonies by British and African slave traders created much inequality and misery

for many years, we fought in the Civil War to re-establish that concept of rights for all and abolish slavery. We passed a Civil Rights Act in 1964 that codified non-discrimination and equality of opportunity into law. But today, we have many who profit from chaos, anarchy, and victimization. They act as if we have done little to change the dynamic of slavery and privilege. Instead, they teach people of color to embrace victimhood and ethnic whites to feel guilty for slavery's evil they had no hand in creating or perpetuating.

- The painful reality is that slavery has existed since the dawn of human life, and only in the last 200 years has it been significantly reduced. We can never succeed in legislating how people choose to feel about their fellow citizens. Still, we have a Constitution, a Bill of Rights, a Civil Rights Act, and lawyers willing to provide redress against those who demonstrate prejudice in the commerce of our society. Let's use those moral avenues and ignore the immoral race baiters profiting from anarchy, chaos, and victimhood.

7. **The Most Prosperity Occurs in a Free Market Economy with Minimum Regulation**
    - Much bureaucratic and needless regulation was eliminated in the prior national administration's embrace of a free market economy. The current administration has reversed much of that, using regulation and mandates to control and stifle the free market. Our country was founded on freedom, but we are ranked 25th in the latest Heritage Foundation's annual survey of economic freedom.[3]

8. **General Education Is Mandated and Considered Essential for Survival**
    - Today, our public schools are not keeping kids interested in completing their education, and too many drop out of high school. The result is that the USA ranks 26th in the world in math proficiency. We do not universally have clear paths for children to follow

based on their interest in getting a job, being an entrepreneur, or going to college to acquire knowledge for specific careers after high school. Regardless of their desired path, high schools should teach basic life skills to everyone while in high school. Not everyone will benefit from or should go to college, and the cost of college has been allowed to be increased astronomically through "unlimited" government loan funding, regardless of cost or benefit.
- This has created a massive student debt load. While states and locales retain some rights relative to education, the federal government still has a heavy hand in it with federal funds, which it can dole out or withhold depending on how DC and its bureaucrats embrace what is being done locally. The Tenth Amendment gave the primary responsibility for education to the states, but that has been seriously corrupted.
- Thankfully, school vouchers are gaining popularity and acceptance. They can positively affect education by creating a competitive level playing field to produce a better educational result (especially for minority populations) than the monopoly of public education and its leftist indoctrination.

9. **Free People Must Stay Strong to Survive**
    - When our country was founded, our strength was visible in many of the new Americans in 4 areas: physical, mental, emotional, and moral strength. That has decayed.
    - **Physical strength**—The National Center for Health Statistics reports that **41.9% of US adults aged 20 and older are obese, and 73.6% are overweight.** For youth aged 12–19 years, 22.2% are considered obese.[4]
    - **Mental strength**—With our waning science interest and math proficiency, we have lost much of our military and space leadership. Many are obsessed with escaping reality or being entertained through video games, TV, streaming, music, movies, Social Media, drugs, gambling, and porn. We have become a borderless country,

and we give children participation trophies to protect them from the sting of a loss. But absent those stings of defeats and the euphoria of winning, we rob our children of the tools they need to survive and thrive as responsible adults.

- **Emotional strength**—Many have become soft, squishy Americans, determined to flee to their safe spaces and be sheltered whenever points of view contrary to theirs are being expressed. Their cowardice is expressed when they put on the cloak of victimhood and anonymously troll Social Media, game apps, and other media. They passionately seek to have contrarians (including their friends and relatives) canceled or "unfriended" rather than engaging in genuine adult conversation.

  Instead of continuing the legal mandate to protect the rights of minorities, we have shifted into having extreme leftist ideas jammed down our throats. We allow minors to be secretly coaxed into gender surgery and biological males to crush biological women in women's sports. Our tolerance of alternative lifestyles has transformed into terrorism against the majority by the minority.

- **Moral strength**—In geopolitical matters, we do not recognize the evil and repression of authoritarian governments. We stupidly use that same "participation trophy" mentality to appease those bullies. That weakens us and the rest of the world and makes us dangerously more susceptible to ever-increasing aggression because bullies do not respect weakness, and appeasement actually encourages more aggression. Placating Hitler is a glaring example, and history has many others. Weakness and appeasement of evil bullies always end badly for the appeasers.

- It can be challenging for us to be strong in the face of the obsession with personal and business profits and personal and governmental power and control. This plays out in people being de-platformed from Social Media, financially and professionally penalized or shamed, and canceled or imprisoned for speaking the truth. There

are countless examples of this truth persecution—like the origins of COVID-19, the Chinese treatment of Tibetan, Mongolian, and Uighur people, mask mandates, COVID-19 therapeutics, and the high value of natural immunity for those who have recovered from the virus. How long can we continue on this path and still expect a good outcome?
- These evaporations of our strength result from our abandonment of **the 3 Rs** implied in this strength principle (**risk, respect, and restitution**). Some weak people want protection from the microaggressions of words from others and are not responsible for the risks they choose to take. They show a lack of respect for individuals and private property, and dishonorable and weak people do not accept the need for restitution for damages and harm they cause.

10. **The Family Unit Is Considered Fundamental to the Viability of Our Society**
    - With poor welfare and other governmental regulations, we have financially discouraged family formation while encouraging divorce and abortion on demand, all of which have shredded this vital fabric of our society.

11. **Federal Debt Is Toxic to Freedom Just Like Being Taken Over by Another Country**
    - After its creation in a time of need (like a war or depression), federal debt was to be eradicated as soon as possible and not passed on to the following generation. Today, the federal deficit and its related interest keep increasing exponentially with no end in sight, and we have not had a balanced budget for many years. We are living off the financial benefit we enjoy of being the world's reserve currency. But as a shock to many, that will likely disappear with seismic-like consequences unless we implement significant financial and other remedies.
    - There are considerations being given to copying China and implementing a US digital currency to take the focus off the inflated

US paper currency or implementing financial discipline. That will allow the government to track everyone's income and spending and penalize those not behaving as they "ought to." Read the book *Undressing Bitcoin* by Layah Heilpern for more information.[5]

This direction will not end well if we continue on this D-S path.

12. **The USA Has the Destiny to Be Exceptional and an Example to the World.**
    - We have had a decent run for nearly 250 years and have done some exceptional things. We sacrificed over 1.1 million lives (many more were seriously wounded) fighting in our own Civil War to end slavery and being the critical domino that won WWI and II, saving the world from control by tyrants.
    - But we never achieved that "Shining City on a Hill" ideal. We are on a downward trajectory and strongly being pulled into the Black Hole of Socialism. Unless a course correction is vigorously pursued, our run as the #1 freedom-loving Superpower will be over long before the climate catastrophe predicted by some. And if the US gets pulled into that void, any hopes for saving the world from climate issues and achieving global peace will be totally destroyed.

***

These are 12 Founding Principles that were key to our birth as a revolutionary new type of government. Our corruption and abandonment of these are primarily responsible for the increasing decline we see today. The next chapter examines how our politics have played a leading role in that corruption and derailing of our quest to become the Shining City on a Hill.

CHAPTER 2

Corrupt Politics Has Hijacked Our Journey

We lost three historic figures within a few short years in the 1960s with the assassinations of JFK, RFK, and MLK. They had the potential to be strong, unifying influences in our country during turmoil, and the wounds to our country's psyche have been lasting. Many of today's politicians are often guided by how to get re-elected from large donations by unions, companies, other organizations, or wealthy individuals. These "public servants" are focused too much of the time on the power and control they can wield, the prestige they want to retain, and the opportunities for personal enrichment. They leave public life financially much better. Despite the Reagan and Clinton years, when bipartisanship poked its head out of the murky DC swamp and some positive legislation passed, that glimmer of hope sank into the abyss with only a rare 9/11 resurfacing.

We must recognize that bipartisanship is dead and stop trying to chase this non-existent relic of the past. Due to the 2024 Democrat-Socialists (D-S) election losses, they will clamor for bipartisanship, and no one should listen. We should remember how they acted in 2021 and 2022 as if they had a mandate, even though their House majority was razor-thin and the Senate was tied. Their ignoring of Republicans must be copied by the Republicans.

All of our major unresolved problems involve some level of tyranny and corruption. That naturally flows from the tyranny and corruption of our politics and government, primarily from the left, with the willingness of too many Republicans to go along for the ride to join the Uniparty. We must rid ourselves of these destructive forces. Let's see how they have infected us.

The Dems and the GOP

The Dems

There are practically no courageous Democrats who possess the JFK Democrat gene and will sometimes stand their ground on principle against the draconian desires of most of their colleagues. Those JFK principles included a strong military for purposes of our defense and deterrence to bolster world peace, top-notch education, lower taxes, strong world leadership and making tough decisions, fighting corruption, and wanting citizens to identify what they could do for the country instead of what the country can do for them. These vestiges of a bygone era are no longer a part of the D-S party and are the opposite of what they stand for. With their rebranding as Socialists, the D-S Party has left these few JFK Democrats and now treats them with contempt and intimidation until they submit or leave the D-S Party.

All the other Democrats are outright Socialists or cowardly go along with that agenda. They do not seek solutions for our country but instead insist on pushing changes that destroy it with their ideology. The result is that these autocrats create or magnify problems. They then try to "solve" them by creating costly mandates and the need for ever-increasing taxes to fund the explosive government growth. The goal is to flex their power by recklessly spending money to look good and buy votes with that bribery. While Dems like to refer to themselves as Progressives, there is nothing progressive or democratic about Socialism.

You will rarely see their preferred but misleading labels used in this book. Democrat or liberal is kindly replaced with leftist or

Democrat-Socialist (a label some of them already use), and Progressive is replaced with wokester, regressive, or repressive. Many are substituting these more correct terms for the misleading false-positive labels that are not now representative of the D-S. Regressive policies actually are a regression to Socialist policies that have never worked and are repressive to anyone other than the ruling class and wealthy elites and oligarchs.

These people often act like animated children, especially when they don't get their way. Many suffer from a toxic malignancy called TDS (Trump Derangement Syndrome). Trump's style, words, and actions ignite hysteria in them, as he is an existential threat to the establishment of the New World Order and their participation in it.

As immature children, they are generally ignorant of the importance of robust national security, fiscal and budgetary responsibility, proper use of cost and benefit analysis in their feeble attempts to make good laws and budgets, and a complete lack of understanding of economics and business (most have had almost no business success). The D-S somehow think Socialism creates a great society, but where are the examples of success?—China, Russia, Iran, North Korea, Venezuela, or Cuba? There are no good blueprints for any country to follow.

D-S politicians do not understand or agree with common sense economics because that goes against their pursuit of power and control. Instead, they rely on the flawed pronouncements of people like their economics "guru," Paul Krugman. His misstatements about climate issues and Red State successes due to lower taxes and effective and appropriate spending controls are easily found online. For just one example, a December 18, 2019 article by Alexander Green titled "Meet the World's Worst Economist" [1] lists several Krugman blunders:

- In a 1998 Time magazine's 100th-anniversary issue, he said that "the growth of the Internet will slow dramatically" and that "By 2005 or so, it will become clear that the Internet's impact on the economy has been no greater than the fax machine's."
- He told a former Fed Chairman to "create a housing bubble to replace the Nasdaq bubble."

- Before one of Argentina's loan defaults, he said that the country was a "remarkable success story."
- He called the US "just a bystander" in worldwide energy just a few months before the US passed Russia to become the world's largest oil and gas producer.

To this must be added his stunning 2023 comment that if the reserve currency status of the USD were lost, it would be "hardly earth-shattering for our economy." [2] With Saint Krugman leading the Socialist pilgrims in praise of Socialist countries and policies and disparaging Free Market Capitalism, it is no wonder his flock venerates him. It is understandable that the faithful on the left are well-versed in Krugman's "Upside Down" imaginary world but totally clueless about fundamental economics.

Another leftist guru made similar bizarre comments about this "exorbitant privilege" the US enjoys from being the world's reserve currency. They said we should borrow as much as we want because the world will gladly give it to us. [3] This ridiculous thinking can bring the "house of cards" crashing down. One day, when the world no longer buys into it, that privilege disappears.

This pot of Socialist stew not only consists of this profoundly flawed economic lunacy but also several D-S earned Party labels along with their toxic ingredients:

1. The **Party of Immigration Insecurity**—No workable programs for illegal immigration just let everyone in and then pass a law later to give them the right to vote (presumably for anyone with a D next to their name).
2. The **Party of Military Insecurity**—Under primarily Democrat Presidents, thousands of American and allies' lives were lost in wars poorly waged in Korea and Vietnam. The current President was responsible for a disorganized and hasty retreat in Afghanistan that cost 13 US lives and abandoned a strategic base we built (at the cost of at least $96 million) next to China's border, as well as billions in

cash and state-of-the-art military hardware, and left behind countless Americans and Afghan supporters of the US. [4] It is next to impossible to find the exact value of items abandoned as that is either suppressed in search engine queries or hidden by Biden's regime. Estimates range from $7–$100 billion.

He stopped a military shipment to Ukraine in January 2022 that could have deterred the Russian invasion or significantly reduced Ukrainian casualties (estimates of 200,000–400,000), millions displaced, thousands of children kidnapped by Russia, and the turning of many cities into rubble. Ukraine asked for planes to control their skies and prevent deaths and devastation, but the D-S foolish "participation trophy" principle that guides them will not allow Ukraine to win and Russia to lose. The US is spending much more than it would have had to if it had supplied the planes at the start, and now we and our allies are not keeping up with the need for artillery that has had to fill the void from the missing planes at the onset. A war must have a winner and a loser, but the D-S mind will not accept that.

They used the same guiding principle with Iran. When King Joseph assumed the US throne, Iran was nearly bankrupt due to sanctions imposed by the prior administration. The people of that country detest the ruthless rulers of Iran and would likely have revolted and ousted them. With little money to pay the military and their affiliate terrorist organizations in the Middle East, peace could have broken out.

However, the guiding principle that there should be no winners or losers resulted in those sanctions not being enforced by King Joseph and his Court. Iran today is funding terrorism and still has cash reserves in excess of $70 billion. They trained Hamas just before the savage attack on Israel on October 7, 2023. Other terrorist proxies funded by Iran have joined it. Joe is ensuring that Iran's ruthless leaders will not be losers.

Our King and his Court are pressuring Israel not to eradicate Hamas, replace the governance of Gaza, win the war Hamas started, or provide for Israel's security. Years ago, Ukraine and Taiwan were coerced to give up their nuclear weapons programs in exchange for the promise of their security. But that is not working well for them with the D-S "participation trophy" principle. The D-S are promising to defend South Korea if they agree not to develop nuclear weapons in response to the North Korean threats.

The D-S despise the military and don't know how to use them properly. They display weakness by trying to compute the exact amount of proportional response to an adversary's aggression. Instead, they should be guided by the US Marines' motto that America should be "No better friend. No better enemy." The goal should be to win a war or conflict as quickly and decisively as possible.

3. The **Party of Science (sometimes)**—That is their claim, but only if it benefits their narrative. If not, it is labeled "disinformation."[5] They even had a new person (who has spread disinformation about stories contrary to the left's narratives) as the head of a new Disinformation Governance Board (DGB—you know, like the KGB). In his prescient book, *1984*, George Orwell called this the Ministry of Truth. This is where the Socialist government tells you what is true or not according to what benefits them. Due to the poor reception this DGB received, it was put on pause but not canceled. The censorship appetites of this administration could not be halted for very long. On June 16, 2022, they announced that Madame VP Giggles herself would lead a task force for this.

Their 6-month goal was to give Biden a "whole of government" outline. That is code for more bureaucracy to permeate and distract all agencies. The first foray is more palatable than before – how to stop internet violence, abuse, and gender harassment. Would it not be simpler to require Social Media (SM) platforms to focus attention on de-platforming people and organizations that post violent and abusive content (that would be clearly defined)? They can easily get the job done, if SM redeploys resources they now use to de-platform people with content they do not like or disagree with. But that shift would not get the D-S any additional voters. After this initial venture is under their belt, you are guaranteed that the D-S will return to their broader agenda of censoring information they don't like.

4. The **Party of Awful Education**—They oppose charter schools and school choice (especially in underserved areas) that would create competition, improve schools and education, and reduce the impact of public school indoctrination.
5. The **Party of (In)Tolerance**—They have no tolerance for ideas other than their unsuccessful ones. They are driven by their insecurity, hatred for those who speak of the alternatives, and loudly telling others to be fearful of and shut down speech about those alternatives.
6. The **Party of the Poor**—By keeping people impoverished and giving them more "free stuff" and dependent on the government, the D-S feel they will capture most of their votes.
7. The **Party of Participation Trophies**—This is a key driver for most of their domestic and foreign policies. Earlier in this section, we shed light on how it has affected their strategy after WWII not to win wars and respond with proportionality instead of delivering a severe blow to the adversary. Unfortunately, that means we are viewed as losers.

   This principle is naïve, senseless, and produces deadly results. But it shows up in domestic policies as well. In the 1950s, significant abuse was exposed at many mental health institutions. Instead of fixing the problems, many people were released onto the streets, and institutions were closed.

   We do not want those people to be stigmatized as losers, so they are free to be homeless and not receive the mental health treatment they need. We don't want anyone to feel unwelcome in our country, so we have wide open borders, and some 30 million are here illegally. They receive all kinds of benefits to not make them feel like losers. The same philosophy is at play with student loan forgiveness funded by taxpayers. Our education system is dumbing down for students, so no one feels smarter or the need to improve. There are many other "beneficiaries" of this gateway to Socialism principle.

Socialism claims to provide equal outcomes for everyone, and there is little incentive to excel. And there are supposed to be no winners or losers – all are equal. But the ruling class, elites, and oligarchs are much "more equal" than everyone else, making them really the winners. And that "everyone else" is equally struggling to get by – basically, they are losers. A Socialist government's promise of equality (parroted by our DEI, ESG, and CRT advocates) cannot create the utopia it promises because it is a fantasy built without a proven foundation and inserts oppression and indoctrination as a poor substitute.

8. The **Party of Power and Big Money**—Slavery was the hallmark of the Democratic South, and that made them powerful enough to form a Confederacy and fight a bloody Civil War. Then, they had a crucial presence in the Ku Klux Klan to continue their racism. They even had racists in Congress, including a Senator who was a former KKK leader. As D-S saw their opportunities for power shifting, they pivoted to hang on and increase that power. They became advocates for free expression, unionization, and civil rights (how ironic). They preach to people of color that they should ignore successful Conservative people of color but vote for any other person of color regardless of their successes or bitter and flawed ideology.

Now, they are on the verge of establishing one-party (the Uniparty) rule by providing a home for disaffected Republicans and Independents and cults, promoting CRT, ESG, DEI, victimhood, reverse racism, legalizing 30 million illegal aliens to capture their votes, and destroying the Constitution and Bill of Rights. They are well-financed by wealthy globalists, big business, and wokesters (many from Social Media). The D-S purposely traded places with the Republican Party by abandoning the working class in favor of securing the Big Money party title to fund their ideologies and increase their power.

All of that leads the way to Socialism, where the rule of law is replaced with the rule of the power to persecute and prosecute political opponents and anyone not following their mandates or dogma. That is from the playbook of the governments in Russia, China, Iran, and all of our other would-be fellow repressive comrades in other countries.

The world premiere of this hideous movie opened throughout the US during COVID-19. Like a chameleon, they have managed a monumental transformation from the Party of Slavery to the Party of Socialism and exploded their power exponentially. With the wide-open southern border, they have reclaimed their Party of Slavery tag since many trafficked across that border wind up as sex slaves (some children) to pay back the Mexican cartels who trafficked them across the border. The D-S can be found chasing power and votes for re-election. All the while, the D-S have managed to fool a lot of Americans. Shame on us.

9. The **Umbrella Party for Cults**—They have fallen in love with the climate and environmental alarmists, extreme transgenderists, social justice warriors, woke globalists, and any other energetic zealots they can conscript as foot soldiers. Those cults are not just exempted from the D-S participation trophy nonsense but actually promoted to win their causes regardless of the consequences. Their environmental solutions are to penalize America (which has done better than most countries) and give a free pass to mega-polluting nations.

    Instead of championing relatively simple things that make a big difference, they seek impractical answers that cripple the US— things like ending our energy independence and preaching about solar and wind power exclusively, along with only battery electric vehicles not adequately supported by the power grid. These policies enrich China, which smartly uses our virtue-signaling appetite to produce and supply most of the solar panels and lithium-ion batteries for electric cars and some of the windmill components.

10. The **Party of Double Standards, Lies, and Lack of Transparency**— The D-S views voters as inconvenient speed bumps to be duped and navigated around and not as most-valued stakeholders to be persuaded with facts and actual solutions to problems. This mindset helps to

hide all of their ineffective policies by drawing attention to the misdeeds (real or concocted) of Republicans while ignoring their own.

They cannot admit their missteps or that they were wrong and made a mistake, unless it was not taxing, regulating, spending, or growing government more. They project any guilt they have onto Republicans and accuse them of the evil they are doing. This is projection, a common psychological occurrence that makes the projector feel good about identifying evil but placing it on someone else and not themselves where it belongs. Churchill once said, "A lie can travel halfway around the world before the truth puts their paints on." Here are a few examples.

- Tara Reid credibly accused Biden of unwelcomed physical contact in 1993 when he was a Senator. The DOJ sealed that warrant from scrutiny, and the *New York Times* was very unsupportive on its website. [6] She sued the NYT, but a left-leaning NY court ruled she had to pay the NYT legal fees. By contrast, Stormy Daniels's claims against Trump were given the utmost respect.
- Doug Mackey satirically poked fun at Hillary Clinton's presidential run in 2016. He was vilified, arrested, tried, and convicted in April 2023 and was facing up to 10 years in prison. [7] He was later sentenced to 7 months in jail for poking fun at an elite member of the ruling class. A known Hillary supporter did a similar election satire against Trump, but there has been no arrest or trial.
- Because authorities ushered them into the Capitol Building, most of the January 6 people might only be guilty of trespassing but have been denied fair treatment. A 2–1 opinion from the DC Court of Appeals said probation and imprisonment "may not be imposed as a single sentence" for a petty offense. This ruling can change harsh penalties against trespassers not involved in destruction or violence. [8] But most rioters, looters, arsonists, and murderers in the summer of 2020 were not even arrested or tried.
- The 1887 Electoral Count Act was considered valid when the D-S used it to object to the results of the 2004 and 2016 elections.

Corrupt Politics Has Hijacked Our Journey 35

However, when Republicans used it to raise objections to the 2020 election results, the D-S rushed a bill through to change that law. [9] That law was good when D-S used it but not good when Republicans used it.

- Gag orders have been issued to Roger Stone and Trump to prevent them from exposing the nonsense involved with their judicial targeting by the left. But Stormy Daniels is free to speak openly about her allegations against Trump.
- Trump's residence was raided with a show of military-style force; even though his documents were packed by the General Services Agency when he left the White House; he had the right to verbally declassify anything as President; he was in negotiations with the National Archives about the return of some documents; and his records were securely stored. His attorneys were prohibited from participating, and the intruders demanded that residence security cameras be turned off. There would be no documented proof of any unlawful shenanigans that occurred.
- By comparison, Biden is the King of Illegally Retained Classified Documents. He allegedly paid expensive lawyers to pack/purge his documents at the Penn Biden Center and his two Delaware homes from his time as VP or Senator; they were poorly secured at multiple locations (including Chinatown and the trunk of a car); he had no right to declassify documents as a Senator or VP: and his lawyers were allowed to go through them (even though they may have had insufficient clearance for handling "top secret" documents). Biden's handling was called "self-reporting," but that involves admitting a crime to authorities, which did not happen. [10]
- The Special Counsel for Biden's illegal retention of classified documents reported that he "willfully" and "knowingly" kept classified documents in inadequately-secured multiple locations and even shared information with a ghostwriter he was using. However, he indicated he would not prosecute him due to his multiple examples of poor memory because a jury would likely

see that as an excuse. [11] That is why the DOJ is sometimes called the Dept of Injustice.
- Referring to the raid on Trump's residence, Biden said, "How one – anyone could be that irresponsible. And I thought – what data was in there that may compromise sources and methods… And it's just – totally irresponsible." Look in the mirror, Joe, and see your own words condemning you.
- Queen Pelosi appointed two Never-Trumper Republicans to her January 6 show committee. The process always followed before was to let the minority party appoint their representatives. [12] These people joined the compromised Swalwell and Schiff, the proven liar. Schiff doctored evidence against Trump's Chief of Staff, Mike Meadows, and repeatedly lied about having strong evidence against Trump.
- Trump's attorney paid Stormy Daniels $130,000 to settle her allegations against Trump. The NY DA has been pursuing Trump for mis-categorizing that payment in his financial records and inflating the value of his properties. He is seeking a wealth transfer of $370 million from Trump to NY even though no lender has lost any money. [13] According to the Federal Elections Commission (FEC), here are just a few D-S election misdeeds. [14]
  o 1996—$719,000 FEC fines for fundraising with foreign nationals to meet with Clinton and Gore (according to the September 21, 2002 LA Times).
  o 2008—$375,000 FEC fine for the Obama campaign for not disclosing 1,300 large donations totaling nearly $2 million (according to the January 7, 2013, US News).
  o 2012—Obama campaign alleged to have received $30 million from a Malaysian charged with embezzling $4.5 billion from the Malaysian sovereign wealth fund and apparently hiding out in China (according to the April 5, 2023 Townhall).

- 2016—$100,000 FEC fine for the Hillary campaign for treating the Fusion GPS role in the "Russia Hoax" creation against Trump as a legal expense.

Remember that most Socialist politicians have had minimal experience with a real job or running a real company. Socialism is just something the cult left gravitates to; it is their primary religion that they cult-like follow passionately regardless of the facts of its failures and oppression. Many of them are lawyers or political science majors interested in creating roadblocks, talking a good game, and getting re-elected. That is why the door has been opened wide for Socialism – people lacking in solution skills have not successfully addressed our problems.

The history of the Democrat Party as the Insatiable Party of Power is a journey from Southern slavery and the Ku Klux Klan to any other cause that can enhance that lust for power. Their moral compass is replaced with a power compass. In the process, they destroy our Constitution and the Bill of Rights, precious governing documents that few countries have. For an eye-opening read on this, consider Mark Levin's latest book, *The Democrat Party Hates America*, [15] or listen to him or Dan Bongino. Both are on the radio, and Mark is also on TV on Fox News.

How do you know if you are a Democrat-Socialist? What follows is not a complete list but some of the more telling signs.

You Might Be a Democrat-Socialist If:

1. You subscribe to identity politics and diversity based on race and gender identity but not on diversity of opinion. It is telling that many D-S foot soldiers never connect the dots from identity politics to the violence it spawns.
2. You seldom apologize because your ideas are a true "gospel," so you can never be wrong.
3. You feel energized, powerful, and patriotic when you "unfriend" or have a hand in "canceling" someone because their beliefs are not aligned with yours.

4. You fully support government mandates to control behavior, regardless of any contrary evidence against them.
5. You believe the D-S government cares for you and always looks out for you in everything they do, especially when they give free or nearly free stuff or provide additional financial support from other taxpayers.
6. You think the current government bureaucracy (especially the federal) is not excessive and that its current size or even larger is needed to oversee the country's well-being.
7. You engage in arguments over issues with the weaponry of emotion rather than clear logic supported by the facts, and you appreciate others on the left who do the same.
8. You avoid confrontation with differing ideas by retreating to your safe space or shouting down those ideas to prevent or disrupt their free speech expression.
9. You deny comedians their free speech to make fun of everything like they have done in the past (as they did in the 1970s televised "roasts" of famous people). Everyone was okay with the humor directed at them and laughed with the audience and roasters because they understood the importance of comedy and laughter. That was the golden age of comedy when comedians were equal-opportunity offenders, and programs like *Saturday Night Live* and *Laugh-In* reveled in that freedom. There was no running to safe places or claiming victimhood. Now, making jokes about leftist individuals or causes is not tolerated, while f-bombs and racist comments directed at whites, Asians, and straight people are enthusiastically encouraged.
10. You support participation trophies where no winners learn the joy of victory from hard work, and no losers know the sting of coming up short and having to regroup to do better next time.
11. You believe your ends (causes) justify any means necessary for them, so no amount of crime, violence, lies, or corruption is off-limits if needed to accomplish your "worthy" ends.
12. You see no problems with the D-S hypocrisy or double standards.

13. You are suspicious of the military, the police, other law enforcement, and successful businesses that do not donate to the D-S.
14. You do not know or understand economics but genuflect at the mention of Paul Krugman, who knows more than you (even though he refuses to change his thinking when his pronouncements are shown to be wrong).
15. You support the D-S playbook that prefers using activist judges, bureaucrats, and Executive Orders rather than legislative courage to amend the Constitution or pass new laws. The exception is for laws representing virtue signaling and helping wealthy donors or spreading more money around as "bribes" for votes and the expansion of government to burden and harass those not in the Uniparty.
16. You disagree with the characterization that the D-S has become an umbrella Socialist "religious" cult of cults, where it has fashioned a coalition of one-issue activist zealots against climate change, environmental decay, gun ownership, and for abortion on demand, LGBTQ⁺ immersion (rather than tolerance and equal treatment), and violence against whites, Asians, law enforcement, and businesses.

    These activist and sometimes violent cults have become religious denominations for their faithful, where they doggedly believe their doctrines, regardless of facts to the contrary. You may even be a member of one of the many "religions" the D-S host. They will do all they can to suppress and shut down any dialog against their doctrines. This is reminiscent of how the leadership of the CCP, theocratic Iran, Russia, ISIS, and other terrorist groups operate and require blind obedience.
17. You believe wholeheartedly in the New Testament of white guilt and shame and Black victimology and support calling whites racist for any reason. Meanwhile, Blacks supporting segregation from whites and making racist remarks against whites is approved.
18. For societal problems, you believe in the leftist simplistic prescription of throwing a few hundred billion dollars at each one and calling them resolved. This strategy has been on steroids since the 1960s. The

Great Society ushered in by Lyndon Johnson has been a colossal flop. The US history of its % of people living in poverty is very interesting.

- 1950—**32.2% or nearly 1 out of every 3 people lived in poverty.** Some think these were "the good old days," but not really for those 1 out of 3.
- 1967—**14.2% This massive reduction of 18% in 17 years** in the % of poverty occurred before any significant government interference from the failed War on Poverty.
- 2020—**11.4% A measly 2.8% reduction that took 53 years and more than $28 trillion of government interference.** And how much of this resulted from just giving individuals stipends rather than empowering them to elevate themselves and their families with job training and opportunities? No business or initiative could have performed as terribly as the War on Poverty and been considered a success story. **When adjusted for inflation, that "Poverty War" spending of $28 trillion is equal to 3 times the cost of all US military action since the American Revolution.**

The D-S would want us to ignore the last 57 years of failures to uplift people and minimize welfare, out-of-wedlock births, single-parent families, violence, and corruption. The magnitude of these problems continues to increase—keep using the leftist playbook and keep spending megabucks because it feels like the right thing to do.

19. You believe taxes should be increased, even though evidence shows tax decreases result in a stronger GDP from all economic groups, and the wealthy are incentivized to invest more heavily in equipment and employment from the added savings.
20. You like the Mainstream Media news, woke entertainment, and woke or corrupt leaders and their virtue-signaling companies. You refuse to believe the latest IRS data dump for 2018. It shows **the top 1% paid 40% of all income tax revenue, which was more than the bottom 95%. And the bottom 50% paid an average of 3.4% tax rate vs. the 25.4% rate paid by the top 1%.** You ignore facts and agree with

giving more "free" stuff to the lower economic rungs and increasing taxes on the upper rungs.
21. You follow the D-S pronouncements, including the ruinous paths outlined by Saul Alinsky and Cloward-Piven in Chapter 3, even if you were unaware of their strategies.
22. You claim to be an Independent or Republican but join this Uniparty by default with your identity as a globalist, squishy Republican, RINO, or Never Trumper, and others who vote based on a politician's style, slogans or soundbites (that are usually not true), instead of the results that they deliver.
23. If you answered yes to many of these, enough said—You are a wokester member of the D-S!

The GOP

Those Republicans who believe in the bipartisanship of the past are living in a past that no longer exists. Politics has become a blood sport game, and mild-mannered, squishy Republicans who want to get along by playing along are falling into the hands of the Socialists and wokesters to join their Uniparty. The "game" should be to solve problems and report progress, not winning elections any way you can. The Tennessee Conservative publishes "the RINO Report." It identifies RINO sell-out actions and real Conservatives and their accomplishments. That Tennessee example should be followed at least annually in every red and purple state. Fortunately, we have some Republican governors who model Solutionism.

Many Republican leaders have lost their spines or have been corrupted by the swamp. They need to encase themselves with a thicker skin and not continue to work with representatives of this failed D-S ideology fueled by hatred. That world view is determined to take down the America we know and replace it with a regressive and repressive power structure where only the elites, oligarchs, and wokesters will be contented and satisfied as long as they behave the way the government wants them to. Democrats have unapologetically made the transition from Democrats to D-S. Recently, in New York, they bragged about the US becoming Socialist.

Even GOP fundraising is pathetic, with endless and irritating texts, phone calls, and emails for many Republican candidates running for office. These current wasteful shotgun campaigns create a lot of revenue for the marketing companies running them. Without a strategic focus each month that donors can embrace and feel good about, donors have to pick which of the numerous appeals they will donate to. Coupled with the D-S now being the party of Big Money, this flawed strategy shows up in the data. 2023 was the worst fundraising year for the GOP since 2013; when adjusted for inflation, it was the worst in 30 years. Yet they kept the same person in charge of the Republican National Committee.

Instead, they should focus on monthly recurring donations and communication highlighting some of the Conservative problem-solvers (not globalists, RINOs, Never Trumpers) that are being supported. There should be four separate funds (for Senators, Representatives, the President and VP, and state and local races).

That change would still leave the door open for individual donations to favorite candidates but would end much of the constant clutter and donor decision-making. For Republicans, whether it is CPAC, the RNC, or some other organization, it needs to have a team of strategists (not one self-serving powerful person).

That team needs to be responsible for the best strategic allocation of donations (which could actually be more significant due to less marketing costs and broader appeal) to ensure as many victories as possible. Each donor cannot be knowledgeable about all the candidates and their races; many good ones are being short-changed because of the current process, and others may be getting much more than they need. This is covered more fully in Chapters 6 and 7 and includes significant financial limits on election interference by wealthy individuals.

Unfortunately, Republicans are poorly equipped to squash this existential threat from the left. They are splintered into squishy Republicans, Never Trumpers, Conservatives, RINOs, and globalists. They need to become Republican Solutionists (R-S) focused on solutions that successfully address issues with critical accountability and reporting aspects.

Except for their stand on raising the debt limit and passing budgets, all of the House legislative efforts they have done had minimal chance of passage by the Senate and being signed by Biden in 2024. That attention should be redirected to D-S corruption investigations and budget preparations. A unified Republican Party can minimize the impact of the D-S Party. The Dems know who they now are; it is critical that the GOP coalesce around a solution-focused identity and terminate their membership in the D-S Uniparty of Corruption.

We should put aside our arrogance and learn from world leaders practicing Solutionism. The new Conservative Prime Minister of Italy, Giorgia Meloni, is focused on changing her Socialist, corrupt government. Italy has partnered with Germany for the innovative construction of a hydrogen pipeline from North Africa to Bavaria. [16] Meloni has been working on other thorny issues like immigration. Almost immediately, the new Argentinian president, Javier Milei, has done even more to reverse his country's failed 100-year Socialist history of bankruptcy, inflation, bloated bureaucracy, and excessive government spending. What has he done, and what are the reactions?

- Devalued the currency by 50% [17]
- Eliminated the Ministries of Culture, Labor, Health, and the DOE [18]
- Fired all government workers hired in the last year [18]
- Is stopping all public projects in part due to rampant corruption
- Plans to reduce energy subsidies and reduce the government % of GDP by 4.2% [19]
- The local stock exchange was up 30% in one month, and the IMF, carrying $40 billion of Argentinian debt, has approved his bold but necessary moves.
- In January 2024, he called on wealthy businessmen and politicians meeting in Davos, Switzerland, to reject Socialism and embrace "Free Enterprise Capitalism." He said Western leaders are "co-opted by a vision of the world that inexorably leads to

Socialism, and thereby to poverty." [20] That sounds very similar to the concepts in this book.
- Of course, the leftist-loving media discredits him and labels him a "right-winger" or even "far right." He is receiving pushback from Argentina's entrenched Socialists in his country's Congress and may have to appeal to his citizens with a referendum. The left's power and control drivers blind them to their country's 200% inflation caused by Socialist policies that do not work.

Many former Dems have left the radical D-S party and joined the GOP. To name a few—Will Pierce, a Dem campaigner; Elon Musk, entrepreneur-owner of X, Tesla, and SpaceX; Brandon Straka, a gay man who started the "walk away" movement 6 years ago; and Tulsi Gabbard and RFK Jr. former Dems who campaigned for President as Dems. We need to give them a more robust alternative to the D-S by minimizing the Never-Trumpers, squishy Republicans, globalists, and RINOs. If Republicans became Solutionists like Meloni, Milei, and Trump, success would breed more success, and leftist dystopia would disappear.

Politicians should be guided by how they can serve the people they represent (not their big donors), solve problems facing our country and the world, and be happy to leave after serving a few terms. Those who make this their life are generally in it for the wrong reasons. If they did a good job, they should be happy to let someone else share their passion to make life better for Americans and return to a career they were trained for. That was the protocol of our country's early leaders, which has been lost, at least in the 20th and 21st centuries. Power, prestige, and personal enrichment should not be parts of their unspoken guiding principles. In Chapter 7, some remedies for governance are laid out to change the rampant corruption in this most critical part of our country's infrastructure.

The 2024 Dems and GOP Campaign Strategies and Tactics

Successful businesses generally follow a form of Solutionism when they prioritize their problems (especially focusing on the most significant threats), itemize the key issues, develop solution frameworks and fill in the details, set metrics to measure success, report monthly or quarterly on the results, and adjust as needed. Before this, they set and create alignment with their vision, mission, values, and strategies. How have the D-S and the GOP campaigned in 2024?

The D-S are nearly 100% aligned with their vision and mission to destroy our culture and Constitution and will use any strategies necessary (especially the ones in the next chapter by American Marxists) to bring about their Marxist dystopia. Only a handful of D-S dare to speak out (at the risk of being ousted). Most are fervent believers in the doctrines or go along to keep their power and prestige. The GOP is not as unified because they have not purified their party as the D-S have. Also, some are actually members of the Uniparty. Despite this, they have effectively focused on registering new voters, early voting, and election integrity. Advantage on alignment to the GOP, whose focus was more productive.

The D-S have passionately set their 2024 priorities: defeat Trump any way they can and win the Senate and House. They know if they win all three, their D-S Uniparty will be enshrined forever in power and control over our lives and our country (with the quick legalization of all 30 million undocumenteds, who will primarily vote D-S). The GOP has the opposite priority concerns and was more passionate since many saw the existential threat of a D-S victory. Major advantage on priorities and enthusiasm to the GOP.

The D-S have identified their key issues for 2024—negatively impacting Trump; improving their odds by dumping cognitively-impaired and scandal-ridden Biden and replacing him on the ballots with Kamala; retaking the House and holding onto their Senate majority; solidifying their support base; increasing their favorable media propaganda; and making societal problems worse to make others more open to D-S phony "solutions."

The GOP has the key issues of exposing the negative impacts of the Biden-Harris administration; informing voters of Kamala's role in those impacts and her Socialist positions; winning the House and the Senate by demonstrating success with a Republican House majority and a unified Senate minority, supporting the Republican presidential ticket; solidifying and expanding their base; and promoting and marketing their positive vision and policies to voters—Advantage on key issues to the GOP whose marketing took advantage of D-S missteps— calling Trump Hitler and his supporters garbage, and lying about their and Trump's positions on key issues.

The D-S identified their tactics for the 2024 elections to:
- cripple Trump financially (using taxpayer funds) and distract him with multiple absurd legal proceedings,
- disparage other Republicans if Trump was ruled ineligible to run,
- accept having a 3rd party candidate for President because they know in a two-person race without any illegal votes, Biden would have lost and Kamala as well.
- continue to spend more than the GOP (because of their brand as the party of Big Money contributors) to win the Presidency, the House and the Senate,
- favor a lack of election integrity by opposing a House voter ID bill (198–5) and promoting easy to cheat practices—mass mail-in ballots with ballot harvesting and drop boxes, and many in-person voting machines that cannot be cross-checked to paper ballots,
- solidify their base of cults in their Uniparty with Executive Orders and speeches,
- increase the favorable propaganda coming from the media, Social Media, their cults, and the Deep State in their Uniparty (particularly focusing on the extreme makeover of Kamala's "do nothing" term as VP, horrible record as Senator, DA, and Attorney General for California, and hiding her extreme Socialist pronouncements),
- continue lukewarm support for Israel and Ukraine,
- and continue inaction against the rampant spending bonanza, unprosecuted crimes, homelessness, people leaving the job market, intimidation of political enemies, and open borders to try

to convince foolish voters that if given a chance, the D-S will fix the very problems they have caused or worsened.

The GOP correctly went after Biden's mental capacity and corruption. In the debate with Trump, Biden's mental and physical deterioration were apparent. The pass and cover-up he had gotten from the media suddenly disappeared. The media feverishly re-branded Kamala as the new shiny object to adore, even though she was an integral part of the Biden-Harris fiasco administration.

But she was heavily responsible for the fiascos of the Biden-Harris administration that she supported. As the VP, she cast the deciding vote on many Senate bills, including $1.7 billion spending monstrosity that unleashed inflation on the country; as the border czar, she has been responsible for some 12 million undocumenteds crossings in 2021-2024; and as the "last person in the room," she is fully behind our disastrous withdrawal from Iraq, tepid support of Ukraine and Israel (including the US campus unrest targeting Jewish students). Domestically, she has responsibility for inflation and migrant cost and crime. Internationally, she had a strong hand in reversing the peace and lack of major wars scenario Biden-Harris inherited, putting the world on the verge of WW III by driving Russia, Iran, China, and North Korea into a strong alliance.

Comrade Kamala (the cackling chameleon) is proposing things to be done in her administration, but why weren't they done as part of the Biden-Harris administration. Why is she not faulting Joey for not doing them, and why did she cover up his declining mental capacity for 4 years. She has lost over 90% of her VP staff due to her management style. Imagine how she will treat world leaders, a Cabinet, and the American people. While her current staff floated complete changes to her radical Socialist positions on many issues before the election, most voters did not buy it—since she claims her core values have not changed. This was just a ploy to confuse voters and collect some of their votes.

Harris is clearly on the record against fracking, ending health insurance and reducing senior healthcare access by instituting Medicare for all (including the undocumenteds), and raising taxes to historic levels to grow government. She has had excellent chameleon mentors in Obama and Biden to demonstrate the technique.

She could never have survived the normal 2 years of campaigning required in a primary and general election. Her IQ, insincerity, and style would have been exposed. This Queen of Word Salads usually speaks only with a teleprompter, because without it, she speaks as if talking to kindergarteners. The D-S strategists knew this and believed their undemocratically forcing Joe off the ticket and limiting her events (especially the unscripted ones) to only 60-90 days could win the day. They were wrong.

The GOP's budget work did not progress well, and unwise and mis-timed retirements in the House minimized their majority there. Senate Republicans are not unified with the presence of Never Trumpers and squishy get-alongers. Republicans are notorious for not having clear, compelling messaging, but they have improved. The GOP focused clear messaging on Kamala's record and her part in the Biden-Harris administration. So, the tactics and messaging advantage went to the GOP.

If the D-S had pulled off victories in 2024, it would have shown that the GOP campaign strategies and tactics advantages that exposed the D-S record of failures, corruption, and cognitive issues could be overcome. How? With the help of an adoring media, celebrity endorsements, shaming by the Obamas, and a $1 billion wealthy donor-benefactors war chest. Fortunately, their flawed plans and strategies did not convince most Americans.

It could have completed Obama's desired transformation of the democratic Capitalist USA into a Socialist authoritarian country during his 4th term, headed by his pick of 2 strong Socialists in Harris and her VP pick, Tim Walz. Obama had been a master in political strategy, and this would have been his crowning achievement, as his surrogates (Biden and then Kamala) speak his words and take his actions.

The Most Recent Impactful Presidents

William Jefferson Clinton's Presidency (1993-2001)

Bill was the last effective Democrat President before they became total Democrat-Socialists. The following is not a complete list, just some noteworthy highlights. [21]

1. He successfully exercised bipartisanship, working with the Republican Congressional majority that appeared in his first mid-term election of 1994.
2. He signed into law most of the Republican Contract with America elements, some of which accounted for at least part of the other positive results of his Presidency.
3. From 1993 to 2001, the economy racked up an average annual growth of 4%, with growth occurring every month.
4. He cut spending and reduced the income tax burdens, and there was the first budget surplus since the 1960s and a paydown of $360 billion of the national debt.
5. Significant drops in poverty and unemployment rates and rises in personal incomes.
6. Crime rate reduced for 8 straight years, with the 2000 rate the lowest since 1973.
7. Enacted the Family and Medical Leave Act.
8. There was a reasonable work requirement for welfare recipients.
9. The lowest teen birth rate in 60 years.
10. Negotiated deactivation of 1,700 nuclear warheads from the former Soviet Union.

On the negative side, Clinton began buying into the Cloward-Piven re-imaging of the Democrat Party into the D-S. He also secured China membership in the World Trade Organization in 2001, which grew it into the world's factory and the superpower it is today that threatens the world.

Barack Hussein Obama's Presidency (2009–2017)

While the Obama Administration gets credit for killing and eliminating future threats from Osama bin Laden, other accomplishments are questionable and unclear. He was the first significant D-S President, but a carefully curated image hid that from many. His engaging demeanor and smile were usually on display, and he often disguised his genuine opinions and feelings. The following list of failures is not complete but highlights some of the more significant ones. [22] [23]

Foreign Policy Failures

1. His Iran nuclear deal trusted a terrorist regime to honor its commitments, allowing them to keep building their nuclear weapons and long-range missile capabilities.
2. He famously called ISIS "the JV team." Later, he said that jihadi groups like ISIS were a "generational threat," and we just need to get used to that.
3. ISIS and al-Qaeda expanded their terrorist reach during Obama's two terms.
4. He told the Syrian President that using chemical weapons against his citizens would be an intolerable red line. Assad crossed the red line, and Obama did nothing.
5. Obama supported deposing Ghaddafi as the leader of Libya. With no plan for the next steps, Libya became a vacuum that terrorists, including ISIS, gladly filled.
6. He refused to use descriptive and appropriate phrases like "radical Muslim" and "Islamic extremist," and he ordered that the word "terrorism" be replaced with "man-made disasters."
7. Obama told the Russian President, "This is my last election. After my election, I have more flexibility." Not long after that, Russia invaded and took over Crimea.

8. He started his Presidency with a world apology tour on behalf of the US. That weakened the US global standing and showed his disdain for the country and the voters who elected him twice to its highest office.

Weaponizing the Deep State

Many before him (including FDR, JFK, and LBJ) have done this, but not on the grand scale of Obama. Here are a few of his political targetings that used the FBI, DOJ, and IRS.

1. Slow walking or not walking at all FOIA requests for information.
2. He has prosecuted more whistleblowers than all prior administrations combined. One example was a US attorney trying to damage a leaker's reputation for exposing BHO's "Fast and Furious" debacle.
3. His Director of National Intelligence told Congress there was no mass surveillance of Americans, which was proven false by Edward Snowden's revelations. This surveillance included members of Congress.
4. Initiated a war on the print media when they did not report favorably; intimidated the *NY Times* when they would not reveal a story source; used the Justice Department to gather phone records of AP reporters to uncover a government leaker; a key IRS figure refused to testify about allegations of the IRS targeting Conservative groups, and the IRS coincidentally destroyed their hard drive, which could have exonerated them or showed their guilt. [24]
5. According to the White House stenographer, Mike McCormick, less than 2 weeks before Trump took office, Obama gave the "green light" to lift the moratorium on federal funding for gain-of-function research, which was officially allowed by the National Institutes of Health in December 2017. Mike called this "Obama's poison pill" for Trump. [25] We will never know, but this may have led the way to COVID-19 and the deaths of 7 million globally, including 1 million in the US.

Trickery, Lies, and Lack of Transparency

1. Obamacare—"If you like your doctor, you can keep your own doctor." FALSE
2. Obamacare— "If you like your own (healthcare) plan, you can keep it." FALSE
3. Obamacare— "is fully paid for and drops the deficit by $4 trillion over 10 years. " FALSE
4. Obamacare—"will lower premiums by up to $2,500 for a typical family per year… by the end of my first term as President." FALSE A typical family saw a $2,200 increase. [26]
5. Obamacare—He seduced Senators to vote for it with "kickbacks" for their states.
6. During his campaign, he was for "marriage is only between a man and a woman" and then "evolved" to be against that sometime after his election. How conveniently timed.
7. Another famous Obama quote: "There was not even a smidgen of corruption" (in his administration). FALSE The Attorney General was held in contempt of Congress for withholding documents about the "Fast and Furious" operation that placed thousands of weapons into the hands of drug cartels in Mexico and wound up being used by illegal immigrants to kill, including a US Border Patrol agent. A prominent Democrat donation bundler and Obama donor received almost $1 billion in tax credits as a part of the Solyndra debacle that ended in its bankruptcy.[27]

Economic Performance

The national debt almost doubled during the Obama years. Obama inherited a much better economy from George W. Bush than Reagan did from Jimmy Carter. Here are their comparative results for the 3rd year of their 1st term. [28] [29]

Economic Growth %	Reagan 1983/84	Obama 2011/12
Apr.–June	5.1%	0.4%
July–Sept.	9.3%	1.3%
Oct.–Dec.	8.1%	1.8%
Jan.–Mar.	8.5%	3.0%
Quarterly 12 Month Average	7.75%	1.63%

Additional Job Growth	Reagan 1983/84	Obama 2011/12
Apr.–June	931,000	389,000
July–Sept.	1,224,000	383,000
Oct.–Dec	979,000	492,000
Jan.–Mar.	1,201000	635,000
12 Month Totals	4,335,000	1,889,000

"Pen-and-Phone" Strategy

He used this to implement his royal edicts/Executive Orders for things he could not get Congress to pass into law. He bypassed Congress to do as he pleased, even though previously he said they limited him.

Power and Influence to Punish America

He always took the side of a Black shooting victim against the policeman involved. He did this even before all the facts were known. This gaslit the racial fires because, as a Black President, he was signaling that white cops have it in for Blacks. Instead of being a healing leader in the image of Martin Luther King Jr., he was still operating as a Marxist community organizer from Chicago. Obama's father was a Marxist, and BHO's significant male figure growing up was an uncle who was a US Communist Party dues-paying member.

And let's not forget the pastor of the church he attended, who was famous for making racist and inflammatory remarks. Or that he launched his political career from the home of two convicted domestic terrorists. Is it any wonder he became the first US Democrat-Socialist President with his anarchy approach to the colonial US for its "slavery sins?" He was reported as saying," I will fundamentally transform America. Soon, it will be unrecognizable." [30] Well done, Barack—mission accomplished!

In retrospect, Obama and his Cabinet were the real "JV team" (not ISIS). On November 30, 2020, on The Late Show with Stephen Colbert, he talked about having more "presidency" beyond his 2nd term. "If I could have a front man with a mic to me, and he could deliver my lines, I would be fine with that." To bolster that aspiration, he never left the Washington DC area. He is the only President to have done that. The others all returned to the state they wanted to retire to. Unfortunately, he and many from his Cabinet have been advising Biden, making Obama's 3rd term a reality.

If Kamala Harris and her Socialist comrade, Tim Walz had won in 2024, that would have been his 4th term and one that would be more radical than the Obama-Biden terms. Obama knew he could never get Kamala successfully through a primary, so he got a very flawed Biden to run as a phony moderate in 2020, surrounded him with many members of his own Socialist Cabinet and then got him off the ticket for 2024 without Kamala having to win a primary or a brokered convention (brilliant strategy).

This clever but undemocratic process fooled some Americans, but many others understood the corruption of installing someone on the ballot who received zero votes in the 2020 and 2024 D-S primaries and zero votes in an open D-S convention. This was anti-democratic and served as a warning of the dictatorial type of country the D-S want to live in, where their Uniparty controls everything. Obama could have then completed his takedown of the USA and its Socialist transformation and decline, with 3 of the last 4 Presidents campaigning as phony moderates but pushing that toxic Socialist agenda when in office.

Donald John Trump's Presidency (2017–2021) and (2025-2029)

Donald Trump had a problem-solver mentality from his hard-nosed business background. He finally decided to run for office after being incensed by the rapid decline in the US in the prior 8 years. Without Obama, there would likely not have been a Trump Presidency. The Capitol swamp had not corrupted him, and he was ferocious to those who impeded him, like the media and the Deep State. The Deep State and media hated his successes and sarcasm and were determined to undermine him as much as possible and get him out. How could someone who did not spend their whole life in politics come in and succeed with new approaches where swamp creatures who were free to ignore and worsen the problems had not? There were phony impeachments and fraudulent accusations of scandals, but he still succeeded with many significant accomplishments in his first term. To name a few:[31]

1. Managed to get COVID-19 vaccines into testing 3 months after getting the genetic code from China and then get them approved and in place in a record time of one year.
2. Negotiated several agreements from a position of strength with our allies and China.
3. Responsible for the lowest unemployment % for minorities and women in decades.
4. Created more federal tax revenue by lowering tax rates.
5. Significantly reduced burdensome regulation.
6. He was the only President to provide permanent funding for historically Black colleges.
7. Created 1,000 enterprise zones to help minority businesses get funded and succeed.
8. Made historic "stay-in-country" agreements with Central and South American countries and built a significant portion of the wall on the US southern border after resolving numerous lawsuits. The result was that illegal immigration became a trickle.

9. Negotiated the Abraham Accords for the historic beginnings of Middle East peace agreements among several countries with Israel.

John Cribb from The Hill made some interesting comparisons between Trump and Lincoln. Here is a quick summary: [32]
- Both were considered by many (including the media and establishment) to be long shots.
- Lincoln had limited government experience, and Trump had none.
- Both were harshly attacked by the media and disliked by the establishment.
- Both were Presidents at a time when our country was very divided and partisan.

While many have enjoyed Trump's bombastic personality and "take no prisoner" speeches and Twitter tweets (before he was de-platformed), they also infuriated some key Independent swing voters, mobilized the far left, and gave birth to the "Never Trumper" kids. That coalition was joined by the globalists, RINOs, squishy Republicans, and the Vast Left-Wing Conspiracy (Media, Woke Business, Sports and Entertainment, the Deep State, Education, and other leftist organizations). They did everything they could to get him out, and they succeeded. If he had a consecutive second term, that would have marginalized the far left and even been an existential threat to their existence. They live off the chaos and fear they create primarily for Americans' safety and economic well-being.

Based on his results-oriented business background, Trump did not realize the negative impact he was having on misguided people who base their voting decisions on what politicians say and their style instead of what they accomplish. Politicians rarely do what they say, so that kind of emotional voting made no sense to him and was not part of his thinking. But politics is like gymnastics, where the results of excellent technical ability can be offset by style, which counts mightily in the judges' scoring. This was Trump's 1st blind spot—some of the electorate vote based on the style and rhetoric and not the results.

The 2nd was that he did not grasp how corrupt and powerful the Deep State swamp was and that it needed much more intense focus to clean up. The 3rd was that loyalty, which is more common in business, is rare in politics. In the political realm, becoming a highly paid TV propagandist commentator or getting an expensive book deal later is more important than loyalty to a President or the American people. His 4th blind spot was viewing China only as a business competitor to be strongly negotiated with, but not as the global threat they really are.

Trump has won the Presidency in 2024. The D-S tried (and failed) to disqualify him just before the election (or significantly soil his character with a felony conviction that survived appeal). Partly because of his successful, long-running TV series (The Apprentice), he enjoys being the Entertainer-in-Chief to *his audience*, but many non-MAGA people do not appreciate that. Great speakers adjust their tone and message to their audience.

In Trump's case, that audience is much broader than the MAGA faithful, and he should consider tweaking (not abandoning) his strong Brooklyn demeanor. Even greater support from Independents and suburban women would happen. "Less is more" when it comes to political speak, and it is better to "walk softly and carry a big stick."

He smartly championed red and purple state election reforms (see Chapter 6). He is on the path to correcting his blind spots and is aware he sometimes provides too much information for criticism and distortion by the left. You can have an opinion on everything, but comments about appearance and clothes lose votes and energize his opposition. Kamala's radicalism and her major role in the disasters of the last 4 years are facts that he wisely focused on to easily win the Presidency.

Opinions are best expressed on important matters in a factual and non-inflammatory way. If not, the messenger's style can impair even a great message. Trump has been our first real Solutionist President and has the potential to be even more effective in his second term.

Joseph Robinette Biden Jr.'s Presidency (2021–2024)

Then along comes Basement Biden, acting like an immature child, expressing his independence by doing the opposite of what his parents said. Whatever Daddy Trump did has to be reversed, regardless of the impact on the country. He was the perfect combination of Manchurian Candidate and Trojan Horse that entered the White House. His carefully scripted campaign was headquartered in the bowels of his basement. He portrayed himself as a calm moderate compared to the bombastic Trump or the Socialist Bernie Sanders. The winning Basement Biden Strategy included minimal campaigning, debates, and responses to questions to hide his cognitive issues.

That Trojan Horse named Joe was just what the radical left needed to win the election and be the perfect empty vessel to fill later. This Manchurian Candidate was someone with a storied career of lies, plagiarism, and allegations of corruption. The hard left could program him with their Socialist agenda that he campaigned against in his primary and would now become his new playbook.

He allegedly has been compromised by his son's shady business dealings with Russia, Ukraine, China, and other countries. It is very possible that Russia and China have leverage on Joe with compromising information. That could explain his cowardly, cozying-up actions that benefit China, Russia, and Iran.

Let's not forget his refusal to take a cognitive mental test and share the results to dispel the concerns of many when they watch and listen to him. That tells us all we need to know about his mental fitness. Then there are his infrequent news conferences with minimal and only pre-approved questions allowed and caustic remarks when he refuses to answer important questions for which he does not have a good answer.

Since 2004, the President has been interviewed annually at the Superbowl halftime, except for 2018 when Trump had issues with the network. Joe has outdone Trump and passed on that for two consecutive years. How about his mixing up foreign leaders' names and saying he recently spoke to people who have been dead for years or even decades? The D-S media covered for Joey until after his debate with Trump. Suddenly that corrupt cabal noticed his deterioration that most of us saw four years ago.

His DOJ says Joey willfully and illegally had classified documents in his possession but refused to recommend prosecution because his memory was so poor that he could not even remember the years he was Obama's VP, and a jury might let him off for that reason. But the D-S still claimed he was fit to run/ruin the country and the world, even though a jury might not. And gaffes-a-plenty Biden claimed to have recently met with two world leaders—one who died in 2017 and the other died three decades ago. Guess Joe is a psychic and learned how to reach beyond the grave for those talks.

Speaking of his hide-in-the-basement campaign strategy, the only reason he made it to the Presidency was China's COVID-19 gift. Without such a gift "from China with love," Trump's accomplishments would have more than offset his bombastic style, and Biden's clueless bumbling and lies would have surfaced in debates and rallies. How has the Biden-Harris administration carefully choreographed regressive policies impacted Americans after four years?

Economic Performance of Bidenomics

1. Bidenflation—The 40-year record-high US inflation of 9.1% seems to have peaked thanks to mercilessly-high interest rate hikes to cool the inflation caused by his reckless spending and energy policies. Some say the actual inflation that people experience is at least 17%.[33] Nice to set records, Joe.

    When he took office in January 2021, the national median home price was nearly $330,000, and the average interest rate on a 30-year mortgage was about 2.75%. Now that the home price for May 2022 is $430,621 and the interest rate is 5.78% as of June 17, 2022. That means in less than 1.5 years of the Biden regime, the cost of homes went up 30.5%, and the mortgage interest rate more than doubled. That costs a home buyer an extra $20,000 for their 20% down payment, an additional $80,000 in principal repayments, an additional $260,000 in interest payments, and a near doubling of the monthly principal and interest payment from $1,077.76 to $2,016.96.

Because Bidenflation continues through 2023 (and likely beyond), these numbers have worsened for homebuyers, with mortgage rates hitting a 2-decade high of 7.5% in October 2023 and mortgage applications declining due to the unaffordability for many. Because of Joey's inflationary policies, all costs have increased, especially food, utilities, gasoline, and material and insurance costs for homes and cars. From January 2020 to September 2023, the purchasing power of the USD has shrunk by 16%. Americans are less prepared for emergencies due to less savings and skyrocketing credit card debt. Does anyone still think the D-S care about US citizens?

2. The US economy shrank (not grew) by 2.5% in the 1st two quarters of 2022, which is the standard definition of a recession. [34] Great job, Jedi Joe.

3. Companies are struggling under the burdens and economic environment Biden's policies have created for them. As of June 15, 2022, the DJIA was down 15.6%, the S&P 500 was down 20%, and the NASDAQ was down 29%. [35] Updated through June 30, 2022, the Dow performance was the worst since 1962; the S&P 500 was the worst since 1971; and the NASDAQ had the worst performance of all time. These are dismal numbers to brag about. All three major indices were officially in bear market territory.

Joe is an accomplished magician because, in front of 335 million Americans, his actions have made $6 trillion disappear midway through 2022 – $5 trillion from the crashes of stocks (many held in retirement 401(k)s and IRAs) and $1 trillion from a cryptocurrency nosedive. As of June 8, 2023, Biden presided over the longest bear market for the S&P 500 in 75 years. He can take credit for the fact that for only the 4th time in the last 50 years, commercial bank lending shrank by more than 1.5%. Look at Chapter 4 under the "Triggers" section to see how these two Biden accomplishments resulted in very dire situations when they occurred for other Presidents.

4. Biden brags about jobs added each month, but he is only about equal to the Trump employment figures before COVID hit, and the vast majority of that growth is from red states, government bureaucracy growth, part-time jobs, and typically low-paying hospitality jobs. 2 million have left the workforce since Biden took office. In June 2023, US manufacturing activity was reduced for the 8th consecutive month. Referring to jobs reporting from the feds, David Rosenberg of Rosenberg Research Associates posted on X, "The downward revisions in 2023 totaled an epic 443,000. More than 40% of payroll growth in 2023 didn't even come from the survey but from the fairy-tale 'Birth-Death' model." [36]

While initial new job totals always look good, the later revisions are always significantly downward. These "job lies" reached new heights in August, 2024. For the 12 months of April, 2023–March, 2024, the new job totals were revised down by 818,000. Guess Forgetful Joe missed telling us about these qualifiers.

5. Since this statistic began being tracked and reported in 1952, consumer sentiment set an all-time low record of 50.2 in June 2022. [37] Another record for Uncle Joey.

6. But this Jedi Knight confidently appears on late-night TV and claims the US economy is the "strongest in the world, in the world, in the world." As the habitual Liar in Chief (LIC), he thinks that if he tells whoppers repeatedly, some will believe it, and even Jedi Joe might. But most voters recognize the lies every time they shop or buy gas. His lie "tells" are apparent when he repeats the same word or phrase three times in a row or uses a stern tone to add phony emphasis to a lie.

His dishonesty is present in his tall tales of his childhood and with ridiculously flattering and untruthful comments about his academic achievements. Let's not forget his multiple instances of plagiarism, using the speeches of others as his own creations.

7. He repeatedly told a whopper that there was "zero" inflation in July 2022. While inflation did not worsen that month, it was still at 8.5% (not zero). To complement his craving for ice cream, he must enjoy a lot of Burger King Whoppers because his burping verbal whoppers seems to re-energize the whopper gene that already courses through his system.

8. Passing a $1.7 trillion COVID-19 relief bill that was unnecessary and followed up with another $740 billion spending bill (just in time to influence/buy the mid-term elections). This is a tried and true D-S strategy – demonize and tax businesses more (which gets passed on to consumers) and spend wildly for green new deals, guarantees for over-the-top pensions, and the forgiveness of student loans ($300 billion and counting without any Congressional approval).

The D-S are the experts in buying votes with giveaways funded by ballooning debt. Unfortunately, free stuff often lures us, even though it is not truly free. These programs always have a bit of merit mixed in with a lot of pork and ideological rubbish. The misnamed Inflation Reduction Act quadruples the number of IRS auditors to harass middle-income taxpayers and small businesses. Pursuing the "fat cats" is too complex, and they can't be intimidated easily.

For the fiscal year 2023, Biden ran up a $1.7 trillion deficit—actually $2 trillion when you include his illegal student loan bailout "reallocation." Government debt interest now exceeds the Defense Department's budget. Because maturing debt is never extinguished but rolled over into higher-interest debt, 2024's interest will exceed $1 trillion. [38]

A September 12, 2022 press release by the House Budget Committee titled "Fact Check: Biden Brags About Deficit Reduction While Adding Nearly $10 Trillion in New Spending That Has To Be Paid for With Higher Taxes and Borrowing And Interest And Inflation." [39] Sorry to inform Joe, but excessive spending causes inflation—that is basic economics.

Foreign Policy Results

1. An embarrassing Afghanistan retreat/surrender of people's lives, money, and equipment (estimates of $7–$100 billion). The Biden regime had 3 opportunities to avoid the suicide bomber killing of 13 Americans and 170 Afghans and acted ineptly with all 3. We had imprisoned the terrorist at the Bagram compound. But the Commander-in-Chief stupidly and abruptly evacuated that compound at the start of our pullout (not the end). The Taliban took over and released that terrorist. A strike on a Taliban facility was requested and denied. Later on the day of the bombing, a US sniper identified the terrorist and asked to take the shot but was denied. Bungled actions cost precious lives. For a complete story, read the book *Kabul* by Jerry Dunleavy.[40]
2. Biden's experience has paid off in overseas alliances. He has taken the potential for Russia and Iran to ally more significantly with China and made it a reality. He has strengthened the Chinese Juan's position to dethrone the USD for trade and as a reserve currency. Several BRICS countries, including Saudi Arabia, agreed to trade outside the traditional USD.

    Joe is too cowardly to deal with the human and drug trafficking from the Mexican cartels and Chinese mafia; or to ask Chinese leadership to open up about the COVID-19 origins, even though a 2018 Wuhan lab document identified a project DEFUSE that was to engineer a bat coronavirus that would be pre-adapted to spread to humans, like COVID-19 did. We are playing footsies with those Mexican cartels and the Chinese mafia and the three main global bullies of Russia, Iran, and China. They are all becoming our BFFs.
3. Pulling out all the stops to get a weak Iran agreement (using Russia to negotiate on behalf of the US) that would continue their path to nuclear weapons and remove sanctions to put billions of dollars in their coffers to metastasize their global terror efforts. Iran's leaders

have repeatedly proven they are not to be trusted and will not follow agreements.

This would be the final "nail in the coffin" of our misguided and dangerous dealing with Iran, starting with Jimmy Carter, Barack Obama, and now Joe Biden. What could possibly go wrong with that appeasement strategy? Maybe the encouragement of more lucrative hostage-taking and imprisonments? No way would a trustworthy country like Iran and its rulers even think of something like that just to gain a few billion dollars to fund more global terrorism.

In September 2023, Uncle Joe found another way to funnel $6 billion to terrorist Iran in exchange for 5 American prisoners. [41] Qatar negotiated this for us. Remember, they are a country that is home to some Middle East terrorist leaders and have funneled billions of dollars to US universities for research (where they keep the intellectual property) and to further pro-Hamas and antisemitic movements on campuses. This was shockingly visible despite the Hamas atrocities of October 7, 2023. Universities' corrupt hunger for money must be stopped when national security is involved.

The unfreezing of $6 billion of Iranian assets occurred in September 2023. On October 7, 2023, the Iranian-funded Hamas attacked Israel, raping women and killing 29 Americans and 1,200 Jews (including children), some by beheading and burning. Considering the much smaller size of Israel, that would equate to 40,000 dying on 911 instead of 3,000. Hostages were also taken, and we are asking Qatar to negotiate their release. The weakness to and appeasement of bully terrorists just produce more terrorism – GI Joe must be a slow learner.

This is in addition to all the propping up of Iran he has done. When Joe took over, Iran had only $4 billion in reserves and might have been toppled by the people there wanting freedom. Prior US sanctions against Iran had reduced their oil production to only 100,000 barrels/day. Savvy Joe has not enforced those sanctions, and they are now pumping and selling 2–3 million barrels/day, mostly going to China, our main adversary. The wealth created by this now shows up in $70 billion in their reserves, even after funding all of their Middle East terrorism.

It was kind of Mr. B to help the struggling Godfather of terrorism re-arm his military complex and his Middle East terrorist affiliates. Iran is now free to sell missiles to Russia for their continued devastation of Ukraine while we and our allies spend money and equipment to help Ukraine. In the fall of 2023, Iran's Navy commander broadcast that they own Antarctica and would build a military presence there. Guess that all makes sense in the mind of our Big Guy.

4. Joe's two-faced support of Israel in dealing with Hamas and Hezbollah since the October 7, 2023 missiles and carnage of 1,200 brutal civilian murders and over 200 hostages taken by Hamas. King B's initial support of Israel has quickly turned into undermining and trying to tell Israel how to conduct a war where they are already doing everything possible to minimize civilian deaths. While our King's streak of faulty strategies remains intact, the Israelis understand the existential threat before them and will not listen to Joey's flawed strategy or threats.

5. Cancellation of a January 2021 scheduled shipment of defensive arms to Ukraine that likely would have deterred Russia's invasion. When large numbers of Russian troops were being staged near Ukraine's borders, the US administration again refused to properly arm Ukraine to protect its airspace from Russian planes and missiles. All the sanctions that have subsequently been taken do nothing to stop the flow of money for Russian oil that supports Putin's brand of terrorism. This tepid policy resulted in a devastating Russian invasion that decimated Ukraine with Nazi-like war crimes and atrocities against the population.

Only after the Russian attack has Biden provided arms to Ukraine. They are just enough to prolong the war, but not the planes and other equipment needed at the onset to prevent or to win it. There have been an estimated 200,000–400,000 Ukrainian casualties; many have been victims of war crimes; millions have been displaced; thousands of children have been kidnapped and sent to Russia to be brainwashed against their country; and many cities have been reduced to rubble.

When this war is over, some part of Ukraine will likely be divided and a part given to Russia.
6. There is a $14 billion backlog of weapons that Taiwan has purchased from the US to defend itself primarily from mainland China. It includes 66 F-16 fighter jets and high-tech missiles. Sleepy Joe has decided to fast-track $500 million for them as of early May 2023, only now that China is acting aggressively in the area. That is only 3.6% of what is due to them.

In March 2024, a "decision" was made to send 100–200 US Special Forces to Taiwan to train them in very short-range drone use. Other commitments for ballistic missiles, tanks, and F-16s were reaffirmed, with some happening in 2024. Just like what he has done in Ukraine, Biden is much too little and way too late. China's harassment of Taiwan has continued, thanks to Sleepy Joe. He did nothing to deter or punish the loss of freedom in Hong Kong and turned Afghanistan over to terrorists and China. Biden's records keep piling up!
7. Stopping the Keystone Pipeline from being completed to safely transport oil between Canada and the US and allowing Russia to complete (with all oil-related sanctions removed) its pipeline to Western Europe. Since then, several European countries have taken a courageous stand against Russian oil, even though the US cannot adequately supply all their needs, which would have been possible under Trump.

This and other presidential actions have made Europe beholden to Russian energy, eliminated US independence on foreign oil, and drove up the US and global costs for gas, food, fertilizer, and many other commodities. Reputable sources have reported that the US may have had a role in the later destruction of the Russian pipeline, causing the largest-ever release per NPR of up to 500,000 tons of methane into the atmosphere.
8. Bumbling Biden has abandoned 6 embassies as of August 2023. Afghanistan was the first. He did not approve a plan to leave 2,500 special operators as a quick reaction force to support the Afghan National Defense Security Forces. From this weak inaction, the

Taliban overran the local troops and quickly took over—something we were told would not happen. Then embassy evacuations followed in Ukraine, Belarus, Sudan, Haiti, and Niger.
9. North Korea's leader talks about re-unifying the Peninsula and preparing for a long-term conflict with the US. He launched more missiles in Biden's first 13 months than in four years of Trump's Presidency.
10. Biden alienated Saudi Arabia, the UAE, India, Mexico, and Brazil.

Domestic Policies

1. Suffering from TDS (Trump Derangement Syndrome), Biden reversed an effective southern border policy in favor of costly chaos for the US economy and its citizens, tragedies for many migrants, and the smuggling of Fentanyl (with ingredients provided by China) that has been killing a record 70,000–100,000 Americans annually and has enriched the Mexican cartels beyond their wildest expectations.

   He even appointed his word-salad VP as the border czar. For an excellent read on the centuries-old Chinese "mafia" behind this, check out Peter Schweizer's 2024 book *Blood Money*. [42] He shows how they ship pill-making machines from China into Mexico, set up shop with some 2,000 Chinese there, and smuggle Fentanyl across the southern border into the US to run the drug operations and massage parlors that employ the trafficked sex slaves.

   This TDS policy is in stark contrast to a speech he gave on August 12, 2007, when he was running for President. The video post can be found on X. "It makes sense that no great nation can be in a position where they can't control their borders. It matters how you control your borders. Not just for immigration. But it matters for drugs, terror [and] a whole range of other things." He added, "So I think the combination of virtual fencing, some fencing [and] additional Border Patrol is important."

   If it appealed to his base in 2007, he was for border security; if it doesn't in 2021–2024, he is not. This is a good lesson King B learned from Obama's flip-flop on marriage being between a man and a woman.

2. Focusing on spending and taxing more to distract from his record of failures, reduce the impact of the private sector, and engorge the government's share of GDP, his administration wants to copy European economies, which are not doing well. But our lefties love the European embrace of green activism, global financial rules and tax policies with high levels of regulation and central planning, and ceding many decisions to unelected bureaucrats in Brussels.

3. Joe, like all good D-S, likes to benefit his donors. Giving a $7,500 tax credit to buy an electric vehicle benefits those who are doing well and can easily afford to be woke with an expensive electric car. It helps the well-funded lobbies for those vehicles, their battery manufacturers, and the charging ports and stations. The administration also pumps billions of subsidy dollars into woke donors involved in undependable wind and solar energy.

4. To boost D-S's performance in the 2022 elections, he drained the Strategic Petroleum Reserve to its lowest level in 40 years and sold some of that oil to China. From the Trump average low price of $1.74/gallon, Biden made it soar due to his actions to a high of $5.01 and artificially drop to $3.05 and creep up again to about $3.50. The Dems nixed Trump's plan to fill the reserve when the cost for 77 million barrels was as low as $18.33/bbl. or $1.4 billion. Because of Biden's actions, he would need to buy 368 million barrels to fill the reserve at a hoped-for price of $75/barrel or $10.3 billion. That is an extra $8.9 billion or more if we faced an emergency.

5. As the Dictator in Chief (DIC), he routinely ignores the Supreme Court and other court rulings he dislikes, like the SCOTUS rulings on the "Remain in Mexico" policy and his illegal student loan forgiveness pandering. It remains to be seen whether he will ignore the unanimous 9–0 ruling by the Court, disqualifying the overreach of the EPA, which wanted to call the water on private property (near a ditch) "waters of the USA" and subject to their regulation.

6. Joe has basked in the authoritarian glow of mandates about vaccines and masks and threatens directly or through his "Vast Left-Wing Conspiracy" (VLWC) anyone who dares to talk about the positive results of natural immunity, off-label successful and inexpensive treatments, some severe adverse reactions to the vaccines, and the inefficiency of cloth masks and most quarantines. Like his subsidies and rebates for wind, solar, and electric cars, his Executive Orders are driven by ideology, votes, and power, not practical solutions.

While the regressives portray themselves as the party of science, they have politicized science to the point that they are the party of non-science (nonsense for short). In his tour of duty as Obama's VP, he was tasked with dealing with the swine flu and bungled that. Luckily, that was nowhere near as deadly as COVID-19, or several hundred thousand deaths could have occurred.

This sterling track record showed up in the COVID-19 death statistics. Before Joe in 2020, without a vaccine and a very virulent COVID, there were 400,000 US deaths. With Joe at the helm, available vaccines (thanks to the Trump administration), a somewhat less virulent COVID, and his mandates, 680,000 lives were lost. People's jobs were lost and their lives ruined when they courageously opted for natural immunity and treatments rather than bow down to King Joe Biden's (KJB) universal, no-exceptions vaccination demands. There have been no apologies from our king and no restoration for the ruined lives.

His National Labor Relations Board is implementing a disastrous policy that makes every employee of a franchise operator also an employer of the franchisor. This creates substantial legal and administrative costs. Something similar was done in California in 2015–2017 at a cost to the economy of $33 billion and the loss of many jobs.

The leadership trio of Winken (VP Giggles), Blinken (the Secretary of State), and Nod (Sleepy Joe) are all aligned with the hard left, while some Europeans are expressing their discontent with failed leftist leaders and voting in more right-leaning leaders. Once again, Joey's direction is wrong for most of the people.

7. Digital Dollar—To compete with the digital Juan and other digital currencies being planned, a Solutionist President would have already been far along with launching a digital USD with built-in protections. In March 2022 (late to the game again), one of Biden's many Executive Orders told various federal agencies to study the potential development of a central bank digital currency (CBDC). In September 2022, Biden announced that policy around CBDC had been developed. Biden told the agencies to meet regularly with the Federal Reserve to design a "potential CBDC." What are the downsides?
    - Unlike Bitcoin, there is no privacy, and every transaction can be tracked digitally.
    - Rules can easily be programmed to control spending on "approved activities." We could be financially penalized or stopped from making automobile gasoline purchases.
    - The government can impose a fee (negative interest rate) for having digital currency balances. Instead of encouraging saving with favorable interest rates, the government can push individuals and businesses to spend on "approved activities."
    - Ownership would be with the government and financial institutions and not citizens.
    - That change in ownership means that instead of our money funding banks to make loans, it funds the government and what it wants to support.
    - Safety rails will be promised for privacy and control over "approved" and "unapproved" currency uses, but that will be a D-S lie to get this dystopian control over everyone.
    - Fortunately, King Joseph was distracted by the coup against him, and US CBDC never happened.

8. There are many other mandates Biden would like to do – Especially close to his heart would be to place the corrupt World Health Organization in charge of declaring whether something in the future

qualifies as a pandemic and dictating what the US response and practices should be. That way, the Basement Biden Strategy could get rolled out again, but this did not happen. There are other strategies the D-S tried (and failed) to win the White House in 2024.

They have already adopted this one—as they analyzed Biden's political and personal baggage, and historic low polling numbers, and replaced him on the ticket with Harris. This should have been done openly at the Democratic Convention in Chicago, but they preferred to have this done in secrecy, so Obama's heavy hand in this would not be exposed. She was so unpopular in the 2020 Democrat primary, that she dropped out before the first state held its primary. How can anyone vote for a party that operates so undemocratically?

There was a well-financed but failed attempt to run a "No Labels" presidential candidate. And there was the 3rd party run by RFK Jr. He realized that he could take popular and maybe some Electoral College votes from the Republican candidate, possibly allowing the D-S candidate to win. Because the D-S have abandoned his JFK principles, he chose to suspend his campaign and support Trump, who aligns more fully with his patriotic and common sense approaches to the country's serious problems.

What did the D-S do to push this Dem royalty to campaign against their nonsense? For openers, they refused to give him any Secret Service protection. Then in every state that he qualified to be on the ballot, they vigorously challenged his presence, requiring some diversion of his time, energy and money. They also denied him the opportunity to be on the debate stage with Biden and Trump.

RFK Jr. also said in his August 23, 2024 impactful speech that this party is corrupt and gave many examples. One was that much of the war in Ukraine could have been averted. Ukraine and Russia had worked well together on a peace agreement, but Biden wanted regime change in Russia and got Zelensky to tear up his agreement. Guess the D-S were expecting some positive "spoiler" impact from him, but never expected a Kennedy to turn against them with such factual vigor.

It was possible in a 3-way race, no one would get 50% of the Electoral College votes. Then, the House chooses the President, with each state delegation getting one vote. The D-S knew that and spent heavily to try to retake the House.

To strengthen their hand, the D-S feverishly worked to increase votes from undocumenteds by granting some of them citizenship just before the 2024 elections; flooding some DMV offices with undocumenteds to get drivers licenses in states that don't require drivers to prove citizenship and then using that ID to vote; and informing others how to vote, even though it is illegal to do so.

Lastly, if the Supreme Court did not rule on Trump's eligibility to run, many Congressional D-S say they will vote to disqualify him on January 6, 2025. The D-S were confident these strategies and the media re-branding of Kamala (just like they did for Biden) would offset the awful Biden-Harris record and deny a 2024 Trump victory.

Corruption Concerns

Obama's stenographer, Mike McCormick, stated in April 2023 that Hunter Biden's overseas business associates visited the Obama-Biden Whitehouse 80 times and made many other damaging comments about Biden's corruption and influence peddling, referring to them as "kickback schemes" and "malfeasance in office." He wants to testify under oath, but the Biden loyalists will do everything to prevent that. In multiple interviews and testimony, Biden's involvement is corroborated by two of Hunter's business partners, Tony Bobulinski and Devon Archer.

Everyone can recall Biden's well-publicized video of him threatening the President of Ukraine to cancel or withhold $1 billion of foreign aid to Ukraine if they did not fire the prosecutor investigating corruption in the Burisma energy company. From 2013 to 2018, that company sent monthly payments to Hunter. What expertise or services could Hunter or any of the Biden family provide for their payments beyond access to the "Big Guy" if and when needed?

Several of Hunter's business partners acknowledge pressure on Hunter to "call DC" to do something about the Ukrainian investigation into Burisma corruption that could have uncovered Hunter and Biden the Elder's involvement. The firing of that prosecutor due to the potential loss of $1 billion of aid was obscured for many years. It allowed Joey not to address this until brought up by Trump and discounted by the media to cover up for him.

This prosecutor's firing occurred about one month after an email on Hunter's laptop from the President of Burisma on November 2, 2015. A multi-million dollar invoice that he received mentions the "scope of work is largely lacking concrete, tangible results we set out to achieve in the first place…for improving Nikolay's case and his situation in Ukraine." It further notes, "If this is done deliberately to be on the safe and cautious side, I can understand the rationale." [43] It is alleged that Hunter and Joe each received $5 million from that Burisma head to change US policy. The basis of this is a June 2020 FBI 1023 report from a credible confidential human source.

On January 20, 2011, VP Biden wrote a letter to Devon Archer thanking him for the "business opportunity." How can any reasonable person believe Biden's whopper that he knew nothing about Hunter's business deals? The dots of this corruption practically connect themselves. More than 150 suspicious activity reports from financial institutions involved several members of the Biden family. How many suspicious activity reports have each of us had? They identify Biden's elaborate web of at least 20 LLCs that funnel money from overseas sources into at least 9 members of the Biden family. This is still being investigated, but estimates are that some $30–50 million has been passed this way, and no one knows the Bidens' expertise to earn that.

If all of Biden's many correspondences (82,000 pages of emails per the National Archives) [44] he had as VP using pseudonyms to hide his identity are provided; if bank records show money going into his control; and if his family is forced to identify what services they offered for the millions they received from corrupt foreign sources; then the powerful circumstantial proof will be elevated to 100% proof of actual corruption of selling out the US for personal gain. If Biden were allowed by the D-S to run, the Republicans would easily have swept the 2024 elections with even stronger results in the popular vote, Electoral College, and Congressional majorities.

Would you believe the entire IRS team investigating Hunter Biden for tax violations had been removed? That is the allegation from an IRS supervisor whistleblower about him and his team. Meanwhile, the IRS Commissioner testified on April 27, 2023, "I can say without hesitation there will be no retaliation for anyone making an allegation or a call to a whistleblower hotline." [45] Those two things seem to conflict and can't both be true.

On September 25, 2023, Jonathan Turley wrote an article for *USA Today* called "Bribing for access: Menendez indictment raises questions about Hunter Biden case and DOJ." It compares the circumstances between D-S Senator Menendez and Hunter. Both allegedly received luxury cars from foreign clients. Allegations are that the Senator received gold bars, and Hunter got an $80,000 diamond. Menendez's wife is accused of being a go-between with those trying to buy the Senator's attention, and accusations against Hunter are very similar. A key difference is that Menendez investigators used many resources to trace gifts and money. However, in Hunter's case, an IRS special agent testified in Congress that the Bidens were informed before planned searches.

Biden would have wanted to be re-elected because a sitting US President cannot be indicted. He is doing everything imaginable to deny, cover-up, and shift the focus to Trump indictments. Unfortunately for Joe, the presiding judge threw out the sweetheart deal David Weiss had cooked up for Hunter.

The DOJ helped JRB by appointing the lead prosecutor, David Weiss, as a Special Counsel to investigate Hunter. That seems like a nice reward for spending years doing little and letting the statute of limitations run out on not reporting significant overseas income. For more great info on this and other recent political financial scandals, read Peter Schweizer's 2018 book *Secret Empires*. [46]

Unlike what the D-S have done to Trump, there seems to be clear evidence of impeachable offenses by Biden. The evidence keeps accumulating from courageous whistleblowers and bank financial records. Of course, the D-S obsession with staying in power closed ranks quickly to take Joe off the ballot to avoid being devastated in the 2024 elections, but it did not work.

Seemingly Racist Comments

Biden has never explained or apologized for these comments.
- 1975—He opposed busing Blacks to white schools for integration since it was a rejection of the "Black awareness" concept and a rejection of "Black pride."
- 1977 (June 30)—He said in Congress that desegregation would cause children to grow up in a racial jungle. He told Democrat Senator James Eastland (a Mississippi segregationist), "I very much appreciate your help in attempting to bring my anti-busing legislation to a vote."
- 1998—In a speech, he called 100,000 juveniles charged with violent crimes (many of whom were Black) predators.
- 2007—Video footage of his reference to Obama as "the first sort of mainstream African-American who is articulate and bright and clean and a nice-looking guy."
- 2010—He gave a eulogy at the funeral for Democrat Senator Robert Byrd, a former Grand Wizard of the KKK of West Virginia. "We lost the dean of the US Senate, but also the state (of) West Virginia lost its most fierce advocate, and as I said, lost a dear friend."

The list of Biden-Harris fumbles goes to infinity and beyond in their four years in office. While Biden may have some positives, like having the 1st of some minority to hold a particular position, that is less important than doing the job competently for the country. It's little wonder that, depending on the month in 2022, up to 88% of Americans believed our nation was on the wrong track.

In 2020, Obama warned us about Joe: "Never underestimate Joe's ability to ____ things up." Also, there were warnings from Robert Gates, Secretary of Defense for Republican and Democratic Presidents. [47] **In his 2014 book,** *Duty: Memoirs of a Secretary at War,* **he said of Biden: "I think he has been wrong on nearly every major policy and national security issue over the past four decades."** [48] The Biden-Harris voters should have heeded the warnings from Obama and Gates about Joe. Unfortunately, his results are disastrous. To characterize him, some have used words like cognitively impaired, cowardly, clueless, compromised, creepy, corrupt, cranky, and continuously dishonest with plagiarism and never-ending lies.

Our Journey Continues to Be Hijacked

In 2022, with a tie in the Senate and a slim majority in the House of Representatives, the radical left has used their intimidation to try unsuccessfully to pass these measures:

- A voting bill that would diminish voter integrity and enshrine permanent power and control with the Socialists.
- A nationwide minimum wage bill.
- Statehood for Washington DC that would give two more Socialist senators to the D-S.
- Packing the US Supreme Court by increasing its Justices beyond the current 9.
- Medicare for everyone. This program is so poorly constructed for seniors that, absent any essential changes, it will be bankrupt in 8 years. This is not a model currently worth expanding.

- Doing away with the filibuster rule in the Senate will eliminate the ability of the minority party to participate in any meaningful way in government.

A 2022 Rasmussen Reports survey showed that 39% of D-S would allow the scandal-ridden and bureaucratic UN to reverse some Supreme Court rulings.[49] 53% of D-S would favor replacing the Supreme Court with a voter-selected court.

Our politicians have given us in the not-too-distant past glimmers of working well, but they are more than offset by financial corruption and the pursuit of power and prestige. The system is broken, and the D-S answers lead to anarchy followed by authoritarianism. Returning to what we had before will only lead us to the same place we are in today, but it will just take a few more years to get there.

The D-S's high levels of taxation, spending, regulation, mandates, erosion of freedom, and imposition of authoritarianism spring from their economic ignorance, the fake cult religions they and their sub-cults practice, and the frustration with unsolved significant problems as a result of the D-S guiding principle of participation trophies and equity with no winners or losers. But their "solutions" do not work and have no place in the government of the #1 superpower.

When the D-S don't get their way, they try to change the rules, like packing the Senate or the Supreme Court and doing away with the filibuster rule (that served them when they were in the minority in the Senate). They have been successful with gag orders on defendants in Trump-related cases, treating Trump's records retention much differently than Biden's worse situation, and changing the Electoral Count Act of 1887 that they used several times but considered problematic when used by Republicans. After examining the results of the D-S actions and their phony moderate Manchurian Candidates, no thinking person should vote for any of these D-S democracy destroyers until they become Solutionists and disavow Socialism.

Many of those who were put off by Trump's bombastic style thoughtfully considered his results as more important than continuing the D-S attacks on freedom and the growing authoritarian Police State. They might even have held their noses when they voted. Many Republicans previously did that for the presidential runs of Romney and McCain.

Starting with the end of Chapter 5, the rest of this book gives a different approach. Our 250th anniversary is on the near horizon in 2026. Trump is poised to get us off that totalitarian path, and using Solutionism can create a culture of success and accountability. That can extinguish that cancerous Socialism that has been plaguing us.

**

Our destination can be reset to create the "Shining City on a Hill," but our governing compass has been corrupted. We can fix that if we embrace the Founders' principles and our Constitution. The corruption of our politics has detoured our journey to scale the hill and construct our Shining City. The lurking Socialist ideology that threatens our vision is covered in the next chapter. We need to understand how awful it is so we are motivated to rid ourselves of it and stay vigilant if it resurfaces.

CHAPTER 3

Socialism and the Alternatives

We have arrived at a crucial fork in the road. The easier path is to continue the authoritarian degradation we are familiar with, which is a short road to Socialism. Our current state of Corrupt Capitalism is unstable and cannot last much longer. It is like a chemical intermediate reaction that will not last long before it transforms into its final condition. We must choose the more difficult journey to laser-focus on solving significant problems, which leads to becoming our Shining City on a Hill, our original destination. Trump's mindset and leadership will guide him to the difficult but more rewarding approach.

This more difficult path requires us and our politicians to become Solutionists for our major problems. That is not about using nice-sounding campaign slogans but being innovative and taking responsibility for solving problems, not ignoring them or just throwing money at them. Prioritize the problems, itemize the key issues, create plans, establish metrics to track progress, and adjust as needed. That will break the threatening grip that Socialists continue to exert more forcefully on us daily. Even though Trump is determined not to let Socialists succeed, he will be out of office in four years. We need to review Socialism's devastation and its influence on the US, so we stay vigilant to keep that door shut.

Why Is Socialism So Awful?

The answers to these questions are too numerous, but here are just a few responses:

1. Socialism minimizes private ownership and endorses primarily government ownership of property and natural resources.
2. It then focuses on the redistribution of the limited supply of goods and services wealth that it controls because it does not have the creative entrepreneurial spark to focus on the creation of more wealth. It plays God and redistributes what it tightly holds in its grasp.
3. It removes most incentives for creativity, entrepreneurism, and merit by producing nearly equal outcomes for all except for the relatively few oligarchs, elites, and the ruling class.
4. It often masquerades as "Democratic Socialism (D-S)," but there is little that is democratic about it, especially with elections that lack strong integrity in order to keep it in power.
5. See Chapter 4 for China's toxic brew of Socialism, Communism, and Corrupt Capitalism.
6. Socialism hosts within itself the DNA of Communism and often acts as its catalyst.
7. Communism creates government control of the production of the quantity of goods and services with a bit of Corrupt Capitalism thrown in to make it appear more palatable to some.
8. Some people refer to the Nordic Model (notably Norway, Denmark, Finland, and Sweden) as a successful Socialist construct. They may have a Socialist kind of high income tax (top rates over 50%) to fund social welfare, but that is blended with a lot of Free Market Capitalism and innovation. They also have a solid work ethic, their smaller size makes it easier to minimize corruption, and it is more culturally appropriate for them. Most would say they are not real Socialists.
9. How about the loss of freedoms in the UK with no right to own a handgun for protection, a flurry of government mandates, and nearly

total facial recognition cameras on every block? What a fall from grace for a country that prospered so well in the 1980s under the Free Market Capitalism of Prime Minister Maggie Thatcher. What about Canada's treatment of peaceful protesting truckers using confiscation, fines, and imprisonment to punish them?

10. The US is no better, as it marches on the path to authoritarianism. Look at how the US has treated the January 6 protestors. They have been called armed insurrectionists, but where were the lethal weapons? Video footage shows Capital Police opening barricades and doors and welcoming and waiving them into the Capitol. President Trump had offered to provide 10,000 National Guard troops to maintain order, but the political elite leadership rejected it. They also dismissed the thought of calling up more Capitol Police or requesting the DC police for help. It appears to many that the purpose was to create a more volatile scenario. The result was the outnumbered Capitol Police killed an unarmed female protestor.

All Capitol Police were presented with medals, including the killer of the unarmed protestor. In violation of the law and their Constitutional rights, the judge and lawyers for the protestors were generally not provided video footage that showed many of them were only guilty of trespassing and not "armed insurrection." These protestors have been held without bail in deplorable conditions, while nearly all 2020 rioters, looters, and associated murderers are idolized and free because they carry the water for the D-S.

Some believe that January 6 was co-opted as a leftist plot to disrupt the proceedings in the House that could have stopped the process of certifying the election of Joe Biden due to contentions of widespread voting irregularities—mission accomplished. To learn more about voting irregularities, rent or buy the compelling movie by Dinesh D'Souza, *2000 Mules*.[1]

There were federal law enforcement individuals (and maybe Antifa and BLM) dressed up as Trump supporters, and we do not know whether they had a hand in stirring up the crowd or even initiating any of the actions of the day. For two years, propagandized footage only showed crowd chaos and mayhem. However, nothing supported the lower criminal activity of trespassing until House Speaker McCarthy released all the video footage to Tucker Carlson, who delivered a fuller picture of the events of that day. Coincidentally, a few months later, Fox fired Carlson, their #1 evening show host. Maybe exposing the radical left comes with consequences.

The release of the Twitter files to an independent journalist showed devious pressure from federal agencies to Social Media (SM) to suppress or ban information the government did not like. Deep State agencies had frequent contact with SM and provided lists of people they wanted to be banned. They used this unholy and illegal alliance to interfere with the elections from 2016–2022. Russia and China would be proud of how their US media comrades have mastered their oppressive tactics. The journalist Matt Taibbi published corroborating evidence of this nearly daily collaboration and conspiracy. Coincidentally, after publishing, he was notified that the IRS was auditing him.

11. Fifty years ago, it would have been weird to be talking seriously about Socialism and Communism as strong political forces in the US. Unfortunately, we have been on a slippery slope of catchy political labels that the left has nestled under while infecting the US with their deadly virus. Since the 1950s, the always nice-sounding leftist terms have morphed from liberalism (focused on rights) to progressivism and wokeism (focused on virtue-signaling, guilt and shaming, victimization, and Corrupt and Woke Capitalism). Socialists use nice-sounding terms to brand themselves, label people, create new words, and rename issues to suit their purposes. When you have garbage results to sell, you need excellent branding and marketing, and they have it.

12. The US is now moving into the Socialist stage. There are many voter rule changes to make election irregularities more common. A senior advisor to Biden is an avowed Socialist who honeymooned in Moscow. You may recall Obama had a Communist in his Cabinet until that was

publicized, and he resigned. Hillary Clinton famously voiced concerns about the non-existent "vast right-wing conspiracy." As usual, caustic accusations from the left result from projection, accusing others of misdeeds they are guilty of but won't admit.

The directionally- challenged Hillary had the concept right, but the direction was wrong. There is a deadly "Vast Left-Wing Conspiracy" (VLWC) laser-focused on changing America into a Socialist country with them in total control of everything. The current administration has strong propaganda associations with the Big Business oligarchs and their lackeys, along with the Mainstream Media, SM, educators/indoctrinators, wokesters, Hollywood, and Sports,

13. Our federal government has a corrupt Deep State that hides genuine truths and speaks non-truths with ease and regularity. Together with their propaganda media arms, they act against non-left people to cancel, threaten, erase their jobs, and sometimes cause unjust, lengthy imprisonments. They established a Disinformation Czar (George Orwell presciently concocted a similar Ministry of Truth in his book *1984*), who was noted for spreading disinformation. Free speech attacks would have been more intense had that action not caused outrage and been put on "pause." Russia and China may have inspired our *Pravda*-like propagandists in the US, but those countries are likely in awe at how seamlessly they all work together in the US.

    A June 2021 poll by Momentive reported that for 18 to 24 aged US adults, 54% had a negative view of Free Market Capitalism, while only 42% felt positive. [2] Extraordinary results for the allied efforts of that corrupt leftist cabal and our version of Corrupt Capitalism to destroy what is left of Free Market Capitalism.

14. The Communist brand of Socialism requires a violent revolution. Millions of lives have been lost, primarily in Russia and China. Russia accounts for at least 20 million, including those dying from starvation and the Gulag labor camps. China slaughtered at least 30–50 million in "The Great Leap Forward of 1958–1962 and another 3–5 million in the "Cultural Revolution" of 1966–1976. China has recently shown

a new path in Hong Kong, where their sheer force and brutality have resulted in an overnight change from a free country to a Communist one with minimal bloodshed.

David Satter, in his November 6, 2017 article "100 Years of Communism – and 100 Million Dead," claims all Communist regimes in total account for 100 million dead. [3] **Rudolph Rummel, a government slaughter demographer, claims the total of lives lost due to Communism was close to 200 million since the Bolshevik Revolution of 1917 that birthed Communism.** To better understand the horrors of Communism, visit the Victims of Communism Museum in Washington, DC.

15. Free Market Capitalism relies on freedoms for individuals to improve their lives, while Socialism requires force and strong coercion to bring about meager outcomes. Our North Star should have been the creation and occupation of our Shining City on a Hill, but we never fleshed out what that meant or a process for how to get there, and we allowed the Socialists to put us on the Road to Perdition.

    A totalitarian state is one where nearly all aspects of public and private lives are controlled by a government without limitations. Good examples are Iran, China, and North Korea. An authoritarian state is a totalitarian-light one with some limited freedoms and a strong leader in charge. Current-day Russia and Cuba are examples. Neither flavor of this toxic brew should be palatable to any country, especially in the US, which, at its origin, valued freedom above all.

    Our first ten amendments to our Constitution were called the Bill of Rights. They included religious freedom, attorney-client privilege, the right to own a gun, and protection against unreasonable searches. The D-S is rapidly stripping those away and deconstructing the Bill of Rights. Socialism is a deadly cancer for nearly every country, but it is especially toxic for the citizens of a superpower or other large nations. Transparent democracy and Uncorrupt Free Market Capitalism in a country cannot coexist with it. Do we really want our BFFs to be our comrades in Iran, Russia, and China?

16. Shortly after World War II, the UK, Israel, and India went strong for Socialism, with Britain nationalizing every significant industry. During the decades of the 1950s and 1960s, all three seemed to do well, but some of that was just due to the boom following the end of the depressing WWII era. However, government central planners could not deal effectively with the demands of global competition and the increasing population. During the lesser-Socialist transition years of the 1970s and 1980s, they saw lower and more incentivizing tax rates and an embrace of Capitalism that better allowed them to deal with global competition and uplift the middle class, especially in India.
    - A former British prime minister, Margaret Thatcher, noted, "The problem with Socialism is that you eventually run out of other people's money." With an earned income tax rate of 83%, income from investments taxed at 98%, and the government sector accounting for nearly 60% of GDP, Britain embraced the monumental change needed. During the 1980s, its growth was more robust than all other European economies except one—mainly due to privatization, lower tax rates, and reduced regulation. One indicator of that progress was that inflation fell from 27% in 1975 to 2.5% in 1986.
    - When the Israeli Socialist economy was near collapse in 1983, President Reagan rescued them with a $1.5 billion grant tied to the abandonment of Socialism and adoption of some form of Capitalism. Inflation dropped from 450% to 20% within one year, and their budget deficit was eliminated. Today, they are a vibrant economy of innovation and a healthy middle class.
    - India began its independence in 1947 with a Socialist playbook with price controls, competition barriers, and other non-productive and non-incentivizing practices. Economic malaise from the mid-1960s through the 1970s characterized those years, with the top individual tax rate eventually hitting almost 98%. By the mid-1980s, dramatic changes were being made, like 3-digit

tariffs being reduced to 2 digits and GDP growing around 5–6%, with some years reaching 7% and 9%. From 2004–2005, India's middle class rose to nearly half its population, from 304 million in 2004–2005 to 606 million in 2011–2012.

17. The transitions of these governments meant they adopted some Capitalism to blend with their other more Socialist ideas as an act of self-preservation. Israel is the most vigorous innovator and capitalist economy of the three. Now, 40 years later, the boots of Socialism and Communism that rest on the necks of several other countries' citizens are hard to remove.

    If you could get people to speak freely in North Korea, China, Venezuela, Cuba, Iran, and others, they would welcome Free Market Capitalism and democracy with minimal corruption. Life in repressive countries is hard, but the thugs that run them are brutally holding on to their power, prestige, and their personal enrichment. Today, they have more technologically sophisticated Police States to monitor and punish opponents with tools that did not exist 40 years earlier.

18. Venezuela is an unfortunate example. South America's most prosperous country with the wealthiest middle class due to Capitalism was upended by a 1999 Hugo Chavez Communist regime. It promised even better results for the lower ranks and was succeeded in 2018 by another Communist, Nicolas Maduro. In 2018, after 20 years of lies, inflation was 1 million %, 80% of the country lived in poverty, and everyone lost an average of 20 lbs. from malnourishment.

19. Muslim theocracies are branches of this authoritarian tree of brutal suppression and control. Their hatred of other religions (especially Christianity and Judaism) is evident in their all-too-common executions. ISIS, which Obama called the JV team, turned Iraq churches into dungeons and facilities for torture. They did this after selling one-of-a-kind artifacts on the black market to generate cash to continue their reign of terror. This JV team crucified Christians (even children) to make an ironic point. Besides these brutal executions

and war crimes, they destroyed Christian sites and monuments, including the "tomb of Jonah" in Mosul.

The Inspirations for US Socialism

There are a few resources that the left has been following in their pursuit of total control: the initial Communist revolutions in Russia and China; George Orwell's *Animal Farm* and *1984;* Saul Alinsky's *Rules for Radicals;* Alinsky's inspiration for the creation and the militant actions in the 1960s and 1970s of The Weather Underground and the Black Panther Party and other offspring organizations today; and a 1966 article by two Marxist professors Richard Andrew Cloward and Frances Fox Piven titled *The Weight of the Poor: A Strategy to End Poverty*. [4] While some D-S may not be consciously following the precepts in these writings, it is hardly a coincidence that many of these ideas are manifesting right before our eyes.

1. The first inspiration is the most obvious—the initial Socialist/Communist Revolutions in Russia and China. While today's Russia is nothing like the USSR that emerged after World War II, its Constitution under Stalin was impressive. It asserted the right to free education, right to work, rest and leisure, social security, free medical care and resorts, care for those unable to work, women's rights, no bias, separation of church and state, freedom of speech, press, assembly and demonstration, unions, arrest requiring a court order, and protection of the sanctity of the home and your personal correspondence.

    These are beautiful concepts, and the people loved the Constitution, but it was a fraud, and they never got those things. Tyrants repackage their tyranny as a utopia to appease the masses, then never deliver. Bernie Sanders' Manifesto of 110 pages has sections that sound eerily similar to Stalin's Constitution with lots of free stuff for all.

If you thought modern-day Socialism began with Russia in 1917, you would need to go back to see where they got their inspiration. That inspiration came from Robert Owen's creation of New Harmony, Indiana. On July 4, 1826, this well-to-do businessman issued his Declaration of Mental Independence from the evils of conventional marriage, traditional religion, and private property (which he eliminated). His new thinking appealed to "intellectuals," and some 800 joined this folly in New Harmony. After 2 years and 7 written constitutions, it was closed down as an abject failure.

But the appeal of private property elimination survives today. It is in vogue with the lefties and the lazy, who are happy to claim their participation trophies in our economy regardless of their contribution. That is what Socialism promises—the flattening of society where all are equal. What is not said is that without winners and losers, all are essentially losers living a meager existence, except for the oligarchs, elites, and the ruling class. This new thinking affected the writings of Engels and Marx in Russia and sparked the ideology of the Bolshevik Party and their Russian Revolution.

That authoritarian state inspired Hitler and Mussolini, who substituted nationalism for Socialism but otherwise used similar playbooks. In 1949, China joined the fold, and by the end of the 1970s, 60% of the global population lived in Socialist countries. While Socialism may have experienced some decline from the success of Capitalism (especially with the breakup of the USSR), it did not disappear.

Because the world's brand of Capitalism was often Corrupt Capitalism and not focused on accountably solving major everyday problems, the yearning for something different has returned. Our US Socialists are especially fond of China, which has fraudulently parlayed their once-backward country into #2 globally, poised to topple the US.

2. In his entertaining dystopian book Animal Farm (published in 1945), George Orwell pitted the pigs and other barnyard animals against the farmer they overcame. [5] The pigs continued to increase their power

and tell the other animals that they alone can decide what is true. They rewrite history, treat the other animals poorly (particularly if they express contrary thoughts), and eventually become even worse than their prior farmer owner. They then dined with the corrupt farmers they had complained about.

This scenario is reminiscent of today's America—rewriting history taught in schools under the 1619 Project; destroying government property (including statues that are part of our history); self-absorbed anonymous trolls that revel in their power to cancel people and ruin their lives; and the corrupting and corrosive influence of politicians that stay in office too long. Our Founders only wanted to serve in government briefly and then return to their businesses. They were smart to understand the corrosive results of being infected with a long affair with power and prestige and the endless temptations for financial or other corruption.

3. Orwell's other celebrated book (published in 1949), *1984*, introduces the reader to Big Brother, an omnipresent voyeur who watches what everyone is doing. [6] The surveillance is stifling, and the Thought Police arrest and make people disappear regularly.

For the first time in our history, we had a presidential candidate and then a President who was spied on with no consequences to the perpetrators. This two-tiered justice system works well for the D-S but not for Conservatives. Non-profits that are conservative were treated horribly by the Obama IRS. Upset parents at School Board meetings during the Biden regime were to be labeled as domestic terrorists by the FBI. SM jumped on board the Biden train to save their Section 230 lawsuit protections by almost daily coordinating with the Deep State of the leftist Executive Branch about what they consider the truth. They banned and canceled mostly those whose thoughts and ideas contradicted the D-S.

4. Saul Alinsky's 1971 *Rules for Radicals* has been a new testament bible for leftists. Alinsky focused on infecting with his deadly virus of discontent and moral relativism the middle class and institutions

like churches, schools, and families to break them for his dystopian transformation. All of the societal evils are blamed on Capitalism's exploitation. Unfortunately, the global pursuit of Corrupt Capitalism makes somewhat of a case for him, but Uncorrupt Capitalism should be the aspiration, not brutal Socialism and Communism.

Alinsky is quoted as saying this about the middle class: "The despair is there; now it's up to us to go in and rub raw the sores of discontent, galvanize them for radical social change." In a 1972 *Playboy* interview, he said he would choose hell if given a choice between heaven and hell. In his book, he includes a comment about Lucifer, who was called by Alinsky "the very first radical" because "he rebelled against the establishment and did it so effectively that he at least won his own kingdom." [7]

Here is a summary of some of his most significant rules, along with some editorial comments for some of them:

a. Make the enemy live up to their book of rules. This creates uncertainty, doubt, and fear.
b. Ridicule is man's most potent weapon, which creates doubt, uncertainty, and fear. Treat the targets (Republicans and Conservatives) with no respect.
c. A good tactic is one your people enjoy. Lefties today like habitual lying, disrespecting non-lefty lives and their property, resisting with physical and verbal violence (even though they claim victimhood and retreat to safe places), hoisting the flag of science, and saluting until it does not support their causes. Examples of disrespect abound with the riots of 2020, rhetoric by Maxine Waters and Chuck Schumer, and physically attacking or chasing Republican leaders out of restaurants.

In an interview, Republican John James stated, "Right now, Conservative speech is considered violence, and liberal violence is considered speech." [8] Any tactic is worth it to accomplish the left's ends, especially masking their true intentions. A

possible example is Obama's being for "marriage is between a man and a woman" during his presidential campaign before he "evolved" that concept after being elected.
    d. Keep the pressure on with changing actions and tactics and always exploit every crisis. Be blind to failures and mistakes and never apologize since they are not viewed as failures. The relentless and meritless attacks on Trump or his associates are good examples.
    e. The threat is more terrifying than the thing itself by creating uncertainty, doubt, and fear.
    f. Create an operations base that controls the activities.
    g. Pick the target, freeze it, personalize it, and polarize it. A good example is blackmailing companies like Target and Budweiser to promote the leftist agenda.

5. Alinsky inspired some of The Weather Underground, especially Bill Ayers. Their 188-page Prairie Fire Manifesto rallied a large following, and they were responsible for some 2,000 bombings with some loss of life in the 1960s and 1970s. Bill Ayers went on to serve in Congress and hosted Obama's transition from a community organizer for the infamous ACORN to running for political office. ACORN was the group that pressured banks into making riskier loans that some contend caused the 2007 housing crisis.

    The Black Panther Party was founded in 1967 and may have taken some cues from Alinsky as they wrote their Ten-Point Plan. These two militant radical organizations likely were the foundations for some of today's radical groups. There are similarities between today's Antifa and their ancestors, The Weather Underground. Similar Marxist genes may have been passed down from the Black Panther Party to Black Lives Matter. Alinsky influenced and was praised by the National Education Association union and many Catholic organizations. He described his association with gangster Al Capone as "heaven."

6. The married duo of Cloward and Piven were both Socialist professors at Columbia University. Alinsky's earlier works inspired them, and they wrote a 1966 article titled "The Weight of the Poor: A Strategy

to End Poverty." The focus is on overwhelming the systems and agencies to the point where there is economic collapse to bring about Socialism. Their strategies were a way to operationalize Alinsky's rules with goals and tactics. Here are their 8 Levels of Control (to move from democracy to Socialism):

a. **Healthcare**—Control healthcare, and you control the people.
b. **Poverty**—Increase the poverty level as high as possible; poor people are easier to control and will not fight back if you provide everything for them to live.
c. **Debt**—Increase the debt to an unsustainable level. That way, you can increase taxes, producing more poverty.
d. **Gun Control**—Remove the ability to defend themselves from the government. That way, you can create a Police State.
e. **Welfare**—Take control of every aspect of their lives (food, housing, and income).
f. **Education and Media**—Control what people read and listen to and what children learn.
g. **Religion**—Remove the belief in God from the government and schools.
h. **Class Warfare**— Divide the people into the wealthy and the poor. This will cause more disconnect, and it will be easier to take from/tax the rich with the support of the poor.

By any measure, we have progressed significantly with the tactics and strategies in these writings by Alinsky and Cloward-Piven (C-P). Obama was heavily influenced in college by Alinsky's classes, taught "Alinsky 101" at the University of Chicago, and wrote positively about Alinsky in his books. Hillary Clinton did her college thesis on Alinsky titled "Alinsky and His Organizing Plan." In December 1982, C-P wrote an article titled "A Movement Strategy to Transform the Democratic Party," and that party has never been the same. They saw a golden opportunity to work with the power-hungry Dems to implement their 8 levels of control.

While Bill Clinton enacted welfare reform, Obama promptly changed that to swell the welfare ranks by eliminating Bill's reforms and incentivizing more people to sign up. Clinton implemented the Motor-Voting Law that dumped many people who were not adequately vetted onto the voting rolls. Cloward and Piven (frequent attendees at the annual Socialist Scholars Conference) were at the signing ceremony as guests of President Clinton.

Implementing the C-P strategy picked up steam when Obama was elected and accelerated the movement, starting with the most essential and initial level, healthcare. He wanted a single-payer plan but settled for what he could get—the (Un)Affordable Care Act. His other actions and those of his acolyte-successor, Joe Biden, have rapidly moved us down the road on all 8 of the C-P levels.

While we were spared a Hillary Presidency, we were saddled with Obama's former VP, Biden. He was so indebted to Obama, China (a benefactor for the Biden family), and the leftists who got him elected that he has let this Socialist poison infiltrate his administration through his speeches, Executive Orders, and Cabinet selections, many of whom served under Obama. What Obama accelerated, Biden has explosively added toxic fuel to, acting as Obama's 3rd term. America woke up and rejected Obama's 4th term under Harris and has returned Trump to the White House. What follows is what he has to reverse.

Checklist to Build a Socialist Country

What would we need to do to usher in Socialism in the US?

1. DONE Significant progress on the eight steps of the C-P strategy to overwhelm the systems, increase dependence on government, control thoughts with educational and media indoctrination, inflame class and racial strife, minimize the impact of traditional religion, family

structure, gun ownership, and gender identity (seen in many of this book's chapters).
2. DONE Poor election integrity with elections often determined by wealthy donors with agendas or corrupt practices (Chapters 6, 7).
3. DONE Authoritarian treatment of everyone with mandates, Executive Orders, and excessive regulations and rules by bureaucrats (Chapter 7).
4. DONE Persecution and prosecution of political enemies of the left (Chapters 2, 3, 7, 8).
5. DONE People are fearful of crime and the government's heavy hand (Chapters 7, 8).
6. DONE Massive growth of government cost and size without improved efficiency and problem solutions (Chapters 7, 11). Good examples are erroneous and changing COVID-19 mandates, the hectic rush (with billions in subsidies) to EV auto manufacturing and purchasing, and undependable wind and solar energy.
7. DONE Militarization of the federal government, opening the door to a Police State (Chapter 7).
8. DONE Erosion of our rights, including freedom of speech, private property rights, and gun ownership (Chapters 7, 8).
9. DONE The ruling class of legislators, judges, and the Executive Branch are well cared for and not accountable for solving problems. The focus is on staying in control for the power, prestige, and personal enrichment opportunities. They have been elevated to be "more equal" and entitled than everyone else (Chapter 7).
10. DONE Neutering our work ethic by rewarding criminals, illegal immigrants, and people who don't want to work (2 million have left the workforce since Biden took the reins of power.) (Chapters 7, 8, 9). A good example is the D-S guiding principle of "participation trophies," with no one feeling bad or like a "loser" needing to improve.
11. DONE Significant progress with replacing traditional religion with passionate environmental extremism, extreme transgenderism and gender identity practices, abortion on demand, organized theft, rioting, and destruction of private and government property (Chapters 8, 11).

12. DONE Many are no longer strong people (Chapter 1) who accept personal responsibility for the risks they take, respect others and their property, or willingly embrace the need to make restitution for any damages they cause. Instead, they enjoy participating in the silencing of voices they disagree with by using cancel culture, unfriending, embracing their victimhood at the hands of oppressors, and retreating to their safe spaces or shouting down opposing views.
13. DONE That weakness also surfaces with the obsession of many to escape reality and be totally absorbed and entertained with video games, TV, streaming, music, movies, Social Media, drugs, gambling, and porn. (Chapter 1).

We have much work ahead to reverse these "accomplishments" of the left, but many are wide awake now and willing to work to make that happen. Trump and his successors must stay alert to ensure the permanence of these reversals.

Conservatives vs. Regressives

1. Regressives/wokesters ask, "What is unfair? What am I owed? What has offended me today? What must my country do for me?" Today, achievement is replaced with aggrievement, and unity gives way to identity politics with friction for all. Conservatives ask, "What can I do for myself, my family, my community, and my fellow citizens?"
2. Regressives have different views of diversity and choice. They believe in focusing on ethnic differences and multiplicity of gender identities, but not in diversity of opinions. Regressives laud choice in many areas but not regarding education or health care. Conservatives believe in school choice to weed out or improve poor-performing schools. They want more choices when it comes to health care instead of the standardized features that regressive lawmakers and their Republican co-conspirators mandate for everyone else, except for their own over-the-top healthcare benefits.

3. There is also a significant difference concerning a nation following laws. Conservatives elect officials they believe in to legislate on things that are important to them. Regressives faced with those laws usually cowardly choose not to be direct and re-legislate them but to use political guerilla warfare tactics. They pursue favorable rulings from activist judges, Executive Orders, and bureaucrats to upend democracy.
4. For a more in-depth view of this summary, review the source, which is www.Heritage.org. Look for "The 3 Big Differences Between Conservatives and Progressives" in their series on America's Biggest Issues.
5. If the regressives' ideas and policies were that good, they would happily debate them openly to win more converts to their thinking. They would take a stand and pass laws when they are in the majority. Instead, they rely on less transparent and accountable methods to achieve results. There are only a handful of real Democrats remaining who have the genes of JFK Democrats. Except for these, they are radicals that cannot be reasoned with or compromised with. Their worldview has no room for Free Market Capitalism that, in its uncorrupt form, would be kryptonite to their Socialist/Marxist ideologies.

Is Free Market Capitalism Better?

In global and national issues, results matter more than some Socialist philosophy with no proven record of success, just totalitarian or authoritarian boots on the necks of everyday citizens. Only cooperating elites and oligarchs do well in those societies. In addition to the dramatic conversions from heavy Socialism already mentioned in India, Israel, and the UK, here are two other snapshots that don't get covered by most media, along with some commentary.

- AEI (American Enterprise Institute) published an amazing chart on July 13, 2015. **Globally, from 1970 to 2005, there was an 80% reduction in the % of people living in poverty. There was 26.8% in poverty in 1970, reduced to 5.4% in 2006.** [9] This period saw

the dissolution of the USSR and other countries adopting more Capitalism in their economies.
- **Since the mid-1990s, 1 billion people have escaped poverty before COVID-19. The World Bank calls this "one of the greatest human achievements of our time."** [10] The Index of Economic Freedom reports that "free" or "mostly free" economies have incomes more than 5 times higher than repressive economies. [11]

While Corrupt Capitalism has negative impacts, that perversion of Free Market Capitalism just needs to be rooted out. We should not "throw out the baby with the bathwater." Let's dispose of this cancerous form of Capitalism that pollutes the waters of Free Market Capitalism. It is only with the help of the Vast Left-Wing Conspiracy (VLWC) that the messaging on Socialism and wokeism has turned them into fake positives. They have created negative messaging on Free Market Capitalism and hidden its uplifting outcomes (even with the corruption attributed to its unholy descendant, Corrupt Capitalism). There are two kinds of this illegitimate offspring:
- Corrupt Capitalism is often the result of an addiction to power, prestige, greed, or returning favors to benefactors (aka major campaign donors). One example frequently cited is the government loan guarantee and $1 billion tax credits for investors in Solyndra (a major D-S donor). They later became insolvent, with taxpayers taking the hit and insulating those who should have taken the loss. Another example is where many politicians enter public service with little wealth but amass veritable fortunes before they leave. Instead of public service, this should more appropriately be labeled "self-service." Does anyone believe they were doggedly working on the people's business, and all just got "lucky" with their investments?
- Wokesters practice another variation. It is the virtue signaling done by individuals, CEOs, and their corporations who ignore atrocities done by countries where their cheap or slave labor produces goods for them to sell. They absolve their guilt by canceling

individuals and entities that do not believe and behave as they do or donating to domestic, violent organizations that have the backing of leftist Socialists. Even if they have been bullied into their actions, that only reveals their cowardice as they navigate the Wokesphere echo chamber they created and inhabit with their comrades.

Corrupt Capitalism is a natural bedfellow with Socialism and Communism, as at their core, they are weak and immoral philosophies that require totalitarian or authoritarian measures to snuff out the small flickering flames of Uncorrupt Free Market Capitalism. They create massive bureaucracies that function like living organisms that fight vigorously for self-preservation and the ability to grow and increase their power and sphere of influence.

Throughout history, tyranny is the global default when Free Market Capitalism degenerates into corruption through a lack of vigilance (like our Founders warned). Trump and fellow Solutionists must demonstrate success and show ourselves and the world a better path for progress, prosperity, and peace.

Shining City on a Hill

Ideas for creating that city's critical national security building blocks are laid out starting in Chapter 6, and they follow the principles of our Founders. Those solutions do not represent a return to the OK days of yesteryear but require an ambitious transformation. Whether we achieve this or not will depend on whether we and the people we elect embrace Solutionism and Uncorrupt Free Market Capitalism. Either way, the USA will transform—into the abyss of the USSA (United Socialist States of America) or into occupants of the Shining City on a Hill. To keep playing footsies with Democrat-Socialists is dangerous and will only forestall that inevitable and disgusting transformation into the USSA. Politicians who think they can resurrect bipartisanship are foolishly living in a bygone era that no longer exists.

The world is very different from the time of Ronald Reagan, and the failure of not achieving his aspirations by solving major problems with a methodology like Solutionism has exposed a gaping hole in the fabric of our society. That has allowed Socialists to intensify their foothold to bring things to a critical tipping point. The Socialists saw their opportunity right before them. Even with their stunning 2024 election losses, they will not be easily deterred. They will continue to hide under the label of Democrat or Democrat-Socialist or other less offensive names to peddle their garbage.

They have changed politics into a blood sport and will use every unethical and illegal trick to create their dystopia. They must be soundly defeated, or our democracy and all other global democracies will be lost. We have to understand that and man up and woman up to this existential threat to our survival as a free society and the world's leading economy and beacon of hope for freedom. If not, the Supermassive Black Hole of Socialism will pull us and the rest of the world into The New World Order that many are absolutely giddy about. They should be careful what they wish for, and God help us and the rest of the world if that dystopia becomes our future. Trump will not allow that to occur on his watch, but his successors must stay alert and stay the course.

Mark Levin has talked on his Fox News program and written extensively on American politics and the dangers of Socialism and Marxism, including his book *American Marxism*. There is also an excellent article on *www.heritage.org/conservatism/commentary* by Mike Gonzalez on September 29, 2022. [12] Mike discusses how the Marxists cleverly adjust their strategy to the country they infect. In the US, it is a black-white relations strategy. In Latin America, it is indigenist-white relations.

In nations with a significant diversity of races (like the US), they also pressure with gender fluidity to fracture society. They push for extreme environmentalism everywhere, using tools like ESG and eliminating fossil fuels to destroy Capitalism. They despise private property, patriotism, the family, and religion, focus on indoctrinating the citizenry, and are often called "cultural Marxists" (in the US, it usually wears the woke label).

New Direction, a Brussels-based think tank formed in 2010, is working to awaken Conservatives globally. Some positive results are seen in their presence at Conservative gatherings and the recent elections of Conservative Solutionists to govern in Italy and Argentina.

***

The next chapter covers China's role in this debacle and how the perfect storm could be forming for the epic collapse of the US. It is almost unimaginable that this could happen to the world's #1 superpower. We were headed for that catastrophe until we re-elected Trump in 2024. We are all depending on him to **wake more of us up and woke down**. He will set sail for the Shining City on a Hill despite the turbulent waters the Socialists have thrown us into. China will be an immense challenge for Trump, and you will see why in the next chapter.

CHAPTER 4

The China Syndrome Facilitating a USA Collapse

The China Syndrome

Like the movie with the same name, this one involves the human traits of ambition, dishonesty, Corrupt Capitalism, catastrophe, intimidation, responsibility, and cover-up. Unlike the movie, this debacle has China playing a pivotal role. This virus is 100 times more deadly than COVID-19 because the added accelerant of the US move to Socialism has made this an existential threat to global freedoms, democracy, and peace that many do not realize. What are the elements of this China Syndrome and the Epic Collapse of the USA?

1. **Ambition**—China has included in its public documents its vision and plan to be the world's largest economy and #1 superpower before 2030. They are ahead of schedule due to the inattention of the US administration.
   - **Military**—China already has the largest navy and standing army of proud, goose-stepping, highly-trained people. They have a cache of weaponry, some of which are better than ours, like their

hypersonic missile, which the US is just now testing. They have 6th generation bombers. One is the JH-XX, which seems remarkably similar to 2 US stealth fighters. The other is the long-range H-20 bomber, which is still being tested and looks like a knockoff of the US B-2 Spirit stealth bomber. In August 2023, they announced they had developed a revolutionary cooling system to allow their high-energy laser weapons to be fired "infinitely."

China bought Russian (and some US) military equipment for many years. China reverse-engineered those and now has created better equipment. **7 of the top 20 global defense contractors are found in China.** Russia has lost not only China as a military equipment buyer but also other countries as well. China's hardware is often favored due to cost, tech, and no fear of international sanctions.

- **Technology**—With their embedded network of spies in the US and outright hacking and theft of US tech, they are rapidly catching up to the US. As shown in the prior two paragraphs, they are equal to or ahead of the US in some critical military technology areas. They appear to be ahead of the US with nuclear fusion and have been engaged with France (and likely others) to assist in their plans to build a fusion reactor. China leads the world in producing and selling supercomputers. It is keeping secret its likely fastest exascale-class supercomputer. Biden's sanctions to prevent powerful computer chips from going to China were once again too late to be effective.

- **Control of Strategic Resources and Global Manufacturing**—China is a low-cost manufacturing behemoth. They have seduced American and other companies to give up their technology for the sweet taste of more profits from cheap labor. They have taken firm control of markets in crucial areas like ingredients for pharmaceuticals, personal protective equipment (medical masks, gowns, gloves, etc.), electric car batteries, and car and appliance computer chips.

Additionally, they have globally purchased operations or negotiated agreements for many strategic materials—things like lumber, steel, their petroleum needs, and most importantly, rare earth minerals used in many applications, including cars, military, aerospace, X-ray and MRI systems, clean energy technologies (electric car batteries and solar panels), and computer screens. In 2017, they reportedly controlled 86% of the global rare earth mineral supply. **Recent estimates show China produces 70% of the world's solar modules, 50% of wind turbines, and 90% of lithium-ion batteries for EVs.**

- **Facial Recognition**—With cameras using facial recognition software everywhere in China and a herd of nerds watching the camera feeds, they can see what everyone does, where they go, and penalize them if they go to a house church or other unapproved activities. Their parents spied-on actions affect their children's ability to attend a top college. This tech is exported to poor African countries and elsewhere to keep authoritarian leaders in control of their populace. This is a despot's dream to keep power via universal electronic spying and intimidation.
- **Digital Currency**—Is there any better way to achieve global dominance than controlling the global currency? The US has been mightily helped to be the top dog in the world with the US dollar's status as the world's reserve currency. That has allowed it to penalize rogue nations for destructive actions with sanctions like have been done against Russia, Iran, Cuba, and North Korea.

The digital Chinese Juan emerged from development and was formally announced in 2019 and test-marketed, including many of the Chinese McDonalds, Starbucks, Subways, and the 2022 Beijing Olympics. It is now used in more than 23 major Chinese cities, has more than 140 million personal wallets opened, more than 1.5 million merchants supporting it, and transactions that exceeded 62 billion Juan. The most current data states that 90% of domestic retail trade uses the digital Juan.

Crypto coins (like Bitcoins, which China is targeting) are protected by decentralized blockchain technology, but the Peoples Bank of China centrally controls the digital Juan without the privacy advantage of the blockchain. This allows the Chinese Communist Party to know what everyone is spending money on. The CCP already knows where the populace goes and what they say and do via facial recognition cameras. With the digital Juan, they will have complete knowledge and control of their people's income and expenditures. George Orwell would be stunned that some country went beyond even the dystopia he wrote about in *1984*.

Because of the sanction actions taken against Russia by Biden (that froze half of their currency reserves), global adversaries at arm's length have come together. Iran is selling oil to China and military drones and missiles to Russia, and China is expanding its influence in Europe, the Middle East and Africa, and Central and South America.

China has done the impossible in getting the ME adversaries of Saudi Arabia and Iran to re-establish diplomatic relationships and has presented a peace plan for Ukraine that benefits itself. Iran, Russia, and North Korea's rogue nations can now skirt sanctions by transacting in the digital Juan. The Biden administration is not enforcing sanctions against Iran, which has been relatively free to sell its oil and get even more money for terrorism than the $6 billion recently unfrozen by Biden.

Because many other countries trade significantly with China, they are being pushed to trade using the digital Juan instead of the USD. If the digital Juan gets global traction for commercial transactions, the US reserve currency status will eventually be hollowed out. At some point, China could dump all or most of its decreasing stockpile of US dollar holdings on the world market and cause a dollar devaluation. While this would cause some economic pain in China, the likely calculation is that this would cause a rush to other currencies, especially the digital Juan (or the coming BRICS gold-backed digital currency), and China would win the currency war.

The US has done next to nothing to prevent this from happening. Instead of keeping the economy and the USD sound, our government is trying to copy China with untamed spending and the minimization or elimination of the use of cash. The US thinks its global status will endure and foolishly plays economic Checkers. Meanwhile, China is skillfully (and often unethically) playing and winning a different game of four-dimensional Global Domination Monopoly.

2. **Dishonesty**—This is clear in many areas. Besides the IP theft and spying previously mentioned, the CCP refuses to acknowledge its harsh treatment of Tibetans, the slave labor, and Nazi-like treatment of the Uyghur minority. The CCP refuses to explain the origins of COVID-19 other than the discredited wet market nonsense.

3. **Corrupt Capitalism**—China has no problem taking plays out of the Corrupt Capitalism playbook and inventing some themselves. That is the magic ingredient that propels China's Corrupt Communism to become the powerhouse they are today— using the lure of financial corruption to beat Corrupt Capitalism. Early in 2020, China recalled shipments of PPE that were sold to other countries so they could be used for China's population or resold elsewhere at a much higher panic-gouging price. Let's not forget their seduction of well-known and lesser-known Americans with generous deals, bribes, intimidation, and threatening blackmail. Or the World Health Organization, which praised China for its COVID lockdowns and transparency when those actions deserved criticism instead.

How about their corruption of our education systems, supporting Socialist division in several areas with CRT indoctrination in K-12, climate hysteria, over-the-top agendas for abortion on demand, LGBTQ+ division and violence, and eliminating the right to own a gun? They understand the change to Socialism/Communism is often strongly supported by energized youth. In high schools and colleges, they are completing their brainwashing of our youth with Confucius studies and other Chinese propaganda.

They want our Westernized youth to be assimilated into the new "shiny object" of Confucius' Eastern wisdom. That can replace Western religion, which has often been riddled with well-publicized corruption that has disillusioned many. The support of the youth is critical to completing the US transformation. Once Socialism/Communism is installed, the champions for CRT, ESG, DEI, climate, environment, and LGBTQ+ will no longer be needed, and they and their causes will be made to disappear, along with Confucius' wisdom. They will all be valuable tools that have fulfilled and outlived their purpose of bringing about the Great Reset and the New World Order.

There was a press release by the National Associations of Scholars on June 21, 2022, titled "Confucius Institutes Rebrand to Circumvent US Policy." [1] "Of 118 Confucius Institutes in the United States, 104 have closed or are closing. But at least 64 colleges and universities have reopened a Confucius Institute-like program under a different name or maintained close relationships with the Chinese entities that co-sponsored Confucius Institutes." While this is a global phenomenon, our focus should be primarily on the US legislation passed to stop this, which has been cleverly made irrelevant by this rebranding from China and their continued financial support to our money-hungry, woke high schools and colleges.

They have bribed some of our military to spy for them and supply valuable military intelligence. On April 8, 2023, Sonya Labosco, Executive Director at Air Marshal National Council, stated two shockers. Biden's JV team requires air marshals to spy on Americans coming to DC. Shocker #2: Air marshals must also allow all of their personal identification information to be passed on to China under penalty of suspension or termination if they refuse. Looks like the Police State is getting stronger and readying to partner with China.

One of the most outrageous examples (and a great return on investment for China) was China's $60 million donation to the University of Pennsylvania. The Penn-Biden Center was set up there, Antony Blinken and Joe Biden earned a few million in their roles there, and the university lobbied the Biden administration to cancel the China Initiative (designed to stop economic espionage by China). Biden illegally possessed and scattered confidential and secret documents in multiple improperly secured locations, including at the Penn Biden Center.

4. **Catastrophe**—The blitzkrieg unleashing of COVID-19 caused a global pandemic like the world had not seen for 100 years. Whether this was done accidentally from poor safety protocols at their level 4 lab in Wuhan or whether it was a deliberate trial run, we will likely never know with 100% certainty. In August 2023, globally, there were 770 million cases and 7 million deaths (of which 1 million were in the US) and hundreds of thousands of business failures.

   If China wanted to test out the effects of a global pandemic, they could not be more delighted with the abundance of valuable data they have gathered at the world's expense. They have also supplied to the Mexican drug cartels large quantities of Fentanyl ingredients earmarked for the US via drug mules crossing our wide-open southern border. They even set up and staffed pill-making factories in Mexico to facilitate their war against the US. **Every year, the Fentanyl amount trafficked into the US is more than enough to kill the entire US population. The result is more annual drug overdose deaths in the US than at any other time—more than 70,000 from Fentanyl. This is the #1 cause of death among men 18–45.**

5. **Intimidation**—Joe Biden knows not to ask Chinese leadership about the COVID-19 origins and, in other ways, knows how to treat them much better than they deserve. Certain other politicians and bureaucrats, business leaders, entertainers, sports icons, educators, and media personnel are very amenable to being woke and not putting China in a bad light. That allows them to keep lucrative business deals with

the enormous Chinese market. Through blackmail, bribes, or other intimidation tactics, China can muzzle nearly everyone of influence.

Chinese immigrants in the US are intimidated into providing information or doing positive lobbying for China due to the veiled threats against their relatives in China. Intellectual property is stolen from US manufacturing in China and desirable tech in the US. This is done with bugging devices, industry spies, and Chinese national students at US universities conducting leading-edge research. They have bought US businesses and farmland (some next to US military bases) to influence a favorable opinion of them, spy on our military tech, and control some of our ability to produce food for ourselves.

American companies in China, like Capvision Partners, are now being raided over phony espionage concerns. How ironic that the country heavily engaged in espionage is now taking attention away from them and placing it on others unfairly. This strategy of the kettle calling the pot black derives from the psychological concept of projection and is heavily used by the D-S in the US. American firms that drool over the revenue and profits to be made in China will regret their greed and wish they had not played with the Big Panda, which is growing progressively more deadly daily. It's time to get out of China!

6. **Responsibility**—China has not accepted any responsibility for the propagation of COVID-19 or any tech theft they have done. Our misguided Congress and White House want to ignore the environmental progress the US has made and saddle us with financially onerous and impractical commitments. Meanwhile, China gladly accepts the moniker it carries of a "developing nation" and is exempt from those burdens, even though they and India are the globe's biggest polluters. Within China, they are building 6 times more new coal plants (two approved every week in 2022) than the total for the rest of the world. They are building or planning 300 coal-fired plants outside China to create profits, expand their global colonialist reach, and create more pollution.

7. **Cover-up**—China has not allowed a proper investigation of the origins of COVID-19, and relevant lab records are either withheld, missing, or destroyed. Several scientists working with the virus at the Wuhan lab are deceased, and patient zero is unknown. This is the same tactic they employed with protestors, where no video clips can be found anywhere of the 1987 killing of the peaceful student protestors at Tiananmen Square.

The Perfect Storm

How does the China Syndrome puzzle piece fit into the Perfect Storm to collapse the US?

1. **Coalescing of More Powerful External Adversaries**—China claims to be neutral in Russia's war with Ukraine. However, in the first six months of 2023, they sold only $200,000 worth of drones to Ukraine but $145 million to Russia—not so neutral. In July 2023, they implemented export controls that prevent further drone shipments. Russia can now enjoy and use the tremendous drone superiority they have obtained from China and continue adding to it with Iranian drones. They are BFFs with North Korea, which is a major supplier of munitions for their war efforts in Ukraine. Russia is getting all the armaments it needs from these critical resources and others. At the same time, Ukraine must continually beg for help and survive with its limited supplies, clever strategies, and courageous fighters.

    China's goal of taking down the US is aided by the distractions from the Iranian proxies' war against Israel and Russia's nuclear threats and massive energy sales to fund its European military adventurism, starting with Ukraine. Russia is now getting much closer to China because of the inept way it has conducted its invasion of Ukraine, the offensive actions that destroyed Russia's Nord Stream 2 pipeline, and the shared feeling of exclusion by "Anglo-Americans."

This last reason seems very similar to the sentiments that created the alliance of Germany and Japan in WWII. Those aligned sentiments are intensified with the hatred of many Muslim countries towards the US and Israel. The Muslim religion believes their messiah, called the 12th Imam, will strangely appear for peace after the destruction of Israel and Jews. It is not possible to make peace with leaders and people holding that belief, and Israel and the US are foolish to try.

Russia's navy has taken delivery of its first nuclear drone Poseidon torpedoes. They can deliver atomic warheads that can cause tsunamis and contaminate large coastal areas. Russia's army has performed poorly in Ukraine, and they are depleting their supply of troops, outdated tanks, and other equipment. Russia sold more oil in 2022 (despite sanctions) than any other year, so Biden's foolish and untimely sanction response did more harm than good. They will continue to move oil to China, likely for a mix of cash and state-of-the-art military equipment. Thanks to Russian invasions in Ukraine, China's One Belt One Road Initiative now includes Mariupol, Odesa, and the Black Sea, connecting Eurasia and Africa.

Mordwitschew, one of Putin's generals, said in a September 2023 Russian TV interview that the invasion of Ukraine is just an "intermediate stage" in a more significant European conflict. "When we talk about attacking Eastern Europe, it will naturally take longer." [2]

Let's not forget the 3rd side of the triangle of evil, Iran. Biden's actions have brought Iran and Russia closer. Iran is selling drones, missiles, and other equipment to Russia, and Russian nuclear firms will likely be enriched working with Iran. Sanctions against Iran had them financially on the ropes at the start of King Biden's reign with only $4 million in reserves (from sales of only 100,000 barrels of oil daily at the end of 2020), and the internal unrest could have toppled that repressive and global-destabilizing regime.

Instead, our King decided not to enforce those sanctions, and their reserves now exceed $70 million. Most comes from oil sales to China—a double-dunce move with much of Iran's 2–3 million barrels/day going to our adversary, China. All of this cash has put their terrorism efforts and nuclear development on steroids. Early in May 2023, Iran seized two oil tankers. This is the same terrorist country Biden wanted a deal with instead of playing hardball with them. While Biden's misguided nuclear pact with Iran appears dead, he has still found a way to appease them. In September 2023, he agreed to deal with this terrorist regime and unfreeze $6 billion of their assets in exchange for 5 Americans, who were basically hostages for such a time as this.

The Nazi regime in Iran has provided significant military and financial support and encouragement for its funded proxies, primarily Hezbollah, Hamas, and the Houthis in Yemen. On October 7, 2023, Hamas took the lead and committed war crimes from their bases in Gaza against Jews and others in Israel, including the savage slaughter of 1,200 Jews and 29 Americans and the kidnapping of over 200 civilians.

You cannot negotiate with evil that delights in brutal savagery that is brainwashed into its believers from a young age. Given a chance (just like ISIS), they would destroy any cultural, historical, and religious sites that are not their own. This lethal evil must be eradicated, and that government must be replaced with one that is not a perversion of religion that promotes hatred, violence, and genocide. Instead, it must form a partnership with Jews and focus on the betterment of its people. Societies based on hatred are toxic for their neighbors and for the brainwashed who do not focus on a better life but on hating and destroying others.

Besides funding terrorism, Iran has also trained Hamas for this war and is calling the shots with Hezbollah in Lebanon to create a 2-front war for Israel. They are green-lighting the Houthis in Yemen to launch more than 150 attacks on US forces and commercial ships in the area with a weak US response. Our response should have been formatted with "shock and awe," but Team Biden does not understand that is the way to deal with terrorist bullies. This is the nice repayment given to Uncle Joe for delisting Hamas as a terrorist organization in 2021. Remember, the **Hamas slogan is "Allah is great, death to America, death to Israel, curse the Jews, victory to Islam."**

In its propaganda newspaper, *Kayhan*, on December 11, 2023, an article appeared titled "Maximum Pressure With A 'Balance of Horror And Fear." It stated, "The only way to confront America's belligerent policy, and to deter and isolate the Zionist regime, is to apply maximum pressure by means of a balance of horror and fear." King Biden still thinks we should negotiate with Iran.

Iran had three reasons for this. Firstly, it derailed or delayed Saudi Arabia's plan to join the Abraham Accords. Secondly, it was part of Iran's strategy to become a nuclear power while they distracted Israel and the US, which has no interest in stopping that. Lastly, **Iran's belief in the appearance of the 12th Imam requires the destruction of Israel and all Jews to occur before he appears.**

None of this would have been possible without the unenforcement of sanctions against Iran. There should be no compromise with this level of hatred, evil, and religious fanaticism. **Iran and other dysfunctional terrorist entities are built on hatred of certain groups and glorify death and destruction, while well-functioning democracies are built on goodwill and tolerance and glorify life and creating a better society.** (That shows how much our country continues to look more like the terrorists and less like the Shining City on a Hill.) King B's uncoordinated and disastrous Afghanistan withdrawal and his nonsensical Iran policies have gaslit wars in Ukraine and the Middle East. He (and his Cabinet) do not want Israel or Ukraine to win, and his actions reflect that.

Arch-enemies Iran and Saudi Arabia are selling oil to China, and China has brokered a deal for them to re-establish diplomatic ties. China's influence in the ME has soared while the US has retreated. Their likely support of Iran's behavior to control the transport of oil tankers in the ME is a danger to global stability. The chaos Iran will increasingly cause (even without nuclear weapons) supports global instability. Biden's actions have made this 3-headed monster now a metastasized mega threat.

Russia's invasion of Ukraine has fortunately resulted in two positive countermeasures. The Nordic countries of Sweden, Denmark, Finland, and Norway have agreed to operate their 250 fighter jets as one fleet. Finland and Sweden have been accepted to join NATO.

What are the major takeaways from these wars in Ukraine and Israel?

- Iran will likely become a nuclear power threatening all in the Middle East, Europe, and the US, while the world is distracted by wars in Ukraine and Israel.
- Expansion of peace in the ME with Saudi Arabia joining the Abraham Accords is delayed and perhaps derailed completely.
- The security of the only ME democracy, Israel, is seriously in jeopardy.
- While the West is providing (in trickles) military equipment support to Israel and Ukraine and depleting its own arsenals, China is ready with its hypersonic missiles and lasers that can fire non-stop to take over Taiwan and any other country it wants in its march to global totalitarian supremacy.

2. **Rapid expansion of China's One Belt, One Road colonialist program and BRICS alliance to minimize the influence of the US and its dollar in global relations and trade and create economic hardship in the US.** China has thousands of projects in 154 countries that expand their influence and pull strategic resources out of those countries, create profits for China by building infrastructure for them, and saddle those countries with expensive loans and agreements to provide China with ports and bases.

Their BRICS program is designed to minimize the use of the USD in global trade and loans and replace the USD as the world's reserve currency with a digital Juan or a likely gold-backed BRICS digital currency. This could cripple the West's SWIFT banking system if it had not launched its new digital platform. There is more about BRICS later in this chapter and Chapter 10.

3. **Destruction of the US from Within**—The prior two chapters showed the US deterioration along many fronts. To name a few: Corrupt and Woke Capitalism, failure to follow the fundamental principles of the Founders and instead re-imagine the Constitution, the powerful Vast Left-Wing Conspiracy from the many propaganda arms of the D-S Party, and no structure or concrete solutions for our problems.

Many critical issues and solutions to those problems involving national security are detailed starting in Chapter 6. They include issues that heavily affect our national security: elections, government processes, crime, immigration, our preparedness for the China threat, and strategic resources. The politicization of the Deep State members (like the FBI, DOJ, EPA, DOE, and the IRS) is extremely serious and eroding our foundational freedoms by harassing and punishing contrarians to leftist ideology.

We have followed the examples of several great powers like ancient Persia, Babylon, Egypt, Rome, Spain, and, more recently, Britain. They all traversed the pathway of expansion and commercial dominance, followed by the rise of pseudo-intellectualism, decadence, decline, and collapse. The US has been traveling this path and is clearly in the decadence-decline phases. We are ripe for being toppled and replaced as the #1 superpower and tossed into the historical dumpster of "has been" great nations. Of course, the US will still exist, but it will be a shell of its former self and be relegated to the status of a junior partner of and highly dependent on China. But how does our hijacked journey compare to other nations or empires that lost their luster?

Comparison to Collapsed Regimes

1. **Government Thinks It is Omnipotent and Benevolent, and Its Mandates Must Be Obeyed.**

- Nazi Germany had many edicts that took away peoples' freedoms, pitted children against parents, non-Jews vs. Jews, labeled non-Jews as victims, and savagely treated and killed Jews. They also masqueraded as benevolent with their youth programs.
- The US has taken away freedoms (e.g., the continued jailing of January 6 protesters without due process); created a sequel to *The Purge* environment where people on the left are free to burn, loot, and murder; used identity politics to divide and pit groups against each other; created two tiers of justice— one for oligarchs, elites, wokesters, and other leftists and another for everyone else; and are happy to have people rat out others who are not behaving in the way our leftist government says they should act.
- The US government mandated (and then kept changing) many erroneous pronouncements, including cloth mask-wearing, which has been scientifically proven ineffective against COVID-19. Government officials openly displayed their hypocrisy and self-exemption from these mandates. Those mandates were supposed to benefit the citizens but are more about acclimating us to their expression of power and control.

2. **Corrupt Governments Co-opt Most Forms of Persuasion for Their Propaganda Use.**
   - The Nazis mastered using the Gestapo, the Brownshirts, print and radio media, the film industry, and the indoctrination of youth in the school system to further their poisonous agenda. The former Soviet Union was infamous for its vicious use of the KGB to silence opposition and its use of Pravda to spread disinformation.
   - The virtue-signaling and Corrupt Capitalism of Entertainment, Sports, Education, Big Media, Big Pharma, and other woke companies are organs of the leftist D-S and often speak with one voice to influence us all. The unholy cooperation of Media with government agencies like the FBI to silence the voices of messages the government does not like is despicably similar to the Gestapo.

Today's BLM and Antifa, with their violence and bullying, are reminiscent of the Brownshirts.

3. **Checks and Balances of the Executive Leadership Are Seriously Eroded.**
    - The Roman Senate was effectively neutered, corruption was rampant, and the Emperor made all the important decisions, along with his Deep State sycophants. Similarly, there were no checks on Hitler or the leaders of the former Soviet Union.
    - Checks and balances from state and local governments have been diminished; the courts have become politicized; the Executive Branch has metastasized and taken power from Congress with Executive Orders that seem to have no boundaries or limits. Financially rewarding or disciplining through Corrupt Capitalism is commonplace.
    - Those Executive Orders continue to roll out and facilitate building our Police State and the elimination of freedoms and rights. They are apparent with immigration, COVID-19 mandates that don't yield results, mandates concerning DEI, ESG, and CRT, gender information and decisions being pushed onto children who are not mature enough to make those life-altering decisions and forcing the Green New Deal on us by pushing us to buy the kinds of cars, appliances, and energy they want.

4. **The Executive in Charge Selectively Ignores Laws and the Protection of Individuals.**
    - Nazi Germany and current-day repressive regimes all have traveled this path.
    - Our Constitution is often ignored or re-imagined rather than requiring legislators to go on the record and pursue amendments or laws that require courageous votes. The Biden regime is happy to ignore (without any consequences) the Supreme Court rulings they don't like (most notably the successful "Remain in Mexico" policy).

5. **People Lose Trust in Government and its Laws, and Chaos and Violence Break Out.**
    - Rome realized that its policies were not helpful to the population. Much of the middle class was decimated because the government farms used slave labor, and independent farmers could not compete. That meant the owners and workers of the independent farms and the other businesses those farms supported became unemployed, and many people were no longer a part of an economy that circulated money. The disenchantment was so great that Rome imported wheat, gave free bread to all, and provided the gory amusement of the deadly "games" at Rome's Colosseum and other arenas around their vast empire.
    - In the US, private property rights and the rule of law are often ignored. Police are vilified, driven out, told not to do their jobs, and sometimes defunded. Looting, riots, burning, and destroying personal or government property are not stopped or prosecuted. Some people are living through real-life episodes of *The Purge*. Unfortunately, this is their reality, not a movie or TV script.
6. **The Elites Are More Equal Than Others, with More Rights, Privileges, and Exemptions from Certain Laws and Mandates, Resulting in Dissension and Scapegoating.**
    - The Romans blamed all government-created problems on Christians, and Hitler blamed all the German problems on the Jews. Both groups of scapegoats were hunted and killed with the encouraged help of neighbors.
    - The US fought the Civil War and passed a Civil Rights bill to provide all Americans equal treatment under the law. The D-S have promoted victimology to scapegoat "white privileged" and Conservative individuals for the problems created by government interference since 1964. They are demanding not equal opportunities but equal outcomes. That is the ultimate participation trophy, absent the joy of winning or the lessons learned from coming up short.

7. **The Endless Feeding of a Bloated, Corrupt, Inefficient Bureaucracy Causes Higher Taxes and Fewer Goods and Services for the Citizenry.**
    - During the Cold War, the USSR diverted people and financial resources to compete with the military spending of the US and neglected the betterment of its people's lives. The result was that it financially imploded and lost most of its empire.
    - A free US market economy with minimum necessary regulations is under increasing siege by the left. They want to decide which companies should win and which should not. That means fossil fuel companies and energy independence need to be sacrificed on the altar to the gods of the environment. Of course, they ignore the significant pain of inflation this causes and the fact that US-produced energy is the cleanest in the world. What is the sense of the US sending currency overseas to buy dirtier oil from repressive bully regimes to damage the environment and imperil world peace?
    - Our total government spending consumes about 50% of our GDP annually and keeps growing, while some flourishing countries consume only 20% or less.
8. **Education's Role in Preparing Children for Life and Work Is Subverted through Indoctrination to Create Lemmings for Government Mandates and Propaganda.**
    - Hitler's Brown Shirts youth indoctrination program was a good example.
    - The US education results are a joke when compared to other industrialized nations. We are a dismal 26th in the world in math proficiency. We are too absorbed in brainwashing the future of our country with victimology, how bad the USA is, white privilege, critical race theory, and other useless and damaging nonsense. Instead, we should teach a balanced perspective of US history, life skills, and preparation to be employed for those not attending college.

- Higher education costs were allowed to increase exponentially through government interference, creating much stress and a student loan debt bomb. The D-S "solution" is to throw taxpayer money to pay student debt (without Congress approval) to reduce the problem they created by herding too many high schoolers to go to college. University bureaucrats were allowed to increase costs without limits and without providing a proper student employment outlook and a return on investment understanding. How many Starbucks baristas (or similar employees not needing a college degree) are now faced with huge college debt for a degree they could not use and did not need for their jobs?

9. **Most Empires Grow from Values of Self-reliance, Discipline, and Hard Work. They Decline When They Focus on Power, Prestige, Comfort, Entertainment, and Greed.**
    - The Roman elites' financial corruption, pleasure, and comfort-seeking were legendary. As mentioned earlier, their fight-to-the-death "games" and free bread were provided for the masses to distract them from the problems the elites created.
    - Many in the US do not resemble the strong people who built the country. Instead, some relish recording a woman being raped rather than coming to her rescue. We do not take seriously the borders that define where we start and other countries end. Many obsess over pursuing power, prestige, greed, comfort, and being entertained. Social Media and cowardly anonymous trolls delight in using their power to cancel people who speak the truth that is not to their liking.

10. **The Family Unit Deteriorates and Is Replaced by the Omniscient Government, Which Feigns Concern for Their Welfare.**
    - Hitler got kids to snitch on their parents if they saw them doing something the government frowned upon. Life was so hard for the non-elites in Rome that many families sold their children into slavery when they could not support them.

- The US family unit has taken serious body blows through nonsensical welfare regulations; deplorable education, teaching children to be ashamed of their heritage; allowing children to make decisions that they are not mature enough to make (and should be made by their parents); despising parents wanting a strong input into their children's education; and not teaching children (who often become parents later) how to incorporate life skills like good relationships and money management.

11. **The Bloated Government Lacks Financial Discipline.**
    - This usually boring aspect is not important until it becomes critical or existential. Mighty (and not-so-mighty) nations think they can ignore the fundamental laws of economics and stay powerful. This silent killer creeps into a country, resulting in high taxes, inflation, crime, unemployment, and urban decay.

        Venezuela was the most prosperous South American country until the corrupt Communist Hugo Chavez took over. Similar deterioration occurred in Africa, Zimbabwe under Robert Mugabe. The USSR had to allow some forms of Corrupt Capitalism to prevent the Communist nightmare from totally collapsing. Many other examples include ancient Rome, China, and Egypt. More recently, since 1990, hyperinflation (50% or more) has occurred in 28 countries on 35 occasions. You can ignore the laws of economics and fiscal integrity only so long before they devour your economy with runaway inflation, currency devaluation, and sometimes total economic collapse.

    - Minimal debt, fiscal responsibility, and annual balanced budgets are generally not considered stylish or essential. Many in Congress think that if they keep throwing more money at problems, voters will like those efforts (even though problems are not solved), and they will get re-elected. The US has not had a balanced annual budget since 2001, prints money with abandon, and spends recklessly with few controls.

- The stimulus payments that were made totaled $5.5 trillion, and the Fed bought up US Treasuries and mortgage-backed securities from the market, totaling another $5 trillion from October 19, 2019 to May 31, 2022. Our total GDP was $21 trillion, so that manipulation amounted to 50% of our annual GDP. How is that prudent or able to bring about anything but high inflation and large debt?
- Added to that toxic cocktail is the addictive lure of higher taxes and complex regulations (another way to increase revenues with fines for violations of complicated regs). Our 2022 debt-to-GDP ratio is over 100%, placing us 7th on the list of countries with high % debt, with Greece, Lebanon, Italy, and others beating us out. That compares unfavorably to the UAE, which has a ratio of only 19%. The total US national debt of $34 trillion in Q3 of 2023 ($35 trillion in 2034) makes us the largest debtor nation in the world, with debt exceeding GDP by 20% and growing.

12. **Most Great and Mighty Nations Are Content to Keep Revisiting Their Past Achievements and Overlook the Traits That Made Them Exceptional.**
    - All of these great nations and empires that fell suffer historical amnesia. Aristotle said, "Republics decline into democracies, and democracies degenerate into despotism." [3]
    - Several leaders have mocked the US's destiny to be exceptional, which is no longer believed by many in the US. Despite global hostile activities and intercepted chatter, our mighty military muscle was unprepared for attacks on December 7, 1941, and September 11, 2001. We could not win wars in Vietnam, Afghanistan, and Korea (not long after we were the primary reason for victory in WWII). Many in the country have been brainwashed to believe that, at our core, we are essentially evil and that Capitalism should be replaced with Socialism. Others are somewhat oblivious to the seriousness of the drastic changes occurring and think that

we are the same great country that was pivotal to winning World Wars I and II. We are not.

Likely Triggers for the Epic Collapse

As bad as the accelerated deterioration is now (with the current national leadership), there still needs to be pre-triggering events followed by one or more big triggers to topple the USA giant. We have an environment of slowing economic growth, higher inflation, low labor participation rates, and worker and consumer goods shortages. Once a noteworthy event marks the beginning of the accelerated decline, the conclusion happens relatively quickly in historical reckoning. Suggested reading: Alfred McCoy, in a prescient Salon article dated December 6, 2010, titled "How America will collapse (by 2025)," compared other collapses and predicted the US collapse 22 years after the 2003 Iraq invasion.

In US history, devastating events were met with a sense of resolve and moral clarity in our fight for independence, World Wars I and II, and 9/11. That unifying resolve and moral clarity are scarce in today's America.

Here are some possible pre-triggering scenarios:

1. Continuing poor economy with slow or negative growth, low labor participation rates, worker and consumer goods shortages, high interest rates, huge budget deficits, and high inflation present in over-valued Wall Street stocks, real estate, and record-high consumer credit card debt. This economic cocktail could decrease the US government credit rating— oops, this actually happened in August 2023. **Since the 1913 Federal Reserve's creation, the dollar's purchasing power has declined to a level where it can only buy 3 to 4 cents of what it could buy then.**

    As for the stock market, from April to May 2022, the DJIA racked up 8 straight weeks of losses, which qualified it as the longest losing streak since 1923. The overall stock market volatility tracks events and sentiment and bounces up and down without a steady and measured upward trajectory. But Apple is a very different story. It took them 49 years to reach a valuation of $1 trillion in 2018, $2 trillion in 2020, and $3 trillion at the start of 2022. Does that make sense to anyone except maybe Paul Krugman and those who profit from this unsustainable phenomenon?

2. The rise of stagflation, which many believe is already in the very early stages. This is a disastrous journey of slow or negative growth and very high interest rates that is extremely hard to get off, as shown by the US during the 1970s and 1980s. Stagflation can also trigger hyperinflation of 50% or more.

3. After 10 years of near-zero interest rates (and excessive federal spending for even longer), the Federal Reserve woke up from its slumber. Its late-to-the-game rounds of severe monthly interest rate hikes will likely combine with other adverse economic factors and push the US into its second Biden recession—some think we are already there. The first Biden recession occurred in Q1 and Q2 of 2022, where the US had "2 consecutive quarters of negative economic growth." [4] That definition of a recession was used for decades, but the Biden administration and the D-S said that is no longer the definition. The lemming media have happily gone along with that re-definition.

4. A cascade of problems and failures with infrastructure like power, water, waste systems, internet, telecom systems, and vehicle fuel. Some or all of this could be caused by cyber warfare or other terrorist actions. Under the current administration, there is no attempt to determine how much is financial crime and how much is adversarial countries like China, Russia, North Korea, or Iran. Regardless, internal confidence would be severely weakened.

This has already happened by hackers, Volt Typhoon, who are linked to China. They operated for at least five years before being discovered. A Cybersecurity Advisory alert issued on February 7, 2024, said those hackers had penetrated the "Communications, Energy, Transportation

Systems, and Waste and Wastewater Systems Sectors in the continental and non-continental United States and its territories."

A few days before that, FBI Director Christopher Wray testified in a House hearing on China's cyber threat that "China's hackers are positioning on American infrastructure in preparation to wreak havoc and cause real-world harm to American citizens and communities, if or when China decides the time has come to strike." At that hearing, it was stated that data "strongly suggest that the PRC is positioning itself to launch destructive cyber-attacks that would jeopardize the physical safety of Americans and impede military readiness in the event of a significant crisis or conflict with the United States. Should we keep playing nice with China?

In 2023, the World Economic Forum Managing Director said, "93% of cyber leaders, and 86% of cyber business leaders, believe that the geopolitical instability makes a catastrophic cyber event likely in the next two years." At the same event, the Albanian prime minister talked about the growth of cybercrime "from $3 trillion in 2015 to an expected $10.5 trillion in 2025." This acceleration continues with no effective deterrence. Read point 7 in the next section.

5. The Russian invasion of Ukraine explodes with tactical nuclear weapons or other "banned" weaponry or aggression against countries supporting Ukraine.
6. China and Iran's military adventurism is accelerating due to US policy coupled with prior failures in Afghanistan, no response to the loss of Hong Kong democracy and sovereignty, the slow and inadequate Ukraine response, no significant response to help Taiwan, and the rush and flawed strategy to make a deal with Iran—a deal that would have been too generous, with no oversight, and one they would not follow. That would not have stopped Iran from transforming from a global bully saddled with unenforced sanctions to a global nuclear bully with little or no sanctions.

Biden's relentless march to create favor with bullies like Iran has found another avenue, as mentioned earlier. He "negotiated" with this terrorist state to give them $6 billion in exchange for 5 Americans held there for just this opportunity. Their terrorist activities will now be re-energized from this successful strategy and will encourage more kidnappings and imprisonments. That already happened on October 7, 2023, with the Iranian-funded Hamas war crimes attack on Israel. Thank you, Joey.

Separately, China will continue its One Belt One Road Initiative of investing in the infrastructure of many countries (154 at last count) to create bases in strategic global locations, swallow up vital strategic resources, and make those countries so financially dependent on them that they will function as colonies of China.

China uses our wide-open southern border to smuggle young Chinese men into the US. That gives China the potential to sabotage our infrastructure or other havoc or violence if and when China gives them an order to. In 2023, 169 men on the terrorist watchlist from multiple countries were apprehended. Because of their stealth, how many others were not caught and are ready to execute some terrorist plan when given the signal?

7. Another pandemic. As far-fetched as this may seem, China is "playing around" with virus strains in their Wuhan lab that are much more lethal than COVID-19.

While these pre-triggers are powerful, they are not enough to topple Goliath. Also, with a more professional Trump administration in DC now, these risks will be addressed more seriously and eliminated or mitigated.

What could that triggering lethal body blow be?

1. Our economy may have been mishandled to create the environment for a recession. Then the Fed may lower interest rates, reverse its tightening course, and print money with abandon, thinking we can print our way out and paper over the mess many administrations

have allowed. Confidence in the dollar would fall due to this unsustainable approach.

Here are some pieces of data that suggest a recession or worse may be something Trump will have to deal with.

- The 10-year Treasury Bond was on target to finish 2023 with a 3rd straight year of losses. This has not happened in the nearly 250 years of our existence. It actually finished slightly higher. Lower rates for new bonds mean the value of existing bonds increases. Our GDP is driven by government-provided suspect job numbers and heavily comprised by jobs from the lower-paying hospitality sector, the government expansion, red state success, and part-timers. The markets expect interest rate cuts in 2024, and the yields for these bonds have only slightly reduced from 3.88% on December 31, 2022, to 3.86% on December 31, 2023.
- In August 2022, wages were up 5%, and inflation was up 9.3%, representing the largest pay decline in 25 years. From January 2021 to August 2023, real wages have fallen each year.
- Our Strategic Petroleum Reserve is at the lowest level in 38 years.
- Over the last 50 years, bank lending has dropped by at least 1.5% only 3 prior times. We now have the 4th instance—as of July 19, 2023, bank lending was down 1.63% from February 15, 2023. After the 3 prior times, the S&P 500 lost about half of its value.
- In US history, 2023 was the 5th decline year for our M2 money supply. This is the 1st one in 90 years. Here's what followed those money supply declines.
  - Depression of 1870
  - Panic of 1893
  - Depression of 1921
  - The Great Depression of 1929 (the largest drop ever in M2)
  - What will follow the recent decline in 2023?

2. However, the Fed may alternatively keep higher interest rates for far too long to tame the inflation caused by their prior loose monetary policy and Biden's wild spending spree. That would seriously

damage the economy, resulting in higher levels of bankruptcies and foreclosures, lower federal and state tax revenues, and higher unemployment. Even worse is the ballooning interest payments on our national debt. Our high interest rates inflate the value of the USD and have negative global impacts on many countries that are trading and borrowing with USD, creating high interest costs for them. This has driven some into the welcoming arms of China, who will accept loans and trades using a mix of the Chinese digital Juan and the other country's local currency.

Since 1960, the lowest rate for a 10-year Treasury note was 0.89% in 2020 but increased to 4.34% in August 2023. With a debt of $35 trillion, the daily interest cost is over $2 billion, and the annual interest cost is $800 billion now, climbing to $1 trillion.

Our national debt borrowing for fiscal year 2023 had to increase to cover the $1.7–$2 trillion deficit created that year by Team Biden. The deficit is on track to repeat in just the first half of fiscal year 2024. The pre-pandemic annual deficit averaged less than half of what the Spendaholics are racking up now. King Biden's Team cannot connect the dots between their Don Quixote spending rampage that is not working and the demise of the dollar they are causing with high inflation and interest rates that are crushing households and businesses.

Eventually, this debt bomb will explode, and confidence will be lost in the US dollar internally. Then other nations (especially China, Russia, and Iran) will look to exchange their dollars for something else, like the digital Juan, and accelerate their bilateral trade agreements with other countries in currencies other than the US dollar. That is already happening—this trigger is being pulled (more on this in the China Threat Chapter 10).

3. The FSB (Financial Stability Board) has a list of "too big to fail" globally based bank corporations. Depending on whose list you look at, the US has 8 to13 of those banks, with another 15 to 20 considered "systematically important." These banks usually have sizeable exposure to derivative commodities contracts from their customers or their own

portfolios. **Global derivatives are estimated at $650 trillion to 1.5 quadrillion dollars. Warren Buffett calls derivatives the "financial weapons of mass destruction."** This could be a devastating tsunami that overwhelms the global GDP, which in 2020 was only $85 trillion. The failure of one or more of these banks (especially in the US) could trigger a dollar collapse and a possible global economic disaster.

Because of the Fed's rapidly high interest rate hikes during 2022–2023, financial institutions holding a significant amount of longer-term government bonds and mortgage-backed securities are at risk since those are worth much less on their financial statements. The 2nd tier banks (just below the "too big to fail" banks have seen 3 failures in 2023 (Signature Bank, First Republic Bank, and Silicon Valley Bank). However, the administration has decided to make everyone whole, including those with deposits beyond $250,000 (the FDIC-insured limit).

Could those banks woke and leftist leanings have been rewarded despite the quality of their financial management and regulatory oversight by the San Francisco Federal Reserve (for two of the three banks)? This is very suspect at Silicon Valley Bank, where many Chinese start-up companies doing business in the US are being made whole when they legally are supposed to be behind US customers' claims.

For more insight into this situation, there is an excellent article by Ambrose Evans-Pritchard on May 2, 2023, in The Telegraph titled **"Half of America's banks are potentially insolvent—This is how a credit crunch begins." It covers the crashing of US commercial real estate, the US bond market, and $9 trillion of uninsured deposits in the banking system. Nearly half of the 4,800 US banks are "burning their capital buffers" and are underwater by $2 trillion. When significant amounts of commercial debt are up for refinancing in the next few quarters at much higher interest rates than they are currently paying, there will likely be many bankruptcies, which further erodes those banks' viability. Commercial**

property values have fallen only 4%, but another 17% is expected, and regional banks typically supply 70% of those loans.

Small and mid-size banks will reduce their lending to avoid situations like the seizure of First Republic Bank, where the FDIC wiped out all value held by shareholders and bondholders. The Fed seems laser-focused on cutting inflation (with historic rate increases and removing nearly $100 billion monthly from the banking system for loan availability). The Fed may cut inflation at the cost of creating a banking crisis, similar to what was done during the aftermath of the 1929 stock market crash. This trigger is being pulled.

4. The actions of the BRICS countries could usher in another attack on the dollar. They are already trading in local currencies with each other and avoiding the USD for trade and loans. When the timing is right, they will launch their planned digital gold-backed currency and divest their USD and US treasury holdings. Their digital currency will benefit from instant transaction settlement, using blockchain technology and hobble the West's SWIFT banking system if it had not launched its coming digital platform.

As a member of the Bretton Woods Committee (the group that created the IMF), George Soros had a hand in its creation. The SDRs are a composite currency basket of USD, Euros, Juans, Yen, and Pound Sterling and create enhanced confidence due to the 2,800 metric tons of gold the IMF has in reserves. SDRs can be used for global transactions like loan repayments and other cross-border commercial purposes. These are formulaically allocated to countries by the elite members of the Bretton Woods Committee.

The allocations and composition of currencies in the basket are changed periodically, and BRICS will likely influence the Special Drawings Rights (SDR). The dollar could be significantly affected if its % of the basket is reduced considerably from its current 41.73% or if more global transactions settle with SDRs, not USD. The USD is already under attack from the BRICS, and this trigger is being pulled (see the China Threat Chapter 10). This trigger helps to pull the next 2.

5. Many countries hold their gold reserves in the safety of the US. A few have demanded and received their gold to store in their countries. If more governments lose confidence in the USD and there is a rush to get their gold bullion back to back a new digital currency or to settle transactions, this will crater the US dollar. This trigger is being pulled (see the China Threat Chapter 10).
6. Gold and silver bullion contracts are backed up by only about 2.5% of the actual physical commodity. That means if people get nervous about the US or global economy and want to hold the actual commodity instead of a piece of paper for that commodity, that would supercharge the price of gold and crash the dollar. The value of paper contracts is discounted compared to physical gold bullion assets, meaning there is now a bias for physical gold holding since April 1, 2019, when gold became a Tier 1 asset with no discount in value.
7. A black swan event like World War III could be launched with an EMP or cyber-attack to neutralize the US military weaponry capability. This might result in minimal bloodshed. This one can be planned for, but others may need responses as they occur. A story by Maggie Miller on April 16, 2023, titled "What it will look like if China launches cyber-attacks in the US,"[5] lays out a good summary. She mentions targeting our financial markets, water and energy infrastructure, as well as our ports, military systems, transport logistics, and other military support companies.

In 2020, FBI Director Christopher Wray said his agency opens one new investigation into Chinese counterintelligence every 10 hours, accounting for half of these investigations. Yet Biden quickly shut down the successful Trump-era China Initiative focused on investigating and closing China's spy operations in the US.

With sound economic policies, Trump can avoid the first 3 triggers. The 4th–6th triggers occur when our country and its economic integrity no longer inspire global confidence. These 4th–6th triggers are occurring with the rapid expansion of the BRICS member countries and their desire to minimize the global use of the USD. The 7th is a black swan event for which we must be prepared. Chinese hackers have already penetrated our critical infrastructures for over five years. China may be using AI to determine its moves toward global domination because its actions and results are uncannily successful, and it adapts and tweaks quickly as needed.

China's CCP celebrated its 100th birthday in 2021 with impressive progress toward global tyrannical supremacy. They have made significant progress in Central and South America, Europe, the Middle East, and Africa, while US leadership appears weak, unconcerned, and uninvolved. China is salivating at the timing of the opportunity to complete the toppling of USA domino to neuter us and ruin our 250th birthday celebration in 2026.

If China can engineer the domino of the epic collapse of the USA to tip over, all the other dominos in their way will also tip over because of the tsunami-like momentum that will be produced. Using their Borg-adopted motto, they will proclaim, "Resistance is futile. Prepare to be assimilated." By outplaying the US, China will have easily won the long game of Global Domination and Subjugation.

The Epic Collapse Timing and Result

Absent any significant changes, this may likely take place during this decade of the 2020s. Sir John Glubb's 1978 *The Fate of Empires* estimated the lifespan of an empire to be about 250 years or 10 generations. That would put our demise at about 2026. In 1997, Neil Howe and William Strauss penned *The Fourth Turning*. Their past research showed that a society goes through 4 distinct repeating patterns called turnings, each lasting 20–25 years or 80–100 years for each cycle of 4 turnings. They identified our cycles starting with the American Revolution in 1776, the end of the Civil War in 1865, and the end of World War II in 1945. They also predicted 2025 as the turbulent end of this current cycle. In 2010, Alfred McCoy similarly predicted a US collapse in 2025.

Others predict dates between 2030 and 2050. Maybe it is coincidental, but `our last nearly fatal collapse was precipitated by the 1929 stock market crash almost 100 years ago. It seems like Sir John, Howe and Strauss, and Alfred McCoy's predictions and the 100-year economic storm cycle are all coalescing during this decade of the 2020s. Because of China's progress on its laser-focused quest to oust the US as the #1 superpower before 2030, a US collapse may occur near our 250th anniversary in 2026.

What would be the likely results if Trump fails to get us off this path of self-destruction?

1. Domestic Economics—Banking would be impacted very negatively, as was the case in the Great Depression, and interest rates would climb steeply; supplies of necessities would not be able to meet the demand; some utilities would be impacted; real estate and the stock market would crater, wiping out trillions of dollars of Americans' wealth (if that had not already occurred); unemployment would soar, while wages would shrink; the US GDP would likely tank by at least 25–35%; inflation could move into the realm of hyperinflation with the continued downward trajectory of the dollar devaluation.
2. Global Economics—There would be global panic, as demand for the dollar and US Treasuries would fall; other currencies would be the beneficiaries, especially the digital Juan or the coming BRICS gold-backed digital currency. One of them will likely become the reserve currency to replace the dollar.
3. World Peace—The world has played footsies with global bullies, and their adventurism has metastasized. The New World Order (aka The Global Reset) sees Iran terrorizing the Middle East even more than they currently do. Funded by oil sales to China, Russia may continue its military adventurism in Europe with armaments from China, North Korea, and Iran. The big winner of the Global Domination game will be China. A digital BRICS or Juan will become the world currency, and they will be the #1 superpower/empire they have salivated for.

Their influence on the rest of the world will be significant, as they will promise the elimination of war, elimination of internal lawlessness, and economic stability. They won't say that the cost is a lack of freedom, enslavement of many, and monumental corruption and propaganda. For 2nd-tier countries in BRICS like Brazil and India, China-based coalitions provide them more prominence on the world stage.

Many other countries (especially weaker ones looking for a strong nation to align with) see the US as untrustworthy, soft, and decaying. They are deciding whether to provide China with bases or strategic resource agreements. They see more attention being paid to them by China. They will likely buy that deal from China without China having to fire a single shot. Many of the 77 Global South countries are in the target zone for China's alliances. These are countries in Africa, Latin and South America, Oceania (except Australia and New Zealand), and Asia (except Israel, Japan, and South Korea).

But the Crown Jewel for China will be the US, which will have been broken from internal and external forces and can be reconstituted however China wants to capitalize on the US's vast natural resources, creativity, business, and military capability.

In the new USSA (United Socialist States of America) and other countries that China absorbs (like the Borg of Star Trek), there will be a winnowing of the elites, wokesters, and oligarchs. Most oligarchs will be safe as long as they parrot the desires of the new overlords as they did for the D-S before. The same will be true for the elites, but they will not need as many of those, and many will fall off their comfortable perches and lose their elite status.

Even less valued are the wokesters. The environmental zealots, climate change faithful, LGBTQ+ community, and other D-S sub-cults will find that the CCP control of their country has no further use for them. People of color will discover that overwhelming racism will take root in this Great Reset. Personal freedoms and the social safety net will be severely diminished.

China will have to decide how long it will keep an alliance with the Iranian theocracy since China tolerates no religion, only blind obedience to the state. Eventually, they will replace that theocracy with their version of corrupt totalitarianism and seek to eliminate the Muslim faith as they do with Christianity or any other religion.

***

Is there a way out of this? The next chapter exposes China's weaknesses that need to be exploited and introduces a positive vision for the US future. We trust that President Trump will understand President Xi's intentions and take strong actions to exploit their weaknesses and prevent the fall of the USA.

CHAPTER 5

The Clash of the Titans

Chapters 1 through 4 Recap

Chapter 1 covered how and why the US got to this pivotal moment. An important factor is the distancing that has occurred from our Founding Principles. Those principles were initially forged using common sense, boldness, and creativity. Most of that chapter concerns the corruption of the 12 most impactful principles.

Chapter 2 covers the critical role politics has played in hijacking our journey. Highlights of the four most recent consequential Presidents are included.

In Chapter 3, what will be replacing our destiny vision is on full display. It is Socialism, and the destructive histories of Socialism and Communism are summarized. Then, the sources of the American style of Socialism are identified. The pathways are significantly lighted and spelled out by Saul Alinksy and Cloward-Piven. Alinsky wrote *Rules for Radicals* and inspired Obama, and he taught classes at the University of Chicago that complimented Alinsky. Hillary was so moved by Saul's "revolutionary" ideas that she wrote her college thesis, "Alinsky and His Organizing Plan."

While Alinsky may have been the godfather of the pathways to American Socialism who heavily influenced Obama, his other great accomplishment was to spawn the works of Cloward-Piven. They wrote a 1966 article titled "The Weight of the Poor: A Strategy to End Poverty." They named 8 ways to overwhelm the US economy to bring about a collapse and leave the door wide open for Socialism/Marxism. In 1982, Cloward-Piven wrote another blockbuster article, "A Movement Strategy to Transform the Democratic Party." When you look at the writings of Alinsky and Cloward-Piven, there is little doubt the Democratic Party has been transformed, and they and their surrogates regularly follow the blueprints laid out in those writings.

Chapter 4 details the epic collapse that these Marxist authors clamored for. First is China's role in facilitating the perfect storm for our economic collapse. Then, a comparison is made to the demise of other historic superpowers. Finally, the potential triggering events for this economic collapse are listed, along with the likely timeframe of this 2020s decade (predicted as early as 1978 by several prominent author-historians). Without far-reaching changes in China or the US, China will neuter the US and realize its goal of world totalitarian domination.

The path the regressives/repressives (with help from weak Republicans and Independents) have put us on continues our country's decay. Those unfamiliar with Alinsky and C-P will keep trying to understand this decay from a rational, common-sense point of view and be baffled. They will attribute current outcomes to incompetence or lack of mental acuity. While these are contributing factors, the real drivers are the intentional implementations of the pronouncements of those American Marxists, Alinsky and C-P.

From that perspective, it is crystal clear that their prescriptions (summarized in Chapter 3) are being purposefully and faithfully followed. They believe this will bring about the economic collapse that is a necessary pre-condition to open the gateways to the "Upside Down" that will unleash the demons and monsters of Marxism that have terrorized citizens of countries like Cuba, Venezuela, Russia, China, and North

Korea. The only way to close those gateways is with the strong force of success by following our Founding Principles and using a methodology like Solutionism to solve (not play around with and worsen) today's issues.

The destruction of our values and culture and our division by race and gender lead to those Socialism gateways. Some would say we are already in the early-middle stages. The left has set up their altars of adoration around:

- Replacing traditional religion with radical climate change, environmentalism, and gender fluidity
- Replacing a solid family influence with brainwashing from the media and education
- Continuing to replace healthcare insurance with government programs like the considerable increases to Medicaid and Obamacare
- Stoking the fires of class warfare on three fronts: the haves and the have-nots; racial identification as victim or oppressor; gender identification with the language of pronouns they consider appropriate
- Rampant crime with a lack of respect for life, property, and the rule of law
- Militarizing many federal agencies in the pursuit of a Police State while continuing to diminish our right to own a gun and defend ourselves
- Excessive government overreach and bureaucratic growth funded by high taxation and government spending (despite poor results), sacrificing the middle class, and increasing poverty and unsustainable personal and government debt bombs
- Massive illegal, non-assimilating immigration
- Elections that do not display the highest integrity
- Wokeism and fake propagandized news
- Constant lies, using science perversely only when it supports their radicalism, and punishment for violating mandates with intimidation, cancel culture, and even imprisonment.

This must all be rejected and reversed, just like the needed reversing of the "Checklist to Build a Socialist Country" in Chapter 3.

The degradation of the US as the #1 superpower and the strong hand that China has to ascend to the #1 superpower throne have been laid out. While this may be overpowering, it is not the complete story. We also need to examine the weaknesses in China's economy (the rest of this chapter) and the positive national security changes the US can make (in the remaining chapters of this book) to win this economic war many deny exists. Before we probe the Shining City on a Hill strategy, let's check under the hood of China's economic engine. Where is it backfiring and susceptible to seizing up?

China's Weak Underbelly

Gordon Chang is an American expert on China. The following points are summarized from 3 of his articles identifying China's weak economic underpinnings.

From The National Interest, December 25, 2016 "Is China's Economy Past the Point of No Return?" [1]

- Foreign investment into China—In 2015, according to Bloomberg, there was a net capital outflow of $1 trillion. Investment in China carries some repatriation risk.
- Dwindling foreign exchange reserves—Inaccurate accounting by China and misuse for long-term investments like the One Belt, One Road infrastructure projects, loans to risky borrower nations like Venezuela, and capitalization of the China Investment Corp, China's sovereign wealth fund. Estimates are this has depleted their forex reserves by some $400 billion and likely put them below the $2.8 trillion the IMF recommends for China.
- China is creating debt 5 times faster than the increase in GDP. Even George Soros noted in January 2016 that their debt to GDP ratio could be as high as 350%, and Orient Capital Research in Hong Kong estimated it to be 400%.

From Newsweek, February 8, 2022, "China's 'Debt Bomb' Is Going Off Under Xi Jinping" [2]

- Real estate—"It would take a middle-class couple 47 years to buy a small apartment ... in Beijing or Shanghai if both husband and wife could save 100% of their salaries for the purchase." The sales value of the top 100 developers dropped 39.6% when compared to the same period in the prior year. The real estate sector accounts for 25–30% of GDP. In July of 2021, Moody's estimated that 70–80 % of household wealth is in real estate. Chinese people cannot easily invest in foreign assets, which minimizing their choices for investing using their currency. Their real estate sector is very risky for the owners and the country.
- "History says the most severe and long-lasting financial crises involve countries that owe money to themselves."

From 19 Forty Five.com, May 21, 2022, "The Chinese Economy Is In A Death Spiral" [3]

- Unfriendly demographics—Population growth is needed to retire debt, but estimates are that China will lose 50% of its population in 45 years. This would be the sharpest decline of any country ever except for war or disease. China moved from a 1-child to a 3-child policy in 2021, but Chinese citizens are not on board.
- Unfriendly economics—From April 2021 to April 2022, industrial output was down 2.9%, retail sales were off 11.1%, new car sales plummeted 47.6%, and river and truck traffic was down 40%. In March 2022, investors divested $17.5 billion of Chinese stocks and bonds. (August 2023 Update: During August 2023, investors sold $12 billion of their holdings of Chinese stocks.)
- Unfriendly real estate—Evergrande Group has $305 billion in debt and is hurting even with the government's full backing. Smaller developers are not supported as strongly. The 4th largest developer, Sunac China, recently missed a bond payment and said it did not expect to make other bond payments. From April

2021 to April 2022, the value of property sales was down 46.6%, and new construction starts were down 44.2%.

The housing bubble is real; only selective government help prevents it from popping. (August–September 2023 Update: These two giant developers above are now in default with their investors. Ocean Sino, another top 20 Chinese developer, has stopped making payments on bonds denominated in USD as it tries to restructure. They have 600 projects across 80 cities, and their stock is now worth $0.08/share.)

- Unfriendly currency value—With the US increasing interest rates, the value of the Juan was down 7% from February to April 2022, with April being the worst ever.
- Stupid lockdown policy—This "zero COVID" approach has dramatically affected China's poor economic numbers.

Michael Schuman expressed similar pessimism in *The Atlantic* on June 29, 2023. The article was aptly titled "The End of Optimism in China."

- The official unemployment rate among 16 to 24-year-olds is 20%, the highest ever.
- Adults starting new businesses dropped from 15.5% in 2014 to 6% in 2022.
- New births dropped by 50% from 2016 to 2022.
- This coincides with the plunge in first marriages by more than 50% since 2013, when China's leader, Xi Jinping, consolidated his power.
- Per the UN Refugee Agency, more than 115,000 Chinese nationals were seeking asylum globally at the end of 2022, a 10-fold increase over the prior decade.

Bloomberg News updated the dismal economy on August 23, 2023, titled "China's Debt-Fueled Housing Market is Having a Meltdown, Again."

- China's largest real developer giant, Country Garden Holdings Co., is nearing default. (Update September 2023: Their 1st half of 2023 results show a loss of $6.2 billion.)

- A third of the 498 dollar bonds issued by Chinese developers are in default, and the $200 billion market for real estate bonds has effectively dried up.
- About half of the state-owned real estate firms reported 2023 losses for the first six months.
- The 10 largest commercial banks are projected to be saddled in 2024 with $120 billion of non-performing real estate loans.

In addition, there was a 14% decline in exports, and the first half of 2023 saw Chinese imports and exports experience several consecutive months of decline. That accounts for another 40% or so of the economy. For decades, there was excessive funding for developers, resulting in many empty apartment buildings throughout China, and many projects have been stopped before completion.

In 2014, China began favoring state-owned enterprises over private enterprises, and much capital has been misallocated. The CCP is now trying to transition from an economy driven by state-owned enterprises and investments focused on infrastructure and exports to one driven by consumer spending. Even fixed-income investments have created significant losses from "shadow" banks called trusts due to inadequate regulation. The Chinese consumer is not on board. They have seen their stocks, bonds, real estate, and currency devalued. The normal inclination for the Chinese to save and not spend has been supercharged now, and they have increased their bank deposits in the first half of 2023 by some $1.7 trillion.

While China may not officially be in a recession, its economy is severely struggling. Many countries like to spend their way out of a recession. The US did this when impacted by COVID-19. Instead, China's solution is to bail out ailing banks that have made bad loans and encourage them to make more loans, but few good customers are willing to take on debt now. Some experts think conditions are ripe for deflation in China, and this contagion could spread beyond its borders.

The US Off-Ramp Before We Crash

China has parlayed a weak hand following the end of WWII into a winning hand today. China's economic-political ecosystem has **150,000 state-owned entities that bring in $10 trillion of annual revenue and comprise 61% of the all-Chinese firms on the Fortune Global 500 list. Every Chinese company with over 50 employees must have a CCP representative on site.**

However, China has shifted focus away from the health and wealth created by its tech companies, as evidenced by its actions against several of those firms and their leaders. China's leader believes that the private sector is a threat to the power of the CCP and that an economy based on finance and property is "fictitious." But their stiff and robotic domestic strategies expose the weakness inherent in their Socialist-Marxist lust for power and control of the masses. Unfortunately, the US left has been mimicking that same lust for power and control to stay in power. But we have an off-ramp if we are bold and courageous enough to use it.

1. We and our allies must jump on this weak internal support for Chinese businesses. We must stop tech sales, close our stock markets to them, end investing in China, and bring back those assets and jobs. This may be difficult due to their currency's declining value, making Chinese goods cheaper. Companies need to control their financial hunger and pass up short-term additional profits in the name of national and global security. We must execute our divorce and eliminate our co-dependent relationship with China.

   With our supply chains running through China and our hunger to sell to the Chinese market, we are in an economic marriage with a partner who is abusive and does not treat us as equals. Our reign as the #1 superpower and defender of freedom and global peace is dying as we stay in the death grip of this deadly relationship. **In May 2019, the *People's Daily* declared a "People's War" against the US.**

[4] **Coincidentally, COVID-19 escaped from China a few months later, killing 1 million Americans and 6 million in other countries.**

We must re-orient our supply chains that run through China (especially for essential goods) to eliminate dependence on them and to starve their economic engine of the financial fuel needed to run it; close the Chinese police stations (aka "aid stations") in the US that intimidate China-born people living in the US; ban the US university education of Chinese nationals (they often participate in leading research and pass the proprietary information back to China).

We must cancel most sales of US land and businesses (especially those dealing with farming and food processing) that were bought by Chinese nationals or Chinese companies and prevent by law any partial or total future sales of US assets or businesses to adversarial countries or businesses. We accomplish that by including a "perpetual clause" that bans any future resales without pre-approval by the US government and must be included in all future sales.

We should also ban all China-created apps (that have a high potential for propaganda, spying and blackmail); and make it illegal for high schools, colleges and universities to accept money from adversarial countries like China, Russia, and Iran, and terrorist and terrorist-supporting countries. The US hand is strong with China's weak economy, but Biden is predictably squandering the opportunity.

2. An even larger Achilles heel for them than their "financial fuel" is their energy demands that power their factories, many burning coal and creating significant pollution. They are the world's largest natural gas, coal, and oil importer, importing 1 million barrels of oil daily. That is why they are cutting deals with oil-rich ME countries and Russia. Their goal is to turn this weakness into a strength.

Chapter 4 identified that their pollution-belching coal factories produce 70% of the world's solar modules, 50% of wind turbines, and 90% of lithium-ion batteries. They have cornered the market on lithium and other rare earth minerals and are getting rich supplying these "sacraments" to the woke faithful. These global zealots are impoverishing their economies as they practice their climate and environment religions on the backs of mining labor often done by children, producing massive pollution and negative environmental impacts.

China's goal is to get rich while transitioning to green energy use domestically. We and our allies must deprive them of these sales to shrink their capital to fund their drives for energy independence, increased military aggression, and the realization of their New World Order. We should accelerate tech for EVs that do not use lithium batteries, which do not have a proper recharge grid, are heavy, costly, and have many other issues (Chapter 11). We must work with allies to accelerate the implementation of sustainable hydrogen-powered vehicles. We must also divorce from China's provision of undependable wind and solar power components. But will the global wokesters abandon their false religions for the greater good? We must lead the way, as this is China's greatest vulnerability.

3. **We must vigorously publicize China's severe economic, societal, and climate deficiencies. They emit more CO_2 than the entire Western Hemisphere.** Their societal brutality against all within its grasp (especially ethnic Mongolians, Tibetans, and Uyghur Muslims) must be trumpeted loudly and not stifled. They use a "social credit system" based on ever-present facial recognition and digital currency; they have no freedom of speech or tolerance for religion, guns, and alternative lifestyles; they support forced organ donation, slavery, and jailing dissidents. **Today, China is 3 times the size of what was "traditional China," but that has not satisfied their appetite.**

With their One Belt One Road Initiative and aggressive trade strategies, they seek opportunities to spread the gospel of their "winning formula" worldwide. We must urge other countries to divorce from China as well. China is the abusive spouse poised to expand the terrorizing of its citizens by enlarging its territory. Hong Kong was just a tasty appetizer. **The world needs to say no to cheap labor and goods to thwart China's quest for global domination. Xi Jinping** told us his "China Dream" to restore China to its prior place of *tianxia* (ruling "all under heaven"). **We must take brutal but deceptive tyrants at their word.**

4. These efforts are part of playing geopolitical and economic hardball with China. The US must end the trade benefit we give China of being a "most favored nation." Their treatment in the WTO as a "developing nation" makes no sense when they are clearly the #2 superpower, and this must also be ended. Developing nation status exempts them from pollution and climate issues which they significantly contribute to. We must work with allies to eliminate the purchase of Chinese drones and Huawei technology and minimize other transactions with China. We cannot let books like *When China Rules the World* by Martin Jacques materialize into our real-life nightmares.

5. We need to wake up Sleepy Joe to the currency actions of China and its aligned BRICS countries. They are focused on settling trades and debts outside of the USD, eliminating the USD's reserve currency status, and obsoleting the SWIFT banking system (owned by the G10 countries). Not addressing this is the easiest way for the US downfall. The US and its other G10 allies must work diligently to make their economies more financially robust and accelerate efforts to upgrade SWIFT to use blockchain tech.

    Also, thoroughly testing one or two primary digital currencies with some gold backing and privacy protections for citizens is essential. This could be launched when needed to counter the coming action of the BRICS to issue their own digital, gold-backed currency. The BRICS trade totals already exceed that of the G7, and their alliance of countries keeps increasing. This threat is real and growing. (see the China Threat Chapter 10 for a more in-depth look at this serious issue).

    We must do all we can to reduce and reverse the acceptance by new members into China's growing BRICS alliance by exposing China's deceitful branding. Part of that involves copying China's alliances that give smaller countries a more prominent voice than

their small voice in the UN or the feeling that the G7 nations seem to be calling all the shots.
6. Besides fighting this economic and geopolitical battle with China, we are also fighting on a 2nd front of internal decay. Fortunately, China has a similar problem with the internal issues mentioned earlier in the chapter. We must re-adjust our compass and create our Shining City on a Hill by consciously and courageously leaving the Valley of Mediocrity and Decline that we and our politicians have languished in for too many years. We need to use the untapped problem-solving power of our Founding Principles to overcome the intense gravitational force of corruption, power, and control that have kept us in the Valley.

That is how we stop the decay and the drive to Socialism and solve our internal national security problems (Chapters 6–8) and external security problems (Chapters 9–11), especially the China threat. We must set the example of a Solutionist country, where Free Market Capitalism sheds the shackles of corruption and massive and ineffective government. That can inspire other nations to fabricate their version of the Shining City on a Hill.

Our Binary Choice Decision

Biden-Harris and Harris-Walz would easily choose the Socialism path we were on (with a big assist "from China with love"). Trump-Vance are keen to blaze a radically different trail to actually solve problems. If you read the first four chapters, you are not in denial of the USA's intentionally hijacked journey. However, some may think we can find some middle ground and return to bipartisanship and the "good old days" (like the 1950s or some other era). That will, after a few years of meager progress, only get us back to where we are now with a more decisive impetus to embrace the Socialist dystopia.

Others may think we should not be polarized and look for solutions and candidates that speak to that thinking. Unfortunately, that is precisely what keeps us stuck and getting worse. Remember, Bumbling Biden said he would be a unifier, a real problem solver, and a kinder President than Trump. How is that working for us? You saw an abbreviated summary of the Biden-Harris 4-year administration in Chapter 2. We must embrace the fact that we are polarized and have clear choices now—the D-S or the Republican Solutionists (R-S). Let's prune those phony Republicans like the D-S did when they purged nearly all JFK Democrats. Our destiny lies in electing leaders committed to positive Solutionist transformations that bloom into success and not electing "get-along" RINOs, globalists, Never-Trumpers, or squishy Republicans.

Socialists are passionate, relentless, and enjoy the enthusiastic backing of the VLWC who support them; they will not play fair and will not lose easily. Vince Lombardi said, "When you've got the momentum…, that is a time to keep going and get it into the end zone." [5] The left is following the words of that great football coach. They will not make a course correction, regardless of what polls say or the damage done to the country.

They must be soundly defeated, and the best way is to enact real solutions to our national security problems, starting with unimpeachable election integrity (Chapter 6). That can shut the door permanently to these cheerleaders of dystopia. When the country and its citizens work successfully and effectively, alternatives to success will be laughed off the stage. That puts us on the winning path for our internal identity war and positions us to win the geopolitical battle with China.

China has many weak spots in its economy, and we must be aware of and exploit them. They have a seriously declining population, reduced level of exports, declining currency value, most internal wealth is tied up in a significantly depressed real estate market, have not recovered from their self-inflicted wound of 2–3 years of thuggish and foolish COVID-19 lockdowns, and have banking and real estate development sectors that are at tipping points. They likely have inadequate currency reserves due to their excessive spending on their military and the tech to support it, the One Belt One Road Initiative, and risky loans to several countries.

This battle is between two powerful but extremely vulnerable titans, and only one can stand as the world's #1 Superpower World Heavyweight Champion. In one corner, the contender CCP with their racism, brutality, intolerance, squashing of freedom, Corrupt State Capitalism, spying, bribery, and intellectual property theft. In the other corner is the USA, the defending #1 superpower with a severe identity problem.

It can continue as the bumbling Biden USA, awkwardly staggering forward to the economic collapse of its Corrupt Capitalism, leading to Socialism. In 2024, voters rejected that and chose Trump to create a reinvigorated and stronger USA to get into fabulous shape by purging the cancers of corruption and Socialism from its body.

Stupidly, the US has supported its own decay and decline and the transfer of the #1 superpower title to China. Can you imagine us doing any of these dumb things (we have done with China) with Hitler and Nazi Germany during WWII?

- Providing $6 trillion in trade deficits that allowed them to build a 1st class military, become a leader in many areas of technology, and control the global supply of strategic resources.
- Educating their young adults at our colleges and universities to learn and steal proprietary technology for use in their home country.
- Financially seducing our high schools and colleges to brainwash our impressionable youth with the adversary's propaganda—today that includes Confucianism and TikTok.
- Allowing the purchases of farmland (jeopardizing our food sufficiency) and US businesses, some of which are curiously near vital US military installations.
- Allowing their companies to be included in US stock markets and not follow US sound accounting and auditing practices. That places the assets of naïve or greedy Americans at risk and supplies welcome capital to an adversary to continue their world domination moves.

Individuals, countries, and the world need to reject the financial seduction of the Corrupt State Capitalism of China and move to de-link from them to thwart their colonialist expansion and build their own Shining Cities. Both China and the US have significant amounts of corruption. Both have bloated governments and weak financial stability, with China's somewhat worse. But China's military is equally strong and more motivated, and its leadership is just as focused as Trump.

Currently, China is winning the match based on points from its flurry of jabs and body blows, but you can't win this contest on points. Someone needs to administer the knockout blow. We have less than 5 rounds left of this 15-round contest, but the US has ample time to expose and capitalize on China's weaknesses, get in top shape, rebuild our stamina, and start solving problems. For additional reference, some knowledgeable authors on China include Gordon Chang, Michael Pillsbury, and Jonathan Ward.

Whoever throws that knockout blow will topple that lead "domino" of either China or the US and start a cascade of other geopolitical dominos. If China wins, they, along with the support of Russia and Iran, will swallow up the world within a few short years, and most freedoms will be lost everywhere. If the US defeats China, the other repressive nations will experience social unrest as citizens clamor for a prosperous and free society like the US.

China's totalitarian and robotic CCP is like *Star Trek's* soulless "Borg," strengthening the Black Hole of Socialism into a Supermassive Black Hole, moving in on its prey. Its intense gravitational force pulls in countries that it entices with its attractive event horizon of Corrupt Capitalism. Then, it absorbs their talents and resources and destroys their identity and freedoms, effectively making them colonies. Through its actions, China has been adopting the Borg's catchphrase, "Resistance is futile, prepare to be assimilated." They have grown their territory 3 times their traditional size and now represent 20% of the global GDP. But they cannot make sweeping changes to fix their problems that they ignore and propagandize over.

In the July/August 2023 issue of *Imprimis* called "Imperialism: Lessons From History,"[6] Victor Davis Hanson gives a great history of the declines of several empires. Two points are especially noteworthy. "The sense of duty sums up the common imperialist mindset: imperialism is a burden, undertaken reluctantly and for the good of the uncivilized. There is little self-serving about it." That is one blind spot. Another is that "empires like to think of themselves as having a lot of friends, but they are often naïve in forgetting the depth of the ill will they incur." China definitely has the 2nd blind spot, even if they are more self-serving to be blinded by the 1st one.

Who will be left standing? China fighting for world domination, or the US fighting one war for world peace (not woke virtue signaling or elevating causes into "religions") and an internal struggle for restoring its Founding Principles and freedoms, the defeat of Socialism, and draining corruption out of Free Market Capitalism. Both countries are emperors with no clothes—their weaknesses have been exposed to you. Our advantage as a still somewhat free society is that we can open our minds, see our nakedness and do what is needed to fix that. And we have a not-so-secret weapon, Donald Trump.

The Journey of Another Way Forward

The good news is that, like frogs in the pot of increasingly hot water, many of us jumped out in 2024. We need to rally around the "Shining City on a Hill" that President Reagan talked about. That journey up the hill will strengthen us by creating those problem-solution frameworks using our Founding Principles applied to today's issues. When we reach the top, we will already have the building blocks needed to construct our version of the Shining City on a Hill and welcome and support other countries, who will be motivated after seeing our results.

Ideas for creating that city's national security building blocks are laid out starting in Chapter 6, and they follow the principles of our Founders. They do not represent a return to the "Happy Days" of the 1950s but require an ambitious transformation away from the destructive change we are currently living through. Whether we achieve this better transformation will depend on whether we and the people we elect to government embrace these solutions. One way or another, the USA will transform—either into the abyss of the USSA (United Socialist States of America) or into occupants of our Shining City on a Hill. To keep playing footsies with the D-S will only forestall that inevitable abysmal transformation. Politicians who think they can resurrect bipartisanship are foolishly living in the past.

The world is very different from the time of Ronald Reagan, and the failure to achieve his aspiration has exposed a gaping hole in the fabric of our society that has allowed Socialists to magnify their foothold and bring things now to a critical tipping point. The Socialists see their opportunity right before them. They will not be deterred, as they try to hide under the label of Democrat or Democrat-Socialist or other less offensive names.

They have changed politics into a blood sport and will use every unethical and illegal trick to create their dystopia. Thankfully, the most extreme Socialist ticket ever in the US of Harris-Walz was soundly defeated. Let's stop wasting our time, energy, and money chasing foolish and detrimental ideologies. This China threat is real and potent, is right before us, and they are laser-focused. We must understand that and man up and woman up to this existential threat to our survival as a free society and the world's leading economy and beacon of hope for freedom.

The following chapters will spell out the things that will begin to make the US the envy of the world and a model for other countries to tweak to create their own Shining City. We need politicians who will use the Solutionism methodology, be accountable, and build our Shining City. If just 75% of the solution frameworks in Chapters 6–11 were fleshed out and implemented from 2024 to 2028, that would start a strong reversal of the relentless death march to Socialism imposed upon Americans by the left. Our Founding Principles and their common sense, creativity, and boldness inspired these solution frameworks.

Some of them you may not initially gravitate to, but what have we got to lose? Continuing on our current path leads to the total loss of freedoms for the US and the rest of the world. This is the most desperate time in all of human history. It is because of the proliferation of the deadliest of all weapons—nuclear missiles and bombs in the hands of tyrants who are prepared to use them to further their ambitions.

Our county is staring at the coming attractions of the abyss that we have allowed the left to put before us. We do not need more 40 or 50-year career politicians focused on re-election, power, prestige, and personal enrichment. We need more people with a successful record of solving problems and accomplishing more with less, who want to serve, fix our problems, and then exit public service. We need more successful military and business leaders who seem to have that gene the most. Our inability to create our Shining City has created the opening for the left to sow its seeds over the past 50 years, and its bitter fruit is now in full bloom for all to see.

Without bold, creative, and common-sense solutions, we are doomed. We cannot stay in the pot of hot Socialist water as it begins to boil. Old "false solutions" of throwing more money at problems without significant results never work. Socialism must not overtake us, with our BFFs becoming our comrades in Russia, Iran, and China.

Most Americans voted for Trump in 2024 because they felt their country was on the wrong track and he would fix that.

***

The remaining chapters explore and address our six most important national security problems using the Solutionism methodology. The next chapter begins with an exploration of the most critical issue of all—election integrity.

PART II

Creating the Shining City on a Hill

The prior five chapters covered how we have deviated significantly from our Founding Principles, squandered our inheritance, and degraded the opportunity they gave us; how our political processes have been corrupted and hijacked our country's journey; why Socialism is the awful path we are rapidly progressing on; how American Socialists began capturing the soul of the Democratic Party and now own them; how we are in an existential struggle with China, and they are winning; what are the likely scenarios that could be the death blow to our democracy; and how we can come from behind and win the struggle.

We are on this ruinous path only because we have fiddled while our "Rome (the USA) has been burning." Since we have not successfully addressed our significant problems, the human spirit is yearning for change, and the perverse lure of Socialism now has a noticeable audience. Many ignore that Socialism, Communism, and terrorist states have no success record for the citizens of any country.

Historically, many superpowers have experienced boredom from the good life and relatively unrestricted freedom. Those "good lifers" are often attracted by trendy new words, new thoughts, new religions, and faux intellectualism. That makes it very challenging for the hard work of real discovery and invention that had been a vital part of their societal progress. That has led to corruption and chaos in the country, its institutions, and its people. Fear and then compliance to tyranny follow because the people are weak. In the 900 years of the Dark Ages, that tyranny was enforced by the coalition of the RAGS: religion, academia, government, and science.

Tyranny springs from internal corruption or externally from more totalitarian regimes. We are retracing that path, and today, some are trading their freedom to pursue life, liberty, and happiness for the authoritarian control they think will give them comfort, "free stuff," and entertainment and amusement. Many are mirroring corrupt politicians, government, and institutions that are driven too often by power, prestige, and personal enrichment.

That same Dark Ages cabal is sponsoring America's tyranny today, but the religion or higher purpose part is being played primarily by cults like the climate and environmental extremists. This oppression is reminiscent of what we suffered under and escaped from 250 years ago. The cycle is repeating and must be stopped—2024's election results provide a golden opportunity to free ourselves. Even though America's internal tyranny and corruption live in so much of our society, Trump is determined to aggressively root them out and creatively solve major problems.

The following chapters identify six major national security problems that have not been significantly and successfully addressed. In each case, key issues and solution frameworks for solving those issues are listed. Those frameworks are linked to many of the 12 Founding Principles in Chapter 1 that were birthed with simple common sense, creativity, and boldness.

What is the core mindset that supports Solutionism?

- **Corruption** drainage and minimization out of the lifeblood of our Free Market Capitalism and institutions. It is particularly present in the uncaring collusion between Big Business and government, similar to the movie *Avatar*. The left hopes to continue to infect

institutions with their flawed ideology that does not work, resulting in totally corrupting or replacing all our teetering institutions.
- **Overwhelm** stoppage and elimination—e.g., illegal immigration. The purposes of the overwhelms are to worsen those problems significantly, paralyze us with too many issues and complexities, and create fear to make us more receptive to phony Socialist "solutions."
- **Risk** acceptance for actions taken, **respect** for the lives and property of others, and **restitution** for any damages and harm caused. These are the 3 Rs from the Founding Principle #9 (being a strong citizenry) in Chapter 1. Those did not have to be spelled out at our founding, as they were part of our DNA then. Over the last 250 years, our societal DNA has been debased, and these three elements have been diminished.
- **Equal** rights and opportunities and not equal outcomes. This is from the Founding Principle #6 in Chapter 1.

Solutionism has five steps often absent in our government processes:
- **Prioritize** the major problems to be addressed.
- **Itemize** key issues and their solution frameworks for each major problem.
- **Compose** the details required to implement each framework.
- **Measure** success with appropriate metrics for each problem and its key issues.
- **Explain** every six months the progress of the metric goals and modify the metrics, goals, or solution frameworks if needed.

If there is no improvement, the metrics, goals, and solutions are evaluated to determine if they need to be changed. The first benchmark indication of progress would be a 10% metric improvement, followed by 25%, 50%, and 75%. A 100% correction is unrealistic, but somewhere between 75% and 90% would be a success. Each problem-solution will have a different success trajectory. For the problems in the following six chapters, sometimes all 5 steps for Solutionism are visible. In other instances, only steps 1 and 2 and parts of steps 3–5 are identified. This is due to the benefits of collaborating with dedicated Solutionists from Congress and the Executive Branch to completely fill out those steps for more complex problems.

We can enhance our Solutionism success by learning from others. We must lose our federal bureaucratic arrogance and bias and learn from and adapt successful Solutionism from other countries, states, or local communities. In Chapter 2, mention is made of Argentina's new President and Italy's new Prime Minister. They are taking significant steps away from their countries' prior Socialist pathways. Ukraine is similarly using its brand of Solutionism courageously and smartly against a much more powerful Russia that wants to erase and absorb it.

We must learn from their creativity, boldness, and common sense and reverse the left's "accomplishments" represented in Chapter 3's "Checklist to Build a Socialist Country." At the state level, we also have the examples of several Republican Solutionist (R-S) governors who have adopted a Solutionist approach to improve the lives of their citizens.

Artificial intelligence is a powerful and relatively new tool in everyday life. It is also a dangerous one that we must use carefully (to eliminate programming bias) as part of many of the solutions in this book. It is as monumental as the discovery of fire. It has fantastic ways to improve our lives, but unchecked (like an out-of-control fire), it can be highly destructive. Nearly all developed nations are using it, and it is deeply concerning when adversarial countries use it for military purposes. We must use it to solve many of our problems (especially to keep our military edge) and will find it helpful to quickly and efficiently deal with our overwhelms.

Some may identify other key issues or solution frameworks that might be as worthwhile as the ones in these chapters. This book is not an exhaustive deep dive into everything. But it is enough to put the puzzle pieces together to sharpen the view of where we are and show how to change course for a better outcome.

Solutionist thinking is not prevalent in DC, so problems go unsolved and often worsen. The leaders and their support teams must inject that problem-solving and accountability DNA into their thought processes.

Many individuals and businesses use a kind of Solutionist approach successfully to accomplish goals. Why not use it for our country?

We cannot afford the luxury of business as usual while our country is in severe decay. There should be no more tolerance for elites that mainly care about maintaining or increasing their power, prestige, and personal enrichment. Doing the same things (more spending, bureaucracy, taxes, and regulation) and expecting a better result is the definition of insanity. We need people focused on and accountable for solving problems to create the Shining City on a Hill that President Reagan envisioned. Afterward, they should be willing to leave DC and return to the productive part of the economy they were in before government service—no more 40 or 50 years of serving themselves and making our problems worse.

Those who understand our dire situation, the unsolved problems, and will benefit from solutions, will likely support these solution frameworks. Leftists, extremists, and others benefitting from the chaotic and damaging current status quo (like criminals, corrupt individuals or organizations, or beneficiaries of the status quo at the expense of most others) will not want to change anything. Also, people who are not the strong ones referred to in Founding Principle #9 will be hard to convince. They should all remember JFK's words: "Ask not what your country can do for you, but what you can do for your country."

There is a broad audience (called by many the "Uniparty") that shares responsibility for the current condition of our country. It lives within the left's Wokesphere echo chamber, created to protect its inhabitants and attack anyone with a contrary view. It includes the beneficiaries of the status quo, globalists, hateful Never-Trumpers, get-along squishy Republicans, and unwitting liberals who think they still have a place in the Democratic Party, all of the cults and Socialists that nestle under and now control the Democratic Party, and the apathetic who sit on the sidelines and may complain but have done little else to support significant positive change.

That last group's dangerous focus has too often been on getting along, saying and being influenced by nice-sounding soundbites, and trying to shield themselves and others from those perceived as shaking things up too much from the status quo. Trump's successes will provide them a chance to abandon their squishy Uniparty membership.

Many have awakened to the issues in the last couple of years. Let's trust that many others will join those voices to embrace a solution-focused methodology that solves our problems and builds our Shining City on a Hill. That will slam the door shut in the face of Socialism and Communism and stop The Great Reset and the New World Order that the restless elites are so foolishly desirous of.

It will inspire the rest of the world to follow our example against authoritarianism and totalitarianism and open the door for prosperity with Free Market Capitalism that squeezes out corruption, dirty tricks, and gamesmanship. Uncorrupt Capitalism can win against corrupt leftist ideologies, but Corrupt Capitalism can never be strong enough to defeat the evils of aligned terrorist, Socialist, and Communist countries. 2024 was an excellent first step to elect leaders that focus on solving our significant problems. At the same time the D-S will do all they can to undermine the GOP efforts so they can get back in power to birth their dystopia.

The transformative terraforming of the global geopolitical landscape from Corrupt Capitalism to Corrupt Socialism and Communism with China ruling over was on track. Biden-Harris re-ignited and accelerated the Socialist transformation of the US. Fortunately, the 2024 extreme Socialist ticket of Harris-Walz to complete the transformation was soundly defeated to derail those efforts at least for the moment.

The D-S hopeful deception was their candidates masquerading as moderates and protectors of democracy. This was done even though they undemocratically pushed Biden off the ticket and installed Harris without her receiving any votes from a primary or open convention. She held no press conferences, had no unbiased or unscripted interviews, and could not express intelligently any actions she would do differently from the Biden-Harris fiasco. Americans overwhelmingly rejected that charade.

We must end this dystopian creep by replacing it with our alternative transformation to the Shining City on a Hill. There are no other choices because it is a deadly zero-sum game. Either Solutionist, Uncorrupt Capitalism wins, ushering in an era of global peace and cooperative problem-solving, or authoritarianism and totalitarianism win, extinguishing the light of freedom everywhere. We must have the courage to pick and implement the transformation we want or live with the result of our inaction.

Returning to our recent mediocre past, where problems were not solved, will only lead to more unrest and continue our journey down the wrong path. In a world that is mainly split between Corrupt Capitalism and Corrupt Socialist, Communist, and terrorist states, the latter coalition will prevail. Their maniacal need for control pushes them to nearly total suppression of freedoms internally and aligning externally with similar repressive and aggressive countries against countries embracing Corrupt Capitalism. Those Capitalists have difficulty joining together and understanding the existential threat before them while they twist themselves in knots, pondering over lesser issues. In an existential struggle, the stronger and more aligned will succeed.

The Supermassive Black Hole of Socialism is fueled primarily by the CCP of China. Its seductive event horizon glistens from a generous serving of specially prepared Corrupt Capitalism. This allows it to reach out and pull in any country it closes in on as it hurtles through our geopolitical universe. It is cleverly setting this up with its bold takeover and bullying tactics in the South China Sea; its support of aggression against democracies in Israel, Ukraine, and South Korea; its colonialist One Belt One Road predatory loans and resource agreements with 154 countries; and its expanding BRICS alliance that gathers and intensifies anti-Western sentiment to minimize the use of the West's SWIFT banking system and the USD in global agreements.

We were instrumental in saving the world from tyrants in World Wars I and II. WWIII has quietly begun many years ago with economic and political battles, and so far, China has an impressive record. Their empire-building using their One Belt One Road strategy is progressing well in Asia, Europe, Africa, the Middle East, and Central and South America.

Do Americans have the will to save ourselves and the world one more time? If we do, we will finally emerge from our cocoon. We have had a mixture of outstanding years and not-so-great times but have never absorbed the ingredients we need to emerge and fully take flight. Our corruption has prevented that, but the 2024 elections have provided a unique opportunity to win WWIII without firing a shot. We can also recapture our squandered inheritance from the Founders and bring about an era of global peace through our strength and successful example.

We must prioritize our efforts to significantly and successfully address these six national security problems in the following chapters. If not, other important issues become unsolvable since we will not be the foremost global power we are accustomed to being. We could become the junior partner to China. Our BFFs will be our RIC comrade leaders in Russia, Iran, and China. President Trump and the newly elected Congress see that stark reality and will not allow that dark future. 2024 must be the year we begin to save America and choose the other Solutionist path with a better destination for us and the rest of the world. "Resistance is futile. Prepare to be assimilated" must not be our future.

***

Chapter 6 covers election integrity, our most critical national security problem. Nothing else is possible without uncorrupted elections.

CHAPTER 6

Elections

While many voting parameters are left to state and local governments, a few global parameters are needed at the federal level to ensure election integrity, minimize the opportunity for fraud, and efficiently produce results no more than 12 hours after poll closings. Voter registers are not universally purified on a regular basis. Voter ballots and identities are not secure from vote thieves. Voter ID is not universally required. Processes are not streamlined to ensure all valid votes are counted and winners announced on election day or early the next day. The voids in our election integrity are easy targets, allowing fraud to happily enter.

Fixing our convoluted voting protocols is the most critical set of solution frameworks for the US. The will of the people is thwarted with disreputable voting processes, just like what happens in authoritarian countries like Russia, Venezuela, and Cuba. Good reforms that create roadblocks for Socialism cannot occur without election integrity.

Some positive election integrity changes for the 2024 elections (like in Florida) are similar to the solutions in this chapter and have already occurred in red and purple states. Now that must be a top priority at the federal level. Without election integrity, we can't enact any other solution-focused changes, even though Blacks, Hispanics, and suburban women are joining the GOP because of the chaos of the last four years. The D-S know that, will fight vigorously, and call these reforms "Jim Crow." The Attorney General in March 2024 said he will vigorously oppose any of these reforms.

Any significant election misdeed (including lack of compliance with enacted solutions (like those listed below) should be a felony if found guilty, with likely fines, jail time, and removal from office (where appropriate). Some of these can only be done at the national level, which is why the integrity of the 2024 election is critical.

We must not continue to tolerate election interference. Nicole Malliotakis (R-NY) received the info asked for in her FOIA request. Shockingly, she discovered that the City of New York requires migrant shelter builders to provide voter registration cards, assist migrants in registering, and promote campaign material within the shelters, regardless of their citizenship status.

Leftists were eager to jack up participation in our election process any way they could because they knew if the D-S won the 2024 elections, our country would be permanently in their grip when they legalized all the undocumenteds. Most of these 30 million new voters could then be mobilized to ensure the reign of the D-S forever. Similar information was printed in Spanish and given to undocumenteds even before they entered the US, encouraging them to vote for the D-S ticket.

A smaller but meaningful army was being created from a Biden "all of government" approach in all his Executive Branch agencies. The goal was to register as many as possible to vote and likely obtain their mail-in ballots for ballot harvesting into drop boxes. This would be especially useful with the prison population. These tactics were the only ways the D-S could win in a 2024 2-way or 3-way presidential election.

These zealous, dishonest efforts were more than matched by election integrity volunteers. Many new concerned voters were registered, took part in early voting, and convinced others to vote also. There was no shortage of volunteers to assist one of the following committed election integrity efforts:

- www.whoscounting.us is the non-partisan Election Integrity Network website. This local and national entity has archived weekly podcasts, brief educational videos, and other resources, including an option to download "Citizens Guide to Building an Election Integrity Infrastructure." Visitors can click on "Join an election integrity working group" and join a group in their state. Some efforts are as easy as being a poll watcher. into@whoscounting.us is their email address.
- A website by a Republican partisan, Scott Presler, www.early-voteaction.com, had the goal to even the score with early voting where the D-S held a big lead. Just in Pennsylvania, his efforts were so successful that Trump won that states' popular and Electoral College votes, and a Republican senator ousted a D-S fixture.
- For partisan voter integrity volunteering, the RNC website provides opportunities at their www.protectthevote.com. They did an amazing job mobilizing volunteers to facilitate election integrity.

Why is this election's integrity so important? Because too many citizens thought it is just another choice between Dem or GOP, woman or man, liberal or conservative. What was really on the ballot were choices to continue and expand wars and conflicts in the Middle East, Europe, and South China Sea or move to world peace; and the transformation of the USA into an authoritarian Socialist country or the Shining City on a Hill that solves its problems. That is what US citizens were voting for—not smiles, captivating lies, bluster, gender, or age.

Key Issues

1. Election day in-person voting and results are not the norms.
2. No standard for those who need to request absentee ballots.
3. Ballot harvesting drop boxes create fraud opportunities.
4. Voter ID is not universally required.
5. Regular purification of election registers is not universally done.

6. Polling places and other repositories of voter and election information do not have universal standards to ensure information integrity, security, preservation, confidentiality, and highly functional processes, including oversight, equipment, and ballots.
7. No national standards to certify voting machines and software.
8. No "gold" standard for voting machines and ballot processing.
9. There is no national standard for candidate participation in debates to inform voters.
10. Corrupt ranked choice voting and jungle primaries are allowed.
11. There is no standard protocol when an election does not produce a 50% vote winner.
12. There are no clear standards for when Social Media, print media, TV, and radio can refuse political ads. That has led to abuse supporting one candidate and silencing another.
13. Political campaign donations are so extravagant that they often determine outcomes.
14. Small political donations do not seem important, even though individuals are harassed with junk mail, texting, calls, and emails.

Key Issues and Solution Frameworks

1. Election day in-person voting and results are not the norms.

    Voting in person should become the norm again. Some inconvenience must be associated with practicing the most essential function in a democracy. We should minimize that with employer-paid (probably 2 hours) state and then national holidays for November elections every two years to minimize the need for early voting and eliminate any excuses (like work-related inconvenience) for not voting on election day.

    The states and counties set hours and locations for voting and counting. However, all vote counting should be completed without stoppage by midnight or, if problems arise, no later than 6 AM on the day after election day. It is suspicious and unreasonable that less sophisticated nations can accomplish this, and the world's #1 superpower cannot. This narrows the window for voting shenanigans and improves confidence in the results.

Voting laws and protocol changes should be made and published 60 days before elections by state legislatures or other responsible entities. Locations for primary, special, and November elections should only be changed if population changes warrant it. Voters should be able to depend on those locations not changing. Public facilities like libraries should be used consistently to eliminate voters showing up at the wrong sites.

2. No standard for those who need to request absentee ballots.

Corruption opportunities explode when the floodgates are opened to allow anyone to request a mail-in ballot. *The Epoch Times* ran a front-page article in their January 24–30, 2024 edition, "Voter Fraud Convictions Challenge Narrative of Secure Elections."[1] It highlighted election irregularities and convictions in 17 states from 2020 to 2023. They quoted a spokesman for the Public Interest Legal Foundation saying, "Michigan still has more than 20,000 deceased people registered to vote."[1] They also cited data from a poll of 1,085 likely 2020 voters conducted by Rasmussen Reports and Heartland Institute and published in December 2023:

- 30% voted by mail or mail-in ballot.
- 21% of those were filled out illegally by someone else.
- 17% of those cast ballots illegally in a state they did not reside in.
- 8% said a person or entity offered to compensate them for voting (also illegal).

Over the past two decades, an ongoing Heritage Foundation study showed 1,500 "proven instances of election fraud," resulting in nearly 1,300 criminal convictions.[2] **When the D-S call voting integrity concerns a big lie, it is they who are telling the big lie.**

Absentee voting must be requested by seniors, the physically disabled, the incarcerated who are eligible and registered to vote, and those proven out of town, like military personnel. These should be the first votes counted on election day and preserved safely for any challenges. Ballots received after election day should not be counted, labeled as "not timely received," and maintained for any challenges. Seniors with severe cognitive issues like Alzheimer's or dementia must be dropped from voter rolls.

3. Ballot harvesting drop boxes create fraud opportunities.

If these are such worthwhile practices, why were these low-tech protocols not implemented before? Because it was clear they were opportunities for significant fraud.

On the Dan Bongino radio show and podcast on January 25, 2024, he noted that America First Legal had discovered strange behavior for CISA, the security entity for the DHS. Before the 2020 elections, they were concerned with the fraud opportunities with mail-in balloting. They also believed there was no significant COVID-19 issue with in-person voting. [3] When others in the country began to express similar concerns, CISA allegedly worked with Social Media to have that taken down as "disinformation."

Ballot harvesting by paid operatives and depositing into drop boxes should be illegal, as would any vote fraud committed by unlawful voters and others. All should be felonies if convicted with a fine of $5,000 per illegal vote and jail time or community service. Illegal alien voting is grounds for immediate deportation. Having state and then national November election holidays eliminates the need for these. The movie *2,000 Mules* [4] shows the impact of suspicious activities of paid ballot harvesters using drop boxes in the 2020 elections.

Ballot harvesting is especially cruel when mentally impaired people at memory centers have their ballots requested and filled out illegally by staff or outsiders. No one should be allowed to enter or leave a memory care facility with ballots. It should be a felony for anyone participating in this fraud. The names of all patients in these facilities must be regularly given to voter integrity authorities in every state for exclusion from voter registers, and no voters with the address of a facility or the ID of a resident there can be included in the voter registers. Similarly, those mentally impaired but not in a facility must also be excluded.

In those states where ballot harvesting and drop boxes are not yet illegal, 24/7 video footage must be maintained for a minimum of 18 months for each drop box, and identification must be displayed for each person depositing more than one ballot.

4. Voter ID is not universally required.

All voters must display federally approved identification, like when they are buying liquor or cigarettes, riding on planes or trains, or using a passport to enter other countries. Passports, free state IDs, or most state driver's licenses would suffice, except for those states that provide licenses or IDs without citizenship proof. Anyone producing, selling, or using bogus IDs should be charged and tried promptly as a felon and a fine of $5,000 per bogus ID.

5. Regular purification of election registers is not universally done.

All states must work with their counties and municipalities to purify and certify their US citizen voter registers annually in early Spring and again as of August 31 (about two months before the November elections). Purification includes the removal of deceased and mentally impaired (especially those living in memory care centers), felons (within five years of their conviction), the elimination of multiple addresses for the same voter, and discovered fraudulent Social Security numbers or other fraudulent IDs. Changes after August 31 must be scrutinized and preserved for challenges. Anyone trying to vote illegally must be charged with a felony and prosecuted as soon as possible to send an important message.

Failure to meet these deadlines or produce significantly accurate voter registers subjects individuals and governments to hefty fines and criminal prosecution. No register changes within the two weeks before an election should be made to allow final voting registers to be prepared and available on Election Day for comparison with voter IDs.

Whenever the D-S creates something that seems good (but is actually a phony solution that makes the problem worse), Republicans should be embarrassed, create their own uncorrupt version, and run away from the D-S version. That is why 8 Republican states that signed onto ERIC (Election Registration Information Center) are leaving or have left, and 3 others are considering leaving. Funded in 2012 by Soros' Open Society (another good reason not to join), it had up to 31 member states.

ERIC can raise members' annual membership costs (which can soar) and have no serious limits on using all personal information collected. It can be utilized to harass people into getting registered. While this may seem good to some, combining this with paid operatives used for ballot harvesting increases voter fraud potential.

Republicans need to stop complaining and join a better alternative program or create ASAP their own database system whose only focus is voter integrity and not intimidation for possible ballot harvesting fraud. The D-S have a 10-year lead with ERIC and have nearly all of the oligarchs of the tech world on their side, but Republican donors do have money. Do they have the will to get this done?

For states that do not prohibit ballot harvesting or do not correctly limit absentee ballots, Republicans must use those tools until this can be made illegal. States and Congress should legislatively prohibit ERIC or any similar entity from forwarding personal information to anyone other than the election authorities within the states. And those authorities must not use the data for purposes other than voter roll integrity.

6. Polling places and other repositories of voter and election information do not have universal standards to ensure information integrity, security, preservation, confidentiality, and highly functional processes, including oversight, equipment, and ballots.

All voting facilities must be staffed equally and only by US-citizen Republicans and Democrats. Interference with the observation by either party or privately handling ballots should be felony voter fraud. There must be standards for the number of polling places needed in each district, testing of voting equipment, adequacy of supplies, and chain of custody for ballots. Civil and criminal penalties should apply.

Security of ballot and voter information is critical. The gold standard should be blockchain technology to change voter registration information or other access to records related to voter ID, ballots, or vote counts. Any views or changes will be automatically associated with someone with the authority to have that access. In a republic or democracy, votes are as precious as gold and must be safeguarded with an impeccable chain of custody.

All records must be securely preserved for a minimum of 18 months. If a lawsuit has been filed, they are automatically kept until the case and appeals are concluded. Standards should be set for what constitutes a physically secure environment with limited access and 24/7 video footage of the ballot counting and storage areas and other identifying information on who, when, and what was done and the reason. It is highly recommended that anyone with IT access or authority to access or change records be given a polygraph test before their information access for each election to minimize people with agendas having that access.

There must be a reconciliation of the records of those who voted by mail with the number of votes by mail counted and a reconciliation of those who voted in person with the number of votes cast in person. Registered voter totals and approved vote-by-mail requests cannot be exceeded by actual votes counted. Before counts can be certified, significant discrepancies require investigation of records handling and possible voting machine issues.

7. No national standards to certify voting machines and software.

Voting machines and software must be certified as to accuracy by the creators and a 3rd party as tamper-proof with hefty financial penalties and considered a felony if convicted of election interference from inaccurate or hacked machines or software. Each election malfunction is punishable with a fine of $300,000 against the manufacturer and/or the software developer and a fine of $150,000 against the 3rd party certifier. They would also pay for a new election if the discrepancies could have reasonably resulted in a different outcome.

8. No "gold" standard for voting machines and ballot processing.

Paper ballots, scanning equipment, and maintaining the chain of custody of all ballots should be the gold standard. Scanners are simpler devices than expensive direct-recording electronic voting machines that require more programming and are more susceptible to malfunctions and security breaches from external sources.

Direct-recording voting machines do not provide an auditable paper ballot trail. Their integrity is more suspect than scanning devices, where archived paper ballots can always be reviewed. A good rule of thumb is if D-S are personally investing in something (like ERIC voter integrity or direct-recording election voting machines), that should be reason enough to flee as fast as possible.

9. There is no national standard for candidate participation in debates to inform voters.

All national candidates for President, Vice President, Senate, and state governors must participate in two to for televised debates that conclude between two and four weeks before voting begins and are available for download. Voters should consider a candidate unworthy if they fail to participate in that great American tradition of in-person debates with moderators, and they should be prevented from running ads in the two weeks before voting begins if they fail to debate. This should also be encouraged for the House, other state-wide, and local elections. Those may not be televised live but should be available for download.

The simplest way to end the delays and posturing over debates for the November elections is to let the candidates pick a moderator who will be a partisan for them. Each candidate knows they will get an equal number of positive and not-so-positive questions. Falsely trashing an opponent with trumped-up charges can be called out by the opponent and their moderator. Lying and cheating to win elections should stop. Let's stop fooling ourselves about moderator independence—they are seldom unbiased, regardless of what they claim.

10. Corrupt ranked choice voting and jungle primaries are allowed.

    A voter uses ranked choice to rank (not vote for) each person on the ballot, which can result in multiple rounds of changes (where fraud can occur) until someone gets 50% of 1st rank votes. Jungle primaries allow multiple candidates from the same party to run instead of the one who won their party's primary and anyone else meeting the qualifications to run. "Ranked choice voting" or "jungle primaries" are unacceptable and perverted voting.

    For primary voting, only registered Republicans should vote for Republicans, and only registered Democrats should vote for Democrats. This ends the dirty tricks of having a party select the candidate they want their candidate to run against.

11. There is no standard protocol when an election does not produce a 50% vote winner.

    Elections should be between one Democrat, one Republican, and any other party's candidate that wins their party's primary or otherwise qualifies. When those elections do not produce a candidate with 50% of the votes cast (for President, that would be 50% of the Electoral College votes), there should be a runoff within 30 days of the top two vote getters. A valid democracy needs winners to have a majority of 50% of the votes.

Unfortunately, under the 12th Amendment, the House of Representatives decides the Presidency if no candidate receives 50% of the Electoral College votes. The voters should decide the President (even if a runoff is needed), not the party controlling the House. The 12th Amendment must be amended to make this a reality. The preservation and improvement of the Electoral College is covered in the next chapter.

12. There are no clear standards for when Social Media, print media, TV, and radio can refuse political ads. That has led to abuse supporting one candidate and silencing another.

    Social media, print media, TV, and radio can only refuse political ads that clearly promote violence or are proven false. They cannot act as champions for one party or candidate by censoring content from others they do not support. Our Constitution recognized the importance of a free press in a democracy. They cannot collude with government agencies to silence, mute, or amplify individuals or messages. This significantly occurred in the elections of 2016–2022 and likely many others.

    A felony conviction on this will result in a fine of $500,000 and a civil penalty to the injured party of $250,000 or more. It may also require the organization to pay for the cost of a new election if the results are close enough to warrant it. Unjustly de-platforming or algorithmic message stifling should bear the same penalties for Social Media and apps (like payment apps) targeted to influence the voters. These fines and criminal prosecutions of the media and government can go a long way to ending this corruption and perversion of the unique role of a free media. They are supposed to be our watchdog on government, not a version of a Russian Pravda lapdog.

13. Political campaign donations are so extravagant that they often determine outcomes.

The corruption of elites, oligarchs, and wealthy wokesters to see who can outspend their opponent to buy elections determines, to a large extent, who gets into office. George Soros and Mark Zuckerberg are the two most egregious examples from the 2020 election cycle.

George Soros has spent $40 million to elect 75 "Progressive" DAs. The result has been that they prosecute/persecute political opponents to his ideology while allowing criminals to be "free range" local terrorists. Chapter 8 discusses how these DAs throw gasoline on the increasing crime wave. You might think that $40 million should be a violation of Federal Election Commission limits. However, elites like him cleverly game the system to stay below the limits in the complex 6x5 matrix of FEC published limits with no overall limitation per year.

Zuckerberg was able to use a "charitable" deduction loophole to significantly influence the 2020 elections by dropping $419 million (some call them Zuckerbucks) in cleverly designed tax-deductible grants to two 501(c)(3) organizations despite their political bias towards mail-in ballots, ballot harvesting, and drop boxes. Combined with other genuine charitable deductions, the only current donation limit for anyone is 60% of their AGI (adjusted gross income).

One organization that received $350 million from Zuck advertised the funds would help "safely serve every voter" during the 2020 COVID election year. There were few limits placed on how localities could use the money. There was a clear bias favoring absentee voting and ballot harvesting, with only a small amount spent on the safety of PPE (personal protective equipment).

There are detailed examples of bias in the distribution of these grant funds in many articles, but especially of interest are the April 5, 2021 article in The Daily Signal by Hayden Dublois and Trevor Carlsen and the website www.fga.org, the Foundation for Government Accountability. The Signal article provides many examples of the Pennsylvania funds bias, where 90% of the grants went to counties Biden won. The FGA website includes examples of biases regarding state funds from Georgia, Ohio, Wisconsin, Michigan, and Pennsylvania.

Perhaps the most succinct information is from David Bossie's article in the Washington Times on April 12, 2022, titled "Mark Zuckerberg's 'donations' rigged the 2020 election." [5] He mentions **the Presidency was decided by 42,000 votes cast in Wisconsin, Arizona, and Georgia for 37 pivotal Electoral College votes; 92% of total grants went to Biden counties; and 25 of 26 grants of $1 million or more went to Biden county wins in Arizona, Georgia, Wisconsin, Michigan, North Carolina, Pennsylvania, Texas, and Virginia.** Lastly, he draws attention to the criticism Zuck took for the 2016 Hillary loss when Trump skillfully used Social Media (especially Facebook) to seal his victory.

It looks like Zuck was trying to make up for allowing that intelligent SM use by Trump in 2016 with Zuck's own immersion into the 2020 election. If his 2020 actions would have helped Trump, he would never have done it and received an even harsher dose of criticism. At least 8 Republican-majority states have banned this use of private money to influence elections.

However, the damage has been done and has likely carried over to 2022 and future elections, even without any new mega-cash injections. The criticism of foolish Republicans against Trump-backed candidates in 2022 that lost is misguided. Many of those races for governor, Senate, and House could have likely been won without 1) the lingering effect of this 2020 Zuck interference that promoted ballot harvesting and other unethical tactics, 2) Republican leadership not adequately funding his endorsements, and 3) the Republicans not blocking or smartly participating in the absentee voting explosion.

While not overtly influencing elections, Michael Bloomberg has, over the past 6 years, pledged $1 billion from his Bloomberg Philanthropies (sounds like another big tax deduction for a billionaire) to Beyond Carbon. Half of that pledge was in 2019, and the other $500 million in 2023. Because Bloomberg Philanthropies supports many worthwhile endeavors, you might think this would fund accelerated research and development of power from nuclear fusion or green hydrogen.

However, according to a September 20, 2023 press release, Beyond Carbon will use the money to "finish the job on coal," "slash gas plant capacity in half, and block all new gas plants." [6] The 2019 funding was primarily responsible for closing 372 of 530 US coal plants, leaving only 30% of coal plants. They want to fully eliminate the US coal industry, which is cleaner than most other countries.

Why not do something positive like operationalizing power from nuclear fusion or green hydrogen or getting the world to shame China and India to change their mega pollution? They are the world's biggest polluters, and China is globally building hundreds of new coal plants every year within and outside the borders of China. Devastating the US economy, its power grid, and energy affordability will have a minimal global impact.

There are many other examples of these non-taxable "umbrella" charitable organizations, providing tax deductions for donors while funneling money to controversial causes or terrorist or adversarial causes and keeping the donors anonymous. Our government even gives tax-payer-funded grants to some of those as well.

Because the umbrella organizations provide tax forms to the IRS, their controversial/terrorist organizations can escape the scrutiny of filing. This nonsense must be stopped. Donor "charities" should be in danger of hefty fines or loss of non-profit status if they support these organizations. All non-profit organizations must file forms with the IRS. No government grants should be allowed to support such organizations.

Neither disguised political donations nor controversial ideological donations should receive tax deductions. Below are the solution frameworks for these devious use of tax deductions for billionaires.

First, because megabucks corrupt our elections, there must be total limits on how much an individual can spend annually on political activities. Those political activities include not only their direct support to candidates or PACs, but also other taxable political entities and not-for-profits that try to portray themselves as voter educators but are really politically partisan.

We should set a reasonable limit of $50,000 per donor (person, business, or organization) and another $50,000 for another company or organization with common or similar ownership. The same $50,000 rule would apply to unions with different locals. Union members should notice their dues reduced due to the reduction in campaign donations. Politicians, wealthy individuals, organizations, companies, donation-soliciting operations, and media profiteers will squeal. We need to end the era of the $100 million political campaigns and stop the buying of elections.

Second, tighten the 501(c)(3) tax-exempt status requirements for organizations with a political focus. The education and focus must be clearly non-partisan, like election integrity or the financial support of carbon capture by Microsoft and Amazon, not donating money to influence elections with mail-in ballots and ballot harvesting in hand-picked districts. This latter group must be transitioned into a revised 501(c)(4) with no charitable deduction allowed for contributors and no tax-exempt status for the organization.

There would no longer be a tax deduction like Zuck got for "donating" $419 million to change the course of the 2020 and likely 2022 (and beyond) elections. Individuals are free to contribute to those organizations as a part of the $50,000 overall political annual limit. But no massive donations or tax deductions for disguised political organizations. These changes would take a lot of corrupt money out of the system. These redefined 501(c)(4) entities should be allowed unlimited lobbying and candidate support, must report all donors (no "dark money" anonymous donors), and pay a 10% flat tax on all gross income received.

Capital Research Center (www.capitalresearch.org) is an organization that has done a great job in following the trails of these 501(c)

(3) organization political activities and 501(c)(4) "dark monies" that currently don't have to report their donors.

Third, besides annual total limits, there should also be a $10,000 maximum contribution limit annually to any one campaign, PAC, or organization that is significantly political.

The damage done by the limitless spending of Zuck and Soros may be long-standing. Cities (mostly D-S) suffer from this gang of 75 DAs that allow criminals to be free-range terrorists with little or no consequences. Rampant crime and political opponent targeting will continue until we eliminate opportunities for people like Soros to buy elections and create chaos. We do this by allowing citizens of every state to recall and remove them from office.

Until voter rolls are purified, mail-in ballots are severely restricted, ballot harvesting and drop boxes are eliminated, and the other needed reforms are implemented, it will be challenging for elections to be won fairly thanks to that one-time infusion of $419 million Zuckerbucks (for which he cleverly gamed the system and got a tax deduction).

It is absurd and corrupt that "limitless" tax deductions are available to the super-wealthy to buy elections or implement their controversial ideologies. This must be stopped, or democracy will be lost. These changes may seem drastic to some, lessening the freedom of the wealthy to buy elections or implement their ideologies and often receive tax deductions. But this corruption fueled by megabucks is a more destructive force that threatens our democracy. We must limit wealthy oligarchs from imposing their candidates and ideologies (and often getting tax deductions) to pervert the will of ordinary voters.

14. Small political donations do not seem important, even though individuals are harassed with junk mail, texting, calls, and emails.

    Limits on wealthy political donations open the door for more impactful contributions from the general electorate. They will feel their small donations can now have a more significant impact due to limitations on how the wealthy can influence elections. A way to boost their patriotic participation is to allow a special itemized deduction or a refundable tax credit (if they have no taxes paid or liability) of up to $1,000 for those who donate for political support, even if they can't itemize deductions.

The parties should be more intelligent with their broader but possibly smaller war chests. They should encourage individuals to make a monthly automatic donation to one or more funds (like for House or Senate seats, state and local elections, and the Presidency).

The parties (or a separate organization like the RNC, CPAC, or some other Conservative group for the Republicans or a leftist group for the D-S) should have a team of strategists to identify which campaigns to fund and by how much and report back to donors.

With smaller but automatic monthly donations, they will reduce the generally unwelcome volume of donation pleas from daily mail, texts, calls, and emails to semi-monthly or monthly with an occasional additional request for specific races or causes. Let's end the daily hassling communication for each candidate or asking voters to participate in a survey and then hitting them up with a donation request at the end. Individual campaigns should still be able to hassle voters, but they should recognize donor request fatigue and limit their frequency.

No longer should a single leader in the House or Senate determine who they prefer to win and how much of that party's donation war chest should go or not go to those campaigns. This was especially detrimental in the 2020 Senate and governor races. One person's preference or corrupt maintenance of power should not rule. That also applies to oligarchs like Zuckerberg and Soros, who have spent hundreds of millions to get election results that benefit their businesses or support their ideologies.

Most Relevant Chapter 1 Founding Principles (FP)

- FP 2 The Right to Govern Derives from the People
- FP 3 Limited Representative Republican Form of Government
- FP 6 All People Are Created Equal, and the Government's Role Is to Protect Their Equal Rights and Not Provide Equal Outcomes
- FP 9 Free People Must Stay Strong to Survive
- FP 12 The USA Has the Destiny to Be Exceptional and an Example to the World

Positive Impacts

Creating impeccable voter and election integrity elevates the USA to the ideal imagined at its birth. Instead, we currently have a third-world situation of untrustworthy voter rolls, lack of universal voter ID, counts being suspended and carried on much after the election night, an explosion of mail-in ballots, paid ballot harvesting dumped into drop boxes, lack of audibility of some voting machines, and other egregious practices.

The way to correct much of this lies with having a paid 2-hour November voting holiday every two years now at the state level and then at the national level. That eliminates the excuses for not voting and removes most of the lack of trust in our convoluted processes and election integrity. Voting is a critical responsibility in our democracy, and it must have the opportunity for corruption to be severely minimized.

We will also elevate the reliability when we create and enforce standards for polling facility operations and certification of voting machines and software. We can further enhance the process by creating common-sense standards for primaries, eliminating the dirty tricks of ranked-choice voting and jungle primaries, and only allowing registered party members to vote in their party's primary. Other common sense changes demand that a primary or general election winner must have 50% of the vote. If not, then a runoff between the top two vote leaders must occur. For the President, that means 50% of the Electoral College votes. We cannot have someone with 35% of the vote win an election for the Presidency or any other office.

In the early days of our country, it would have been unthinkable for a candidate to avoid engaging in a public debate of critical issues with their opponent(s). We have seen the disaster of electing candidates that evaded putting their thoughts out to debating scrutiny, and we will be better served by eliminating that "Basement Biden" option.

Allowing small donations to gain more importance while minimizing the impact of larger donations to "buy elections" or "implement favorite ideologies" (sometimes with substantial tax deductions) will restore a much-needed balance. Stopping the media from silencing campaigns and candidates that they do not like will be therapeutic to our democracy.

Some of these positive changes can be made at the state level, and some involving the US Tax Code or the 12th Amendment (for presidential elections when no one receives 50% of the Electoral College votes due to the votes for 3rd parties) can only be done at the federal level. The key to solving any other problems and changing our dystopian direction rests on having elections with high integrity. Without that, there is no chance of affecting positive changes to become the Shining City on a Hill.

* * *

The next chapter covers the second internal security issue—government processes. The corruption, inefficiency, and costly bureaucracy are huge, but significant reforms can be made.

CHAPTER 7

Government

Why do we continue to see daily headlines about poverty, inadequate healthcare, struggling seniors, poor quality education, serious global threats, government corruption, out-of-control immigration, spending gone wild, tax inequities, skyrocketing crime, crumbling infrastructure not worthy of a superpower, a poor safety net for underserved citizens, the out-of-balance condition of environment and energy, and a heavily-biased entertainment and media, tearing apart our culture and canceling people, companies, and institutions at will?

Too many in power and control focus on personal agendas, not the country's issues. Politicians and bureaucrats have allowed our government processes for all three branches to accumulate "barnacles" of corruption, bureaucracy, and inefficiency that have contributed mightily to our highjacked journey in the last nearly 250 years.

The first 60 appointees of the Biden-Harris administration have a combined business experience (our economy) of only 2.5 years (most have zero). Their business literacy is lacking, but they are in charge of regulating the people's business (the economy of the #1 superpower). When the Biden-Harris administrations took over, we were told, "Now the adults are in charge." How has that worked out for us domestically and for the chance of a more stable and peaceful world?

These are really the JV team with a roster of petulant, arrogant, and spoiled kids (many left over from the Obama regime) who must have their way. It is as if kids are in charge of our candy store, and with no business or financial skills, they are bribing us to come inside and telling us everything is free. Of course, it is not truly free, but we fall for it. Without common sense business skills, this house of cards will come crashing down and the store will shut down because of the giveaway's and raising prices (taxes) on others to pay for the "free stuff." Shame on Americans for putting these corrupt and geopolitically and economically ignorant leftist kids in charge.

Democracy, especially for the #1 superpower, is a delicate balance. All governments need strength and force domestically to maintain law and order and internationally to maintain peace and respect, but those need tempering with tolerance of opposing views. Repressive Socialist/Communist and terrorist regimes minimize tolerance and are heavy-handed with their strength and force. The US balance is similarly lopsided, tolerating lawlessness internally and internationally while using its strength and force domestically against those opposed to the coming New World Order. We need to correct that imbalance by fixing our dysfunctional government. This must be a high priority for Trump's second term.

Executive Branch

Key Issues

1. All presidential nominees requiring Senate approval are not timely vetted by the FBI and voted on by the Senate.
2. Executive Orders (EOs) can often be a way to legislate without Congress, but they are too broad, are often unconstitutional, and without limits.

3. While the United Nations and other global governing bureaucracies may have had sincere altruistic goals when they were formed, several aspects (like many other institutions) have become corrupt.
4. The State Department administers foreign aid and negotiates international treaties and "accords" without appropriate and consistent guardrails against bad-actor nations.
5. DC corruption, bureaucracy, and tax complexity are major threats to our democracy that have been ignored for too long.
6. All well-run large businesses produce an annual report, and the US, the world's largest economy, publishes a lot of data but not an impactful, comprehensive, and easy-to-read report.
7. The Deep State is real and has grown exponentially and corruptly.
8. We are significantly increasing funding for and militarizing federal agencies while defunding, reducing, and de-weaponizing local law enforcement. Simultaneously, Biden-Harris took incremental steps to create unauthorized gun lists that could eventually allow the removal of guns from lawful, mentally competent citizens. We have been building a National Police State.

Key Issues and Solution Frameworks

1. All presidential nominees requiring Senate approval are not timely vetted by the FBI and voted on by the Senate.

    All nominees by the President for positions requiring Senate approval must be vetted by the FBI within 60 days of their nomination and voted on by the Senate within the next 45 days. Vetting should include an investigation and a written report with an executive summary of key findings. Every nominee and the President deserve to have their nominations vetted and voted on within a reasonable period.

    The President needs to get their Cabinet in place to properly govern and not have nominations languish due to Senate politics or investigative incompetence. Organizations like the FBI have vast resources to do this job, which needs to be their top priority with a new administration or new nominees. No nominee or President should be forced to wait 6 months or longer for approval.

In a related circumstance, when an individual in the Cabinet or any other government service leaves their post, their security clearance designation should become "honorary" to maintain the recognition of that achievement. However, they should no longer have access to various levels of classified information that should be reserved for those in active government service.

Otherwise, they can access confidential information, which they often will corruptly spin to make money for a book or TV deal. We are allowing more opportunity for classified information to be insecure, like what happened with classified docs from Biden's Senate/VP days that were insecurely and illegally in his possession in 2023. Keeping confidential/top-secret information is prohibited for Representatives, Senators, and VPs.

2. Executive Orders (EOs) can often be a way to legislate without Congress, but they are too broad, are often unconstitutional, and without limits.

There need to be limits on the number of new EOs to prevent a President from legislating without the Legislative Branch's involvement. However, eliminating prior presidential EOs should not count toward that. At a minimum, all global and other significant treaties should require the approval of the Senate, and this should not be circumvented by simply calling them agreements or accords.

Secondly, any new departments, projects, or strategies with significant financial costs or onerous regulations should be approved legislatively. A prime example is Biden's "American Climate Corps." It would hire 20,000 youth to continue their indoctrination and climate activism to become paid clergy for this ideology. Congress has not explicitly authorized this annual cost of hundreds of millions.

These changes will reduce the volume of EOs that create a dictatorial rule that neuters the built-in checks and balances.

3. While the United Nations and other global governing bureaucracies may have had sincere altruistic goals when they were formed, several aspects (like many other institutions) have become corrupt.

The Executive Branch and Congress should be wary of the corrupt parts of the UN and other global bodies and subjecting us to them. If we rightly lead by example, there is no need to shackle ourselves to unelected international bureaucrats thousands of miles away who may be biased against us. We must call out the UN when it carries the water for China or other repressive regimes or terrorists.

This includes having repressive countries pass judgment on other countries' human rights while continuing unchallenged repression in their nations. In particular, countries with repressive human rights records, including terrorism, a lack of religious freedom, and high levels of pollution, should be economically penalized by a coalition of democracy-loving countries if the UN cannot agree to do so itself. Corrupt UN organizations should not be funded by the US and as many allies as we can partner with.

There are many examples of corruption in the UN. One example is the funding of UNRWA with its support of global terrorist activities often perpetrated by Hamas. Because of that, the Trump administration stopped US funding of UNRWA. But King Biden reversed that and has poured $730 million into UNRWA for "refugee assistance" in the West Bank and Gaza. Since Hamas terrorists control and influence much of what goes on there, most of that "assistance" is stolen by Hamas to support its military. The US is now listed as the largest financial supporter of UNRWA.

We are funding terrorism via UNRWA and the nonenforcement of economic sanctions against Iran and all of its terrorist activities. We are also supporting the victims of terrorism in Ukraine, Israel, and elsewhere. How dumb is that to fund both sides of wars and conflicts? Teachers working for UNRWA use antisemitic textbooks. As the brutality of the savage killing, raping, and kidnapping of Jews on

October 7, 2023, was being reported, some of those teachers cheered, according to transcripts of a UNRWA Gaza online group.

When it comes to carrying water for China, it is hard to find a more egregious example than the World Health Organization, which praised China for its COVID-19 handling. Biden-Harris wanted to have (probably by Executive Order) the corrupt WHO tell US citizens how to live if the WHO declares there is another pandemic. This could repeat the successful Basement Biden COVID-19 lockdown strategy.

4. The State Department administers foreign aid and negotiates international treaties and "accords" without appropriate and consistent guardrails against bad-actor nations.

    Just like we should be doing within the UN and with our allies to economically penalize bad actor nations (in the prior key issue), we should be consistent within our own State Department's international actions. Consistency of economic penalties for bad-actor nations can have a positive result, as money often has a way of changing behaviors.

5. DC corruption, bureaucracy, and tax complexity are major threats to our democracy that have been ignored for too long.

    The President should appoint three independent czars to clean up serious issues.

    - A Tax Czar to simplify taxes and close loopholes and abuses.

        Taxation rules include the Tax Code, IRS regulations, IRS revenue rulings, and applicable court cases (as published by Commerce Clearing House). When last examined in 2017, it totaled over 80,000 pages of 36 million words. This strangles our efficiency and costs millions of dollars in compliance, fines, and court proceedings. We need a simpler approach with fewer exceptions that is less susceptible to fraud and errors. The Czar should end up with a fair simplification that results in at least 50% less volume of rules and regulations.

Surely, intelligent, uncorrupt people can simplify the 14 types of 401(k) plans to two or three plans with many common regulations. How about one tax rate for dividends instead of two? Should we tax Social Security since it was taxed when withheld from earnings and is barely enough to live on? What about raising the earning thresholds needed to increase Medicare premiums? Can't we simplify the 401(k) required minimum distribution rules?

An underappreciated fact is that not-for-profits provide societal needs (like food banks, thrift shops, and job transition support) more cost-effectively than government programs since they often use volunteers instead of paid government employees. A recommended way to recognize this is to allow a special itemized deduction or a refundable tax credit of up to $1,000 for those who donate to them but cannot otherwise itemize deductions.

- A Corruption Czar to weed out people with private agendas for personal gain or to benefit an ideology vs. performing their job.

Unfortunately, bureaucrats are no longer rewarded based on the results of their work but on the number of years they collect a paycheck. There are many outrageous examples. How about the $125,000/yr. EPA worker watching porn for 4 hours daily while at work? Or IRS agents who receive bonuses even if they are guilty of tax misdeeds or other misconduct?

A Wall Street Journal article by Michael Siconolfi on October 11, 2022, exposed the magnitude of the suspicious financial trades allowed within the Executive Branch during the six years of 2016–2021.[1] Investments were made in companies that were lobbying their agencies. The revelation included 200 senior officials (out of about 600) from the EPA. Similarly, Defense Department officials bought stocks ($1.2–$3.4 million) of aerospace and military contractors. The FDA allowed one official to own dozens of food and drug stocks on its "non-buy" list. 70 officials traded options, with some trades between $5–$25 million.

These people are doing a lot of work to grow their financial wealth, but is there much time or interest in solving our country's problems? The WSJ looked at 31,000 disclosure forms for 12,000 senior officials. Shockingly (or not), the feds don't keep a database of these mandatory forms. The WSJ had to create its own to analyze the corruption.

Other corruption includes Deep Staters who act like a shadow government, leaking confidential information, creating false stories, and destroying records. The accused should be placed on leave and, if convicted, lose their security clearance and civil service status and are dismissed with a felony conviction on their record. Terminating a federal employee is next to impossible, and that must change.

The independence of the Corruption Czar will also allow them to look at the Legislative and Judiciary Branches cooperatively with them.

- A Bureaucracy Reduction Czar to streamline accountability, processes, operations, and decisions.

The Deep State does exist, and we have nurtured it with the defective DNA of an endless supply of additional funding each year to do more of the same rather than do better, more efficiently, and actually solve problems. Like many businesses, it often needs fresh eyes to find ways to improve; and Trump's second term can provide that.

Utah represents an excellent example of Solutionism at work, but in 1998, Congress legislatively prevented any other states from adopting their successful integration of workforce development and the safety net. Greg Sindelar and Daniel Erspamer reported this in the New York Post on January 1, 2024, in an article titled "The simple reform Congress can make to move millions from welfare to work." Unfortunately, the federal Workforce Innovation and Opportunity Act traps people into federal government dependence.

Utah requires those applying for unemployment insurance, food stamps, Medicaid, or other welfare to go through the Utah Department of Workforce Services. An individual plan is created to get each person back into the workforce. Many sources, such as the US News and World Report, disclose that Utah's economy is the strongest in the country. After COVID, they replaced almost two jobs for every one that was lost—the best in the US. Utah has extremely low unemployment, the highest labor participation rate, and a poverty rate of 8.6% vs. 12.8% nationally.

The rest of the country's 40 million on food stamps and 80 million on Medicaid are mostly not connected to workforce development. We like massive federal government dependence programs that produce terrible results. The Bureaucracy Czar could find and fix this and many other examples of unproductive, costly programs.

The Rahn Curve plots government spending as a % of GDP, and the results are available for many countries. Some say the optimal range of efficient government spending is between 15% and 25%, but the US federal % is about 40%, with another 10% for state and local government. The history of this metric in the US showed it to be 10% or less until the Great Depression. Interestingly, the period from the end of the Civil War until the early 1900s represents the highest US economic growth.

Most European and other Westernized developed economies are now in the same ballpark or higher with the metric of the Rahn Curve, some with their government spending % of GDP surpassing 50%. While we are in the good company of other bureaucratic allies, this is not admirable. Hong Kong (before China swallowed it) was at about 16%, and Singapore and Taiwan are also below 20%. In the Heritage Foundation's 2024 Economic Freedom Rankings, Taiwan placed 4th, Singapore 1st, and the US was a mediocre 25th. Government spending is often for "transfers" or "consumption," and these expenditures typically result in poor economic performance.

China would likely prefer to extinguish these other two bright flames of Asian Free Market Capitalism so that no other positive alternatives to their totalitarian bureaucracy can outshine them in the region.

Scott Fitzgerald, a Republican House member said, "The total annual cost of regulation is almost $2 trillion or about 8% of the US GDP. If US regulations were a country, it would be the world's 8th largest economy." [2] No doubt regulations are necessary, but Congress (not the unelected bureaucrats) must be accountable for its $2 trillion annual cost, using specific authorization in budgets and law clarifications.

Bureaucrats have different agendas than Congress and don't have to worry about being voted out of office for egregious spending. Scott Fitzgerald sponsored a 2023 bill that aims to stop the Executive Branch from regulating as it pleases as it interprets the enforcement of laws and effectively makes new laws. That practice has neutered Congress in its oversight and law-making role.

Taxpayer-funded bureaucratic intervention in the economy can never account for all individual and group situations and the unintended effects of their "brilliant" policy actions/blunders. In a June 20, 2019, article on www.*adividedworld.com* by C. B. Thorington, he believes that "the Great Depression of the 1930s was caused by a change in monetary policy by the Federal Reserve, Lyndon Johnson's War on Poverty caused great damage to many families." "The Great Recession of 2008–2009 was caused by a misguided federal housing policy." [3]

6. All well-run large businesses produce an annual report, and the US, the world's largest economy, publishes a lot of data but not an impactful, comprehensive, and easy-to-read report.

Collaborating with Congress and the Judiciary, the President should issue an annual report on the USA with supporting charts and graphs. It should be posted on the Internet to include significant and noteworthy "report card" items like:
- Important Executive, Legislative, and Court Actions.
- Metrics that reflect progress on major problems and key issues like eliminating the annual deficit and reducing the accumulated national debt.
- Financial Reports of the US government for the prior year and the Budget for the next.
- How the US has helped our communities and the world through actions by the federal (and state if available) government, non-profit organizations, corporations, and individuals.

7. The Deep State is real and has grown exponentially and corruptly. Examples are everywhere.

IRS: They destroyed 30 million taxpayer returns because we are told its expensive systems and procedures could not handle them. And not one of the D-S Senators would vote for a bill that clarified that the extravagant $80 billion extra annual funding for 87,000 new IRS agents would not be used against anyone with income below $400,000 like the D-S claimed. Let's not overlook a prior administration's use of the IRS to target Conservative groups to diminish their influence before an election.

DOL: One of Biden's new labor rules (without legislation) was being administered by his Department of Labor. It would result in many independent contractors having to be treated as employees. More funding will be needed for the DOL to monitor and implement his mandate. After a similar 2019 law in California, many employers could not afford the extra costs, and many jobs were lost. Biden expanded that "successful" concept nationally—way to go, Joe. Many contractors enjoy the independence and freedom that status gives them, but the Deep State does not care about them—only more power, control, and funding for themselves (from higher taxes to support the ever-expanding bureaucracy).

DOJ: How about Biden's Department of (In)justice indicting Trump for possession in one secured location of classified documents (that he is entitled to verbally declassify) and which he was negotiating with the archive authorities? All Presidents have such records, and none have been indicted. Meanwhile, Joey had classified documents in multiple improperly secured locations and was allowed to have his lawyers (who may not have the proper security clearance to look at classified documents) purge through the files at his multiple residences. There may still be other locations that have not been searched.

As a Senator or VP, he legally cannot retain such records. That is blatantly illegal, and no similar "Trump" treatment has been given to him. The extensive coordination between the DOJ and Soros-elected corrupt DAs to go after Trump would be unimaginable to our Founders. Look at how they coordinated new Trump indictments on the same day or within two days of more damaging announcements of the evidence for the alleged Hunter-Big Guy corruption.

CIA: What about the significant roles just before the 2020 election of the Central Intelligence Agency and the Biden Cabinet? They got 50 intelligence leaders to sign a cleverly worded document saying that the Hunter Biden laptop authenticity story had "all the earmarks of Russian disinformation."

FBI: Who knows how long they have been involved in election interference? Let's review just recent history. They gave a free pass to Hillary Clinton just before the 2016 election for her deleting thousands of emails, illegally conducting government business with her personal email addresses and personal cell phones and keeping an unsecured server in her home for those emails. Of course, Hillary said those deleted emails were innocent and personal (yoga, grandkids, etc.). If that was true, why go to the trouble of using sophisticated software so they could never be recovered, and why physically destroy the cell phones she used?

Who can forget the Russian collusion hoax that the FBI knew was unverifiable, but they still used to get the FISA Courts to grant spying on Trump's campaign and then his Presidency? Even though the FBI used the FISA courts to spy on Americans over 200,000 times in 1 year, the Republicans foolishly went along with extending this corrupt practice as part of the funding for the Department of Defense just before the end of 2023.

The FBI tricked (and laughed about it) Mike Flynn into an interview without legal counsel and wound up harassing and costing him hundreds of thousands of dollars for statements they construed as lies.

Both the FBI and DOJ are famous for slow-rolling or not rolling at all documents requested by Congress in its oversight role. When they begrudgingly produce the documents, they are often so heavily redacted that they are of limited value. Unredacted versions should be available to appropriate Congressional leaders in the SCIF.

Military: Trump offered to have at least 10,000 National Guardsmen go to the Capitol to secure the premises on January 6, 2021, but that was turned down. The military and Congressional leadership will not admit their roles in the fiasco from that refusal.

There is so much more (enough for an entire book on the Deep State corruption), but the purpose here is just a refresher of some of the egregious corruption of the Deep State. Senior leadership in the Deep State with private agendas must be identified, flushed out, and replaced with patriotic, hard workers committed to doing their job and solving problems without political bias.

Homeland Security and Secret Service: Homeland Security failed to provide adequate Secret Service protection for Donald Trump despite requests for added protection. Fortunately, a July 13, 2024, assassination attempt on him was unsuccessful. They also had provided no protection for RFK Jr. There must be serious consequences from the new Trump administration for those responsible.

NSA: There is an intriguing 2022 book by Bruce Brill, *Deceit of an Ally: A Memoir of Military Anti-Semitism, NSA's Secret Jew Room and Yom Kippur War Treachery.* The book claims the presence of a secret anti-Semitic "Jew Room" in the agency that has provided false and corrupted intelligence to the Israeli government. If true, this, along with other corrupt elements within the Deep State, must be eliminated.

8. We are significantly increasing funding for and militarizing federal agencies while defunding, reducing, and de-weaponizing local law enforcement. Simultaneously, Biden-Harris worked with EOs to take incremental steps to create unauthorized gun lists that could eventually allow the removal of guns from lawful, mentally competent citizens. We have been building a National Police State.

    It seems like the trend is to reduce and eventually eliminate private gun ownership, neuter local law enforcement, and supersize the military capability of federal agencies to intimidate the citizenry. Open the Books (www.openthebooks.com) has done a great job obtaining spending information on various government agencies. Particularly eye-opening is the enormous spending to militarize many branches of our federal bureaucracies. Here are a few tidbits from their extensive reporting in "The Militarization of the US Executive Agencies" and its update on the IRS, dated May 1, 2023.

    - Besides the Defense Department, 103 agencies spent $2.7 billion on military equipment, guns, and ammo between 2006 and 2019. This includes "$4.4 million on grenades/launchers, $7.9 million on unmanned vehicles/aircraft, $8.75 million on projectiles, $11 million on buckshot, and $37.6 million on Tasers."
    - 27 of those agencies are traditional law enforcement, but 76 are "pencil-pushing regulatory agencies" like the EPA, SSA, VA, IRS, HHS, DOT, and USDA.
    - There are now more federal agents (200,000) with arrest and firearm authority than US Marines (186,000).
    - Since 2006, the IRS spent $35.2 million on guns, military equipment, and ammo.

- The current IRS special agent headcount of 2,159 (before Biden's massive spending for the IRS and new personnel) would rank in the top 50 of all US police departments. In their job description, they must be willing to use "deadly force." They own 4,500 guns (including sub-machine guns and semi-automatic shotguns) and 5 million rounds of ammo. That doesn't sound like the kinder, gentler IRS that had been talked about.

Removing guns from lawful and competent citizens eliminates their ability to enjoy their legal use for recreation or hunting or protecting themselves from criminals who have no problem getting firearms from the black market. Despite these cleverly incremental EO steps, they do not escape the notice of most and should not be tolerated. Building a Police State to enforce the deconstruction of our society, culture, and institutions and transformation to an authoritarian government is the opposite of our founding based on principles of freedom.

Dan Bongino and Dinesh D'Souza collaborated on a movie, *Police State*.[4] It is an excellent portrayal of our leftist authoritarian lurch.

Judiciary

Key Issues

1. The number of Supreme Court Justices is subject to the whims of Congress.
2. Cognitive or physical health issues may have compromised the effectiveness of some SCOTUS Justices.
3. Some significant financial, constitutional, or cultural impact cases may not be fast-tracked to SCOTUS as they deserve.
4. It is often questionable whether justice is blind, especially when attorneys illegally shop for politically favorable venues, judges, and juries.

Key Issues and Solution Frameworks

1. The number of Supreme Court Justices is subject to the whims of Congress.

    The number of Supreme Court Justices should be fixed at nine and not be subject to change without a constitutional amendment.

2. Cognitive or physical health issues may have compromised the effectiveness of some SCOTUS Justices.

    Supreme Court Justices should not be a lifetime appointment. They should have terms like 16 years, a mandatory retirement age of 80, and pass an annual cognitive test every year beginning at age 65 and every six months starting at age 75.

3. Some significant financial, constitutional, or cultural impact cases may not be fast-tracked to SCOTUS as they deserve.

    Fast-tracking cases to the Supreme Court should be reviewed to ensure that far-reaching, financially huge, or critically urgent decisions can meet that standard.

4. It is often questionable whether justice is blind, especially when attorneys illegally shop for politically favorable venues, judges, and juries.

    There may have been a time when most judges (federal, regional, state, and local) were not political. That time of Lady Liberty being impartial has long passed, and we should acknowledge that it is now mainly in the rearview mirror. We can accept that reality by having each judge listed as Democrat or Republican, or whatever party they align with. Each state has different rules as to whether they are appointed or elected.

    Federal and regional judges should have terms of 6 years and may continue to serve as long as they are re-elected (even though they may have initially been appointed). State and local judges should have terms of 4 years or less and may continue to serve as long as they are re-elected (even if initially appointed).

Records of a judge's judicial highlights should be published at least one month before their re-election voting begins. Left-leaning and right-leaning areas deserve judges whose records they are satisfied with.

Investigative journalism was praised (and won awards) in its golden years of the 1970s and 1980s. The most noteworthy such TV program was *60 Minutes*. Now, organizations doing undercover work are trashed by the left, routinely taken to court in front of leftist judges in leftist jurisdictions and are financially punished instead of getting awards. While Project Veritas had allegations of financial mismanagement that tainted their excellent undercover work, it is a shame that their voice was silenced and shut down in 2023.

Venues should be where the business or individual is based. Still, leftists try to bring cases into left-leaning jurisdictions with lefty judges and juries. Because of institutional bias, some court venues (like Washington, DC, which votes at least 90% Democrat) should be replaced for important cases.

Congress

Key Issues

1. Congress has put itself above the law by exempting itself from many prosecutions that regular citizens can face, opening the door to much corruption.
2. In addition to generous salaries, perks, and the lure of financial corruption, they leave DC with generous pensions that average Americans can only dream about.
3. Lobbying is out of control and can easily lead to corruption.
4. Term limits have been discussed for years, but the addiction to power, prestige, and personal enrichment has been too great for any change.

5. There are no mental competency testing requirements for those serving in Congress, the Supreme Court, the President, Vice-President, and leadership in the bureaucracy.
6. The issues of a line-item veto by the President and overriding a President's veto with the approval of two-thirds of the Senate and House do not seem to work well.
7. The Congressional gamesmanship and dirty tricks are often praised as clever when they are just a perversion of doing the "people's business."
8. The filibuster rule is controversial and poorly understood.
9. Bills are passed without periodic measures to assess whether they work as intended.
10. Most people condemn the potential corruption of Omnibus Spending Bills.
11. We have no annual plan to reduce annual deficits and the accumulated national debt.
12. Politicians looking to gain permanent majorities for their party have talked about increasing the number of states beyond the current level of 50.
13. These same politicians have clamored to minimize or eliminate the Electoral College, which constitutionally determines the President.
14. Laws do not adequately set tight goalposts for the bureaucracies to carry out those laws.
15. The concepts of secession and Constitutional amendments are vital but poorly understood.

Key Issues and Solution Frameworks

1. Congress has put itself above the law by exempting itself from many prosecutions that regular citizens can face, opening the door to much corruption.

    All laws that apply to the populace must also apply to Congress. They can no longer mandate programs and laws for others that they are too elite to be subjected to. The frequent ability to enter Congress "broke" and be enticed to vote or legislate for their own enrichment should be better policed, resulting in a felony if convicted. There have been similar proposals, and it is time to make that happen.

We must be wary of separate laws for elite corruption to which they may find exceptions. The Corruption Czar should investigate alleged violations and turn the information to the courts for processing. Business Insider revealed that 72 members of Congress did not report financial trades as mandated by law, with no consequences. That must not be tolerated.

2. In addition to generous salaries, perks, and the lure of financial corruption, they leave DC with generous pensions that average Americans can only dream about.

   There should be blind trusts for leaders and enforcement of insider trading rules for those in the DC national government. Except for the President and the Vice-President, they should not have pensions, but 401(k)s like the rest of the country. The difference is that retirement accounts for leaders are placed into separate blind trusts for most investments, and they cannot influence the purchase or sale of those investments other than by replacing their chosen trust manager. All 401(k)s should be simplified to allow immediate participation and 100% vesting with no forfeitures. These changes would require some level of phasing in and grandfathering.

   If a politician is convicted of an infraction of these rules or insider trading on their non-retirement investments, that should be a felony. All reasonable blind trust fees for retirement assets are reimbursed to the leaders. No blind trust is needed if they invest in government bonds, mutual funds, ETFs, and indices. The Corruption Czar will investigate violations and turn the information to the courts for processing.

3. Lobbying is out of control and can easily lead to corruption.

Millions of dollars are wasted (often corruptly) hiring former government officials or providing perks to them to influence legislation. At a minimum, limits must be established; some even suggest banning lobbying altogether to prevent this and other corruption in the above two key issues.

4. Term limits have been discussed for years, but the addiction to power, prestige, and personal enrichment has been too great for any change.

    Term limits are overdue. Senators should be limited to 2 or 3 six-year terms; House members to 4 or 6 two-year terms. That means someone could spend 20–30 years in Congress, which is still more than they should, but at least these are achievable limitations instead of the current "lifetime" situation that can last 40–50 years. This has been a scarlet letter and not a badge of honor. Term limits are necessary to eliminate politicians serving themselves (instead of the public) with the associated power, prestige, and personal enrichment instead of solving problems and returning to being a productive part of the economy.

    To stop the sense of entitlement that seems to contaminate much of the Senate due to their lengthy service of six years compared to House members who serve for two years, a Constitutional amendment should change the term to four years. How many times have we been stuck with disappointing Senators for six years? When passed, that should modify the term limits for Senators to 3 or 4 four-year terms.

5. There are no mental competency testing requirements for those serving in Congress, the Supreme Court, the President, Vice-President, and leadership in the bureaucracy.

    All DC leaders should be required to undergo and pass a standard mental competency test annually beginning at age 65 and every 6 months starting at age 75. A test failure should require a confirming test; if confirmed, a retirement should occur within a reasonable period. Also, if a government leader has suffered a severe health event (like a stroke) that might cause mental impairment, they must complete the testing every 6 months. Besides cognitive impairment and term limits, mandatory retirement should occur at age 80.

6. The issues of a line-item veto by the President and overriding a President's veto with the approval of two-thirds of the Senate and House do not seem to work well.

    There seems to be room to compromise with the current situation by lowering the threshold for overriding a President's veto from two-thirds to three-fifths (In the Senate, that would drop from 67 votes to 60). The other part of that compromise would be to allow some presidential veto discretion, even if not a full line-item veto like what is given to most governors.

7. The Congressional gamesmanship and dirty tricks are often praised as clever when they are just a perversion of doing the "people's business."

    Holding up voting for Executive Branch appointments; blocking a vote on a bill that has properly been sponsored to avoid having their vote go on the record; refusing to take up and vote on a bill that the other Chamber has passed; and conducting most of the Senate business by unanimous consent to avoid having the Senators' votes be on the record. These corrupt tricks must be ended.

    A particularly obnoxious game is earmarking. Earmarks and other unrelated measures piggybacking their pork onto other bills must be eliminated. Those projects are often designed to get politicians re-elected and not solve problems. They should be voted on their merits separately, and those voting for "pork projects" can be spotlighted and not hidden.

    The "reconciliation process" is an annual out-of-control trick that must be reined in. It is another gamesmanship ploy used to add things to the Budget that should have been voted on separately, but cowards prefer this devious route.

Another egregious example is pushing legislation through a lame-duck session of Congress. This session should only act on emergencies and not on regular business. The purpose of this currently-allowed game is two-fold. It allows a party that lost control of one or both chambers of Congress to saddle the new Congress (not yet sworn in) with legislation they would not have approved. It allows cowardly politicians to postpone controversial legislation voting until after the November elections, where they could have lost some election votes if that legislation had been passed before the election.

These kinds of trickery, gamesmanship, and corruption have no place in our government and must be stopped. No one should be praised for their cleverness in executing them.

8. The filibuster rule is controversial and poorly understood.

The filibuster rule was a prime target for elimination by the D-S who thought they would win the 2024 elections. Let's give them what they wanted, so the Trump administration can get their legislation passed instead of blocked by the minority party.

9. Bills are passed without periodic measures to assess whether they work as intended.

Each bill should be cost-benefit analyzed as part of the bill, and that analysis should be included in the yearly Budget for the involved area, along with an executive summary. Solutionism protocols should also be followed: prioritization of the problems, itemization of the key issues and solution frameworks for those problems, composing the details to implement the frameworks, deciding on measures of success, and reporting on them every six months.

10. Most people condemn the potential corruption of Omnibus Spending Bills.

The Budget for each of the 12 large budgetary areas (like the Department of Defense) should be a separate bill required to be individually voted on. When combined with all other budgetary areas, this becomes the Annual Budget for the country. 1998 was the last time this was done to start the year. We must return this financial sanity and common sense to the budget process.

Omnibus ("everything but the kitchen sink") spending bills are often passed with minimal time to read their 4,000 pages. That makes them ripe for corruption, and they need to be eliminated, as they are not designed to solve problems (with metrics to track success) but to provide funding for pet projects, get favored lawmakers re-elected, and fund the status quo regardless of its effectiveness. Omnibus Spending Bills are a lazy and cowardly power grab and do not empower legislators to thoughtfully "do the people's business."

For any of the 12 appropriation bills not passed on time, there could be a safety valve like with a 2% automatic spending cut until the budget is passed. An exception would be the Department of Defense. Failure to pass all 12 appropriation bills before the start of the new fiscal year will result in a 5% Congressional pay cut that will stay in place until all 12 are passed. A separate 13th critical bill should be a separate Infrastructure Bill since corrupt pork barrel "earmarks" will be eliminated. These projects should be ranked and justified.

11. We have no annual plan to reduce annual deficits and the accumulated national debt.

    The annual deficit should be reduced with the goal of a balanced budget within 2–3 years. The Penny Plan, where most budget areas are reduced by 1% annually, is one way to reach this goal, along with some solutions from the Tax and Bureaucracy Czars.

    All of our out-of-control spending has created annual deficits since the revenues can't match the ravenous appetites of politicians to spend our tax dollars in a greater amount than they take in. This is demonstrated with pork barrel projects, inflating the size and bureaucracy of the federal government, and the annual deficits for SS, Medicare, and other existing programs. **In 2021, Biden-Harris** tax revenues were $4 trillion, and spending was $6.8 trillion, producing a huge deficit that added almost $3 trillion to the national debt in just one year. (If you were able to annually spend $68,000 every year and you only received an income of $40,000, it would not be long before your financial house of cards would collapse and devastate you.)

Those deficits are financed by printing more money and selling Treasury Bonds. The accumulation of those yearly deficits rose $1 trillion in just 3 months to produce a national debt on December 29, 2023 of $34 trillion (currently, over $1 trillion per year in interest payments, often to our adversaries). In 2020, interest payments were $527 billion, only about half the current amount.

A Boston University Economics professor researched the "real" national debt that included all USA liabilities, including unfunded liabilities for things like Social Security, Medicare, federal pensions, and other items that were not included. All in, he computed the unreported obligations amount to $200 trillion. That would mean our total debt is 9 or 10 times our annual GDP. This would be like a household with a yearly income of $100,000 trying to pay debts of $1,000,000 (which keeps growing yearly). If the US were a business, we would not be very credit-worthy.

Research has not provided one source for the details of this $200 trillion. However, researching three sources and adding the results produces a total "real" national debt of $201.4 trillion. Here are those resources:

Unfunded Federal Debt (rounded) from www.usadebtclock.com updated July 7, 2023
- $123.3 trillion for total federal unfunded liabilities for Medicare, Prescription Drugs, Social Security, and National Healthcare. Because **the Supreme Court ruled in 1960 in Flemming vs. Nestor that the government has no legal obligation to repay any specific amount for SS and Medicare,** politicians use this

gimmick to hide these unfunded future liabilities. Some countries use sound accounting practices to report unfunded liabilities, but not the US.
- + $35.0 trillion, the nationally reported amount without the unfunded debt
- = $157.3 trillion federally funded and unfunded liability

From www.mauldineconomics.com by John Mauldin on March 21, 2019, titled "The Real US National Debt Might Be $230 Trillion,"
- + $3.1 trillion state and local government debt

From the Federal Stability Report for 2022 table of business and household debt
- + $23.0 trillion business debt
- + $19.0 trillion household debt (loans and credit card debt)
(And an annual 2022 GDP of $26.1 trillion)

The total US debt from all three sources amounts to $202.4 trillion, not quite the $235 trillion projected, using the Economics professor's amount of $200 trillion unfunded plus the $35 trillion that the government reports. But if current data was readily available, the totals would likely exceed $235 trillion.

Here's what those three levels of debt mean:
- Using only the $35 trillion amount, visualize a stack of $1 bills going to the moon and back 9 times, and each US taxpayer's share of the debt would be $470,890. If the government were to pay back the principal at $1 million per hour (without any interest), it would take 3,863 years.
- Using the $157.3 trillion amount, including all federal unfunded liabilities, visualize a stack of $1 bills going to the moon and back 43 times, and each US taxpayer's share of the debt would be $2.2 million.

- **If adding the Economics Professor's unreported national debt obligations of $200 trillion amount to the $35 trillion, that would equal $235 trillion. Visualize a stack of $1 bills going to the moon and back 65 times, and each US taxpayer's share of the debt would be $3.2 million. If the government were to pay back the principal at $1 million per hour (without any interest), it would take 26,590 years.** This is staggering and unimaginable, reflects the misconduct of our elected leaders, and must be corrected.

While even the smallest of those three amounts seems absurd, the enormity of this shows that we must stop ignoring the mess we have allowed our politicians to get us into. We must start being Solutionists and turn this ship around. When the Biden-Harris administration says their massive spending (produced nearly a $3 trillion deficit in 2021 alone) does not create inflation, they demonstrate their basic economic illiteracy.

Without any positive changes, the nonpartisan Congressional Budget Office projects our annual deficits will double over the next 10 years, our interest cost will triple, and for every dollar we borrow, half of that will go just to pay the interest. In 10 years, interest payments will exceed what we spend on national defense—oops, we are already there.

A few years ago, several sources stated that total US spending on social services ranked 2nd in the world at about 30% of GDP, just slightly behind France at 32%. Has our 1st class welfare spending produced 1st class results in moving many people from welfare to work?

Consider downloading the annual report to Congress dated May 2023 by the US Government Accountability Office called "The Nation's Fiscal Health." At least read the first three pages. The first sentence sets the tone: "The federal government faces an unsustainable long-term future." US debt has often increased during war or recession, but this unprecedented debt increase happens during economic expansion and rising interest costs.

Our reckless spending with poor results, annual deficits, and massive debt creation has not worked. We must use common sense, stop doing what we have always done and expecting better outcomes. It starts with budgets for each of the 13 major budget areas (including infrastructure and no more 4,000-page Omnibus Spending bills) to reduce and eliminate annual budget deficits and begin to create surpluses to reduce the national debt.

The federal national debt can be systematically reduced with spending and bureaucracy controls and appropriate taxation to reduce the accumulated national debt by 50% in 7 years or less. Our % of federal government spending to GDP of 40% should be reduced to no more than 30% within 7 years, setting the example of less cost and better solutions for the states and local communities.

12. Politicians looking to gain permanent majorities for their party have talked about increasing the number of states beyond the current level of 50.

    The number of states should be fixed at 50 and only changed by constitutional amendment or the near impossibility of secession.

13. These same politicians have clamored to minimize or eliminate the Electoral College, which constitutionally determines the President.

    48 of 50 US states award Electoral College electors on a winner-take-all basis. That means the Presidency may be determined by the heavily populated states and big cities (which are often D-S) to impose their views on the rest of the country. States like New York and California (with more House members due to their high undocumented population) and major crime-ridden cities like Detroit and Chicago remind us of King George of colonial times deciding the fate of the whole country. This concentration of power was precisely what the Founders were concerned about and did not want to have repeated.

    This should be stopped at the state level until a Constitutional amendment can be passed. The Supreme Court should take up a case on this issue and identify the subversion of the Constitution by this trickery. Consideration should be given to using that Founders' concept selectively to strengthen the voice of smaller states and moderate the impact of larger states. The 30 smaller states, the District of Columbia, and Puerto Rico would be allowed to practice that "winner take all" strategy for selecting the electors for the Electoral College. But the top 20 most populous states should allocate the elector selection proportional to the votes cast—no winner-take-all.

14. Laws do not adequately set tight goalposts for the bureaucracies to carry out those laws.

    Too much latitude is given to agency bureaucrats, which often tramples individual freedom and enlarges the bureaucratic control of our lives, resulting in more taxes to cover more government employees and more regulation and oversight. Nullifying bureaucracy rules should be done more frequently using the 1996 Congressional Review Act (CRA). Approval by the House, Senate, and President is needed to make that happen. This must be used often to rein in the unaccountable bureaucracies that have been given too much freedom to set and change their goalposts based on their political ideology and not legislation for which Congress would be held accountable by the voters.

    Laws must be clear regarding what can and cannot be done with each agency appropriation and new laws. A perfect recent example of overreach was the EPA's attempt to classify a private property drainage ditch as "Waters of the United States." That would allow them to regulate that drainage ditch. Similar examples can be found in every agency trying to enlarge its reach and gain more funding and higher pay levels (just like any living organism wanting to survive and thrive).

15. The concepts of secession and Constitutional amendments are vital but poorly understood.

    The secession of counties to other states starts with the citizens' petitions. There are now 11 counties in Oregon where voters have voted to leave Oregon and join Idaho. They must get both legislatures to approve and then get Congressional approval to redraw state boundaries. The town of Buckhead, Georgia, is proceeding with its efforts to secede from the Atlanta metroplex, which takes its tax dollars but does little for them and does not represent its views.

If successful, these could be good models for other areas within states that feel trampled on by governments they disapprove of. Whether successful or not, this process must be simplified and made easier to empower citizens and wake politicians up to the reality that the mistreatment of constituents can lead to impactful results.

States have a higher bar to leave the USA—a super-majority Congressional vote of two-thirds to amend the Constitution and the approval of 75% of the state legislatures. That is how our Constitution received 27 amendments. While success with that process for new amendments is nearly impossible today, without those rights, entrenched elites in government are free to trample on their subjects like King George did to ignite the American Revolution.

The other alternative for changing the Constitution that our Founders allowed is convening a Convention of States per Article 5 of the Constitution. This requires two-thirds (34) of the state legislatures to agree to meet and 75% (38) of those legislatures to agree to any proposed amendments. Because of this, if only 13 states object, an amendment would not pass. This is so difficult that it has never been tried. Until current political realities change, neither of these avenues makes sense to invest time, energy, and money to pursue.

However, many patriotic and well-meaning people are invested in pursuing a Convention of States. We should focus energy and money on conducting and winning high-integrity elections to change laws and processes. With a successful track record and gaining the majorities needed, amending the Constitution by either of the two methods can become more likely. The D-S governor of California supports this Convention idea. Once again, if the D-S support something, they have found a way to gain an advantage with their ideas that worsen our country. Let's not allow them to pass things they could not get through Congress and block any proposed R-S Constitutional amendments.

These amendments and the Convention of States' paths are theoretical exercises that will produce no positive changes now. Meanwhile, the D-S are busy going after low-hanging fruit to win elections without strong election integrity, practicing "limitless" spending, installing corrupt DAs, creating Executive Orders, and successfully using the Judiciary by appointing and venue shopping for leftist judges and jury rulings. We should stop playing that "Convention of States" game that has little chance of success now (but feels good, like a virtual reality game) and copy the successful tactics of the D-S, focusing first on winning elections but with opportunities for fraud minimized.

<u>Most Relevant Chapter 1 Founding Principles (FP)</u>

- FP 1 Inalienable Rights
- FP 2 The Right to Govern Derives from the People
- FP 3 Limited Representative Republican Form of Government
- FP 4 A Written Constitution to Be Followed
- FP 5 Private Property Rights and the Rule of Law
- FP 6 All People Are Created Equal, and the Government's Role Is to Protect Their Equal Rights and Not Provide Equal Outcomes
- FP 7 The Most Prosperity Occurs in a Free Market Economy with Minimum Regulation
- FP 9 Free People Must Stay Strong to Survive
- FP 11 Federal Debt Is Toxic to Freedom Just Like Being Taken Over by Another Country
- FP 12 The USA Has the Destiny to Be Exceptional and an Example to the World

Positive Impacts

Reforming our three branches of government to minimize bureaucracy, corruption, inefficiency, gamesmanship, dirty tricks, lack of transparency, and cost will elevate our trust in government. Term limits and mental competency testing beginning at age 65 will make DC less entitled and more competent and accountable to the citizens they serve. Giving a President's Cabinet and other nominees a swift and thorough vetting and vote in the Senate is essential to end this gamesmanship that both parties participate in. Stopping political and ideological targeting will end the ungodly reigns of the Department of (In)justice, FBI, IRS, EPA, and the other Deep Staters.

Reforming agencies into problem solvers worthy of removing their Deep State identity is critical. De-militarizing federal agencies like the IRS and restoring respect, tools, and funding for local police will deconstruct the National Police State we have been building.

Being an active member of the UN but choosing to lead with successful problem solutions rather than be bound by unfair agreements. Those deals often take away our freedoms and hurt us economically. At the same time, they reward bad actors (terrorists, high polluters, and human rights and religious freedom violators) with a lifetime "get out of jail free" card to carry on their bad behavior. Stopping terrorism funding from Iran and UNRWA will be a giant first step toward a more peaceful world. With the cooperation of allies, there can be economic penalties for high-polluting and freedom-squelching countries. We need to use leverage to persuade others to be better global citizens.

We can have an Executive Branch that accomplishes defined goals but does not play the role of King George with limitless Executive Orders to rule over the citizenry. We will proudly have a US annual report that details significant accomplishments, including the generosity of the US for domestic and international needs, our 13 individual major department budgets (no more Omnibus Budgets), and our progress on significant problems, including eliminating annual deficits and reducing the national debt.

Acknowledging that Lady Liberty is no longer blind is a sad reality. But that will allow us to stop the practice of venue shopping and force judges (except SCOTUS) to be re-elected with a D or R (or some other party affiliation) after their name and publication of a summary of their record. That will give the people an essential input into the too-often corrupt judicial system. Creating criteria that ensure all crucial cases are fast-tracked to SCOTUS will be a much-needed financial relief to many and serve our country well.

Treating Congress with the same standards applied to the citizenry will go a long way to ending that "elite" badge that too many like to wear to blaze their trails for power, prestige, and personal enrichment. Placing limits on lobbying is vital to reduce the corruption that it often brings. Transitioning DC (except the President and VP) from pensions to 401(k)s with blind trusts will remove that "elite" identity and end the "Golden Age of Political Enrichment" that has gone on far too long.

Congress can be restored to take its proper seat in the three branches of government with its corruption rooted out, its focus on laws that solve problems, and reporting on metrics that show that progress. They will reclaim their "checks and balances" role over the Executive Branch by placing reasonable limits on Executive Orders and ensuring that those EOs that have significant economic or cultural impacts are only activated by the passage of laws. They will notify agencies when they go beyond the scope of their Congressional authorization.

Eliminating the Senate filibuster rule (as the D-S vowed to do if they took the Senate majority in 2024) will allow sensible and necessary legislation to not be blocked by the minority party.

Instead of gutting the Electoral College, we can strengthen it by requiring the 20 largest states to award electors based on the % of popular votes or districts won and allowing the 30 smaller states to enact a winner-take-all approach. This could give the citizens of smaller states a counter to the behemoth states. This was a serious concern for the Founders.

Our country can survive and be re-invigorated past 2026, our 250th anniversary, and inspire the rest of the world with a better blueprint for becoming the Shining City on a Hill. A key component is re-engineering our government by cutting away its corruption barnacles and infusing it with a Solutionist approach to its work.

***

The next chapter covers the last most pressing internal security issue of crime. Criminal justice is seriously malfunctioning, but there are remedies.

CHAPTER 8

Crime

Why is criminal behavior tolerated and encouraged to grow significantly? Why are we prosecuting and persecuting non-crimes?

The main focus of the federal statutes should be on crimes of corruption, dishonesty, fraud, and violence that are physical or otherwise expressed against individuals, companies, organizations, and private or governmental property. The voter fraud penalties are separately covered in Chapter 6 and not repeated here. The unjust inhibiting of a person's exercise of personal freedom (that is not maliciously and significantly harmful to others) must be stopped. "Harmful" should not mean "they don't think like me."

Key Issues

1. Wealthy individuals like George Soros have spent extravagantly to get 75 "Progressive" (opposing imprisonment and thereby encouraging crime) prosecutors elected.
2. There is no clarity in the law to prevent or minimize prosecutorial misconduct in going after individuals who are not aligned politically or ideologically with the prosecutor.
3. There is inconsistent treatment and punishment for murder.

4. There is inconsistent treatment and punishment for the violent crime of rape.
5. There is no sensible plan to reduce school shootings and disease transmission.
6. A person's right to exercise non-harmful personal freedom in their daily expression of life, liberty, and the pursuit of happiness is under attack.
7. We are fooled into thinking protests are genuine when many are just paid to protest.
8. "Anonymous" sources often are the sources for leaks and are sometimes not even real.
9. Financial fraud, scamming, spamming, and hacking account for millions of dollars taken from victims and millions of hours of wasted time and stress.
10. There is inconsistent treatment and punishment when firearms, other deadly weapons, or drugs are involved in a crime.
11. For much of the country, homelessness is not successfully addressed.
12. There is inconsistent treatment of restitution for the financial losses of the victim.
13. Innocent people who give nervous testimony can be too easily convicted, and criminals who present themselves well can be too easily found not guilty.

Keys Issues and Solution Frameworks

1. Wealthy individuals like George Soros have spent extravagantly to get 75 "Progressive" (opposing imprisonment and thereby encouraging crime) prosecutors elected.

    According to the Enforcement Legal Defense Fund, 75 "Progressive" prosecutors are now in office. George Soros, a lefty billionaire, contributed over $40 million to elect these anti-incarcerationists. What are the results of his victories?

From a 2022 Heritage Foundation report entitled "The Blue City Murder Problem," policies filtering down from this gang of 75 DAs include:
- Refusing to prosecute misdemeanors like theft, drug possession, shoplifting, breaking and entering, property destruction, disorderly conduct or disturbing the peace, resisting arrest, and receiving stolen property
- Forbidding prosecutors from enhancing sentences due to prior convictions or special circumstances for heinous crimes
- Forbidding prosecutors to seek the death penalty or life without parole
- Forbidding prosecutors to prosecute teenagers as adults for crimes of murder, child abuse, and rape
- Forcing prosecutors to ask for the release of violent felons after serving 15 years
- Prohibiting or limiting prosecutors from asking for bail or considering the criminal's prior record to ensure their presence at the next court hearing

AMAC's July–August 2023 magazine had an article titled "A Tale of Two Cities." It compared Portland, Oregon (a self-proclaimed "hotbed of Progressivism") with Naperville, Illinois (a more Conservative community).
- Portland had more crime than 99% of the country (with crime affecting 66 of every 1,000 residents), set another homicide record in 2022, and had a poverty rate of 12.2%.
- Naperville has less crime than 83% of the country, with crime affecting only 4 of every 1,000 residents, which is 16 times less than Portland.

Where would you rather live and raise a family? —in "progressively blue" Portland or "neighborly red" Naperville?

The World Population Review released statistics in 2022 that showed which world cities have the most homicides per capita. The #1 world superpower made 4 of those top 50 spots, along with the excellent company of cities in Latin and South America that account for the rest of the top 50 most dangerous cities in the world. Those 4 US cities are Saint Louis (#15), Baltimore (#23), Detroit (#46), and New Orleans (#50). We must have harsher penalties, especially for homicide, and stop the illegal influx across our southern border that is often from these high-crime areas of Latin and South America,

You can see the skyrocketing violent crime this is causing in cities and wonder if it is intentional. In 1992, Soros "broke the British pound" with his speculative shorts against the pound, and he walked away with a nice profit of $1 billion (a lot more in today's dollars). He also strengthened his reputation as the top currency speculator in the world. Since that was 30 years ago, could he be trying to re-energize his reputation with a "last hurrah" by taking down the USD and setting us up for the New World Order he and other globalists are anxious for?

Wealthy individuals using their wealth to buy elections must be stopped. In Chapter 6 on elections, there is a solution framework with strong limits on this corruption.

We must have the right to recall, fire, or defeat any official, especially this gang of 75, which is not prosecuting and allowing deadly criminals to terrorize citizens, especially in disadvantaged areas. Every state should have laws that empower citizens with the right democratically to recall officials, as well as create a referendum on an issue to pressure legislatures, and the right to submit an initiative that proposes a law or state constitution amendment. States should meet those standards to qualify for related federal funds.

Shoplifting exceeding a certain amount (like $250) must be prosecuted. Stores should be free to employ without consequences any reasonable deterrents and defenses to protect their goods, their property, and the safety of their employees.

2. There is no clarity in the law to prevent or minimize prosecutorial misconduct in going after individuals who are not aligned politically or ideologically with the prosecutor.

   Rogue prosecutors and persecutors have gone after ideological or political opponents with the intent to smear their names or ruin their careers or finances. Here is one of the countless examples.

   The 65 Project is a 501(c)(4) dark money group that does not have to disclose donors and is going after 111 lawyers in 26 states that had been a party to 65 lawsuits filed to challenge the 2020 election results due to fraud. This group spends millions anonymously filing and publicizing local ethics complaints with ads in Arizona, Michigan, Pennsylvania, Wisconsin, Nevada, and Georgia.

   David Brock, founder of the leftist Media Matters, is an advisor to the group. He told Axios "the idea was to "not only bring the grievances in the bar complaints but shame them and make them toxic in their communities and in their firms." [1] So disbarring is not enough. Like all leftist/Socialist/Communist entities, their philosophy and its results are so pathetic that they must crush and silence any opposition. That is why they will seldom debate a Conservative.

   There must be carefully thought out statutes with severe criminal, financial, disbarment recommendations, and removal from office penalties to prevent situations like the 65 Project and the meritless suits against Trump and other Conservatives. Legislation should remove anonymity for donors to 501(c)(4) political organizations. That "dark money" needs to see the light of day, and donors should be limited to $10,000 per political entity and $50,000 overall per year. The tax-exempt status of these organizations should be removed, and they pay a 10% tax on gross income. Reducing the impact of large donations to swing elections and punish opponents is critically important.

3. There is inconsistent treatment and punishment for murder.

   When murder is a charge, and the DNA evidence or witnesses' testimony is unimpeachable, the penalty should be capital punishment.

Attorneys are given a 6-month window that cannot be extended to bring a strong defense. This must be the highest priority for the attorney, as a person's life is at stake, and shoddy defenses will be punishable by severe fines and likely disbarments.

If convicted, there is another 6-month window to return with a vigorous appeal. If the conviction is upheld, capital punishment is carried out within 90 days unless a credible 2nd appeal is granted based on new evidence. Anyone who lies and provides false information that significantly impacts the conviction should be charged as if they committed a murder. While financial compensation is required for murder, no amount can adequately compensate for the loss of life and the impact on the victim's family.

Some may think this is too harsh but committing the most anti-social act of causing a death during a crime (usually with a deadly weapon) needs the harshest of consequences. Years of free lodging, food, clothes, and activities are inappropriate consequences for murder. Three of the main religions have considered capital punishment as a fitting punishment. Wokesters and other elites will likely claim we have evolved from that, but how well has that worked out for us?

4. There is inconsistent treatment and punishment for the violent crime of rape.

    In 8 states and several European countries, the administration of testosterone-suppressing drugs ("chemical castration," whose effects are reversible when stopped) has been shown to reduce repeat offenses. Without the medication, recidivism is 97%, and with the drug, it is only 3%. If our D-S cities and states were not content to let crime and chaos run amuck, they would work to nationalize a successful solution that is right in front of them.

5. There is no sensible plan to reduce school shootings and disease transmission.

There are four primary problems: many schools are soft targets for shooters and disease transmission, people are not reporting those who post on SM or otherwise communicate dark and deadly inclinations, mentally disturbed people have access to guns, and there is inadequate treatment for those with mental illness.

There should be national standards for making new schools hardened physical targets for shooters and disease transmission, including more robust HVAC systems and funding to revamp existing schools as close to those standards as possible. We must educate kids that they must protect themselves and others by providing evidence of dark and deadly conversations or postings to law enforcement as soon as possible. As mentioned in key issue #10 below, promising treatments for many forms of mental illness should be fast-tracked, approved, and available.

Teacher unions liked the paid time off and remote learning they enjoyed during the COVID-19 lockdowns. They don't want HVAC systems that capture and destroy airborne pathogens and eliminate the need for those niceties they had during COVID. Corrupt politicians and unhinged greenies desire infrastructure spending to fund their sexy dogmas of solar, wind, and battery electric cars. Spending to make schools safe does not have that same glitz and would take away their other goal to disarm Americans. Even if they were successful with disarmament, the black market would still supply guns for criminals and the mentally disturbed. How does that solve the problem?

Our Founders saw the importance of the right to bear arms. Even the pacifist Gandhi favored that also. He said of the British rule over India: "History will look upon the act of depriving a whole nation of arms as the blackest." [2] However, the power-hungry left is highly motivated to disarm mentally competent individuals and not really protect children. If they genuinely cared about child safety, they would push these above approaches, but continuing to destroy our Constitution and Bill of Rights is more important to bring about the radical changes they fervently pursue.

6. A person's right to exercise non-harmful personal freedom in their daily expression of life, liberty, and the pursuit of happiness is under attack.

   Our Declaration of Independence spells out a person's right to (exercise non-harmful personal freedom in their daily expression of) life, liberty, and the pursuit of happiness. We must criminalize strong-arm tactics like cancelation, loss of a job, protesting in front of a person's house, harassing their family and neighbors, and similar repressive regime tactics.

7. We are fooled into thinking protests are genuine when many are just paid to protest.

   Protesting must be a groundswell of passionate individuals who come together voluntarily without compensation to express their views. Otherwise, we are letting wealthy billionaires bankroll protests they favor and let the public think these people act out of their personal convictions rather than being compensated. Paid protests are frauds and should be felonies if convicted for the protestors and the people providing money and resources.

8. "Anonymous sources" often are the sources for leaks and are sometimes not even real.

   We need to recognize that "anonymous sources" provide no credibility to a story because the consumer of that "news" does not know if it is accurate or made up by the journalist masquerading as an anonymous source. Instead, the story should be that the author believes something but has not found anyone willing to come forward publicly under the protection of whistleblower and anti-retaliation statutes. Because of these statutes, no one should be intimidated to come forward. It should be a felony to compensate leakers or publish stories from "anonymous sources."

   Whistleblower protections and anti-retaliation statutes should be strengthened to provide greater protection and compensation awards to the victims, along with more substantial criminal and civil penalties for the retaliators and their organizations. Because severe retaliator punishment is not happening yet, we continue to see abuses by the Deep State. A law with funding to cover the financial devastation happening to whistleblowers should be enacted ASAP. Once retaliators are severely punished, these offenses will be greatly reduced.

9. Financial fraud, scamming, spamming, and hacking account for millions of dollars taken from victims and millions of hours of wasted time and stress. We are inundated with spam and scams for products and services with fraudulent and unproven claims. Despite virus protection, hacking of accounts is an epidemic that little is done to prevent or punish.

    Financial fraud, scamming, spamming, and hacking should have more resources focused on thwarting, prosecuting, and punishing them. Spamming and scamming should have more substantial financial and criminal penalties. Domestically sourced hacking and invasion of computers and systems with viruses must be treated as a serious felony with hefty jail time and lifetime restitution requirements. For foreign-sourced hacking and viruses, we must partner with allies, capture and punish the criminals, and impose severe economic pain on countries that provide safe harbor to these digital terrorists.

    We are still blazing a trail in AI, but there should be some basics we should move forward on. Voice cloning should be disclosed before such an audio is played. This can reduce the volume of ransom scams that use this to extract money from concerned relatives over a tragedy that never happened.

    Clever scammers can even alter their caller ID to display the family member's name they want. Those should be felonies with serious jail time, and voice cloning for non-ransom scams should likely be a misdemeanor. Deep fakes of people saying and doing things that did not actually occur must be clearly disclosed before the video is played. If not, they should be charged with a felony. Like in any other crime, restitution must be applicable for any losses incurred by the victims.

We can do a better job of minimizing these types of fraud, or we can continue to do little and allow this staggering level of victimization to proceed with minimal consequences.

10. There is inconsistent treatment and punishment when firearms, other deadly weapons, or drugs are involved in a crime.

    When firearms, other deadly weapons, or drugs are involved in a non-deadly crime, the punishment should be double the sentencing guidelines if convicted. Increasing the penalties for gun crimes will do more to reduce them than harassing and creating gun lists of mentally sound people who lawfully own guns and use them responsibly.

    The extra penalty can be eliminated if they agree to participate in medically supervised treatment with safe plant-based "cures" for these anti-social crimes that often involve addiction, mental health issues, and some homelessness. There have been numerous studies and success stories of using plant-derived substances to cure PTSD, OCD, addictions, violent aggression, depression, and other mental health issues. Our bureaucracy and Big Pharma appear to work together to prevent significant testing to allow for the medical use of these substances.

    Our agencies must fast-track the testing of promising plant-derived substances despite Big Pharma not being able to profit significantly from them. If those tests are successful, that could reduce the use of pricey and, at times, deadly prescriptions, and some long-term therapies could require many fewer visits. There is a very informative book and Netflix series, *How to Change Your Mind,* by Michael Pollan. [3] He covers four substances, with the most promising being psilocybin and MDMA, which is being allowed to be tested but has no financial support from the NIH for the $100 million required for testing.

11. For much of the country, homelessness is not successfully addressed.

    A high % of homelessness has mental illness as a component. Fast-tracking the approval of the plant-based substances identified in the prior point has the potential to make a significant and positive impact on homelessness and the crime and blight associated with it at a reasonably small cost.

12. There is inconsistent treatment of restitution for the financial losses of the victim.

    For all crimes resulting in proven financial losses, restitution must be made to each victim or organization at 1.5 times the loss. This would be evidenced by an automatic lien on all assets and garnishment of future earnings of the criminal until paid in full without being able to avoid that through bankruptcy, asset sales, or asset transfers. Consequences can be a good deterrent, and bankruptcy should not allow criminals to avoid their responsibility for restitution.

13. Innocent people who give nervous testimony can be too easily convicted, and criminals who present themselves well can be too easily found not guilty.

    DNA testing has significantly reduced the inaccuracy of false convictions. Are there other tools we generally overlook that could further reduce the frequency of these situations when DNA evidence is unavailable?

    Polygraph testing should be allowed as evidence from the accused, witnesses, victims, and law enforcement. If anyone refuses to take a correctly set up polygraph test, that is admissible as a matter to consider. The polygraph test accuracy is about 90%, and we should look for ways to get that % even higher. It is actually 94% in Utah, which can serve as a model for a uniform standard.

    That standard to improve the accuracy can include greater use of computer AI to reduce subjectivity, provide an appropriate environment, account for language issues, disability, and medication, and eliminate any possibility of the presence of alcohol or other substances that adversely affect the results. It could be complemented with the use of body language experts. In many cases, polygraph testing coupled with body language analysis should be elevated as very important but not definitive tools.

Most Relevant Chapter 1 Founding Principles (FP)

- FP 1 Inalienable Rights
- FP 2 The Right to Govern Derives from the People
- FP 3 Limited Representative Republican Form of Government
- FP 4 A Written Constitution to Be Followed
- FP 5 Private Property Rights and the Rule of Law
- FP 6 All People Are Created Equal, and the Government's Role Is to Protect Their Equal Rights and Not Provide Equal Outcomes
- FP 7 The Most Prosperity Occurs in a Free Market Economy with Minimum Regulation
- FP 9 Free People Must Stay Strong to Survive
- FP 12 The USA Has the Destiny to Be Exceptional and an Example to the World

Positive Impacts

Retooling our criminal code to focus on violence, corruption, fraud, dishonesty, and the impairment of citizens' rights to life, liberty, and the pursuit of happiness should be welcomed by most. Providing strong deterrents, including mandatory restitution, will do much to reduce crime and reverse our decline into Socialism. Those who commit the worst anti-social crimes involving the death of another still deserve a timely, vigorous defense and appeal.

Stopping political and ideological targeting will end the reign of the Department of (In)justice. Making our schools safe and providing more accessible and cheaper mental health treatments for potential school shooters, criminals, and homeless people will result in communities with much less crime and better safety.

Crimes can be treated more consistently and effectively, especially rape and murder. We can trust that protests are genuine and not funded by wealthy individuals with agendas. "Anonymous" (often phony) sources will disappear from our language, especially if we strengthen the whistleblower statute protections.

Doubling the penalties for crimes where drugs or deadly weapons were involved will do more to stop gun violence than the relentless march to disarm lawful and mentally competent gun owners. Significantly reducing spamming, scamming, and hacking can save millions of dollars and hours for would-be victims. Allowing high-quality polygraph testing can be another valuable tool to enhance the criminal justice system's results.

When our country was founded, we sought to strengthen the rights of crime victims, as well as those suspected of committing a crime. We have seriously lost our way by punishing victims, criminalizing non-crimes, and going soft on actual criminals. We can return to common sense reforms and eliminate the corruption often brought about by wealthy oligarchs, elites, faux intellectuals, and the looney left Socialists.

***

Chapter 9 covers immigration, our most pressing external national security issue. The status quo is unacceptable, and there are remedies to replace all the hand-wringing that currently passes for dealing with the many aspects of this significant issue.

CHAPTER 9
Immigration

If we do not solve our external threat issues created by our intentional Socialist creep and lazy leaders, we will not have a viable country. This chapter and the following chapter on the China threat present the most critical problems after election integrity that must be addressed early in the next administration.

This issue produces several other C-P overwhelm areas to take down the US: education, medical care, housing, and welfare, just to name a few. The solution frameworks are built on the four core mindsets and the five elements of Solutionism (as noted in the Introduction).

Illegal immigration and the carnage it inflicts economically and in the lives affected must be stopped, and there must be consequences for not respecting the rule of law in the US. The abuses of chain migration, birthright citizenship, and a porous southern border must be fixed. The monthly billions of dollars we enrich Mexican criminal cartels and Chinese mafia with must cease. We need to solve the issue of illegal immigrants already here and create different paths for those here for many years and those who have been here for a shorter time.

Key Issues

1. Current immigration is out of control. "Catch and release" has brought 3 million illegal immigrants annually from our southern border just since 2021–12 million in 2021–2024.
2. They are spread throughout the country without notice to the states or communities and without disease and DNA testing (to ensure a legitimate family relationship).
3. Some immigration policies mirror failed European policies
4. Chain migration and birthright citizenship are curses that no other country endures.
5. We have enriched the Mexican criminal cartels and Chinese mafia with billions of dollars monthly by consenting to their human trafficking (some as sex slaves and some raped on the journey) from 170 countries and their export of deadly Fentanyl (with ingredients and pill-making equipment sourced and staffed from China).
6. We have no solution for illegal aliens in the USA for a long time.
7. We have no policy for illegal aliens in the USA a short time.
8. Agriculture needs seasonal workers who are often illegal aliens.
9. Construction, manufacturing, and hospitality are also employers of illegal migrants.
10. Employers do not have to use E-Verify to ensure workers have valid Social Security #s, and some states and cities (like New York City) do not maintain information on undocumenteds.
11. Government services are often given to many who are not legal residents, turning on a giant magnet for the undocumenteds and the states that score additional federal funding, representatives, and Electoral College votes from the undocumenteds in their state.
12. Visa overstays are not effectively caught and corrected.
13. Immigration claims processing can take 1 to 5 years for legal immigrants and up to 12 years for undocumenteds, both of which are unacceptably long.

14. Many grumblers think our country is irredeemable and pursue violent actions or rhetoric to express their displeasure.

Key Issues and Solution Frameworks

1. Current immigration is out of control. "Catch and release" has brought 3 million illegal immigrants annually from our southern border just since 2021—12 million in 2021-2024. From the Office of Field Operations and US Border Patrol for the fiscal years of 2021-2024 (through August), the data on single adult encounters show horrifying numbers from countries that are hostile to the US—508,000 from Venezuela, 302,000 from Haiti, 152,000 from China, and 78,000 from Russia.

   When illegal immigrants evade capture and cross into a border state, they often create significant property damage to the fencing, facilities, livestock, and crops of farmers and ranchers. Besides those looking for better lives, their ranks include criminals, drug mules, sex slaves (some are children), and terrorists, some of whom are on the terrorist watchlist (169 of them caught in 2023).

   That 169 is more than in the prior decade, and how many terrorists were gotaways who avoided apprehension and being included in that total? Many border citizens need firearms for protection from illegal immigrant crimes. Daily apprehensions averaged 800–1,500 at the end of the prior administration. At the start of 2024, Biden can boast he averaged 12,000–15,000 daily. Queen Kamala (aka The Border Czar) should claim the credit for this fiasco.

   The southern border wall must be completed. Without effective borders, respect for laws, and a common national language, history shows a country is on the path to implosion. Catch and release must be eliminated, using the remain-in-Mexico policy as mandated by the US Supreme Court.

   This has been ignored by King Biden and Queen Kamala, who disrespect the other branches of government when they do not do as he and his handlers want. New illegal entrants not fleeing from persecution must be identified, fingerprinted, and deported. They should never be allowed to apply for temporary or permanent visas unless they agree voluntarily to leave the US. Border control agents must be supported to apprehend and return illegal entrants to the other side of our southern border.

Biden strikes again: In August 2023, his Department of Defense arranged with Gov Planet to auction at fire sale prices the last 250 miles of border wall material that was prevented from completing the wall due to lefty lawsuits. Now Biden is talking (probably not seriously) about completing the wall. Guess those two things make sense in the Big Guy's brain.

Looking the other way and encouraging illegal immigrants to violate our laws in the hopes of soon gaining their votes in exchange is blatant corruption in plain sight. This is the ultimate trump card that the D-S are saving to play at the right time to acquire permanent control of election results by legitimizing another 10% of voters.

Those here for the 2020 US Census increased the number of US House members for states like Illinois, California, and New York and their electors that elect the President. If they sweep the 2024 elections, the undocumenteds impact will explode as many will vote "D." It will complete the authoritarian takeover of the US and usher in the New World Order the left is so giddy for. Most of us will simply wring our hands and say we did not see this coming.

But we should have seen this coming. A current Dem Senator from Connecticut showed us the hand the D-S is playing with in an interview with MSNBC's Chris Hayes on February 7, 2024. He said that "the Democratic strategy for 30 years"..." has failed to deliver for the people we care about most, the undocumented Americans that are in this country." [1] Clearly, they care because of the permanent power grab they will have when they legalize and create a tsunami from these 30 million voters. That is necessary to more than offset their voter losses with Blacks, Hispanics, and all other working-class Americans.

But the D-S were not waiting for the 2024 elections. Nicole Malliotakis (R-NY) received the info from her FOIA request. Shockingly, she discovered that New York City requires migrant shelter builders to provide voter registration cards, assist migrants in registering, and promote campaign material within the shelters, regardless of their citizenship status. Leftists are eager to jack up participation in our election process any way they can because they knew if they had won the 2024 elections, our country would be permanently in their grip when they legalize all the undocumenteds. These 30 million new voters would then be mobilized to ensure the reign of the D-S going forward. Hopefully, the 2024 elections have permanently derailed this.

2. They are spread throughout the country without notice to the states or communities and without disease and DNA testing (to ensure a legitimate family relationship).

They are often transported in the middle of the night to avoid transparency and scrutiny, and these individuals have a high likelihood of COVID-19 (and maybe easily spreading its new variants) and other diseases due to the low vaccination rates in their home countries and the lack of health testing for them in the US.

In prior administrations, DNA and disease testing were required before any undocumenteds could be released into the US. King Joseph and his Court did not like the optics of long lines at the border, so those common-sense protections were stopped. Some minors are brought in by their sex slave masters, and people with communicable diseases may be infecting Americans.

Governors must be given the respect due to their states and approve in advance before any immigrants are disbursed to their state. DNA and disease testing must be resumed.

3. Some immigration policies mirror failed European policies.

On May 21, 2023, Peter Caddle wrote for *Breitbart* about an interview with France's Minister of the Interior regarding the upcoming Summer Olympics. The Minister identified Sunni Islamist terrorism as the "largest terror risk to the games." [2] That is in contrast to the US obsession with white supremacy. He cited our withdrawals from Afghanistan and specific African areas as giving the radicals needed territory. It doesn't take much imagination to see the value of that to organize, recruit, train, and plan terrorist actions. The article highlighted the increased surge of Arab migrants into Europe—26,000 to Italy in Q1 of 2023. This was greater than the increase in 2015–16 that preceded deadly terror incidents in France.

Another article by Gopal Goswami appeared in Firstpost on April 2, 2023. The title is "As Europe is fast becoming Eurabia, The West must reassess its refugee policy." [3] It provides some good context for the problem. Here are some highlights.

- Most Muslims coming to the US and Europe are only Sunni Muslim males.
- Some are acquiring a passport from major European countries, which allows them to travel to 167–186 countries, generally without needing a separate visa. A US passport allows visa-free travel to 186 countries (nearly everywhere).
- **The size of the problem in Europe is staggering. 70% of refugees are males under age 35. They will likely marry European women, and by 2050, that population will be sizable enough to impose Shariah law.** According to the International Organization of Migration, 10 million refugees arrived in 2015. Many millions more have come since then, including illegal border crossings.

Angela Merkel had candidly admitted the failure of Germany's immigration policy. Much of the horde of Muslims there have not assimilated into the culture and are responsible for much of the unrest and violence. **Unless Europe changes its immigration policies,**

it will become Eurabia and lose its distinctive and appealing cultures.

With the US's wide-open southern border ushering in 3 million annually, we are speeding to a similar apocalypse. Stupid immigration policies were the downfall of ancient Greece and Rome. Europe and the US should wake up and not be added to that list. All countries should encourage family formation with tax relief or other incentives to create stable populations. Our child tax credit is an excellent example of a good incentive. Immigration should be based on population stability shortfalls, needed skills, emergencies, and fleeing war or persecution. Immigrants must be assimilated into the culture with mandatory proficiency classes in the country's language and history.

The drop in our family birth rate from 2.1 to 1.6 should not be a reason to welcome un-assimilating foreigners. You have to wonder what the birth rate would have been without the impact of the abortion of 64 million since Roe v. Wade. By the way, US abortions have actually increased since the Supreme Court ruled the issue is to be decided by each State.

4. Chain migration and birthright citizenship are curses that no other country endures.

    Chain migration and birthright citizenship need to be abolished immediately. If an asylum claim is approved, only the immigrant and their immediate family of spouse and children can immigrate. We cannot allow endless chains of migrants with some apparent connection to the original migrants to flood into the country.

    It is also absurd that pregnant women are coming here to have their child, and then the parents (if staying in the US to care for the child) are declared US citizens. The lucrative "birth tourism" business supporting that needs to go out of business.

5. We have enriched the Mexican criminal cartels and Chinese mafia with billions of dollars monthly by consenting to their human

trafficking (some as sex slaves and some raped on the journey) from 170 countries and their export of deadly Fentanyl (with ingredients and pill-making equipment sourced and staffed from China).

In a *Washington Times* article by Stephen Dinan on September 27, 2022, the human smuggling fees for the cartels produce an estimated "$20 billion payday" yearly.[4] Many (including former Senator Diane Feinstein) estimated the global drug smuggling trade at $500 billion annually, with a significant amount pouring into the US from Mexico.

A robust southern barrier will reduce the enrichment of the Mexican criminal cartels and Chinese mafia and the carnage they inflict on immigrants and the US economy and annual US drug deaths of 70,000–100,000. The deaths of 100,000 in just one year is more than the total number of lives lost in the entire Vietnam War. These cartels must be labeled terrorist organizations, and we must do everything we can to stop their threat to our national security.

Our current government's reactions reflect their lack of concern for 100,000 young people dying annually from the collaboration of the criminal cartels with China's mafia. To see the complete picture of this unholy alliance, read Peter Schweizer's book *Blood Money*.[5]

6. We have no solution for illegal aliens in the USA for a long time.

    We should have expedited hearings, temporary judges, and the use of AI to handle our overwhelming immigration case backlog. Anyone not appearing voluntarily or in response to an order is subject to apprehension and removal with no chance of gaining legal US status.

    The idea that once they are here (primarily due to the D-S pining for their votes), they must be allowed to stay is not logical. There needs to be a red line, perhaps 10 years. Anyone proven to be here for more than 10 years (including the years of their US ancestors) without a felony conviction, having a job, and not on welfare could be allowed to stay. They must enroll and complete English proficiency classes. They must also pay a fine for the 1st two generations of illegal immigration. That fine of $5,000 per person would not continue past these 1st two generations.

Comparing the benefits provided in the US to the thousands paid to the cartels to bring them to the border and abuse them along the way, this cost is a bargain. The penalties will go towards the cost of claim processing, border security, government services they received previously, and possibly needed health screening and vaccinations. Payment plans should be offered if they are unable to pay in full. If they refuse to pay the fine or complete the English proficiency classes, they are subject to deportation.

English will become the official language of the US, and all everyday commerce and government transactions will be conducted only in English one year after widespread ESL classes are available. Using currencies other than the dollar within the US for everyday commerce would be too inefficient and bureaucratic. Similarly, why should we allow different languages to transact that commerce? We must align the economic currency with the linguistic currency for commerce and government transactions. After completion, they will get a green card and become citizens after the standard five more years. They will have a pathway to legalization and no longer have to hide in the shadows.

7. We have no policy for illegal aliens in the USA a short time.

Those here for less than 10 years and their families will be deported (and can never return) if they have a felony conviction. Those not immediately deported will have the same expedited claims process as those here for over 10 years. However, their ability to stay is heavily influenced by the US-needed skills of the immigrant or their proof that they were fleeing war or persecution (like Ukrainians). Their asylum claim can be accepted up to authorized limits. They will incur the same fines and English proficiency requirements as those here for over 10 years. They can also be given a green card and become citizens after 5 more years.

The left is depending on the sympathy of Republicans to allow the completion of their devious plan for permanent government control from their Uniparty. Welcoming illegal immigration to accomplish the left's thirst for power to implement their Socialist dystopia cannot be allowed and rewarded by our stupidity.

8. Agriculture needs seasonal workers who are often illegal aliens.

    We could reduce the workers needed if we aggressively pursued more greenhouse farming (like the Netherlands highlighted in Chapter 11). However, there will still be a need that may not be able to be met without importing temporary agricultural workers. Temporary agricultural employment should be expanded to meet the needs of US farming and help the livelihood of those in Central or South America. After passing all criminal screening and health evaluations (which employers or immigrants must pay for), immigrants will be granted temporary visas (for them only and not their families). They must show proof of a family in their home country to prove that employment will benefit that family.

    Those visas allow them to legally work for one or more employers for one year. After they return to Central or South America, they may apply for a one-time renewal for one more year. At the end of that, they return to Central or South America. This special visa will benefit their family financially in their home country. They would be subject to arrest, fines, and deportation if they violate the terms of their visa. Employers must ensure they are enrolled in English classes, provide basic healthcare, and are encouraged to give respectable housing to the immigrants. They are not eligible to apply for any other government benefits.

9. Construction, manufacturing, and hospitality are also employers of illegal migrants.

    High schools are often an assembly line to move as many students as possible to college, where their leftist indoctrination can be completed, as they incur significant student loan debt they will struggle to repay. Instead, many of those should be introduced with curriculum in high school to possible employment in these areas, along with others who have not completed high school and have limited skills should be sought for these jobs.

Whatever needs still remain could be met with programs similar to the temporary agricultural visas program.

10. Employers do not have to use E-Verify to ensure workers have valid Social Security numbers, and some states and cities (like New York City) do not maintain information on undocumenteds.

    Cities like New York routinely destroy documents used by illegal immigrants to apply for ID cards to qualify for government services that should be reserved for US citizens.

    Records from undocumenteds must be preserved. Except for temporary work visas, employers must use the E-Verify system. The incentives for states and illegals must stop.

11. Government services are often given to many who are not legal residents, turning on a giant magnet for the undocumenteds and the states that score additional federal funding, representatives, and Electoral College votes from the undocumenteds in their state. An awful example is New York City, which provides them with debit cards loaded with up to $1,000 per month, in addition to providing housing. The governor of New York changed the safety net rules to allow these additional funds.

    While illegal immigrants create some tax revenues, their costs to our economy are enormous. The Center for Immigration Studies analyzed the 2022 Census Bureau Survey of Income and Program Participation. 59% of illegal-headed households are using one or more welfare programs compared to 39% of US citizens. Besides opening the border for terrorists and criminals, we have become a dumping ground for other countries failed Socialist governments.

The undocumenteds are improving their standard of living—free housing, free healthcare and education, and extra welfare cash. It is a no-brainer and like winning the lottery. When given the chance, they will vote D-S because that is all they know, even though Socialism has not worked for them in their home country.

Instead, we should help them improve their literacy, education, low skills, and poverty in their countries, where the costs would be cheaper, and they would not need assimilation. At the same time, oversight would be required for the spending to minimize corruption and encourage Uncorrupted Free Market Capitalism. Here are the annual costs for undocumenteds from a few years ago from several other sources.

- $1 billion—prison cost for them (who have committed 1 million sex crimes and represent 30% of the inmate population)
- $2.5 billion—Medicaid
- $17 billion—anchor baby education
- $12 billion—other illegal immigrant education
- $45 billion—sent to immigrants' home country
- $134 billion—welfare, social services, food assistance
- Subtotal of the above items = $211.5 billion in hard costs
- $200 billion—estimated suppressed American wages from illegal immigrant workers
- $411.5 billion total annual cost—Updating this for the increasing costs and accelerated high levels of border crossings, the amount easily exceeds $500 billion annually. These numbers seem too low. According to Todd Bensman at the Center for Immigration Studies, $400 billion is just the initial cost to "feed, house, clothe, and resettle" them. The cost per US individual taxpayer (based on filers in 2022) is at least $2,562 annually. Would you vote for that use of the taxes you paid?

Educating children must be done only in English. By first completing free ESL classes and becoming proficient in English, children of legal migrants will be able to keep up with other children in the classroom and not feel different and subject to more mistreatment. This change will stop impeding the pace of education due to the mix of English-speaking and non-proficient English-speaking children in the same classroom. Dumbing down the education results may be a goal of the left, but it should not be the goal for any parent.

Availability of federal, state, and local services should require proof of green card or citizenship status. Absent that, we are continuing to create a magnet for illegal immigration and increase taxes and deficits to fund that. All legal immigrants with a green card or a temporary work visa must have a guarantor (an individual or organization) provide a forfeitable escrow that they will not apply for or receive any "welfare" benefits for 5 years. The guarantor is responsible for any illegally obtained "welfare" benefits during that period, including if those benefits exceed the escrow setup.

Only citizens, tourists, or immigrants with green cards or temporary work visas can send personal money to another country, probably with a 5–10% government fee. If they are here illegally, no transfers are allowed. Anyone who provides fraudulent documents for work, welfare, or transferring funds to another country is subject to immediate deportation and can never return. The creator and seller of the fraudulent documents should be tried as felons with a minimum sentence of 5 years per fraudulent document and a hefty fine if convicted.

12. Visa overstays are not effectively caught and corrected.

In June 2023, the Department of Homeland Security issued its annual report titled "Fiscal Year 2022 Entry/Exit Overstay Report." The rate of overstays tripled from 2019 to 2022, from 1.2% to 3.67%. The left has failed to implement exit procedures for these overstays, which often are another means of illegal immigration. This is dangerous, risky, and irresponsible because the 9/11 tragedy was executed by people who overstayed their visas. Even without the terrorism potential, we cannot let this be a lazy way to look the other way on illegal immigration. Bureaucrats must do their job to protect our sovereignty and direct visa enforcement to apprehend, fine, and deport.

13. Immigration claims processing can take 1 to 5 years for legal immigrants and up to 12 years for undocumenteds, both of which are unacceptably long.

    With the immense bureaucracies in DC, resources should be reallocated and processes streamlined. The goal for legal immigrants should be to process and reach a decision between 6 months and 1 year, with more complex cases taking one and half years.

    All illegal immigrant claims for those already here must be adjudicated within two to five years with the help of AI. An effective southern border barrier will prevent any new illegal immigration, and future processing must be done in their home country. No more enriching Mexican cartels and Chinese mafia for all the carnage they cause.

14. Many grumblers think our country is irredeemable and pursue violent actions or rhetoric to express their displeasure.

    As we begin to implement the solution frameworks in this and the other chapters of this book, that cadre of violent leftists will grow as they see their Socialist dystopia fading. They must be prosecuted and not coddled. We need a better solution for these agitators.

    Anyone seriously disappointed in this country should be given the option of a free coach flight and a reasonable amount of baggage to travel permanently to the country of their choice, where they believe their lives will be better. Those serious people taking up this emigration offer will ensure the nation they pick will accept them, and they will renounce their US citizenship and can never reclaim it. This respects their sincere disdain for the US and allows them to be happy in a place that fits their worldview.

    If they cannot find such a country, that means there is no successful model among the 195 nations of the world, and their thinking is deeply flawed. These people are different than those actors and influencers making phony pledges that if someone they don't like is elected, they will move to Canada, France, or some other country (which they never do). In 2024, they mistakenly thought their fans were so loyal that they would take their voting cues from these phonies.

Most Relevant Chapter 1 Founding Principles (FP)

- FP 2 The Right to Govern Derives from the People
- FP 3 Limited Representative Republican Form of Government
- FP 4 A Written Constitution to Be Followed
- FP 5 Private Property Rights and the Rule of Law
- FP 6 All People Are Created Equal, and the Government's Role Is to Protect Their Equal Rights and Not Provide Equal Outcomes
- FP 9 Free People Must Stay Strong to Survive
- FP 11 Federal Debt Is Toxic to Freedom Just Like Being Taken Over by Another Country
- FP 12 The USA Has the Destiny to Be Exceptional and an Example to the World

Positive Impacts

Completing the southern wall and re-instituting the Remain in Mexico policy will stop the monthly enrichment by billions of dollars for the criminal cartels and mafia whose annual human trafficking to the US of 3 million includes the "gotaways" and raped and sex slave women (and children) and annually kills about 100,000 American youth (primarily from Fentanyl). This measure will significantly enhance border security and ensure a small, manageable influx of legitimate asylum seekers. New cases will be initiated in their home country and resolved under the guidelines of 6 months to 1.5 years. Working with governors to agree on where allowed immigrants will be settled provides the respect for states that has been absent in the current mess.

We can align with the rest of the world by ending chain migration and birthright citizenship and focusing on skills and prompt processing of legitimate asylum claims. Requiring employers to use E-Verify before hiring removes that magnet for illegal immigration. Excluding welfare benefits to illegal immigrants will further de-magnetize the hordes pouring into the US and make those benefits more available to those here legally. The $500 billion annual cost of undocumenteds can begin to be eliminated.

Dealing with those already here illegally is a necessary part of the immigration solution, with financial consequences for those immigrants and a path to citizenship, especially for those here for more than ten years. Additional temporary judges and the use of AI will be needed, and they will resolve within five years the considerable backlog of current cases that prior and present administrations have created.

We can supercharge efforts to successfully use technology and fill jobs in agriculture, construction, manufacturing, and hospitality within our borders to improve our employed workforce. Unmet needs can be determined, and work visa programs for temporary help will be established for those remaining needs.

Requiring fines and proficiency in English with free ESL classes provided will create a fair assimilating approach for those allowed to stay and make classrooms more productive. Angela Merkel said that Germany's efforts to develop a multicultural country had "utterly failed" and that immigrants must assimilate better. These changes should help us reverse our similar course that mirrors the outcome she decried and result in better multicultural assimilation. We can be a model for successful multicultural assimilation, which no large country has ever achieved.

While we can sympathize emotionally with those looking for a better life, the US cannot be the dumping ground for the world. Most compassionate people have a common-sense side to their reasoning and should be able to embrace these solutions. The economic well-being of our citizens below the poverty level is often equivalent to the lower or middle class in poor nations. That realization creates the magnet that fuels illegal immigration from those other countries.

We must set an example of successful, Uncorrupt Capitalism focused on solutions for these people. We can provide funds to motivate them to change their corrupt and often Socialist governments to improve their lives in the country they grew up in and love (like the first Americans did in the American Revolution). Let's stop encouraging them to take the easy (but dangerous) way out and flood into the US. Illegal immigration is critical for the Cloward-Piven strategy to take the USA down (as mentioned in Chapter 3), and that needs to be reversed.

Besides closing the floodgates for illegal immigration at our southern border, we can stop and penalize visa overstays with better tracking, fines, and prompt returns to their countries.

Reducing the illegal immigration claims processing time from 1–5 years to ½ year to 1½ years is what would be expected for a developed or superpower country.

Giving people dissatisfied with our country a free "get out of the country" emigration opportunity to a country that is their image of "perfection" is more productive than the riots, looting, destruction, and all the other violence they might promote and participate in.

***

While it is critical that we address these 30 million who have illegally taken residence in our country, we must not overlook the serious external threat posed by China. The next chapter examines the illegitimate picture they paint of themselves, how we enabled them to now be that threat, and how unprepared we are to address it.

CHAPTER 10

Are We Prepared for the China Threat?

As existentially important as successfully addressing the China threat is, without election integrity (see Chapter 6), we have no chance of winning this war. China and the D-S know this and are aligned. Be prepared for more 2024 election tricks from both sources.

This chapter will make more sense if Chapters 4 and 5 are read first since the threats to the US and the rest of the world are laid out there, as well as China's weaknesses. Only some of that will be repeated here. We must counteract China's threat and exploit its weaknesses. Their goal is not to win a competition with us, as Biden claims. They are focused on surpassing and weakening us to the point that we become Socialist and autocratic (we already show many signs of this) and pose no threat or deterrent to the real prize for them of global domination.

China's Fictional New World Order

China has previously proposed a New World Order called the G2 to several US administrations, where the US would be #1 and China #2, making the G7 irrelevant. Now, they are driving hard to become #1 by making the US a much weakened #2 with our tepid foreign policy, internal strife, and self-destruction. This diabolical scheme reminds us of the words of the French poet Charles Baudelaire: "The greatest ruse of the devil is persuading you that he doesn't exist." [1]

Since 2013, when President Xi took the reins of power in China, he has been under the radar, quietly talking about this Global Reset. In the last ten years, they have boldly taken moves to weaken the US and strengthen themselves, some of which are chronicled in Chapters 4, 5, and later in this chapter. China now considers itself at least equal to the US and is no longer under the radar. In September 2023, they published "A Global Community of Shared Future: China's Proposals and Actions." [2]

It is a lengthy, feel-good document that has all the buzzwords that will enthrall struggling nations, globalists, squishy people, independents, faux intellectuals, leftists, environmental extremists, and the other cults of the D-S. Like Stalin's Russian Constitution, it is filled with lofty ideals that no one can argue against. Like that Russian document, those are just a tyranny's way to sell itself by candy-coating it with lies that will never be realized. They paint themselves and others as victims of the West and that they will be the saviors from that and usher in world peace. Instead, the heavy hand of tyranny will occur, not just in one area but worldwide. They will install a new "iron curtain" that will be more unyielding than the USSR version.

That propaganda document talks about "humanity at a crossroads," "an answer to the call of the times and a blueprint for the future," "the shared home of humanity," "building a global community of shared future," "lasting peace through dialogue and consultation," "an open and inclusive world through exchanges and mutual learning," "make our world clean and beautiful by pursuing green and low-carbon development," and "work together in harmony and unity." "Only when appropriate attention is paid to the collective future of humanity is it possible that the wishes of every country, people, and individual come true."

It concludes, "We can build an open, inclusive, clean, and beautiful world of lasting peace, universal security, and shared prosperity, and jointly create a better future for all of humanity." It also brags about China's programs: the One Belt One Road Initiative, the Global Development

Initiative, the Global Security Initiative, and the Global Civilization Initiative. AI likely wrote this "wonderful" piece of propaganda. Even the best BS artists could not have done such a masterful con job.

How do these lofty concepts square with China's actions?

- They have enslaved or mistreated Uighur, Mongolian, and Tibetan ethnic minorities to show their intolerance and bigotry for their subjects, who display differences from the homogenous robots they desire. They want to pick the Dalai Lama, the religious leader of Tibet. How clever for a regime opposed to any religion to try to control (and eventually eliminate) one that has had a leader for 800 years. In most official documents, they have changed the name from Tibet to "Xizang." They are pressuring the rest of the world to accept their tactics for cultural erasing and rewriting and to ignore their mistreatment of minorities, which they deny.
- Their onerous lending agreements to struggling countries make them de facto colonies that provide materials, ports, and bases to China in exchange for some infrastructure, and they are beginning to squeeze those who cannot repay the loans with added fees, interest, rewriting loans to be a 99-year lease. This will become a perpetual lease since China will not walk away after 99 years. This is how they are turning small and mid-size countries into colonies.
- Their efforts for world peace include supporting Russia's invasion of Ukraine, Iran and its terrorist tentacles attacking Israel, shipping Fentanyl ingredients to kill 100,000 US youth annually, and bullying countries in the South China Sea. They have harassed Philippine fishermen and poached and damaged a fishing area internationally recognized as belonging to the Philippines.
- Their record on the environment is horrible, creating the most pollution of any country and building over 300 new coal-powered plants annually in China and worldwide.
- Their irresponsible escape of COVID-19, which has taken the lives of 7 million globally, is paired with their refusal to take ownership of that and transparently provide all the data on its origin. They

appear to continue doing gain-of-function research on an even much deadlier virus at the same lab in Wuhan.
- Many have identified China as a practitioner of the 3 Rs: rob, replicate, replace. They steal other's technology, replicate it, and then replace it.

Do you want to believe their nice AI-generated inspirational words or your own eyes observing their actions? Reality should be preferred over propaganda that tells the world what it wants to hear.

According to the Economist, China is a "superpower that seeks influence without winning affection, power without trust and a global vision without universal human rights." [3] The US must be thoroughly prepared to address this and stop its internal decay because the rest of the world has no ability to stand up to China. Peaceful coexistence and "live and let live" with free countries are not part of the Chinese Communist vocabulary. Instead, the CCP postures itself as a victim turned savior, not the world leader of global totalitarianism.

The US complacency to bask in our past accomplishments and current-day Corrupt Capitalism has put us behind China, which has been busily expanding its global stature. At the same time, ours is diminished by weak leadership with no attainable vision. We must show the world the successes of Solutionism fueled by Uncorrupted Capitalism for them to imitate. And not let them all become de facto colonies of China, suckered in by their AI-generated inspiring soundbites, unsupported by their aggressive behaviors.

Let's see how the US enabled China's rise and our preparation to deal with them now.

China's Unimaginable Journey

Nixon was the first US President to play geopolitical two-dimensional Checkers with China, thinking he could successfully play this game due to our strength and their weakness. He believed he could change this

Communist country into a Capitalist democracy and be a counterbalance against Communist Russia. This was a fool's errand, since Communism will never embrace freedom. This nonsense started with Nixon's visit to China in 1972. He was concerned about the Vietnam War and wanted China to stop supplying arms to the North Vietnamese and bring about a conclusion. At the time of that meeting, 57,000 American lives had been lost, along with many others from allies and the seriously wounded and disabled.

How many thousands of US and other lives have been lost in unsuccessful conflicts with North Korea and Vietnam thanks to the military support they received from China and US ineptness? Those countries remain Communist nations today thanks again to that support.

Nixon was willing to trade the long-term freedom of Taiwan for getting out of Vietnam. He started the "One China" policy, so Taiwan is considered a part of China. He got next to nothing for this major giveaway and betrayal of Taiwan and started the US and China hurtling down this one-way street that has put us in the unenviable place we are today.

Jimmy Carter made the next major blunder by signing an agreement in 1979 to share scientists, students, and scientific and tech information and documentation for agriculture, energy, space, health, environment, earth sciences, engineering, and other areas of science and technology. **Our National Science Foundation has been transferring discoveries to China** since then, and over 19,000 students have studied in the US and taken leading-edge tech info back to China.

Carter was taken in by the outwardly humble demeanor of Deng Xiaoping, the prominent leader of mainland China from 1979 to 1989. This Chinese strategy was later named "hide and bide," meaning hide your capabilities and bide your time while rapidly progressing using a new combination of Corrupt Capitalism mixed with Corrupt Communism. Deng was called the "Architect of Modern China." Today, President Xi is a blackbelt in this deadly art.

Even Reagan added to this by providing Mark 46 advanced torpedoes to China in 1985, along with many other advanced armaments that made the People's Liberation Army a first-class force. Reagan also helped develop China's robotics, AI, biotech, lasers, supercomputers, and space tech industries.

The Clinton administration was responsible for agreeing to let China join the World Trade Organization, which began to supercharge its growth with this economic jet fuel to accelerate China's ascendance. In 1987, Clinton started the "1000 Talents Initiative," which allowed more Chinese students to study in the US, participate in research, and return to China with the tech they learned. This was especially nonsensical, with some students participating in nuclear research at New Mexico's Los Alamos National Laboratory.

No President has ever canceled Carter's or Clinton's lop-sided agreements or Nixon's one-sided "One China" policy. This has left Taiwan a sitting duck while China grows stronger thanks to our misguided policies. We pushed Taiwan and South Korea to give up their tactical nuclear weapons. They are now without that leverage and easier targets for China's voracious appetite.

For many years, China has been allowed to practice its 3 Rs. Now, they have a diminished need to do that, and they are pursuing their "Borg" strategy of swallowing up countries and assimilating them using the threat of their military might or enslaving them with one-sided agreements. How has China paid the US back for its stupidity all these years? China often significantly misses its agreed commitments for the purchase of US goods. They do not respect our weakness and foolishness, as their might is now on a par with us. Their schools teach that the US is evil and trying to hinder China's rise and culture. No mention is made of all of the support (foolish though it was) that the US gave China to grow into the behemoth it is today.

The analogy for this is that of a successful global company (US) observing a few ruthless international gangs (Russia, Iran) that threatened its operations and the world. That organization thought it best to help the local ruthless gang (China operating in Asia) see the benefits of Capitalism, renounce their thuggish behavior, and later help fight the two other bullies. That local bully has become the world's biggest bully, with Russia, Iran, North Korea, and a few others as junior partners. The sick python we felt sorry for and nurtured has grown immensely and is now strangling the one who pumped new life into it.

If we left China isolated, one has to wonder what would have happened. Without their military might that we enabled, would the citizens have grown tired of the oppression and been more successful in overthrowing their oppressors and seeking our help to set up a democracy?

While China has mishandled its economy, they have strategically made all the winning moves thus far for global domination. In November 2023, AidData estimated that 80% of China's loans to the developing world were to countries suffering financially and that the principal owed on all loans was more than $1.1 trillion. In some cases, China increased the late payment penalty from 3% to 8.7% on these predatory loans.

The total number of projects is a staggering 21,000, comparable to the $1.3 trillion US Marshall Plan after WWII. The One Belt One Road Initiative agreements require providing China with ports, bases, or mining of strategic minerals. That aligns with China's goal to acquire global assets and resources to win Global Domination Monopoly. Most of these projects have little regard for the carbon footprint they are laying down and are not loudly criticized by environmental extremists.

Here are some notable and concerning China's achievements.
- The US has 120 Fortune 500 companies; China has gone from none to 140.
- China's billionaires now outnumber the US.
- China has a presence on the mineral-rich far side of the moon, and we do not.
- China has a functioning hypersonic missile, and the US does not.
- The US and Russia have an unratified nuclear weapons limit of 1,500, but there are no limits on China.
- China has more ICBM missile silos (and increasing) than the US.

- China has the world's largest Navy and Army.

Good resources are the 2015 book by Michael Pillsbury, *The Hundred-Year Marathon,* and Mark Morano's 2022 book, *The Great Reset.*[4]

Key issues

1. Our military is focused on things other than being the best with the best equipment and technology to provide a credible deterrent to China and any other rogue nation or terrorist group.
2. Presidential leadership and military support for Ukraine and against Russia are potent examples of our JV team's ineptness.
3. Presidential leadership and military support for Israel against Iran and its proxies are additional examples of our JV team's ineptness.
4. Presidential leadership and military support for Taiwan against China are more examples of the Biden-Harris team's ineptness.
5. Other military performances and leadership from Biden-Harris demonstrate where wokeness leads, which isn't admirable: Hong Kong, Afghanistan, China's spy craft flying over the US, and China setting up a base in Cuba are just a few more glaring examples.
6. China's facial recognition to control the Chinese population and also to export to despots, along with their One Belt One Road Initiative in other countries to secure their rights to bases, ports, and strategic materials.
7. There are areas of tech and equipment where China has an advantage over the US.
8. China has spies and facilities for them in the US.
9. Manufacturing chains running through China threaten the US, especially for strategic resources, which gives them leverage over us.
10. China is building several successful alliances to wage a currency war against the US dollar as the world's reserve currency.
11. Because of China's goal to take down the US, they have a critical financial presence in the US, including exchange-traded instruments,

individual China-owned stocks (not independent of the CCP), and their presence in ETFs, mutual funds, and indices. They also have freely purchased US farmland, food processing, and other businesses.
12. Will China win Global Domination Monopoly or go bankrupt trying?
13. Other nations (especially China) are catching up to the US in space dominance.

Key Issues and Solution Frameworks

1. Our military is focused on things other than being the best with the best equipment and technology to provide a credible deterrent to China and any other rogue nation or terrorist group. Our focus on white privilege, CRT, etc., is laughable to the CCP. The US Navy Professional Reading Program has a book on Critical Race Theory by Ibram X. Kendl, which states, "Capitalism is essentially racist," along with other outrageous comments. [5]

    The result of this corruption is evident in our military recruitment shortfalls. In 2022, the Army missed its goal by 25%. For the fiscal year beginning October 1, 2022, the Navy, Air Force, and Marine Corp. were 50% "below the normal recruiting numbers. Focusing on CRT, ESG, and DEI creates more bureaucracy to soak up funding, taking our focus off our values and preparedness.

    Our Marines have stopped this nonsense and are now doing much better with reaching their recruitment goals. Hopefully, our other branches will wake up and woke down. The Heritage Foundation's latest annual military strength index rated our preparedness as "weak." Adding to this misguided focus (likely responsible for many recruitment shortfalls), courageous military personnel who refused the vaccine were dismissed. These missteps must be reversed.

    The 2023 DOD budget requested $34 million to root out extremist (aka Conservative") political activities. A DOD study showed that less than .005% of the 2 million active military personnel were linked to what they considered extremist activity. This is an example of using a $34 million sledgehammer to crack a nut and feel good about it. These practices must also be reversed.

We need an ombudsman group (see the Corruption and Bureaucracy Czars in Chapter 7) to ensure that the best tech, equipment, and training are provided to our military at a fair price with no more $300 toilet seats.

The US Armed Services should be respected as a first-class, honorable profession that is allowed to tell its story at high schools and colleges. China has the world's largest standing Army. We will never match that, but we need to do better. We harm our military capability by teaching soldiers that they are either oppressors or victims. We need our military to get along on a one-to-one basis, regardless of skin color and all other differentiating characteristics, and discipline those who violate that concept. Another reversal is required for this Biden administration bungling.

2. Presidential leadership and military support for Ukraine and against Russia are potent examples of our JV team's ineptness.

We should have supplied Ukraine with the planes they requested as Russia amassed troops by the Ukraine border (before the Russian invasion) to allow Ukraine to protect its airspace, cities, and citizenry. Putin would have either never invaded, or his carnage on cities and citizens could have been significantly reduced by stopping many missiles and planes from dropping bombs.

There have been an estimated 200,000–400,000 Ukrainian casualties, millions displaced to other countries, a whole nation extensively destroyed, and we are spending over $100 billion belatedly on equipment significantly less effective than what Ukraine had initially requested. Weak US leadership from the D-S has resulted in our providing Ukraine with costly drips of help to prolong the devastation and deaths, but not enough to win. We also specify where the weapons we provide can be used. Remember the D-S governing participation trophy strategy: there should be no winners who celebrate or losers who feel bad.

The lack of early tank or air support has hobbled the 2023 Ukrainian counter-offensive. The promised US Abrams tanks have not arrived in time to support that effort. Also, the planes they are finally getting were not be ready to include in operations until Q3 of 2024. Biden is forcing Ukraine to operate with one hand tied behind its back. It is doubtful that Ukraine or Russia will be totally successful. The most likely outcome is that some of Ukraine's territory will be lost, and there will be a massive rebuilding effort for the saved part of Ukraine that may likely become a part of NATO.

The Biden-Harris ineffective leadership and slow-rolling of aid efforts ensure they will not have the airpower to protect their troops, stop further devastation, and actually win. The war may be over by the time the promised planes are available for use by Ukraine. Did you know Ukraine has identified nine US companies as "international sponsors of war?" They support the Russian war effort either militarily or in other ways make money by supporting the Russian economy. Why is the Biden team not loudly outing them to stop their support of Russia?

Some think Russia's invasion of Ukraine started World War III. While it began with the attack of one country against another, it has become Ukraine, supported by most Western democracies pitted against Russia, backed significantly by Iran, North Korea, and China. Let's hope Biden's Ukraine missteps do not lull the world into a genuine WW III.

Before Russia's Ukraine invasion, Biden and his lackeys crowed about how Russia's pipeline for oil to Europe would be destroyed if Russia invaded. On Feb.7, 2022, Biden said, "If Russia invades—that means tanks or troops crossing the border of Ukraine, again—then there will be no longer a Nord Stream 2."[6] "We will bring an end to it." Then, when that happened, they denied they had any role in creating the explosions that spewed 300,000–500,000 metric tons of methane gas into the atmosphere.

This was the most significant release of greenhouse gas in a single event ever. It equals the annual emissions of 1 million cars because methane can be 81 times more potent than CO_2. The greenies have not been clamoring for understanding whether to blame the Russians for blowing up their own source of revenue or another country like the US, either with the help of others or solely with our Navy. This was alleged by Seymour Hersh, Pulitzer Prize–winning author on Substack and then the New York Post.

Instead, they use it as a rallying cry for more unreliable renewable energy. Just like our military dithering and fumbling in Afghanistan and improperly and too late arming Ukraine, we may have had a role in direct action against an evil international regime that was not threatening us and could result in retaliation by a country with a nuclear missile arsenal as large as ours. If this occurred, as Hersh alleged, this was not a responsible use of our military because providing Ukraine the equipment it asked for to control its airspace and prevent death and devastation would have been the correct action.

3. Presidential leadership and military support for Israel against Iran and its proxies are additional examples of our JV team's ineptness.

That same participation trophy philosophy is in action with our Middle East policy. Publicly, we support Israel (especially after the Hamas brutality unleashed on them on October 7, 2023). Privately, we work diligently to undermine Israel's determination to eliminate any future threats from Hamas, Hezbollah, and Iran directly. We work to undermine Netanyahu's government by meeting with his Cabinet and opposition leaders. Our leftist administration is resolved to carve out part of Israel as a reward for Hamas terrorism. This would ensure the elimination of Israel.

After the events of October 7, 2023, the leadership and people in Israel are smarter than Sleepy Joe. They know the Iranian proxies in Gaza, Judea, Samaria, and Lebanon are existential threats to their existence. It is a zero-sum game—the two-state solution assures the continuation of terrorism and the destruction of Israel and its citizens, and they will not be on board.

The Biden strategy is the dumbest strategy we could employ because we saw the brutal carnage and war crimes perpetrated from Gaza by its terrorists who infect the citizens, culture, and governance. Gaza was allowed a lot of self-determination, and that model is a total failure and must not be replicated again. Because Palestinians have been indoctrinated and financially rewarded for expressing their hatred of Jews with murders and war crimes, most Middle Eastern countries don't want those hate-filled people in their countries. The foolish two-state "solution" with the slogan "from the river to the sea" means the elimination of Israel. After destroying Hamas, Israel must not be deterred from replacing hateful indoctrination with real education and cooperation in Gaza.

US leadership is applying the same "participation trophy" strategy it is using in Ukraine to Israel to prevent Israel from winning a war where its very existence is threatened. The Biden team is delaying weapons they need and telling them how to conduct their war.

4. Presidential leadership and military support for Taiwan against China are more examples of the Biden-Harris team's ineptness.

There is a $14 billion backlog of weapons that Taiwan has purchased from the US to defend itself primarily from mainland China. It includes 66 F-16 fighter jets and high-tech missiles. Only now that China is acting aggressively in the area has Sleepy Joe decided to fast-track $500 million for them as of early May 2023.

That is only 3.6% of what is due to them. In March 2024, a "decision" was made to send 100–200 US Special Forces to Taiwan to train them in very short-range drone use. Other commitments for ballistic missiles, tanks, and F-16s were reaffirmed, with some happening in 2024. Just like what he has done in Ukraine, Biden is much too little and way too late. When this book is published, Taiwan and some parts of Ukraine may be lost, thanks to Sleepy Joe.

5. Military performance and leadership from Biden-Harris demonstrate where wokeness leads, which isn't admirable: Hong Kong, Afghanistan, China's spy craft flying over the US, and China setting up a base in Cuba are just a few more glaring examples.

    The lack of a meaningful response to the Chinese takeover of Hong Kong and our disastrous and disorganized withdrawal from Afghanistan gave the world a real-time view of that misguided focus. It also encouraged bad actors across the globe not to be fearful of the incompetent leadership of our President and his military.

    How responsibly did we react to China sending a 200 ft. 2,000 lb. spy balloon to collect information from sensitive military installations? It was not even mentioned until a Montana civilian posted a video. Then, it was acknowledged and allowed to continue its mission (from Alaska and across the US mainland) to gather and transmit data before it was shot down in the Atlantic. It would have been better to intercept it and bring it to the ground intact for easy retrieval of its components and mission identification or at least shoot it down over sparsely populated areas of Alaska—another display of American weakness. To date, there is no data-driven clarity from the Biden team about the mission of the balloon.

    Later, the US story changed to the balloon was being observed since its launch in China. This shows even more weakness in our handling of this national security issue. Because Biden & Co. were embarrassed, they quickly shot down several smaller balloons that were detected later and told us they were a threat. They were small civilian balloons used by hobbyists and educational organizations. That should have been done with the first spy balloon before it completed its spy mission and transmitted the data, but we were too timid or corruptly compromised.

Because the Biden-Harris administration seemed weak when they allowed a large 200 ft. Chinese spy balloon to complete its surveillance across the country, they used $200 million fighter jets and $ 1.6 million for 4 missiles to take down 3 hobby balloons that cost $12–$180 each. We should all be appalled by the actions of Biden-Harris and their JV team, falsely thinking this makes them look strong.

What will we do about China setting up a base in Cuba 90 miles from us? We know what JFK did, but our current JV team is not cut from the same cloth.

6. China's facial recognition to control the Chinese population and also to export to despots, along with their One Belt One Road Initiative in other countries to secure their rights to bases, ports, and strategic materials. They are the world leader in this technology.

   An example in our backyard is China's dealings with Panama concerning its loans for infrastructure and operating agreements involving aspects of the Panama Canal. That leverage gives China a lot of influence over that famous canal that the US built in the ten years ending 1914 at the cost of thousands of lives and, in today's dollars, $6.7 billion. Another bumbling President, Jimmy Carter, signed an agreement that gifted the Panama Canal to Panama and ended our perpetual lease. The vast majority of traffic through the Panama Canal comes to the US, and China could use its leverage to choke the flow of goods into the US.

   We must use our leverage to sidetrack these efforts to increase the number of global "lifetime" despots using China's facial recognition tech and reduce China's relentless march for worldwide influence and dominance with its One Belt One Road Initiative. They are a geopolitical Borg in the early stages of absorbing every country they can.

7. There are areas of tech and equipment where China has an advantage over the US.

The latest "Critical Technology Tracker (Appendix 1.1)" was prepared by ASPI (Australian Strategic Policy Institute). It shows that **China is leading the US in 37 out of 44 key tech areas and that for some of these, all of the world's top 10 research institutions are in China. They also produce 9X more "high-impact research papers than the 2nd ranked country.** This is particularly concerning in defense and space-related technology.

We must increase research and close those gaps, especially with hypersonic missiles and hydrogen and nuclear fusion energy. **China has recently built a compact hypersonic generator that can power hypersonic missiles, lasers, rail guns, and microwave weapons. They also announced a cooling technology that will allow infinite firing of their lasers by overcoming the massive heat they generate.**

Historically, China had a small arsenal of 50 nuclear missiles. They now have 300 new silos under construction, which would exceed the US stockpile when completed and filled. We should seek a nuclear arms treaty with this growing atomic powerhouse and expose their unwillingness to enter such a critical agreement for world peace.

8. China has spies and facilities for them in the US. In the prior administration, the US launched the China Initiative to discover and stop China's spy operations within the US. Because of that, China's Houston embassy was closed due to its spying operations. Biden, infected by the Trump Derangement Syndrome (and possibly compromised), shut that down. There are Chinese coercers who are in the US (in "aid stations" that are effectively mini-police stations) to intimidate and harass any influential Chinese Americans who have family in China.

    They are intimidated into providing information or positive lobbying for China with veiled threats against their relatives in China. Intellectual property is stolen from US manufacturing in China and desirable tech in the US. This is done with bugging devices and spies in industry and Chinese national university students conducting leading-edge research. They have purchased US businesses and nearly

400,000 acres of US farmland, some conveniently next to US military bases, making it easy to spy on our military tech. This must stop.

Besides spies and saboteurs already here, more keep coming. In 2022, 55,000 Chinese came to the US on work visas. Our Border Security personnel also encountered another 45,437, half through the wide open southern border (86% of these were single adult males). We need to deport or prosecute spies, illegal Chinese border crossers, and the Chinese military in the US (the US military would not be allowed a presence in China.

Only recently has the threat of the TikTok and WeChat apps to spy, blackmail, and disseminate propaganda gotten the attention it deserves. TikTok created propaganda favorable to the Hamas savagery of October 7, 2023. This caused foolish college youth to be urged on by Hamas representatives at those campuses to support Hamas's barbarism. We must minimize or eliminate their presence in the US. Other US-based apps can happily fill that entertainment void without those concerns.

All universities and colleges should annually report all foreign donations (with firm country limits in place). They should be forbidden to accept any from adversarial countries like China, Russia, and Iran or terrorist-harboring countries like Qatar. We must stop Chinese national students from studying in the US since they often get involved in leading-edge research directly or indirectly and too often pass the tech info back to China.

9. Manufacturing chains running through China threaten the US, especially for strategic resources, which gives them leverage over us. US companies have been seduced by the low-cost or slave-labor cost of producing goods in China. The US obsession with bottom-line profits has created a significant imbalance in trade and strong dependence on China. That can probably be tolerated for inexpensive, non-essential things like toys, but definitely not for strategic materials. In 2022, we

imported $537 billion from China and exported only $154 billion to them, creating a trade deficit of $383 billion in just one year.

In 1999, with Republican support, Bill Clinton reached an agreement to normalize trade with China and pave the way for their 2001 entry into the World Trade Organization. This began its march to become the "world's factory." Since then, our trade with China has allowed them to catapult their military prowess and transform their country by transferring $6 trillion in cumulative trade deficit dollars from the US to China. We must end their status with the US as a "most favored nation."

This was also done on the backs of American manufacturing and their workers, as millions of jobs were lost to China. China has taken advantage of its WTO "developing nation" status to avoid pollution reductions other nations must follow. That status is inappropriate for the #2 Superpower and must also be terminated. The WTO's antiquated rules have not changed in 25 years, and now China has made the WTO barely relevant. They have also corrupted the World Health Organization and have them firmly in their camp.

We must urgently bring back China supply chains for pharmaceutical ingredients, personal protective equipment (like medical masks, gowns, and gloves), computer chips, and energy components. We must compete with them in negotiating agreements or setting up more operations in the US and elsewhere for strategic materials for steel, lumber, fossil fuels, rare earth minerals (used in cars, military, aerospace, X-ray and MRI systems, and computer screens) and clean energy tech (like electric batteries and solar panels). Recent estimates are that China produces 50% of wind turbine components, 70% of the rare lithium supply for EV batteries, and 90% of solar modules.

In November 2023, China announced mandatory mineral export reporting. They will know who is getting supplied and by how much. This will allow them to turn off or on those spigots for countries at any time. The announcement came after they already had the reporting in place and began weaponizing these resources. Their export in

August 2023 of gallium and germanium products was zero compared to July amounts of 5.15 and 8.1 metric tons. In 2010, they weaponized that strategy against Japan, reducing their shipments of rare earth minerals to them. Their targets now are the US and its allies, and China is incrementally taking one step at a time. We must increase our domestic critical minerals mining ASAP.

China uses many rare earth minerals for Chinese EV auto batteries. The balance gets sold at excellent profits to nations anxious for EV car batteries. They are doing the same electrification with light commercial vehicles and buses. Along with high-speed rail that minimizes the need for domestic flights, these actions will reduce its vulnerable dependence on imported oil, which now supplies 70% of its oil needs. While this will eventually reduce its carbon footprint, its strategic goal is ending its dependence on oil importation. If they cared about the environment, they would not be annually building hundreds of coal plants domestically and overseas.

Once the world has been fervently led and enslaved to buy most windmill, solar, and EV components from China at great profit to China and cost to other countries, they will flip the script. China will transition to energy solutions like nuclear fusion for their grid and home and transportation solutions like hydrogen that are next generation and continue to increase their profitability, eliminate their oil import dependence, and continue to drain capital out of the rest of the world with its products that are "sexy" for the woke environmentalist Western nations. The West will make an even larger wealth transfer to China that will financially enslave them and render them impotent against China and its allies' aggressions.

We and our allies must wake up and woke down to stop enriching China at our expense. The feverish pursuit of climate extremism will have an existential impact on world peace and individual freedoms. Oil-rich countries like Iran, Russia, and Saudi Arabia that align with China today to meet its oil needs will experience significant impacts to their economies when Chinese oil needs are minimized.

China also controls 90% of the ingredients needed for generic antibiotics. There is a similar situation with other generic drugs. In March 2020, their official news outlet threatened that they would use "strategic control" over medical products to "ban exports to the United States" in the event of a conflict. [7] Because of their monopolistic 90% control over antibiotics, in March 2021, China increased the cost of antibiotics and acetaminophen to India by 100%. It seems like simple economics eludes the world in its greed for the lowest cost and most profits. That eventually leads to a monopoly supplier, exorbitant monopoly prices, and ruthless control of the supply for those not aligned with the monopolistic supplier.

We and our allies must admit we are in an "economic war" with China and demand and incentivize US firms to return jobs and facilities to the US. Traveling to despotic countries or stationing US citizens there is dangerous and not responsible, and our ability to protect them in adversarial territory is minimal. So, DON'T BE THERE. We must loudly and regularly publicize those US companies that invest in the US and avoid the tasty Chinese elixir of "cheap labor." We must firmly nudge allies and others to also decouple from China. There will be short-term pain that avoids devastating longer-term geopolitical pain later.

10. **China is building several successful alliances to wage a currency war against the US dollar as the world's reserve currency. This is the easiest way for China to become the #1 superpower and defeat the US without firing a single shot.** How has China been waging this war?

What Has China Done Within China?

China is replacing its internal paper currency with its digital Juan and encouraging visitors and trading partners to use it. 90% of China's internal retail payments are already done this way. Standard Chartered Bank in China is now a part of the pilot testing that uses a foreign bank. They are working with City Bank Clearing Services to offer digital Juan currency services to customers.

The digital Juan differs significantly from crypto coins like Bitcoin, which enjoy a decentralized blockchain's protection. The digital Juan has no such security and is controlled centrally by the Peoples Bank of China, which has no meaningful constraints. As it completes the internal transition, it will be able to know and control the income and spending of every person in China. They have gained valuable information on operationalizing a digital currency to create their desired controls.

What Has China Done Externally?

China has used that intel from their digital Juan to gain its traction globally with newly-forged significant trade with Saudi Arabia, Iran, Malaysia, Turkey, and France, along with the other members of the initial BRICS alliance countries (Brazil, Russia, India, and South Africa). The current BRICS countries account for more trade than the combined G7 countries. 6 new countries have joined the BRICS since 2010: Saudia Arabia, the UAE, Iran, Egypt, Ethiopia, and Pakistan. Two US "allies," India and Egypt, have moved even closer to China and are no longer settling trades in USD.

Middle East oil producers are distancing themselves from the weak US and aligning with a more assertive China. 20 other countries have submitted applications to join BRICS, and many others are also interested. This growing movement is rapidly moving away from using USD, euros, pounds, and yen. It is in the early stages of wreaking currency mayhem on Western democracies and, most significantly, the US. BRICS is a political, trade, and currency movement that could become a military alliance.

In the 1970s, Saudi Arabia agreed with the US to settle all their oil trades in USD in exchange for security guarantees from the US. Subsequently, the rest of OPEC went along with this, and their revenue became known as "petrodollars." Because of Biden's rhetoric against Saudi Arabia and the perceived weakness of the US, they are now accepting payment for oil sales in currencies other than the USD. All of this fits in perfectly with the BRICS de-dollarization strategy.

China has cleverly expanded its influence in several ways. First, its creation and continuous expansion of the BRICS membership make it a force to be reckoned with. Second, it is the largest trading partner with the Eurasian Economic Union of 5 post-USSR countries (including Russia). Third, it has created and hosted two other entities besides BRICS.

- One Belt One Road Initiative—China provides loans to countries to use China to build infrastructure for them in exchange for ports, bases, or rights to mine minerals there. As of now, 154 countries (many impoverished) have taken this bait, making many de facto colonies of China as they struggle to repay those loans, interest, penalties, and fees or restructure into 99-year (aka perpetual) leases.
- Shanghai Cooperation Organization—Founded by Russia and China in 2001, it is a political, economic, and security entity for Eurasian countries. It has 8 members, 3 observer nations, and 14 dialogue partners. It accounts for 40% of global GDP and 60% of the Eurasian land area.

While China is the critical player in all these alliances, other influential countries like Iran, India, Pakistan, and Russia are involved in more than one of these alliances, increasing China's bond with them. China has gotten countries that are not friendly with each other to join these associations. Examples are India and Pakistan, and Iran and Saudi Arabia.

China seduces these countries by creating an equal playing field and making them feel more important than just bit players. **If China can coordinate the actions of their alliances (BRICS, Eurasian Economic Union, One Belt One Road Initiative, and the Shanghai**

Cooperation Organization) that represent 85% of the global population, they are practically unstoppable.

Initially, BRICS members are satisfied to trade with other group members using their currencies to avoid the SWIFT system that has created economic sanctions against countries. While it may seem justified against Russia for its invasion of Ukraine, many countries perceive this as autocratic. They also see the US as a financial concern with its huge and growing status as the world's largest debtor nation. Some have stopped or are considering stopping using US Mastercard and Visa credit cards.

China is quietly influencing BRICS members to launch a digital currency that will likely be heavily based on the digital Juan and backed by some gold. China can dump its $1 trillion on the market whenever it wants. It has greatly influenced making the same happen in other countries since it is the largest trading partner of more than 120 countries. Many countries are increasing their gold and other commodity reserves and reducing their USD and US Treasury (UST) reserves.

Any country's loans based on USD are more costly to repay (due to the inflated USD and increasing interest rates), and their holdings of UST have declined in value as new Treasuries are issued paying higher interest. And while financial sanctions against Russia may be morally right, many countries see the US as weaponizing its reserve currency status against anyone they want and are concerned they could be next. Had the US given Ukraine the planes they requested at the onset, no sanctions against Russia would ever have been needed. When the timing is right for them, members of BRICS will bring their gold reserves to their home country and dispose of their USD and UST.

The focus is to reduce global trade and loan settlements with US dollars, reduce the 41.73% of US dollars allocated to Special Drawing Rights (SDRs) used for international transactions, and avoid any US sanctions impact. They don't realize that their passion for "de-dollarization" and dethroning the US as the reserve currency and #1 superpower will only result in installing China in that vacated spot. They will be unable to escape China's brutal grip as it completes its victory in the Global Domination Monopoly it has been so skillfully playing. Once the US is dethroned, the Supermassive Black Hole of Socialism (powered primarily by the CCP) will absorb the rest of the world. The accommodating image it projects to them now will be replaced with "Resistance is futile. Prepare to be assimilated."

What Has the Rest of the World Done?

Gold had been a tier 3 asset, and banks would have to discount their gold holdings by 50% on the reserves portion of their financial statements. Then, on April 1, 2019, physical gold was reclassified to a tier 1 asset, no longer requiring that 50% discount. While other reasons may also play a role in their decision to de-dollarize, this certainly reflects their lack of confidence in the future value of the USD and their Plan B if the USD craters. **The USD status as a reserve currency eroded in 2022 at 10 times the rate of the past 20 years, according to Eurizon SLJ Asset Management.** Total global holdings of USD reserves dropped in 2022 from 55% to 47% in just one year.

90% of the world's central banks are researching the creation of their own CBDC (central bank digital currency), and 40% are already engaged in pilot programs. The SWIFT system has tested a new platform for use with different countries' digital assets and hopes to launch that service in one to two years. Meanwhile, these countries are buying gold and other commodities and currencies while lightening their holdings of USD and UST.

Some of these central bank actions were triggered by freezing 50% of Russia's currency reserves and shutting most of their big banks out of the SWIFT banking system by the US and its allies after Russia invaded Ukraine. Financial systems are based on trust, but if used for retaliation, that trust can be seriously eroded. Other countries hold $16 trillion and $8 trillion US Treasury securities. Those can be expected to reduce significantly, putting pressure on the US, the world's largest debtor nation.

Western Responses to China's Actions

Germany sees the danger of a digital currency heavily influenced by China and its allies. They are pushing hard to initiate a digital euro, but not all in the EU are as concerned. These necessary efforts may not happen due to the foolish short-sightedness of some.

The US is not prepared and will wring its hands. They will blame China for the misdeeds of the Biden-Harris administration. But their explosive government spending and money printing causing massive domestic inflation and the bubble of inflating US assets; the high interest rates that hurt the US economy and cause foreign debts to inflate; and its use of sanctions against Russia (instead of giving Ukraine the planes they asked for and desperately needed to minimize the devastation that has occurred). This last action created mistrust by using the reserve currency status to punish those taking steps the US and its European allies didn't like.

There is an interesting August 10, 2023, two-part YouTube interview by Michelle Makori of Andy Schectman, a respected precious metals expert and thought leader on geopolitical and economic changes. [8] Watch those two segments if you can. Andy has a plausible theory for the US ineptness in this area besides the usual reasons for most Biden administration blunders. Biden's Council of Economic Advisors has two members with provocative agendas. One actively lobbied to eliminate the US reserve currency status; the other is a strong proponent of a US digital currency and not a fan of banks.

Losing our reserve currency status is a big deal and will produce catastrophic results, especially within the US, as noted in the next section. In Government Chapter 7, it was pointed out that the $35 trillion debt talked about is just the tip of the debt iceberg. Much of

Social Security, Medicare, and pensions are not fully funded, and a sizeable portion of our debt is owed to people in this country.

When the economic tsunami of losing our reserve status washes over us, we will become fearful and sign onto a digital currency that will undoubtedly not have privacy or other protections but gives us the "assurance" of being made whole. Banks will likely be made irrelevant, and the Federal Reserve will control everything. Central planning, here we come.

This "purposeful" inattention and too late of a response will be Biden's biggest blunder and cause the downfall of the US and please all those rooting for this Great Reset to the New World Order.

The Result of Our Inadequate Response

If we do not hinder this momentum-gathering debacle, what will happen? A digital currency from the BRICS will create a new system for global trade financing that settles transactions instantly, will replace other currencies held in banks, and may impair or replace the SWIFT system for international trade settlements by reducing costs and time lags. A new digital currency for global trade will rapidly expand and seriously erode the USD 96% use over the last few decades.

An international banking crisis can occur, and the status of the USD as a reserve currency will significantly diminish or be totally lost. Our annual deficit financing of 15–20% of our annual GDP will be very problematic on top of the accumulated and growing stated deficit of $35 trillion. The value of the USD will reduce significantly, which could lead to hyperinflation.

A recent pronouncement by the left's patron saint, Paul Krugman is very disturbing. He believes the US will not lose its leadership currency position, but it would be "hardly earth-shattering for our economy" even if it did. This could be his most significant economic misstatement and blunder of all time.

A Better US Currency Response

We and our allies must aggressively discourage and impede China's alliances and efforts to globally popularize the digital Juan and the coming BRICS digital currency by loudly publicizing China's weaknesses (Chapter 5). This includes exposing their fictitious vision that is not backed up by their actions, as shown at the beginning of this chapter.

We must not be too proud to copy China's alliance strategy, which gives smaller and mid-size countries a more prominent voice to be heard than their small voice in the UN or the feeling that the G7 nations seem to be calling all the shots.

We should work with the other G10 nations to fast-track our readiness for one or two primary digital currencies with some gold backing that addresses privacy and other concerns to counter the coming BRICS digital currency.

We must work with our G10 allies to accelerate the SWIFT system's platform modernization with first-rate blockchain technology to allow for more instant settlement.

We must strengthen our USD, and our allies must do the same with their economies. That will maintain our reserve currency status, its high % in SDRs, and the other currencies' % in SDRs. Many US currency-strengthening actions involve the tax and spending reforms that the Tax and Bureaucracy Czars from Chapter 7 would recommend. Unfortunately, that is missing from the DNA of Biden or any D-S.

11. Because of China's goal to take down the US, they have a critical financial presence in the US, including exchange-traded instruments, individual China-owned stocks (not independent of the CCP), and their presence in ETFs, mutual funds, and indices. They also have freely purchased US farmland, food processing, and other businesses.

Their securities do not follow US accounting standards and subject US investors (including our military) to significant risks while providing capital to an adversary and its military. How bright is that?

The Chinese Communist Party controls Chinese companies. Their goal of world dominance is only possibly hindered by the US, and they are laser-focused on debilitating the US. We must not stupidly fund our downfall at the hands of a totalitarian government. **Pensions, profit-sharing plans, IRAs, or 401(k)s must be prohibited from investing in any security with Chinese assets or ownership.** Financial advisors and other fiduciaries should be responsible for identifying those and not selling them to clients or risk prosecution.

In 2022, Chinese firms tried to buy Forbes (with its significant financial influence and its database) but were stopped by Congress. In 2023, Russian interests were involved in trying to do the same, with a young tech billionaire as the frontman for a consortium they had ties to. We must ban our adversaries from buying US assets. The greed of American businesses (aided by greed-driven investment bankers and fund managers) to sell to adversaries in a "friendly" takeover and the ability of those adversarial countries to execute "hostile" takeovers must be legislatively prevented. Common sense about national security being compromised must take precedence over unfettered freedom to maximize profits.

We must end their participation and presence in our financial markets and ownership of businesses and land. **They have purchased US businesses and over 400,000 acres of US farmland** (some next to US military bases) to influence a favorable opinion of them, control some of our ability to produce food for ourselves, and spy on our military tech. **They control our pork supply due to their $4.6 billion acquisition of Smithfield Foods.** Who knows how much farmland they control in the rest of the world?

We must prevent China from owning more land or businesses in the US and arrange for a disposition of those they already own. For the sale of some assets or a portion of a business, there must be a clause that forbids sales to nationals or companies controlled by countries we determine are national security risks.

There must also be a perpetual clause to prevent future resales of those assets or portions of the business to US adversaries by requiring the pre-approval of the US government. We must accept that we are adversaries with China (the CCP) and that they are systematically working to take down the US, the only threat to their dystopian dream of world domination. We cannot provide support to an adversary to improve their ability to take us down. Because Biden would not do this, some states are taking their own banning actions. Agriculture, non-residential property, and a few industries provide critical needs like food, and they must be owned by US entities. So, even companies from "friendly" nations should not have the ability and temptation to divert critical resources to their countries.

Another member of the leftist coalition is the governor of Michigan, who is incentivizing China with $700 million to build a battery plant in her D-S devastated state. This will require a member of the Communist Party to be involved with the operation daily, as that is required of all Chinese companies with 50 or more employees. 250 Chinese nationals will be brought in to work there and provided housing at a local university. The site coincidentally is excellent for spying on a nearby military installation.

12. Will China win Global Domination Monopoly or go bankrupt trying?

China and the US have spending and debt issues, and one of us will become a financial disaster. As we fix our problems, we must exploit China's issues. According to a Newsweek article of February 8, 2022, "China's Debt 'Bomb' Is Going Off Under Xi Jinping," it would take a middle-class couple 47 years of savings to buy a small apartment in Beijing or Shanghai if both saved 100% of their pay.

China is creating debt 5 times faster than its increase in GDP. Experts have said the debt-to-GDP ratio could be 350% or even 400%. Some of this is due to their long-term investment, like the One Belt

One Road Initiative projects (a global march to provide infrastructure to countries in exchange for ports, bases, and rare earth mineral rights), loans to risky borrowers like Venezuela, and funding the China sovereign wealth fund. Estimates are this has depleted their foreign exchange reserves by $400 billion, putting them below the IMF recommendation of $2.8 trillion.

China has told us through its words and actions that it is playing Global Domination Monopoly and intends to win. Their empire today is 3X their traditional historical amount. **Xi Jinping told us his "China Dream" to restore China to its prior place of** *tianxia* **(ruling "all under heaven"). In May 2019, the** *People's Daily* **declared a "People's War" against the US. Coincidentally, COVID-19 escaped from China a few months later, killing 1 million Americans and 6 million others.**

Global Domination Monopoly strategy is like regular Monopoly: acquire as much property as possible through clever negotiation, extract as much money as you can from your opponents with the assets you acquired and made more valuable, and don't go bankrupt in the process. China is playing well, but "the emperor has no clothes."

We need to vigorously publicize their colonialism, and their financial, environmental, and human rights problems, South China Sea bullying, support of war and terror, and research to make viruses more potent than their virus that killed 7 million worldwide. Chapter 5 covers more of China's weaknesses.

13. Other nations (especially China) are catching up to the US in space dominance. If China gains a strategic advantage in space, it will threaten and destabilize the world.

    Whoever wins in space wins the world. China's expansionist moves (see Chapter 4) across the globe are naturally advancing into space, where they can threaten the entire planet. Numerous sources say China is focusing on setting up a permanent moon base and claiming the most mineral-rich parts as theirs. They are even working on having a robot build bricks out of moon soil. That outpost could also be a launch site for further space exploration or a military option against adversaries on Earth. For the security of the US and the world, the US must be dominant in space technology. We must work with allies to prevent China's claims to any part of the moon.

Most Relevant Chapter 1 Founding Principles (FP)

- FP 3 Limited Representative Republican Form of Government
- FP 4 A Written Constitution to Be Followed
- FP 8 General Education Is Mandated and Considered Essential for Survival
- FP 9 Free People Must Stay Strong to Survive
- FP 11 Federal Debt Is Toxic to Freedom Just Like Being Taken Over by Another Country
- FP 12 The USA Has the Destiny to Be Exceptional and an Example to the World

Positive Impacts

It is critical to have a Commander-in-Chief who will provide our military with the best training and technology at fair costs, focus on closing our tech gaps with China, and re-focus the military on its primary security role. That will result in more effective US Armed Services branches. Allowing them (and law enforcement) to tell their stories at high schools and colleges will inform our youth and provide considerations for career paths they might not have considered. We must repair and reverse the recent reputational damage we have amassed in Afghanistan, Hong Kong, Ukraine, the Middle East, and Taiwan.

Global security is only possible with a strong US that thwarts all the moves that China is making for global dominance and the emasculation of the US with internal turmoil and external pressures. Working with our allies to curtail reliance on China (especially for scarce and strategic items) will not allow them to economically blackmail many countries as they did during the pandemic they caused. That will create more jobs in our countries and strengthen relationships with our allies. It will also strengthen our hand and weaken China's quest for global domination.

Partnering with allies to thwart China's export of facial recognition software and their colonialist One Belt One Road Initiative that stifles freedom and enslaves poorer nations will make the world better. Stopping China's many forms of surveillance, IP theft, and propaganda that undermine the US are common-sense actions that must be taken for national security.

Ending the ability of Chinese or any other adversarial country's companies or nationals to own US land, non-residential property, or business is more common sense. They should not be able to blackmail the US, especially with food production and distribution. We must end their ability to be on our stock exchanges or included in our mutual funds, indices, or ETFs. That will likely prevent significant losses from their misleading and undependable financial reporting. Any investment with Chinese assets or ownership will be disqualified from investment by pensions, profit-sharing plans, IRAs, and 401(k)s. Stopping the funding of an adversary with these measures is sensible. Economic war can quickly transform into military conflict. We would not have allowed Hitler or the Japanese emperor that opportunity to mess with our economy for their benefit.

We can stop China's progress toward global dominance by working with allies to loudly expose China's financial, environmental, and human rights shortcomings, their support of war and terrorism, global colonialism, and the irresponsible experimentation with making viruses more potent than COVID-19 that killed 7 million worldwide. This can have a chilling effect on the growth of China's BRICS and other alliances as we wake up the world to China's ambitions. With these same alliances, we can counter their war against the USD, strengthen our currencies, and test one or two digital currencies (with solid privacy protections) to rival the coming BRICS digital currency.

Working with allies to prevent colonialist China from claiming any part of the moon and reclaiming our space dominance will thwart China's ambitions to exploit and intimidate. A more successful and much less corrupt vision from a reinvigorated US focused on solutions will cause terrorism and the tyranny of Socialism and Communism to wane as we show the world a much better alternative to China's counterfeit vision. We have a lot of work to do to bring this about, and with the proper leadership and a Solutionist focus, we can make it happen.

**

Chapter 11 is the last major external threat, having an abundant supply of clean water and energy. These are actually both internal and external issues because some aspects can be out of our control and make us dependent on other countries. Politicians are spending exorbitantly, often misdirecting to faulty ideological or political purposes. They seem to ignore our serious water issues and do not significantly support better energy alternatives than undependable wind, solar, and electric cars with their many associated problems. That chapter is longer than any other in this book. If you have gotten this far, do not overlook it. It will be a valuable use of your time.

CHAPTER 11
Strategic Resources

A country cannot be a world leader and influencer without an abundant supply of clean water and energy for the innovation, personal, household, commercial, industrial, and agricultural needs of daily life. If we continue to not adequately supply these internally, we will be captives to other nations (like China and ME oil-rich countries) or resort to harsh conservation measures on ourselves. Can you imagine the desperate actions we may take when our clean water supply gets lower than it is now due to contamination and depletion of reserves?

Our government worked hard in the prior administration to achieve energy independence, where we were no longer dependent on others. The Biden-Harris administration has been seriously infected with TDS (Trump Derangement Syndrome) and wanted to please their sub-cult of BANANA Greens (Build Absolutely Nothing Anywhere Near Anybody). They depleted much of our Strategic Petroleum Reserve to artificially lower gas prices and help win an election. That left us soliciting authoritarian regimes afterward to sell us higher-priced and dirtier energy to make our required sacrifices on the altar of our past environmental sins.

We cannot allow the false religion of environmental hysteria to financially ruin our country when more reasonable and environmentally better approaches are possible. Most EVs have serious issues with battery efficiency, performance, cost, lithium supply needs, human and environmental impacts, infrastructure for expanding the household grid, and creating a network of convenient, extensive, and reliable charging stations. Scientific investigation is blossoming new technologies that are more efficient, less costly and complex, and in the very near future. However, we focus on promoting a flawed woke agenda, the interests of the enormous lobbies for EVs and their lithium batteries and charging ports, and the lobbies for expensive wind and solar that have demanded and received increasing subsidies for over 20 years.

Another result is the littering and debasement of hundreds of thousands of acres of our landscape with windmills and solar power farms with severe drawbacks. We also are lining the pockets of the CCP in China in its quest to control the world commercially, culturally, politically, and militarily. Now is the time to stop the regressives from bribing and mandating problematic technology while banning tech they don't like. We need to re-focus on accelerating innovation for future technology that needs a bit of research and optimization to realize those benefits. As those technologies become cost-effective in the next few years, their benefits won't require bribing, mandating, or banning other tech.

Summaries of what seems like the best solution frameworks come at the end of these sections on water and energy. There is so much innovation that the best ones that surfaced needed to be separately summarized. Priorities and changes may likely happen from new innovations or reviews by those who are more scientifically immersed.

Water

Key Issues

1. The US and the world's waters (and land) are significantly polluted by the 9,000 varieties of PFAS (also called "forever chemicals"). One estimate says 200 million Americans drink water contaminated with PFAS, and nearly all have PFAS in their blood.

2. The US and much of the world's waters (and land) are significantly polluted by pharmaceuticals and personal care products (PPCP).
3. Our efforts for recycling and reclaiming plastic are not worthy of our country and should be significantly improved. The average person in the US creates about 220 lbs. of plastic waste annually—globally, that is 380 million tons annually, and only 5–9% of all plastic is recycled. Much of this degrades and becomes microplastics that impact our landfills, bodies of water, and their sea life (and the humans that consume them).
4. Water sold in plastic bottles is a serious problem. Many are not easily recyclable into useful products, and the volume is too large. Some developed countries promote reusable water bottles, but that market is only $9 billion compared to the single-use plastic water bottle market of $283 billion in 2021.
5. Our efforts for recycling, reclaiming, and safe disposal of toxic items should be significantly improved.
6. Reservoirs (lakes, rivers, streams, and other visible retention) are seriously declining.
7. Groundwater basins (sub-surface aquifers that are a source of clean drinking water) are getting depleted, and not enough is being done to publicize and reverse that process.
8. Government rollout of conservation and individual voluntary efforts are not well-publicized to make the necessary restorative progress.
9. We are not fast-tracking promising research on plastic and other pollutants, replacing aging water infrastructure, and replenishing our water supply. These are critical, as many would argue that a plentiful clean water supply is our most precious yet depleting natural resource.

Key Issues and Solution Frameworks

1. The US and the world's waters (and land) are significantly polluted by the 9,000 varieties of PFAS (also called "forever chemicals." **One estimate says 200 million Americans drink water contaminated with PFAS, and almost all have PFAS in their blood.**

This contamination from PFAS chemicals is very serious since they contaminate the environment and the human body and can last for decades. This affects our clean water supply and the sea life within the waters. Clean water is our most precious natural resource.

PFAS chemicals are everywhere: in fire-fighting foams, water-resistant clothing, paint, cosmetics, photography, pesticides, microwave popcorn bags, stain-resistant products, fast food packaging, non-stick cookware, and personal care products. They have been linked to kidney and testicular cancer, thyroid disease, and immune problems.

Testing in many states reflects the presence of these toxic substances. In South Carolina, three years of testing of several bodies of water showed two-thirds contained these chemicals, even though those PFASs tested for have been banned since 2016. Sludge fields close to rivers and streams had levels above the federal limit. Many wells and surface water intake pipes were within a few miles of the sludge sites. Strangely, 80,000 South Carolina agricultural acres are approved for using sludge to irrigate and fertilize crops that wind up on the dinner table.

There are over 700 US military bases, and in a 2023 report, the Department of Defense has so far confirmed PFAS contamination at 455 of those bases. That document also reported a further study of 295 of that group and that 275 of those, or about 90%, had released those toxins "in the proximity" of drinking water supplies for neighboring communities.

The EPA guidelines state that less than 1 part per trillion (ppt) in drinking water is safe and is considering changing its legal maximum limit to 4 ppt. Some levels have been found by the testing to exceed 2.25 million ppt. Currently, the military provides surrounding communities with clean drinking water that exceeds 70 ppt. This is shameful, and we need to be more concerned about our base neighbors' health, get alternatives for PFAS, and create decontamination processes.

All "forever chemicals" should be banned within three years, except where there is a critical need and no other technology is currently available. We should work hard to get PFAS substitutes for those vital needs. Manufacturers must be required to prominently label their products as PFAS-free or that they have a temporary exemption for use in their products. There should be excellent collection and safe disposal efforts for discarded products that contain them, along with accelerated research to de-toxify PFAS in the environment.

2. The US and much of the world's waters (and land) are significantly polluted by pharmaceuticals and personal care products (PPCP).

A 2022 University of York study found that wastewater treatments cannot completely eliminate the presence of drugs. Especially harmful are substances for epilepsy, diabetes, caffeine, nicotine, pain, contraception, and antibiotics. These are not only the result of improper disposal but also the residual parts that are not absorbed by the human body but passed out. The testing included 1,000 sites from 258 rivers and more than 100 countries. More than 25% of the tests had active pharmaceutical ingredients considered "unsafe for aquatic organisms." This affects the development and reproduction of fish and increases the potential for developing antibiotic-resistant bacteria.

"Treatment Trends and Combined Methods in Removing Pharmaceuticals and Personal Care Products from Wastewater—A Review" was published in the *National Library of Medicine* on January 27, 2023. [1] It said that PPCPs become microorganic contaminants and are among the largest groups of emerging pollutants.

"Human, animal, and aquatic organisms' exposures to PPCPs have linked them to... carcinogenic, mutagenic, and reproductive toxicity risks." "Contemporary wastewater treatment plants do not effectively remove PPCPs," They can end up in landfills or stormwater and seep into groundwater. They can also be inadequately processed at wastewater facilities to produce fertilizers and irrigation, which plants take up and are consumed by animals and humans. This article identifies many scientific processes to remove these PPCPs.[1]

Our infrastructure spending should allocate significant sums to these processes to make them cost-effective and operational for wastewater processing and treatment of water areas and landfills. That will result in healthier humans and animals and clean water for everyone and the environment.

3. Our efforts for recycling and reclaiming plastic are not worthy of our country and should be improved. **The average person in the US creates about 220 lbs. of plastic waste annually—globally, that is 380 million tons annually, and only 5–9% of all plastic is recycled. Much of this degrades and becomes microplastics that impact our landfills, bodies of water, and their sea life (and the humans that consume those organisms).**

Microplastics comprise different plastics, including PVC, PET, and polystyrene. They have been found in many foods we consume, like fish, shellfish, and water.

According to Statista, annual plastic disposal in the US is about 40 million tons, with 85% going to landfills that can often leach into our waters. We should monitor bodies of water for microplastic levels and publish the results. We could trap more microplastics with better filters in wash machines and factory storm sewers and push industry away from unrecyclable plastic.

A 2023 study by the University of Toronto concluded 10 years of testing the Great Lakes waters. 90% of the samples had a level of microplastics (less than 0.2" long) unsafe for wildlife. That is likely caused by the estimated 22 million pounds of plastic debris entering the Great Lakes annually. This contamination significantly affects our health because 90% of the US freshwater comes from the Great Lakes. High levels of this contamination were present in the fish living in and the products made using the Great Lakes waters.

The University of Barcelona found artificial grass accounts for 15% of larger plastics found in samples within a half mile of the shoreline between 2014 and 2021. This did not focus on microplastics, as their sources are more challenging to determine. The polyethylene in artificial grass lasts 10–20 years and is hard to reuse or recycle; it breaks down into smaller pieces of plastic, harming the soil, the waters, and the sea life injured by it or consuming it, thinking it is prey.

In 2023, the Environmental & Science Technology Journal reported a pilot study of 15 patients undergoing cardiac surgeries. They used electron microscopes and infrared images. They found 9 types of microplastics and up to thousands of these plastic pieces in tissues from most areas of their hearts. This study and a few others show the presence of microplastic not only in externally exposed body areas like the skin but also in internal organs.

There are many pieces of low-hanging fruit to improve the situation. Things like plastic straws and bags, unrecyclable takeout food containers, and plastic-lined paper hot and cold cups are already being replaced by some businesses and need to be universally done. "Baggie-type" items are now available in a biodegradable form. Universal adoption should be accelerated ASAP.

Another low-hanging fruit is the six-pack rings. Some grocers and others are accepting these for separate recycling since they tend to contaminate other recyclables if mixed with them. This should be more uniformly adopted. Some breweries have six-pack rings that are compostable and edible by sea life. This should be reviewed carefully for universal adoption. Of course, it would be best if those rings never made it to our waterways, but changing the materials is much easier than changing human behavior.

Wherever possible, all sewer and other runoffs that go into bodies of water should be more universally tested and treated for the presence of microplastics, PFAS, PPCP, and other known toxins than is being done. We deserve to know how polluted our waters have become and redirect spending to fix them ASAP.

4. Water sold in plastic bottles is a serious problem. Many are not easily recyclable into useful products, and the volume is too large. Some developed countries promote reusable water bottles, but that market is only $9 billion compared to the single-use plastic water bottle market of $283 billion in 2021.

   While the bottled water market and its lobby are enormous, and we love convenience, we must do what we can to shift that market into reusables. Marketing and innovation are needed. For example, MIT recently invented a briefcase-size purification system to turn seawater into drinking water. This could reduce the need to supply bottled water to undeveloped and developing countries. We also need to provide them with scalable, clean drinking water systems to end the need for much of their plastic bottled water and with gauges so they can make sure not to lower and deplete their water table.

   Another step being considered in the US is to end the sale of single-use plastic items in our national parks. That would include plastic bottled water and other beverages, plastic bags and cutlery, plastic-lined paper cups, and non-recyclable food containers. It would be a small convenience behavior change that could have a not-so-small impact. That could set the standard for the rest of the country with a small convenience sacrifice that can go a long way.

5. Our efforts for recycling, reclaiming, and safe disposal of toxic items should be significantly improved. This is particularly an issue for landfills where much of this ends up and may leach further into water areas. This pollution is caused by waste disposal by individuals, businesses, and industries.

   An October 2, 2023 article was in the *USA Today Network* by Keith Matheny, "It's a toxic dump: Michigan has become dumping ground for US's most dangerous chemicals." This is important because landfill seepage of dangerous elements can contaminate groundwater. More disturbing information in that article merits reading in total rather than a summary, but the title tells you what to expect. The report provides a good insight into the results of not significantly treating and removing contaminants, many of which have toxic impacts on the environment and everything and everyone in that area.

Michigan is cozying up and enriching China with a $700 million inducement to build a battery plant. Why not have those federal funds repurposed to create a state-of-the-art remediation operation for most or all contaminants in their landfills? The simple answer is that it is not as sexy as a battery plant for EVs, which is part of the left's religion. It is difficult to do hard science compared to the ease of building a clone of existing battery plants. People's health and very lives are willingly traded away for a woke agenda.

In addition to Michigan, we should examine other landfills and dumping grounds to discover processes that reduce the volumes and provide some remediation of those sites where possible. While landfills are problematic due to their toxic and poorly biodegradable items, their issues magnify when they migrate to waters and add to the problems there.

Abandoned telephone cables have been contaminating our soil and waterways for decades, and little has been done about it. That is covered in the Wall Street Journal article of July 9, 2023, "America is Wrapped in Miles of Toxic Lead Cables." [2] We know about lead poisoning and its terrible effects and have eliminated lead paint, but not this obvious danger. **A sample from Lake Tahoe showed 2,533 times the EPA limit for drinking water. The company responsible for leaving 8 miles of degrading phone cables that affected the lake settled a lawsuit against them, but the cables may still be there.**

The fracking industry has improved our energy independence, but at a significant cost to the environment and the health of many. According to the American Geosciences Institute, **the water needed to frack a well is between 1.5 million gallons and 16 million gallons.** The process creates a strategic energy resource by consuming an even more strategic water resource.

Toxic benzene and several other chemicals are injected with water and large amounts of sand to fracture rocks, allowing

trapped oil and natural gas to be released for capture while also releasing trapped radioactive radium. Efforts to safely reuse or decontaminate the billions of gallons of wastewater produced annually are not highly successful. **The resulting salts often make the ground toxic to plant life.** A higher incidence of earthquakes and soil subsistence occurs near the wells.

A study done in Texas covering the last ten years found 150 million gallons of toxic wastewater from oil and gas operations was spilled state-wide, contaminating soils and waters. Related research has been done in Pennsylvania. An EPA and NIH study found that Pennsylvania children living near fracking facilities were two to three times more likely to be diagnosed with leukemia at ages 2 to 7 than those not living near oil and gas operations.

An article written by Julia Mehalko was published in Savvy Dime on March 8, 2024, "Abandoned Water and Oil Wells Are Exploding in Texas, Destroying Land Owners' Properties." [3] A 2021 Interstate Oil and Gas Compact Commission report states, "About 310,000 to 800,000 undocumented wells may be around the country." [4] Some of these wells were dug nearly 100 years ago, and record-keeping was not very good. When pressure causes these wells to explode, they spew out high-salt content water, killing the soil. One theory is that this could result from fracking pressure, causing water to move through underground channels. Another theory is this is actually some of the fracking water that was used.

Steel processing has its own toxic waste production issues. The Pittsburgh Water Collaboratory issued a report (over four consecutive seasons) based on samples from 25 tributaries and sewage areas that feed into the Ohio, Allegheny, and Monongahela rivers. A high cadmium concentration was present in fish caught and eaten from those waters. Cadmium is a by-product of coke production used to make steel. In high doses, this can cause kidney, liver, and heart disease. The testing also showed the presence of pet waste, raw sewage, and high levels of phosphorus and nitrogen (common components of fertilizers).

Almost daily, you can read stories (not generally covered by TV media) about other ground and water contamination that threatens our health and abundant supply of clean water. Just one example is the pollution of well water (especially in Minnesota and Wisconsin) primarily due to nitrates from runoff of commercial fertilizer and manure used by large agricultural farms. This kind of adulteration also comes from slaughterhouses and meat processing plants. It is estimated that animal sewage is twice the amount humans produce in the US. Gastrointestinal problems and cancers have been attributed to nitrate contamination.

We must prioritize being good corporate citizens with effective programs to stop polluting the environment and damaging the genetics of the wildlife and people near the pollution. This is more impactful than the merit badges pursued for DEI, ESG, and CRT.

Proper disposal of toxic items and recycling and reclaiming programs must be prioritized for better results. Unneeded paint, toxic plastics, and outdated or no longer needed medications should be more universally available for easy collection and safe disposal. All electronic waste should be reclaimed for the value of its metals and the reduction of the volumes in our landfills.

Lastly, there should be pressure on all countries to sign agreements not to transport their trash to other nations. Those countries receiving trash are often impoverished and will create more global land, air, and water pollution due to insufficient processing. When all countries are forced to deal with their trash within their country, they will find ways to do a better job, and the US should be the leader.

6. Reservoirs (lakes, rivers, streams, and other visible retention) are seriously declining.

    Ian James wrote about an important example of this in the *LA Times* on February 18, 2023, titled "As the Colorado River shrinks, federal officials consider overhauling Glen Canyon Dam." [5] The drying up of the Colorado River has resulted in Lake Powell (our 2nd largest reservoir) being at the lowest levels since the 1960s at 23% capacity.

The last time it was considered "full" at 100% was 50 years ago in 1983. It is 320 miles upstream of Lake Mead (our largest reservoir). Less water is flowing into the Grand Canyon and debasing Lake Mead towards becoming incapable of passing water to Hoover Dam and downstream to several states. One drastic solution is decommissioning Glen Canyon Dam and draining Lake Powell into Lake Mead. **Our largest 2 water reservoirs are in jeopardy.** How many of us knew about this?

Duncan Phenix published an update in *News Nation* on April 25, 2023. The melting of the significant winter snow season has produced a rise in Lake Mead and Lake Powell levels from 23% to 26% full—still too close to dangerous levels. [6] Lake Mead rose 20 feet in 2023 but is still 160 feet below its full recovery level. One good year does not fix the problem. There are 7 states and Mexico that share this water supply. Curiously, Mexico is required by agreements to supply water to the US and is withholding it, depriving our agriculture of much-needed water. We need to respond appropriately.

One of those states is Colorado, which has plans to turn off the water to 25,000 farmland acres before 2030. If that is insufficient, then another 500,000 acres of well-water land may be the next target.

The Department of Interior withdrew its "request" to reduce water demands by 25% from those served after Biden threw money (the most favored D-S tactic) to cities, tribes, and water districts to "pledge" to reduce their water usage. Where is the strong leadership to mandate water conservation and provide sound recommendations? Guess they are too busy sacrificing our lives on the altars of environmental extremism (with solar, wind, and EV mandates and rebates) to actually work on real solutions for our depleting water supply. This is a rare case where mandates are needed.

On April 9, 2023, Dan Stillman reported in the Washington Post on the similar plight of the Great Salt Lake. The article was titled "**The Great Salt Lake** seemed like it was dying, but there's been a 'miraculous' shift." [7] **It is at record low levels of 4,189 ft above sea level, with a loss of 70% of its water level since 1850. Even with its record winter snowfall melting, it is still 6 ft below the minimum levels for sound ecological and economic health.** A February 2023 assessment by Utah researchers found that 67–73% of the water level decline "is due to natural and human water use." A BYU ecologist says, "**To replenish the Great Salt Lake, we need to reduce our consumptive water use by 40 to 50%.**" [8]

The El Nino weather pattern helped California's reservoirs. As of September 30, 2023, they are at 128% of the historical average due to intense winter snowstorm melting in Spring–Summer. These are occasional gifts from Mother Nature and cannot be a signal to ease up on increasing the amount of clean water availability. California recognizes that and still has permanent water use reduction requirements for each of the 274 water utilities in the state.

Unfortunately, this key issue is not just a US problem but is being felt globally. Australia experienced its millennium drought in 1996–97; Sao Paolo, Brazil's 2014 reservoirs were at 5%; in January 2018, Cape Town, South Africa had 3 months left of water after 3 years of drought; Catalonia, Spain has had severe drought conditions; Mexico City may run out of water by summer of 2024. In the 1990s, there were 16 water-related military conflicts, and over the past 5 years, there have been 73.

7. Groundwater basins (sub-surface aquifers that are a source of clean drinking water) are getting depleted, and not enough is being done to publicize and reverse that process.

While some of this may be due to changes in our climate, a significant amount is due to excess demand from the increasing population and not robust conservation efforts. In *a Live Science* article by Elizabeth Howell, dated July 8, 2015, titled "Earth's Groundwater Basins Are Running Out of Water,"[9] she captures the size of the problem. **Of the 37 largest aquifers in the world, 21 have exceeded sustainability tipping points and are in depletion, and 13 are in severe decline.**

We are pumping so much from groundwater sources that we are significantly lowering the water table, which removes support for the ground. It sinks and results in a scarred surface full of cracks. This is especially noticeable in Arizona, Utah, and California.

Globally, this impact may have changed the planet's tilt by 1.7" per year from 1993 to 2010 or 28" in total) and contributed to a rise in sea levels. The US Geological Survey estimates more than 1,000 times more water is underground than in all the global lakes and rivers above ground. These often feed those lakes and rivers, and their ability to do that is compromised. The staggering estimates for those 17 years are that we have pumped 2,150 gigatons (1 gigaton=1 billion tons) of groundwater, equal to 5.5 million Empire State Buildings. We need water to survive, and we should not act like drunken sailors, but we must begin to treat this as the indispensable and precious survival commodity that it is.

Per the UN, by 2050, 70% of the global population will live in cities vs. 55% now, creating more stress on underground aquifers due to the ground heating caused by the massive amount of concrete. As droughts and high usage empty aquifers, the structure of the sand and clay in them changes and begins to collapse. Even if they refill, they can never hold the volume they once did. Of course, this also sinks the ground above them. **From 1900 to 1970, California's Central Valley dropped 28 feet. In parts of Jakarta, land is sinking at 10 inches annually. Sinking and cracking ground affects the infrastructure of pipes, bridges, and building foundations, and lower areas become more prone to flooding.**

There is an unfortunate story about the government's well-meaning but disastrous efforts to implement the woke agenda as they practice their climate and environmental religions. It is chronicled by Oliver Wainwright in The Guardian on May 21, 2023, titled "How solar farms took over the California desert: An oasis has become a dead sea." [10]

The Mojave desert has 150,000 acres (10 times the size of Manhattan) called the Riverside East Solar Energy Zone. In this area is an ocean of blue solar panels that stretches for miles in all directions. The facilitation of this project falls to the federal Bureau of Land Management (the other BLM). **They naively treated this as a barren area, overlooking that it is a rich and fragile habitat for endangered species. It hosts thousand-year-old carbon-capturing woodlands, ancient native cultural sites, and hundreds of people's homes.** What are the results of this solar panel mania?

- Two wells are dry, mainly due to the solar plants' water demands.
- Constant noise pollution from pounding supporting metal posts into the ground.
- Frequent dust storms create allergies, skin, and respiratory issues for residents caused by the loss of thousands of acres of cryptobiotic desert crust (a thin layer of bacteria-rich soil) that retains water and nutrients and slows erosion.
- Frequent bird kills when they mistake panels for water and dive into them.
- This massive array blocks endangered species' natural movement.
- They are destroying scraggly-looking small desert shrubs that form a vast underground network (150 ft below the surface) of natural carbon capture. Some of these bushes can live for 10,000 years, and the Mojave yuccas can be up to 2,500 years old. Robin Kobaly (a botanist and author of *The Desert Underground*) says, **"By digging these plants up, we are removing the most efficient carbon sequestration units on the planet and releasing millennia of stored carbon back into the atmosphere."**[10]
- Indigenous sacred sites have been bulldozed or damaged, and heritage experts testified that "17,000 sites within the Southern California Desert Region will potentially be destroyed."

In addition to California, Arizona, Nevada, and New Mexico have done similar projects in what looks to the untrained eye as totally barren land. The projects may involve data center operations, bitcoin mining, or giant solar farms, as the proponents chase green energy merit badges, huge profits, and brag about how many homes are being provided with green energy.

They overlook that the sparse rainfall has much less chance of reaching the ground, and insects, native plants, and animals have their habitats ruined by these projects. The loss of thousands of acres of bacteria-rich soil has also produced considerable cracks in the earth in these states. There are still 120,000 acres available in California to destroy with ugly solar farms and use up precious groundwater. These projects should prove a positive environmental impact or be canceled.

Just like in the movie *Avatar*, it is the government and greedy big businesses that do not care about the people or the environment—just ferociously fulfilling their woke agendas and making lots of money. These enormous mistakes will become "scarlet letter" episodes for Wokeism Gone Wild.

At www.coppercourier.com in December 2023, a report appeared: "Arizona communities sink after Saudi Arabia pumps water out of the state: It's horrific. McMullen Valley had seen some areas sink at least 3 feet since 1991, with a foot of that since 2015, when corporate drilling for groundwater began. [11] In 1957, farmers and corporations had to drill 107 feet in McMullen Valley for water. Now, it is 542 feet, and the well-funded Saudis can pay for that drilling that is depleting water and damaging homes for the soil subsistence.

In a June 6, 2018 article by the US Geological Survey for Water Science School titled "Groundwater Decline and Depletion," [12] it was said that we are depleting our groundwater and lowering the depth needed to reach the underground water table. They gave an example of one county in Oregon where that depth was 160 feet in 1960 and increased to 260 feet in 2005. **Land subsistence (collapse) happens when subsurface water is removed. And the deeper you** go, the greater your chance of encountering salt and not fresh water. Groundwater loss affects flows to streams, lakes, rivers, reservoirs, and wetlands. The depletion rate from 2000–2008 is 2.6 times the rate from 1900–2008.

8. Government rollout of conservation and individual voluntary efforts are not well-publicized to make the necessary restorative progress.

We must better promote and recognize water conservation efforts by individuals, farming, and businesses. We should evaluate having home sales require a diagnostic of the water pipes' integrity, a certification of toilets not leaking, and toilets that meet the standard of 1.3–1.6 gallons per flush (compared to older toilets that use 3.5–7.0 gallons per flush. Toilets account for 27–30% of indoor water usage, so these water savings would be huge.

According to the EPA website, "If all old, inefficient toilets were replaced with WaterSense labeled models, we could save 360 billion gallons of water per year or the amount of water that flows over Niagara Falls in about 9 days." [13] Leaking from toilet flappers wastes 180 gallons per week or about 10,000 gallons yearly. From other news sources, that is equivalent to a slow leak, but a medium leak would be approximately 250 gallons per day or 90,000 gallons per year, and a large leak even more.

We often waste water waiting for the hot water faucet to deliver hot water. We should evaluate where needed, promoting for existing and requiring for some new construction, to have an "instant" hot water recirculating system (with a small pump with an on/off switch at the furthest fixture) to minimize that waste. All hot water pipes that should be insulated could be narrower to 3/8" or 1/2", "and the hot water tank should be placed as close to the kitchen and bathrooms as possible. While these processes consume some energy, enhancing our supply of much scarcer clean water makes it worthwhile.

An excellent resource to check out your personal and household water footprint can be found at www.watercalculator.org. [14] They also provide conservation tips. Here are some interesting water usage and infrastructure stats primarily from the Texas Rural Water Association:

- **Only 1% of the global water supply is drinkable water.**
- **The US is funding only 33% of its water infrastructure needs.**
- 36,000 gallons/yr. used for each landscaping area of 3,000 SF per www.denverwater.org.
- 11,000 gallons/yr. of water loss for the average US home due to pipe leaks.
- 29,000–36,500 gallons/yr. for the average American use of 80–100 gallons daily.
  - 25,550 gallons/yr. for a daily bath (70 gallons to fill an average bathtub).
  - 3,600–9,000 gallons/yr. for a daily 5-minute shower (10–25 gallons per shower).
  - 2,000 gallons/yr for 1 load/week for an average wash machine (41 gallons/load).

Water bills should reward water conservationists. It is OK to have a low billing threshold (like 8,000 or 10,000 gallons/month) for low-volume users. However, anyone below that usage should be rewarded and billed per gallon, not a flat minimum that has them subsidizing others who use more water but still fall within that low bill threshold.

Reducing demand through achievable conservation efforts can significantly begin to refill groundwater basins to meet current and future water demands. We must ensure our infrastructure spending allocates sufficient funds to aging water systems and leaks rather than the lust for problematic electric vehicles and other ways to destroy fossil fuels without good alternatives. We need to take steps to fix problems rather than creating climate change hysteria and fear. But where is the push to do this? Guess it is better to scare everyone into being docile lemmings who give in to the fear being preached.

9. We are not fast-tracking replacing or repairing aging water infrastructure, increasing our water supply, and promising research on plastic and other pollutants. These are critical, as many would argue that a plentiful clean water supply is our most precious yet depleting natural resource.

Water Infrastructure Renewal

In Spain, at least 25% of water is wasted due to aging and poor infrastructure; in Montevideo, Uruguay, the water network losses are even higher at 50%.

Much of the water infrastructure in the US may be 100 or more years old. Jackson, Mississippi residents have lived through many water pipe leak problems and have often been told to boil water because tap water was unsafe to drink. There are two water plants: one built in 1980 and one in 1910. A significant leak began in 2016 under a golf course. The leak produced a geyser that wasted 5 million gallons daily (enough to supply the water needs of 50,000 people daily). The leak continued until 2022, when the Justice Department ordered the city to bring in an outside manager to run the water department properly. That leak has been fixed, but others keep popping up.

It is understandable that replacing aged infrastructure that has lost effectiveness is not as "sexy" and woke as getting drivers into EVs or building monstrous solar farms and wind infrastructure, but those are not critical. Protecting our water supply is critical, but unfortunately, no woke campaign donors can be repaid for this spending. We need uncorrupt politicians to address this.

Increasing Our Water Supply

The UN claims **water consumption has been double the population growth of the last century. One thing that is being done (and should be responsibly expanded) is the practice of commercial** greenhouse production. **Some of them are vertical, and all use less water, fertilizer, and generally no pesticides.** They are well suited for arid or salt-contaminated dead ground and can better control runoff. The Netherlands, which is only the size of Maryland, has led the way with greenhouse farming and globally is 2nd behind the US in agricultural exports.

This concept is being scaled up in the arid, oil-rich Middle East. This was covered by Rebecca Cairns on CNN on March 13, 2024, in a story: "This 'GigaFarm' in the desert of Dubai could produce 3 million kilograms of food." [15] Dubai is complementing its existing 1 million kilogram vertical farming operation with this even larger facility. They produce leafy greens, herbs, and vegetable seedlings for Dubai's smaller farms. The recycling of food waste and sewage into compost, animal feed, clean water, and energy is the secret sauce that makes this a financial homerun.

Hydroponics allows plant growth using LED light and compost instead of soil. Sensors monitor operations and manage light, temperature, humidity, water, and nutrient levels. Crop growth is faster, less land is used, the operation is unaffected by growing seasons and weather, and water usage can be reduced by up to 98%. The clean water produced is enough to run the vertical farm, and the fertilizer created is a natural replacement or reduction of chemical fertilizers. An interesting byproduct of the waste treatment is ammonia. In the energy section of this chapter, ammonia is identified as a good source for creating hydrogen power.

The UN also states that **80% of water usage is for agriculture and livestock, so efforts to make that more efficient will have a significant positive impact.** Commercial greenhouses are one efficiency. Another is meat curated from animal cells. That currently has limited but expanding US availability and is being improved to make the experience like the meat we are used to. If done right, the water savings are significant. Estimates are that traditional cattle raising takes 1,500–1,900 gallons of water to produce one lb. of beef.

Eric Ralls wrote a story that appeared in *Earth* on June 15, 2023, titled "New hydrogel can extract unlimited amounts of water from the air, even in deserts."[16] MIT improved the absorbability of hydrogels that are used in disposable diapers. They tweaked the hydrogels with lithium chloride to absorb 24 times their weight in water. This can be a game changer when operationalized to capture water from the air. Combined with better water usage management, this can help refill our above-ground waters and the below-ground aquifers that feed them. It can even be effective in deserts, and we can work to recycle hydrogel and lithium chloride for optimal efficiency.

Another discovery comes from a study by the Federal Institute of Technology in Zurich, Switzerland (ETH) and was published in *Nature Sustainability*. They used a metal mesh coated with polymers and titanium dioxide to purify atmospheric water in fog.

The Pacific Institute issued a report on February 29, 2024, citing **the amount of stormwater that goes uncaptured across the country is roughly equal to 53 billion gallons per day. On an annual basis, that 19.3 trillion gallons of precious water lacks a coordinated strategic focus for capture, treatment, storage, and use.** Systems should be designed to capture and clean most of this. What cannot be stored and reused should be discharged cleanly into waterways or ground areas (but not the ocean) that can handle it.

If the US and the rest of the world focused on capturing this stormwater, treating it, and releasing it other than into the ocean, there would be a significant global increase in clean water availability. That would also begin to reverse the rising sea levels that threaten so many humans, wildlife, and plants near the coastlines. Instead of the required burdens of DEI, ESG, and CRT, we should require state and local governments to have sound programs for a clean and abundant water supply. Why are we not supercharging those efforts with big dollars from infrastructure spending?

Promising Solutions to Water Pollution

Plastics were never created with the idea of recycling them when they were initially designed. There are ten noteworthy new technologies to replace or eliminate many plastics from staying I our environment and one natural CO_2 removal process.

One discovery is from Solutum, a company that has created a plastic-like material from environmentally friendly materials that biodegrades readily with water. The 2nd operation is a bacteria named C. testosterone that has an affinity to naturally "eat" plastic and can even create new plastic material to reduce the need for oil to manufacture new plastic. That bacteria is readily available in soils and sewage sludge. Thirdly, scientists are investigating adding hydrogen to plastics to break them down into recyclable components.

A fourth discovery is from a consortium involving UC Berkeley Labs, the DOE, and the Joint BioEnergy Institute that has created **a new plastic abbreviated as PDK, which can be recycled infinitely without losing quality.** Their first focus is on car parts and electronics and scaling those operations. They then plan to turn their attention to single-use plastics that litter our landfills and waterways.

A 5th discovery at Virginia Tech College of Agriculture and Life Sciences was awarded a $2.4 million grant from the USDA. They have successfully demonstrated transforming food waste into biodegradable plastic that can be molded for many uses. US annual food waste is estimated at 19 billion pounds, winding up at landfills with some seepage into waterways.

The 6th development comes from the University of British Columbia. Their test of combining sawdust with plant compounds called tannins removed 95.2%–99.9% of microplastics in a water column.

Princeton Engineering reported a seventh discovery in March 2023. **It is a material that can remove 98%–99% of microplastics in testing. Our oceans are estimated to have 24 trillion pieces of these microplastics, which find their way into our food and** fresh water supply. Their discovery is the protein in egg whites. As research continues to move from testing to a scaled-up operation, what a dramatic impact that can be if we prioritize it.

The 8th development was reported by researchers at Rice University in October 2023. **They have developed a 4-second high-heat process to produce clean hydrogen from plastic disposed of without the need to wash or sort. It also produces (without any CO_2 emissions) another valuable byproduct, graphene.** Graphene is used in electronics, energy, healthcare, and the food and transportation industries. That byproduct more than covers the cost of production.

A ninth process from North Dakota State University can remove 27–57% of salt pollution from soil using the same Prussian Blue material that conservationists use to eliminate salt from historic sites.

The 10th development comes from a Stanford research team to eliminate toxic heavy metals from ground contamination. They use the same EDTA compound that is used to treat lead or mercury poisoning in people. So far, it has worked on lead, cadmium, and copper, and hopefully, it can also work with other heavy metals like mercury.

These are all examples of our scientific curiosity used to solve big problems, with the likelihood that a few of them will have significant positive impacts. More promising discoveries will continue to pop up. Meanwhile, as we should be financially supercharging these innovation efforts, let's go after the existing low-hanging fruit noted earlier.

Lastly, kelp farms have flourished in cooler coastal waters around Korea and Japan for centuries. California has found that wild kelp forests can shelter more than 800 marine life species and improve biodiversity. Kelp, seaweed, and other algae are high in minerals and fiber, suitable for cosmetic use and vitamins, and food for humans, farmed fish, and livestock. Kelp reduces the acidity of the oceans and absorbs CO_2, nitrogen, and phosphorus to produce its beneficial substances. It can potentially remove billions of metric tons of CO_2 from the air.

Many good things are happening with organizations addressing the proliferation of plastic in the environment. Here are just a few.

- On www.oceanconservancy.org, in January 2022, the U.S. Plastics Pact's List of Problematic Items to be Eliminated identifies a comprehensive list and 2025 goals. [17]
- The Intergovernmental Negotiating Committee for Plastics has been meeting semi-annually and plans to have a global treaty draft by the end of 2024.
- www.endplasticwaste.org focuses on recycling, processing, and collecting plastics.[18]
- There are many other dedicated efforts to identify, quantify, and propose solutions to the proliferation of plastics in the environment, especially in oceans and other waterways. One good example is www.pewtrusts.org with their project "Preventing Ocean Plastics" and their report "Breaking the Plastic Wave." [19]

There are many innovative and common-sense things we should be doing robustly to reduce the strain on our waters, restore them to prior levels, and remove much of their contamination for our benefit and that of the sea life and wildlife they impact. They will only be done by a DC government that uses a Solutionist approach to prioritize our problems and holds itself accountable with solution frameworks and reporting on the success of metrics that track the progress. These have not been the protocols of the current or most other administrations.

Best Clean and Abundant Water Ideas

After reviewing the preceding info, the following seem to be the best ideas to address the inadequate supply and contamination of waters sometimes caused by nearby landfills or other contaminated land. More scholarly scientific input might adjust these. Funding from the polluters should be combined with the $26 billion of pork barrel/earmark spending that should no longer be allowed in order to achieve an abundant clean water supply.

This water and pollution focus should be a separate significant budget priority that Congress funds and sets priorities and goals for in collaboration with the agencies involved. Some may not want to embrace all of these solutions, but doing what we have been doing only continues our path to clean water scarcity and drastic measures.

a. Refilling our water supply in reservoirs and groundwater basins. Create funded national and local plans to capture, clean, and store 19.3 trillion gallons of annual stormwater. Create annual funded water infrastructure budgets that prioritize repairs and replacements. Create incentives to grow, where possible, more vertical hydroponic farms that can reduce water consumption by up to 98%. Instead of shutting down small farms by depriving them of water (like in Oregon), we should fund them to shift to vertical farming. The D-S may be targeting smaller farms because they are not likely voters for them, and the campaign donations from large farms or associations are more welcome and they are easier to control.

Great examples in the Netherlands and Dubai should be copied. Besides the water reduction, they use little or no fertilizer or pesticides and process sewage and food waste (19 billion lbs. annually in the US) to produce compost, animal feed, clean water, energy, and ammonia to process for hydrogen. Because agriculture and livestock account for 80% of water usage, we should promote the expansion of meat curated from animal cells. Tradition cattle raising uses at least 1,500 gallons of water to yield one lb. of beef.

After revisiting our energy strategy, consider stopping new land-based solar and land and water-based wind projects and repurposing some existing giant solar farms to reverse the environmental damage, including the serious water impact. Create and publicize campaigns for mandatory and recommended water conservation programs. Create reasonable depth limits for well water drilling until the water tables are restored. Create models to show how new technologies for capturing water from the air can be done without adversely affecting needed rainfall. Within the US and globally, expand the use of personal seawater purifiers and scalable groundwater systems with depth gauges that produce clean water without exhausting the water table. That can drastically cut the need for plastic water bottles.

b. Replacement of non-biodegradable plastic food containers and utensils. Since some businesses already have these in a biodegradable form, it seems these could become universal—straws and bags, takeout food containers and utensils, hot and cold beverage cups, baggies, and six-pack rings.

c. Store-bought items that contain toxins like paint, non-recyclable plastic, medications, electronics, or products with PFAS. Let's copy successful programs of some communities to make the collection easy and the processing and recycling or safe disposal effective.

d. Testing and reporting on the amount of contaminants in lakes and rivers, treated wastewater, and stored stormwater. The focus should be on microplastics, PFAS, PPCPs, and other toxins.

e. Plastic pollution. Supercharge the optimization of the Rice University 4-second high-heat process to recycle plastic (without the need to wash or sort) into clean hydrogen without CO_2 that makes valuable graphene as a byproduct. Accelerate the focus of the infinitely recyclable PDK plastic into single-use plastic beverage containers. Identify and publicize the uses of biodegradable plastic, and prominently identify all plastic containers as recyclable or not.

f. Water used for fracking. We should require a plan for decontamination (including the radium) and reuse of the thousands of gallons used for each frack with no contamination to nearby ground and water, exploding wells from pressure or subsurface damage or surface cracking due to soil subsistence.

g. 300,000–800,000 abandoned and undocumented wells. Some of these are exploding and fouling the soil. We need a government strategy to prevent this from happening.
h. Ocean acidity and algae. Expand kelp farms wherever possible to reduce acidity and absorb CO_2 and the nitrogen and phosphorus from fertilizing to produce beneficial compounds and products. Focus US and global efforts to collect and recycle what is feasible from the trash in the oceans and use the remedies available (especially for microplastics) to further detoxify the oceans.
i. Treat polluted waters and remediate landfills and contaminated soil. Heavy metal extraction for recycling (including lead and cadmium from steel processing and batteries) can be done using EDTA (which is used with poisoning victims to remove their lead or mercury toxins). Salt ground pollution has been surfaced and collected with a 27–57% effective rate using Prussian Blue, which conservationists have used to cleanse historic sites from salt.

    Complete the research and scale up microplastic elimination using sawdust and tannins or the protein found in egg whites. We have processes to remove PPCPs and should be optimizing them. We need to develop methods for removing other toxins. We must create a state-of-the-art landfill remediation and recycling operation with Michigan as the likely 1st site so that it can relinquish its title of "the dumping ground for US's most dangerous chemicals."
j. We need to offer a significant "prize" and share in the royalties for removing PFAS contamination. We need to develop a label that says that products are PFAS-free or have a temporary exemption for 3 years. It seems they are particularly useful in semiconductors, and with a robust recycling program, applications like that could continue.

Energy

Key Issues

1. We have rushed into battery electric vehicles (BEVs) without the necessary infrastructure or innovatively thinking about better HFC technology that is just around the corner.
2. Our current energy policy is detrimental to our national security, the economy, and the well-being of US citizens. It focuses almost exclusively on undependable solar and wind and dismembers oil, natural gas, and clean coal.
3. Pipelines are environmentally a safer method of transporting oil but are being sacrificed on the altar of climate change.
4. Some budding energy alternatives exist, but like all new discoveries, they must overcome a few hurdles to become operationally efficient.

Key Issues and Solution Frameworks

1. We have rushed into battery electric vehicles (BEVs) without the necessary infrastructure or innovatively thinking about better HFC technology that is just around the corner.

Benefits of an Alternative Hydrogen Fuel Cell Vehicle

Most of the following analysis of the benefits and comparisons of hydrogen fuel cells (HFC) to other energy sources like battery electric vehicles (BEVs) are from the website www.twi-global.com. Their article is titled "What are the Pros and Cons of Hydrogen Fuel Cells?" [20]

   a. **Renewable/readily available** hydrogen is the most abundant element in the universe.

b. The **byproduct of burning green hydrogen is water**—it has zero carbon footprint. This is superior to BEVs that require strip mining for the metals used in the heavy batteries, often using child labor, and contaminating soils and water to secure the minerals mined to enrich China, which controls those markets. NASA is working on using hydrogen fuel and capturing the water it releases for astronauts to drink.
c. **No expensive catalytic converter** to dampen performance or get stolen, since there are zero greenhouse gas emissions. It's the same for BEVs.
d. **More powerful and energy efficient** that is 3X better than a gas-powered car. Highly efficient compared to other energy sources, requiring much less fuel. BEVs experience a reduction in power as the battery discharges while driving.
e. **Fast charging times for HFC vehicles are under 5 minutes,** compared to BEVs of 30 minutes for direct current level 3 chargers or 8–10 hours overnight for a level 2 home charger. Many public BEV charging stations are level 2, so you just want to get enough to get home. Level 1 home charging can take 4 days for long-range EVs to go from empty to full. Times are also affected negatively for BEVs with hot or cold weather.
f. **No noise pollution** (just like BEVs) for vehicles and commercial applications compared to the noise created by wind power.
g. **No visual pollution** since HFC production has much less space requirements than wind, solar farms, and biofuel plants, which can be eyesores.
h. **Better durability, less impacted by weather and usage times**—BEVs are affected by outside temperatures and significantly deteriorate in cold weather. HFCs and gasoline cars go the same distances but with a smaller tank and minimal impact by temperatures.
i. **Better for use in remote areas** that may have less fuel availability.

j. **Versatility of more uses** because hydrogen could be used for large-scale heating systems and other applications besides vehicles.
k. **No impact from power outages,** as a station can operate with a cheap generator.
l. **Democratization of power supply**—nations will not depend on importing, discovering, and processing fossil fuels.

Other Information About a Hydrogen Fuel Cell Vehicle

a. It has a smaller supplemental battery for when an extra power surge is needed.
b. Major car makers Toyota, Hyundai, and Honda have produced HFC vehicles. In the next few years, they will be joined by BMW, Kia, Jaguar, Rolls-Royce, and Land Rover, along with more models from Honda, Toyota, and Hyundai.
c. **The Toyota Mirai set a Guinness world record by traveling 845 miles in August 2021 on one tank of hydrogen, averaging 152 mpg.**
d. 40-ton HFC trucks are better suited for long-haul transport and temperature variability than electric vehicles. While Nikola Motor Company still has challenges with this, Toyota has partnered with PACCAR to make Kenworth and Peterbilt trucks available with this tech.
e. The EU is serious about hydrogen and requires a hydrogen fueling station every 93 miles along its transportation network.
f. Ryan Callahan wrote an article published in Topped in February 2024: "10 Things to Know About Toyota's Hydrogen Fuel Cell Technology." [21] The whole article is worthwhile, but here are a few of the more interesting facts:
    o NASA has used fuel cell tech to power spacecraft since the 1960s.

- o Toyota's HFC research began in 1992, resulting in the Mirai in 2014 and a 2nd generation Mirai in 2020. They recirculate the water produced to provide the necessary amount needed for its patented tech.
- o Toyota's hydrogen generators have lit up the Eiffel Tower and powered its Energy Observer boat, the first hydrogen ship to circle the globe. They have also developed a prototype for a hydrogen-powered train for the EU.
- o Toyota partnered with FuelCell Energy to create the tech for its Tri-Gen plant at the Long Beach, CA port. It produces 1,400 gallons of clean water and 1,200 gallons of liquid hydrogen daily for electricity needs. The port's annual carbon footprint should be reduced by 9,000 tons of CO_2.
- o Fuel tanks and refueling stations have safety and sensors built into them, and existing gas station infrastructure can be retrofitted instead of creating a new infrastructure like for BEVs. Hydrogen cannot readily catch fire from pooling on the ground like diesel or gasoline.
- o HFC tech provides longer driving ranges, simple refueling, and zero emissions.

g. GM and Honda have partnered for HFC tech, and their operation in Brownstown, Michigan, produces hydrogen fuel cells in a state-of-the-art processing facility.

h. Hydrogen is more flammable than gasoline, but safety measures have been built into the construction of HFC vehicles, and they have had an excellent safety record.

i. There are three issues for hydrogen to knock off BEVs. (In the solution frameworks for key issue 4 near the end of this chapter, some discoveries that can solve the first two of these issues are identified.)

- o Hydrogen production costs are high and need to be done in a greener way than by using fossil fuels.

- Transportation costs and safety from production to fueling stations.
- Availability of fueling stations. In Japan, Toyota has successfully modeled retrofitting existing gas stations, so we have a roadmap available to us.

Other Information About BEVs

a. In 2020, charging an electric vehicle was much more expensive than a gasoline one. The Biden administration has intentionally depleted our Strategic Petroleum Reserve and impeded investment in US drilling (while groveling for dirtier Venezuelan oil). This resulted in gasoline costs rising from a low in 2020 of $1.74/gallon to a doubling to $3.42/gallon in February 2023. That interventionist fervor has artificially made it cheaper in some areas to charge an expensive electric car with all of its battery issues, including the lack of a reliable national power grid to support it.
b. **Replacing an EV battery can cost $5,000--$20,000.**
c. Pricey BEVs will become more expensive as fossil fuels (used to mine the minerals needed for BEV batteries) are depleted, less available, and more costly.
d. 5% of BEV batteries are recycled, and their toxic elements can wind up in landfills.
e. **Building an EV emits 70% more greenhouse gases than an internal combustion engine (ICE) vehicle and consumes 6 times more minerals in the build process.**
f. Electric vehicles are 15–30% heavier than ICE cars, so the tires wear out 20 to 40% quicker and produce more particulate emissions. Michael Buschbacker, who worked in the Justice Department's Environment Division in 2020–21, said, "Today's cars are so clean that almost all of the particulate matter (emissions) comes from tire wear." [22] A study by Emission Analytics showed tire wear emissions into the air are 1,850 times more

for BEVs than tailpipe emissions of gasoline cars. That seems to imply that driving a BEV might make the air dirtier.

g. **Outside temperature is a key factor for BEVs.** For optimal efficiency, you must charge that battery at temperatures between 60 and 70 degrees. Charging in frigid weather takes twice as long, and the driving range is cut by 41%; and continued exposure to very cold weather can permanently degrade the battery. Hot weather and AC usage cut the driving range by 17%. Similarly, charging in hot weather can also permanently degrade the battery. **The optimal operating range for EVs is between 32 and 80 degrees, but how many drivers live in such a place?** The brutal winter of January 2024 showed this negative impact for BEV owners.

h. The best state of charge for an EV battery is between 30%–80%, and 100% should be avoided unless the car is driven immediately afterward.

i. There may be a shortage of trained BEV technicians, causing longer times to diagnose and repair a BEV.

j. Estimates of EV market share are about 1% of the 250 million cars registered in the US. In 2023, their share of new car sales in the US was 6%.

k. According to a study published in *Nature* covering 2012 to 2019, **20% of plug-in hybrid drivers and 18% of full EV drivers returned to gas-powered cars** for their next purchase. [23] The most recent **Consumer Reports annual car reliability survey of 330,000 car owners reflected that BEVs are less reliable than gas or hybrids, with 79% more issues.** And JD Power's EV owners' satisfaction survey scores have dropped.

l. The finicky electric motors interfere with AM radio frequencies, and several car makers are doing away with AM capability in their new models. While buying a streaming service may lessen some of that impact, emergency broadcasts may not get out if internet access is affected by the emergency.

m. The **flammability of the batteries** may have made them more prone to catch fire and get "totaled" at some charging stations. In February 2022, The Felicity Ace, carrying about 4,000 cars (some were EVs), caught fire and sank. While the source of the fire is unknown, lawsuits are in progress, and some vessels have refused to transport EVs.

BEV car fires usually engulf the car, release toxic smoke, and can kill a trapped individual. **Hydrogen fires are more confined, release no toxins from the hydrogen burning, and only raise the inside vehicle temp by 1–2 degrees F,** while the outside temp of the car is about equal to that on a sunny day. **The individuals of a hydrogen car fire are only burned if they come in direct contact with the flame.**

BEV fires can vent toxic gases like hydrogen fluoride and carbon monoxide, and the smoke can contain hydrogen cyanide and chloride. Intense flammability is due to "thermal runaway," which can result from charging too quickly, overcharging, or under freezing or high-temperature conditions, installation damage, or from an earthquake. Recent battery storage fires reported in Florida and New York may have been triggered by power surges or lightning strikes during a storm.

On February 17, 2024, a French **lithium battery warehouse experienced a fire** for 900 tons of lithium batteries collected for shipment to be recycled. It required 70 firefighters to control the blaze. A proposal to build one of the largest battery storage facilities in Europe in Buckinghamshire, England, is being opposed by residents whose homes could be as close as two city blocks away from this sprawling 26-acre parcel.

Firefighters detest putting out EV battery fires. Those require 20,000–40,000 gallons (compared to 500 gallons for ICE cars) to extinguish and can reignite while the vehicle is towed. The "thermal energy" created causes lithium-ion batteries to reach 4,500 degrees Fahrenheit. The hydrogen fluoride and hydrogen dioxide gases produced are toxic and require firefighters to use breathing devices. There are even occasions where they **have melted part of the road they were on.** With a current inventory of 2.4 million BEVs, this is a big deal due to the water wasted, the total destruction of the cars, trapped passengers, and nearby areas, and the toxic gases that impact the firefighters and air pollution. **Imagine if we were 100% BEV cars.**

n. Another battery issue is the **significant weight of the battery.** A Ford F-150 truck is 2,000–3,000 pounds heavier than its non-electric version. **Collisions** involving these "tanks" with gas-powered cars will result in **higher insurance claims and costs** due to more damage (about $1,000 more) and damages for the non-electric cars and occupants.

o. The weight of BEVs can affect older parking structures that may not be able to handle the extra weight. This is a genuine concern in the UK. There is also a negative impact on bridges and roads that must carry the additional weight. Imagine if the woke mob got their way and all vehicles were BEVs. **How much damage and costly repairs would be needed for many parking facilities, bridges, and roads not designed to carry that extra weight?**

p. Adding to the woke dystopia of 100% EVs, **some experts think we don't globally have enough lithium to replace every gas-powered car with a long-range EV and still meet all other needs for lithium.**

q. **The impact on the nation's power grid would be significant** with many more EVs. The grid is abandoning fossil fuel sources in favor of solar and wind, which are unavailable 24/7. Some additional nuclear fission plants may be planned, but that takes many years to become operational and produces toxic waste that could fall into terrorist hands. **Expect more blackouts and higher energy costs, along with regulations restricting home charging use and other home power demands, because 90% of BEV owners have home charging tech that draws from the grid.**

r. **The public charging infrastructure is inadequate** and cannot support the massive army of EVs many are pining for. Some charging facilities are plagued with non-functioning ports (and some have significantly damaged the cars). King Biden is handing out $15 billion to build more stations and ports. These funds wind up in the coffers of 30 private companies, with 3 controlling 2/3 of the EV station and port market. To reach the King's goal of 50% of car sales in 2030 being ones with zero greenhouse gas emissions, there needs to be at least 50,000 new charging ports built each year from 2022 to 2030.

   If all cars in the nightmare of the left were BEVs, to keep the current ratio of BEV public charging stations per vehicle, we would need 200 times more stations than we currently have. That is nonsensical. **Would it not be easier, less costly, and environmentally better to supercharge the hydrogen solutions and then simply retrofit hydrogen pumps into the existing network of gas stations?**

s. **Ford Motor Company lost $1 billion on BEVs in Q2 of 2023 and expected to lose $4.5 billion for all of 2023.** It has lowered its expectations for BEV building and pushed out indefinitely its goal of 2 billion BEVs per year by the end of 2026. It is profitable only because its ICE and commercial vehicles are profitable and offset **the BEV reported losses of $66,000 per sale**. It has to lower prices to move BEVs and loses thousands on each sold. Despite this record and all the issues with BEVs, Biden's DOE salivates at every opportunity to show its woke credentials and gave Ford a $9.2 billion loan to build 3 BEV battery factories.

t. An article by Henry Cesari was published in *MotorBiscuit* on 2-24-24. The title was "Toyota's Leaked 1:6:90 Rule Reveals Why It's Not Wasting Lithium on EVs." [24] It explained the rarity of lithium and the environmental damage caused by its mining. **Toyota told their dealers that the same amount of rare minerals needed for just 1 EV could alternatively be used to build 6** plug-in hybrids or 90 hybrids. They said, "The overall carbon reduction of those 90 hybrids over their lifetime is 37 times as much as a single battery EV."

u. **Roughly 80% of the Highway Trust Fund revenues come from gasoline taxes.** Our politicians, who are bribing consumers to buy BEVs, are starting to see dwindling gas tax revenues. Not to worry, our government is so concerned about running deficits here that they will likely pass a law for a tax based on vehicle miles traveled. That could be monitored with a GPS tracker. Big Brother is alive and well as he continues to invade our lives. **The coming vehicle miles driven tax will quickly consume all those BEV gas tax savings. It will be even higher because of the extra weight of BEVs and their impact on the roads and bridges, which will cause more wear and tear and maintenance costs.**

Changing BEV Battery Tech

Used BEVs have poor resale value due to discounting, rebates, and selling new vehicles at losses and discoveries that change the battery technology. Because of BEV issues, most consumers are not rushing to buy them, and dealer BEV inventory is very high at about a 4-month supply. A sad example of the resale value was provided for a used 2018 Tesla Model 3 selling for $58,000 in December 2022, and 1 year later, the value dropped to about $38,000. Hertz is selling off one-third (20,000) of its BEVs and replacing them with more dependable, less costly to own and maintain ICE vehicles, which most customers prefer.

If these issues with BEVs have not deterred you, consider waiting a few years for the commercialization of these coming battery enhancements. Unfortunately, these still produce big profits for China: the first one from direct car sales and the others from lithium mining.

a. China vehicle maker BYD is creating sodium-ion batteries as an alternative to lithium car batteries for short-run micro vehicles.

While not as efficient, they work better in cold temperatures and can handle more charge/discharge cycles.
b. Tesla's Model 2 should debut in the US in 2025 at a price between $25,000 and $30,000. That will put it within reach of more customers and create an extensive charging and infrastructure mess if it replaces ICE cars with its BEVs. BYD took over the top sales spot globally with 3 million vehicle sales in 2023. They have several models under $30,000. What will happen to Tesla if BYD is allowed to sell into the US without significant tariffs?
c. Swedish battery maker Northvolt is a leader in battery research. They developed an EV battery using sustainably raised and harvested wood to replace graphite in their batteries' anodes, but they still need lithium.
d. A ONE Gemini battery ran a Tesla Model S 752 miles before needing a recharge and uses fewer rare earth minerals. It is considered by some to be a "semi-solid state battery." It uses iron and manganese, which are more abundant to lessen our need for more expensive and rarer minerals: 20% less lithium, 60% less graphite, 75% less nickel, and no cobalt.
e. A solid-state lithium battery that is more fire-resistant, weighs less, charges faster, and has a longer lifespan. This tech can even be used in smartphones and laptops. Toyota is using this tech to produce EVs in 2027 with a 600-mile range and 10-minute charging time and earlier in 2026 with a 500-mile range and 20-minute charging.

A good article appeared in *Top Speed* by Ebenezer Ugorji on March 13, 2023, titled "10 Ways Solid State Batteries Will Change EVs Forever." [25] It covers issues like reducing battery weight, increasing the driving range, safety and stability, cheaper materials and manufacturing costs, reducing charging time to 10 minutes or less, greater battery durability and longer lifespan, and smaller environmental impact by eliminating cobalt and nickel. These minerals are often mined in deep-sea operations or child labor countries. Unfortunately, it will still need lithium, but instead of using it in a liquid form, it will be in a solid form. There are 9 other car manufacturers investing millions in this tech, working with two battery manufacturers.

f. Graphene was created in 2004. A layer is 1 million times thinner than a human hair. It could charge EV batteries, cell phones, and laptops in minutes, not hours. It is lightweight, produced environmentally-friendly, and reduces energy usage.

   The Lyten company modified graphene and came up with a 3D version. It is focused on using it to build lithium-sulfur batteries that deliver twice the energy that lithium-ion batteries produce. They are 40% lighter and can be sourced and manufactured in the US, improving our supply chain, lowering costs, and not enriching China. Their automated battery operation in the US is in pilot production in 2023 for defense applications. They have other applications, but the batteries for BEVs are their next priority.

g. Pennsylvania EC Power has reached mass production of its FastLion lithium iron phosphate battery to supply a charge in 10 minutes for a 250-mile range. They scaled up from publication to mass production in 11 months. They are now partnering with Ampcera, which was awarded a part of the $42 million Biden Bucks from his DOE to develop better BEV batteries. They will combine their tech with Ampcera's solid-state tech. Their battery is designed to be not combustible during charging, discharging, or if a short circuit occurs.

Solar Technology for Cars

In December 2022 in Australia, students set a certified Guinness world record in their Sunswift 7 solar car by traveling 621 miles (1,000 km) on a single charge in just under 12 hours (averaging 53 mph). In a limited way to enhance their woke credentials, several automakers are incorporating solar collectors into the body of their BEVs that will slightly improve their driving range.

More significantly planned for 2024–2025, a California company (Aptera) and a German company (Sono Motors) are each introducing solar models with embedded solar collectors at affordable prices. Aptera's model can get 1,000 miles before needing a recharge (about 2.5 times the range of a Tesla Model 3). The first 2-passenger cars are small, reduce the trips to the time-consuming charging infrastructure required for EV vehicles, and have the cleanest and cheapest (free) fuel.

If parked outside, it can collect enough solar energy to run 40 miles without a charge. It has a top speed of 112 mph and can go 0 to 60 in 3.5 seconds. They have taken reservations for 40,000 cars at $33,200 each and have secured $33 million in funding to start early production, as it is near the end of the product development stage.

We should be leaders or heavy investors in operations advancing the next generation of alternative-powered vehicles instead of extravagantly building an infrastructure for a technology that began in the 1990s and may be obsolete in a few years.

The Way Forward

Stop the wasteful spending that satisfies the interests of BEV car and battery production and the entrenched 3 giants that control two-thirds of the public charging stations and ports. Hydrogen fuel cell vehicles can overcome their few issues compared to the myriad of problems plaguing BEVs, and green hydrogen production and use are 100% carbon-free. More funding should be going there. It is time to make a hard stop on the $15.6 billion of tax dollars for EV loans and subsidies and about $6.8 billion in consumer EV rebates. We are bribing auto manufacturers to push out patched-up and repackaged tech and consumers to buy that problematic tech.

We should allow the free market to decide as it did with the Concorde supersonic airliner. After massive government spending, the issues of cost, disturbing sonic booms, and other problems still could not be overcome. Usage was primarily by the wealthy elites, just like the BEVs. Instead, we seem to be copying the old VHS-Betamax tape wars of the 1990s-2000s. Betamax had the better product, but huge dollars went into marketing VHS tapes and buying market share, and they won the war.

This war has more dire consequences, as **the BEV path leads to a disastrous woke financial and geopolitical destination for the US and its allies without realizing our clean energy and climate aspirations for 2030 and 2050. Some of the freed-up $22.4 billion can be redirected to hydrogen tech development and optimization that other countries are now leading.**

What if solar tech was combined with hydrogen fuel cell tech for cars? This is the technology that we should be smartly focusing on operationalizing. Once processes and costs are addressed, we would simply retrofit hydrogen pumps into the existing dependable and convenient gas station infrastructure. This would eliminate the rare earth and other minerals that enrich China at significant human and environmental costs.

Let smarter technology progress with a bit of help. We should not let the lobbies for expensive lithium batteries, charging stations, and lithium battery EVs squash solar and hydrogen fuel cell EVs. As these solutions become commercially viable, the gas-powered car lure will organically significantly decline. We must stop demonizing gas-powered cars until there is a reliable, affordable next-generation choice that is in use. Let's get behind HFCs.

If you are not looking to change cars, there still is something you can do. If your vehicle has "Eco" mode, use that, and you will reduce your CO_2 emissions by 26% and save fuel. This is based on a study done by Toyota and summarized at www.carbuzz.com by Karl Furlong on May 21, 2023. The title is "Toyota Study Shows We Don't Need EVs To Dramatically Lower Carbon Emissions."[26]

2. Our current energy policy is detrimental to our national security, the economy, and the well-being of US citizens. It is focused almost exclusively on undependable solar and wind and dismembering oil, natural gas, and clean coal. This has minimal impact on the global climate, while the woke mob gives the world's most massive polluters (China and India) a free pass. We have rapidly shifted from an energy-independent country in 2020 to one that pleads with OPEC and other unsavory nations to produce more oil (that is dirtier than ours) for US and global needs.

   Liquified natural gas (LNG) has some climate issues, but it emits 50–60% less CO_2 than oil or coal-fired plants (which China and India are aggressively building). It can make sense for emergencies, limited use, or less-developed countries (like Brazil), where it is plentiful until renewable energy sources are more available.

   As many as 60 LNG vessels could not offload to European ports to support their urgent energy needs in early 2023 because the infrastructure was not built sufficiently and was at 93% capacity. Germany and a few of its EU neighbors have moved quickly and taken significant steps to improve their LNG capability following the Russian invasion of Ukraine and the destruction of the Russian pipeline.

   Wind and solar take a toll on the environment by littering hundreds of thousands of acres for their monstrous solar farms or towering windmills. They also require mining (using machinery that runs on fossil fuels) the minerals needed for their equipment and all of the concrete necessary for wind farms. We must end the 20-year subsidies to wind and solar. It was $15.6 billion in 2022, more than double the $7.3 billion 6 years earlier in 2016. If they can't make it on their own with high energy prices now, it is time to admit they are not cheap and may never make economic sense even with subsidies, especially if prices drop.

   Those subsidies, the lure of big dollars from governments, and the desire to earn woke merit badges have created negative impacts on our land and sea wildlife and plants and the people displaced or impacted by them.

Wind and solar collection drop off at sunset, requiring fossil fuels to pick up the slack in the evening. Strangely, sometimes wind and solar produce too much power, and the excess may have to be wasted. However, power companies still paid the generators of the excess energy $ 20.8 billion in 2022, which is 56% higher than the $13.3 billion in 2021.

During high power usage, major business power users like crypto miners have been paid millions of dollars to not "mine" instead of limiting their time and charging them extra. These wind up on utility users' higher energy bills to fund these dumb, unnecessary payments. To combat this, additional cost and land will be needed to build battery storage projects to hold excess power until it is required. We are undoubtedly #1 globally in wasting money, and these wastes should end.

Wind research should be done to minimize the number of birds killed by giant windmills. Wind is an inefficient, fluctuating, low-density power source compared to a nuclear plant, using a small machine to create a lot of energy from a dense energy source on demand as needed. When you triple the blade length of a windmill, you can generate 9 times more power, so greed has set in. And in our profit-driven tax credit rush to hastily build more enormous windmills that kill even more birds, the structural tech hasn't been understood, and they are collapsing worldwide.

Some of these monoliths are over 700 feet tall (many are taller than the Statue of Liberty and the Washington Monument). These Tower of Babel monstrosities tend to fail within one year of completion (some fail during construction). Smaller turbines produce 25–50% of the power of the behemoths and typically fail within 5 years. These failures drive up insurance and other operating costs, making this energy source less attractive and not cheap.

The wind farm industry is cratering despite record subsidies and high energy prices. No bids were received at a 2023 UK auction for the right to build offshore wind farms. 10 major offshore wind farm projects in the US and UK worth $33 billion are in trouble. Siemens, a major player in wind farm equipment and management, reported a loss of $783 million in 2022 and projected losses in 2023 to be much larger.

To try to make lemonade out of lemons, Siemens is repositioning somewhat into wind-to-hydrogen tech using seawater and its offshore wind energy to continuously make hydrogen and ammonia to refuel ships. Absent any sea life impact (especially on whales), this could be a good tech.

According to some estimates, solar panels attract and kill 50,000–100,000 birds annually, and windmills kill an estimated 700,000 birds annually. Most environmentalists don't seem very concerned about that. Little mention is made of the solar panel attraction for birds, resulting in their nesting under the panels of some of the brands, stealing roof insulation for nesting, defecating on and scratching the panels (causing loss of efficiency and having to be replaced earlier), and insect population increasing under the panels and into the attic. The deadly Texas cold snap in the 2021 winter (causing over 200 deaths when power was unavailable to many) showed the fallacy of the over-reliance on wind and solar.

Who is speaking up for our majestic whales? In 2022, 18 humpback whales washed ashore along the US Atlantic coast, a trend that has continued into 2023. While there have been a few calls by the greenies for investigation, it is muted compared to its traditional over-the-top fossil fuel rhetoric.

There likely may be a linkage from offshore windmill emissions of strong underwater sonar signals that can disrupt the whales' hearing and equilibrium. The greenies seem unconcerned about whales, birds, or anything else that gets in the way of the practice of their climate change religion. If they cared, their voices would be vigorous and intense, calling for an immediate suspension of new projects to address issues while seeking remedies for existing damage being caused.

Despite the shortcomings of solar, there are a couple of bright spots with very good uses for solar power. Elevating and angling panels above the height of crops can still provide enough sunlight for growth, shielding them against high heat, drought, and storms and less water evaporation by 5–15%. Yields of some produce have doubled or tripled. Secondly, California is testing something that works in other parts of the world, protecting canals from drying out. Solar panels over the canals produce energy, conserve water by reducing evaporation, keep the water cooler, and create a better environment for life in the canals.

When nuclear fusion or other energy technologies become operational, we will regret how our Don Quixote and land-based solar manias have littered our landscape and caused societal, environmental, and economic issues as we rushed to earn our woke merit badges and huge profits. We have ignored the arable impacts on the landscape, the visual pollution, the killing of whales off our East Coast, the killing of hundreds of thousands of birds annually, the high financial costs, the environmental impact on other wildlife whose habitats are compromised, and the societal and poisonous impacts from the mining of the minerals needed.

Despite all those sacrifices, we will never hit 2050 net zero goals from these energy inputs. Here are some reasons why. **95% of global transportation currently runs on fossil fuels—changing that to zero is too massive to be realistic. Discoveries of new deposits of fossil fuels and minerals have likely peaked, and they are furiously being mined and depleted for BEVs.** Professor Simon Michaux from the Geological Survey of Finland estimated that **this transition would require mining 4.5 billion tons of metals, including copper, zinc, silver, nickel, lithium, cobalt, and vanadium. The demand to mine lithium would increase 46 times to meet that goal.**

Chris Martenson's book *Crash Course* [27] is filled with staggering figures to make this quantum leap. 380 million acres of solar farmland are needed to produce a gigawatt-hour of solar power at a rate of 2.8 GWh. **We would need 586,000 electrical power stations, not the 46,000 we have today. This carbon-neutral religion is not based on the science of what is achievable with solar, wind, and BEVs.** It ignores the factual projections of its impossible achievement but sounds wonderful as we earn praise for our wasted sacrifices.

Another great resource is James J. Puplava's *"The Beginning of the End Part III: Green Energy Realities."* It was published on October 6, 2023, at www.FinancialSense.com. [28] It states that **75% of the world's population (primarily China, India, Africa, and South America) is increasing fossil fuel reliance, including building many of those types of power plants.** Meanwhile, the Western developed countries are quickly moving away from traditional sources of nuclear, coal, and gas and becoming dependent on solar and wind, which are weather-dependent. China and India are leading in using diverse power for their electricity grids with nuclear, coal, gas, and renewables.

The US approaches lack thorough planning, engineering, and scientific principles. California refuses to accept its role in impeding controlled burns for forest debris clearance, water storage adequacy, and erosion control. He also points out our dependence on Russia for uranium for our nuclear naval vessels and nuclear power plants and our need for China's computer chips for our guided missiles and elsewhere in our economy.

Limited land-based solar and wind energy production needs to share (not replace) the US energy table with the other energy sources that we have in abundance. We must act smarter with our focus and investment in innovation for the near future of all our energy needs. **We can achieve a zero carbon footprint with nuclear fusion power and green, blue, and white hydrogen, which is impossible with land-based solar, wind, and BEVs.**

We must stop and redirect subsidies and rebates for undependable wind and solar power of $24.6 billion annually into limitless fusion power (covered later in this chapter. As we return sanity to our energy strategy, we should end our dependence on China to manufacture wind and solar products, encourage allies to do the same, and slash enormous trade deficits with them. They invest their vast profits in achieving military superiority and building coal-fired energy plants in China and worldwide.

We are paying China to use high-polluting energy to produce cleaner but problematic products for us to absolve our climate guilt. At the same time, we are restraining the use of our vast (and cleaner than other countries') oil and gas reserves and not realizing the benefits of fusion and green hydrogen. **We are funding China to be the world's largest polluter and to pursue global domination and military adventurism.**

Much of this is covered in a July 8, 2022, Daniel Turner article titled "Power The Future," which reveals how China's coal-powered plants produce energy to make most of the US solar and wind power devices. [29] China harvests a lot of US dollars to supply our wind and solar energy while they bring 1 new coal energy plant online every 10 days. They use dirtier, cheaper coal for their domestic needs and exports, laughing all the way to the bank.

The US has cut emissions by 25% in the last decade (78% in the previous five decades) and more than met its goals for the Paris Climate Accord, which we withdrew from due to some countries getting a "free pass to pollute;" and then Biden put us back in the Accord. We should not sign on to unrealistic and strangling policies, regulations, and accords when we have already shown our effective response to climate issues. Financially crippling the US will have no significant global climate impact.

In 2019, China was responsible for 27% of all greenhouse gas emissions, compared to 11% in the US. **From 2000 to 2018, China's CO_2 emission tripled, and India's increased by 157%. These largest**

CO_2-emitting countries must be pushed and not coddled to reduce emissions significantly. That will greatly and positively impact the environment because, according to the EPA, 76% of greenhouse gas emissions are from CO_2.

A relevant article by Lee Ying Shan on January 10, 2024, on www.cnbc.com is titled "World's two largest coal consumers won't be weaning off the fossil fuel anytime soon." [30] Due to their own coal burning and China's construction of hundreds of coal plants globally, **worldwide coal usage in 2023 set a record of 8.5 billion tons. 60% of China's power comes from coal; for India, it is 75%. "China's share of global electricity consumption ... is set to jump to one-third by 2025."** While they have set aspirational renewable energy targets for 2030 and 2050, would you bet they will achieve them, or do they just excel in saying the words the woke mobs want to hear? India's and China's coal consumption will likely increase for at least a decade.

A scholarly book by S. Fred Singer, *Hot Talk, Cold Science*, [31] provides data to combat the climate hysteria we have been bombarded with. Similarly, an article by Bjorn Lomborg on www.InsideSources.com and published by Tribune News Service on September 14, 2023, accomplishes the same. The title is "POINT: No need to panic on climate change." [32] Here are a few highlights:

- **Global governments have promised "net zero" carbon emissions at a cost beyond $5.6 trillion annually.**
- Per a Lancet study, global cold deaths of 4.5 million were 9 times greater than the well-publicized heat deaths.
- France adopted a resilience approach to warmer weather by mandating air conditioning for care facilities and "reduced heat deaths 10-fold."
- Despite what we are told, land area fires are less frequent than in the early 2000s.
- Controlled burns, better zoning, and forest management are more effective tools for preventing fires.

- The UN Climate Panel's latest report has "low confidence in general statements to attribute changes in flood events to anthropogenic climate change."

An article by Naveen Athrappully in *The Epoch Times* on August 29, 2023, was titled "Over 1,600 Scientists Sign 'No Climate Emergency' Declaration."[33] That scientist group is the Global Climate Intelligence Group (CLINTEL). Here are some highlights:
- The signers include two Nobel physicist laureates and 321 signatories from the US.
- Many doomsday predictions have been made since 1970, none of which have happened.
- Our buying into the activism has led to Biden regulations on ceiling fans, gas stoves, gas generators, and a ban on incandescent light bulbs.
- Climate models "exaggerate the effect of greenhouse gases" and "ignore the fact that enriching the atmosphere with CO_2 is beneficial." Extra CO_2 boosts crop yields and plant biomass.

If we were serious about climate change, changing China and India's coal use would be the key we would be turning to unlock climate improvement. However, we are too corrupted and fanatical to do this one thing that will have a massive impact. **That would make all the doctrinal and corrupt practices around wind, solar, and BEVs irrelevant. We have been brainwashed that we must keep living with more mandates, even if the science is not there. Scientists say the Western nations' frenetic activity has not moved the needle because the big polluting and impoverished countries are dramatically increasing their fossil fuel usage.**

3. Pipelines are environmentally a safer method of transporting oil, but that is just another sacrifice on the altar of climate change. While Biden stopped pipeline construction in the US, he greenlighted a

pipeline from Russia, making Europe dependent on Russian oil, which is more expensive, dirtier, and of poorer quality than the US LNG.

It was recently disclosed that the US Navy might have been involved in destroying that Russian pipeline to Western Europe. While the US denied any role in that, Biden's lackeys spoke differently before the invasion. Biden even said on February 7, 2022, that "we will bring an end to it." [34] Estimates of that destruction range from 300,000 to 500,000 metric tons of methane released into the atmosphere. It was the largest release of greenhouse gas in a single event ever and has been reported by experts as a clear case of sabotage by someone.

It would have made more sense to keep the Trump-era ban and sanctions on completing the pipeline, but the administration's TDS blinds them to anything Trump. They may have preferred to "cut off their nose to spite their face" and hurt Americans and Europeans. If reports are correct, we may have had some involvement in a risky, provocative war action against a country run by a ruthless, aggressive dictator with a sizeable nuclear arsenal. Our strategy on pipelines, energy, China, and nearly everything else is being created and implemented by people lacking strategic, common sense thinking.

Making Europe dependent on Russia for energy by allowing the Russian pipeline construction to proceed and then allegedly having some role in destroying it are the most bizarre actions the US could have done when the pipeline had already been successfully stopped. Because of this supply disruption and Russia's invasion of Ukraine, the EU has modified its level of "greenism." The EU is expanding existing LNG terminals, building new ones, and supplying them from the US and Qatar. LNG now represents 25% of their energy needs.

Our pipelines need to be finished, along with additional drilling (with sensible environmental protections), to return the US to the energy-independent status it had in the prior administration.

4. There are some budding energy alternatives, but like all new discoveries, they need some hurdles to overcome to be operationally efficient.

Hydrogen

Hydrogen has made impressive progress that many are not aware of. The Japan 2020 Olympics used hydrogen power for cars, two stadiums, a hotel, and the Olympic Village. Japan's hydrogen commitment is also visible in the large hydrogen fuel plant in Fukushima. It generates 10,000 KWs of clean energy annually, producing 900 metric tons of hydrogen to help power hydrogen cars, buses, and forklifts.

Hydrogen exists globally, with estimates as high as 150 trillion metric tons that could last hundreds of years. A town in Mali is powered exclusively by naturally occurring hydrogen. **Digging for this "white/gold hydrogen" gas could be done with lasers, not with equipment that runs on fossil fuels. It can be compressed or converted into liquid ammonia for transport via pipeline or trucking, where safety protocols already exist.** When hydrogen is made from fossil fuels like natural gas, it is called grey hydrogen. Making it without using fossil fuels (like using water and renewable energy like wind and solar) would be green hydrogen.

An article by Nick Paschal for *The Cool Down* on May 29, 2023, is titled "Scientists just discovered an 'astonishing' way to create energy out of thin air: 'The sky is quite literally the limit.'" [35] Australian scientists produced a hydrogen-consuming enzyme from a common soil bacterium. The enzyme called Huc converts hydrogen from the atmosphere into electricity. It is very stable and can easily be grown in scalable quantities, making it highly sustainable.

US subsidies for clean energy have caused a Norwegian manufacturer to build a $500 million factory to make the equipment that uses electrolysis to extract hydrogen from water.

Successful developmental research is happening around converting seawater into hydrogen. The International Energy Agency projects global production of low-emission hydrogen to rapidly increase by 2030 from these and other projects to 38 million tons annually.

Some seawater projects require costly desalination and elimination of microbe contamination with special membranes.

One process developed at Columbia University does not use membranes and results in another valuable byproduct of magnesium hydroxide, which can be utilized to create carbon-negative cement. The Saudi Arabian city of Neom is planned to use the seawater conversion tech to daily produce 600 tons of green hydrogen for all of its power and drinking water needs.

GenHydro+ broke ground on December 6, 2023, on a pilot project to bring renewable electricity to Burle Business Park in Lancaster, Pennsylvania. They have **a proprietary process that repurposes aluminum metal waste residue using a chemical accelerant, high pressure, and high heat. This frees up hydrogen gas and produces recycled steam to continue the pollution-free process. GenHydro believes this tech will make green hydrogen more widely available at a low cost and help industries transition to cleaner energy. This is a great way to cleanly produce hydrogen by eliminating and recycling industrial waste and not touching any water resources.**

It is possible to extract hydrogen from ammonia, a compound with existing safety protocols for storage and transportation. An article by Science X staff in Tech Xplore on February 29, 2024 was titled "Zero carbon dioxide emissions: Successful production of ammonia-based clean hydrogen." [36] It highlighted the work at the Hydrogen Research Department of the Korea Institute of Energy Research. A research team developed a clean hydrogen production tech based on ammonia decomposition, requiring some heat and a catalyst. To be totally green, a carbon-free energy source must produce the heat.

The Institute of Chemical Research of Catalonia (in Spain) developed a process that converts the main element of urine into ammonia with no CO creation. This is a big deal because water treatment plants struggle to break down all of the urine before the "treated" water is released. Depending on where the water is released, it can result in toxic algae blooms and threaten some of the sea life. This still needs optimization, and we should be helping, as this could be another way to create hydrogen for transportation needs.

Another development was reported by researchers at **Rice University in October 2023. They have developed a 4-second high-heat process to produce clean hydrogen from waste plastic without the need to wash or sort. It also creates a valuable byproduct, graphene (without CO_2 emissions). Graphene is used in electronics, energy, healthcare, and the food and transportation industries. That byproduct more than covers the cost of production.**

The UK created its Hydrogen Strategy in 2021 to make it the world's leading hydrogen power by 2030. Japan plans to have a network of 900 hydrogen stations by 2030 to support 800,000 hydrogen fuel cell vehicles. Germany, Italy, France, and the Netherlands have also set up hydrogen station networks, as they can see the future for HFC cars. Germany and Italy are collaborating to build a pipeline from North Africa to Bavaria to transport 11 million tons of hydrogen by 2030. They all understand the abundance of hydrogen and its place in a common-sense approach to clean energy and restoring the environment.

South Korean scientists at the Ulsan National Institute of Science and Technology replaced expensive metal with very affordable nickel as a catalyst to create hydrogen through electrolysis with a 200% increase in output, working for 1,000 straight hours without degradation. This would be green hydrogen production at lower costs and end the need to transport hydrogen. Gas stations could create their green hydrogen onsite, powered by solar energy, only needing water and cheap nickel-iron. South Korea also has a Hydrogen Industrial Strategy, and its spending for hydrogenation is just behind Germany and Japan. Following the lead from Mali, they have three cities as pilot tests for transportation, industry, and space heating using hydrogen.

Why are we not partnering with Japan, Germany, the UK, and South Korea to accelerate green hydrogen production instead of bowing to the one-dimensional climate extremists, the BEV wokesters, and all the enormous lobbies for BEVs, lithium batteries, and charging ports? Hydrogen is the clean transportation medium, but we continue to head down a no-win path with BEVs. Most Americans are not buying into that BEV mania with all their problems, but that has not cooled our government's love affair with BEVs.

Non-Land-Based Solar

Technology is booming in the renewable energy space. Engineering professors at the Australian National University wrote a paper in 2023 suggesting that **floating solar panels in equatorial waters with little wind or waves could generate more than 6 times the current global energy needs of 8 billion people.** Major assessments of the impacts on sea life and sea traffic on the surface are needed, but if those are minimal, that could be a significant, positive development.

If you search www.solarisfloat.com, you will see the company's first patented actual use of this concept in the Netherlands. It is a floating island of solar panels that can reposition the panels' angles to maximize solar energy capture throughout the day. According to *Interesting Engineering* and SolarisFloat, algae pollution is reduced, and evaporation of lake water is decreased by 60%.[37] **Solar land farms require 40–45 times as much land as coal plants and 90–100 times as much land as gas power plants. Floating solar farms can free up precious land.**

In January 2023, Caltech launched into orbit the Space Solar Power Demonstrator that carried a microwave array to **collect sunlight 24/7, turn it into electricity, convert that into microwaves, and send it wirelessly back to Earth. It can go wherever needed, and no infrastructure on the ground is necessary to receive the power beamed to it.**

Other Battery Technologies

There is an interesting August 3, 2022, article by Courtney Flatt titled "The US made a breakthrough battery discovery—then gave the technology to China." [38] It chronicles the $15 million of taxpayer funds to support the research at UniEnergy Technologies in Mukilteo, WA. They were building a vanadium redox flow battery based on a design from two dozen US scientists. It could power a house, last for decades, reside next to their outside AC unit, and connect to solar panels.

Our Department of Energy gave the tech to a Chinese company in 2017, and they have built a considerable facility in China and have ramped up production. After years of complaints, the license seems to have been revoked, and perhaps a US company may still be granted a license. There is a lot more to this story, but it only adds to the already-rotten taste this gives us for our government's mismanagement and perhaps corruption.

The DOE gave a $400 million loan to startup Eos Energy for a zinc-bromine battery storage system to produce 8 gigawatt hours of storage capacity for 130,000 homes annual needs by 2026. Their Pennsylvania facility produces 540 megawatt-hours annually and is still in a scale-up stage. The batteries can last 20 years, and zinc is much more available than the relatively scarce lithium. It works more seamlessly and efficiently with the grid. This could be an energy win to offset many of our fumbles.

Other Technologies

Zero Petroleum is a UK firm that set a 2021 Guinness World Record by using its synthetic fuel to power an aircraft, the first use of synthetic fuel for an aircraft. It produces a carbon-neutral fuel in a proprietary process that uses carbon dioxide from direct atmospheric capture and hydrogen from water electrolysis using renewable electricity.

The UK's Royal Air Force has agreed to have them supply all of its aviation fuel needs. Its first plant was opened in June 2023, and its next plant could open as soon as 2025 with production at commercial scale levels. It is one of just a few companies that create carbon-neutral synthetic fuels for gasoline, diesel, and jet fuel applications. While there may still be hurdles with large-scale carbon capture, green hydrogen production, and cost, they could be promising developments for truck and jet fuel applications.

However, on September 25, 2023, Lufthansa's Carsten Spohr said switching to sustainable aviation fuel (SAF) would absorb half of Germany's electricity supply to make the fuel. He also stated, "If the Lufthansa Group were to use all of SAF currently available, it would only be able to fly for just under two weeks." [39] Another voice of reason to ensure this is done with an understanding of the math and depletion of energy components needed for production.

European jet manufacturer Airbus is aggressively pursuing a more promising development. They are developing hydrogen tech to use as the jet fuel for their A380 planes. It will have near zero environmental impact compared to the significant emissions of current jet fuel.

Firefly Green Fuels has chemically created a kerosene-like fuel that is a "near zero carbon emission biofuel." **While some energy is consumed in the processing, there is a 90% carbon savings compared to fossil jet fuel production.** Independent testing in Germany and the US confirmed the high similarity to fossil-based A1 jet fuel. The UK government has given them a $2.5 million grant to build a full-scale demonstration plant. Get ready—the secret ingredient is human waste. While this may seem odd, what a great way to take what is a major pollutant now and recycle it into a greener replacement for polluting jet fuel.

The opposed-piston (OP) engine has primarily been used in tanks, trains, subs, ships, and some planes, but not cars. It has no valves, cylinder heads, or camshafts, making it simpler and cheaper to construct and operate. The leading developer today is Achates Power, which claims its gas engines can deliver **37 MPG for a full-size pickup truck** and 65% fewer NOx emissions than the standard set by California for 2027 without the need for expensive electric batteries. There would be major fuel savings due to the significant efficiency for truck fleets. **They are tweaking a version to work with hydrogen fuel cell cars.**

Looking to the Future

Our National Ignition Facility in Livermore, CA, on December 5, 2022, achieved ignition, where more energy was created than consumed in fusing atoms. $5 billion (details can be seen in the Fusion Industry Association's annual report) of private capital flowed into several companies in this sector in 2022 as investors saw the potential.

Microsoft signed an agreement to buy fusion fuel from Helion Energy, which is planned to go online in 2028. It seems like the technical hurdles could be overcome and operational sometime in the next few years. On September 25, 2023, DOE head Jennifer Granholm stated the US aims to create a nuclear fusion facility within 10 years. If Microsoft and their vendor are successful, they will beat our DOE by 5 years.

Ambrose Evans-Pritchard wrote in The Telegraph on March 13, 2024, "Nuclear fusion for the grid is coming much sooner than you think." [40] Peer-reviewed papers confirmed that Commonwealth Fusion Systems in Boston broke the record for the strongest magnet (needed for fusion). An MIT professor said that **"it basically changed the cost per watt of a fusion reactor by a factor of almost 40."** [41]

The CEO for Commonwealth said the tech "scarcely existed 10 years ago and was still in its infancy five years ago." **"Much stronger magnets mean that we can build a plant that is 40 times smaller."** [42] Fusion reactors will be like hospitals that use tiny amounts of deuterium-tritium, which is minimal compared to the radioactivity of components for fission reactors. Some fusion facts:

- **Produces 4 million times more energy than fossil fuel with no CO_2 or methane emissions, almost no long-term waste, and creates a useful byproduct of helium.**
- **Produces industrial high-grade heat to decarbonize glass, cement, steel, ammonia, hydrogen, and other industries.**
- **Requires minimal land and water, can run continuously if needed, and its fuel is limitless for thousands of years.**
- Only small amounts of deuterium are needed from seawater or tritium from breeding small quantities of lithium.

There is an October 13, 2023 article by the *Associated Press*, "Biden awards $7 billion for clean hydrogen hubs across the country to help replace fossil fuels," by Matthew Daly and Marc Levy. [43] Each hub seems to be using a different approach. We may wind up with six not-so-great hubs and, hopefully, one very efficient one. Bill Gates called clean hydrogen a "Swiss Army knife of decarbonization," and Bjorn Lomborg, a responsible climate scientist, agreed.

Gates (along with several others) is investing significantly in carbon capture technology that can capture CO_2 from factories, the air, or grey hydrogen production from fossil fuels, making it "blue hydrogen. White, blue, and green hydrogen are all environmentally friendly versions of the coming hydrogen boom. Although hydrogen is colorless, "colors" are used to categorize the different hydrogen production processes.

Carbon capture, storage research and optimization have collected many investment dollars and are being used globally. On February 18, 2024, Jeremiah Budin wrote in *The Cool Down* an article, "Developers plan to build a first-of-its-kind energy storage system that will set global records: The expansion of energy storage infrastructure is key." [44] It stated that Alliant Energy and WEC Energy Group had received a grant of up to $30 million to **create the first**

US compressed CO_2 closed-loop energy storage system, which releases no CO_2 and needs no additional CO_2.
The initial CO_2 gas is changed into a liquid for easier storage. When energy is needed, it is changed back to a gas, which powers an electricity-generating turbine and captures the CO_2 produced. A smaller version of this is operational in Sardinia, Italy with a 75% efficiency.

Ameya Paleja reported on February 19, 2024 in the South China Morning Post that Huazhong University of Science and Technology had created a process that transforms CO_2 in the atmosphere into useful chemical products. The article is titled "New tech turns CO_2 into chemicals with 93% efficiency, runs record 5000 hrs." [45]

There is a Department of Energy (DOE) initiative called the **"111 Program" to reduce the cost of green hydrogen by 80% to $1 per 1 kilogram in 1 decade.** This should result in efficient green hydrogen production, storage, and transport. **Those lower costs could allow existing gas stations to include hydrogen, making it more convenient for drivers who now have limited fill-up options (primarily in California). This will solve our transportation and possibly other energy needs and be a responsible transition from fossil fuels compared to the current panic.**

Regardless of this bright future, we must mine lithium in the US to eliminate the blackmail opportunity for China. But it must be done responsibly with no toxic chemical leaks like what happened in China, killing animals from contaminated drinking water; no air and soil contamination; and restoration at the end of the mining cycle. Even without lithium batteries, that rare mineral is still needed for nuclear, military, medicinal, optical, and many other uses.

The subject of **nuclear fission power plants** has proponents and opponents. The reality is that 32 countries have 436 fission reactors, of which 92 are in the US in 35 states. **The US sites have accumulated some 88,000 metric tons (194 million lbs.) of spent nuclear waste,** which increases by about 2,000 metric tons annually. **They**

produce nuclear waste that must be stored safely for hundreds of thousands of years till it loses its radioactive toxicity. According to an article by Alexander C. Kaufman on January 9, 2024, in the Huffington Post, the US plans to increase its nuclear fission plants with the next generation of fission reactors using low-enriched uranium. [46]

The US used to supply its fuel source for fission reactors by enriching uranium fuel. But getting Russia to dismantle some of its nuclear weaponry in the 1990s came with a deal to buy cheaper Russian enriched fuel. That put every US enricher out of business and made us dependent on Russia. **A start-up company, Curio, focuses on recycling the spent rods of our nuclear reactors (every two years) since they contain 97% of their original energy. Estimates are that recycling our nuclear waste could power the US for 100 years.**

This could significantly reduce the toxic nuclear waste that requires safe long-term storage, reduce the uranium mining demands, and provide fuel for existing and any new reactors. The US has provided $38 million to companies for nuclear recycling research, including $5 million to Curio.

The downside is there will still be toxic material that can result in an accidental or terrorist disaster if not vigorously protected with safety protocols. The best answer is nuclear fusion power without any of those safety concerns. But this can be a good solution for all the existing stored waste and any new waste generated. We should have fusion power in a few years, so constructing those new fission plants may not even be needed.

Over the next few years, more appropriate sizing, innovation, and protection for birds and whales from wind and solar can allow them to be a portion of our energy needs. Just like the JFK goal of putting a man on the moon, we must laser-focus on the goals of hydrogen and fusion for our transportation and energy needs. Let's redirect the current wasteful dollars focused on wind, solar, and BEVs. They will never reach the aspirations we have for 2030 and 2050.

With that redirection, fossil fuel use will decline as hydrogen and fusion become the clean energies of the world. Looking back 30–50 years ago, all of the alarmist prediction dates of climate Armageddon have proven to be fear-mongering rhetoric designed to birth the mandates for the environmental climate religion but lacking in solid science. Let the free market and innovation make that transition happen without flawed policies that are not workable today and will be obsolete in a few years. **The best ideas for abundant clean water and energy should be accelerated with funds that are now wasted on wind, solar, and BEVs.**

Best Clean and Abundant Energy Ideas

a. **Transportation**—Redirect the $22.4 billion annual subsidies, loans, and rebates for BEVs, their batteries, and charging ports to research for green hydrogen production and accelerated research on solar and hydrogen fuel cell transportation. Fund research into Rice University's 4-second high-heat process to recycle plastic into clean hydrogen without CO_2 or the need to wash or sort the plastic and create graphene as a byproduct. Fund expanded research for GenHydro's repurposing of aluminum metal waste that releases hydrogen gas and steam that can be recycled for more electricity.

Let's work with the Institute of Chemical Research of Catalonia (in Spain) to optimize their process of converting the main element of urine into ammonia with no CO creation. This can improve our water treatment plants' struggle to break down all of the urine before the "treated" water is released. This could be another way to create hydrogen for transportation needs. We must work with South Korea's tech to efficiently decompose ammonia into hydrogen.

Our ocean levels are rising, threatening many who live nearby. Why not provide funding for Columbia University's tech that uses seawater to produce hydrogen and magnesium (to create carbon-negative cement)? Validate the feasibility for the US of the hydroponic and vertical farming successes in Dubai that produce hydrogen and other valuable products from seawater and waste. Help small farmers transition into those rather than shutting them down.

Fund research into Achates Power's opposed-piston engine that can get 37 MPG in a full-size pickup with 65% fewer emissions, fewer moving parts, and can be tweaked for HFC vehicles. We can learn from Japan how to retrofit hydrogen pumps into existing gas stations.

California has agreed to purchase 10 hydrogen trains from Stadler, a Swiss rail manufacturer, with the first one expected to operate in 2027 between Merced and Sacramento. Spain and Quebec are also starting down that road. Toyota will be supplying Peterbilt and Kenworth with hydrogen trucks. Determine the viability of the UK's tech for processing human waste into jet fuel. If we develop good processes for scaling the production of green hydrogen, we should determine the viability of Airbus' tech to use hydrogen for jet fuel.

We must commit significant funds to support all the green hydrogen production technologies to meet the needs for air, rail, trucking, and, most significantly, cars. That will create a truly green transportation solution without bowing to the BEV lobbies that support problematic vehicles. We should work with partners in South Korea, Germany, Japan, and the UK to make this happen sooner and more efficiently.

b. **Solar and wind technology**—After 20 years of providing subsidies and rebates now exceeding $24.6 billion annually, it is time to end them and redirect them into limitless fusion power. We have been funding havoc to the environment, while we blindly practice a flawed climate religion. All solar and wind farms should be required to have scientifically accurate information on plans to severely limit bird and whale deaths with no new permits until those are in place and working.

One of the best actions we can take is to end China's status in the WTO as a "developing nation." That will make the #2 Superpower comply with pollution standards they now avoid with all their coal-powered plants. Similarly, we need to use allies to economically shame China and India to stop their proliferation of coal-powered plants. This impact will be significant since India and China are the world's largest polluters.

We need to validate the data or accurately refute the claims that we will never hit our 2030 and 2050 goals toward net zero emissions, despite the global annual spending in excess of $5.6 trillion. Determine the viability of ocean and space-based solar collection and transmission. Stop wasteful payments by utilities (that wind up being paid for by customers) for solar power that cannot be used and for high energy users like crypto miners if they don't mine. Instead, they should be charged penalties and experience reduced service if needed.

c. **Nuclear fusion**—Commonwealth Fusion Systems created the strongest magnet to make the fusion process work. It is so powerful that it will reduce the size of a fusion reactor to 2.5% of what was considered normal. AI has been used to monitor the reaction and adjust in milliseconds for potential instabilities.

Fusion creates 4 million times more energy than fossil fuels with no CO_2 or methane emissions. It also produces industrial high-grade heat to decarbonize the glass, cement, steel, ammonia, hydrogen, and other industries. Microsoft's agreement to buy fusion energy from Helion Energy beginning in 2028 looks more realistic today. Since the process uses minimal land, water, and fuel to create limitless green energy, helium, and no nuclear waste, we need to support this strongly and ensure all safety protocols are in place. This will obsolete windmills, solar farms, and fossil fuel energy, and they will all lobby hard to oppose this.

d. **Nuclear fission**—Older nuclear technology creates waste that stays radioactive for thousands of years, creating safe storage and nuclear theft problems. We must strongly support Curio's nuclear waste recycling from these fission reactors. Once operational, priorities should be developed, especially targeting early on those with more compromised storage. We don't want to have deteriorating storage accidents or terrorists stealing materials. We have 194 million lbs. of this material that still has 97% usability in the recycling process that Curio has developed, so this could last 100 years.

e. **Other**—Complete US pipelines that have been stalled. Any traditional drilling should have sensible environmental protections built in. The issue of fracking is covered in the prior water section. Before banning appliances, we must identify the annual global impact of each action.

CO_2 capture using the Chinese process to transfer it into valuable chemicals should be evaluated. Alliant Energy and WEC Energy Group's closed-loop CO_2 energy storage system that creates energy and recaptures the CO_2 for use again should be assessed after it is operational to see if this should be replicated. Determine the viability of expanding Eos Energy's zinc-bromide battery storage system and its use with the existing power supply.

Most Relevant Chapter 1 Founding Principles (FP)

- FP 2 The Right to Govern Derives from the People
- FP 3 Limited Representative Republican Form of Government
- FP 4 A Written Constitution to Be Followed
- FP 5 Private Property Rights and the Rule of Law
- FP 7 The Most Prosperity Occurs in a Free Market Economy with Minimum Regulation
- FP 9 Free People Must Stay Strong to Survive

- FP 11 Federal Debt Is Toxic to Freedom Just Like Being Taken Over by Another Country
- FP 12 The USA Has the Destiny to Be Exceptional and an Example to the World

Positive Impacts

General Focus Concerns

Focusing the world on pressuring China and India to significantly reduce greenhouse gas emissions will be the most attainable and crucial success factor in climate moderation. That will be more effective than financially crippling Europe and the US (which has already significantly reduced its emissions). Our and Europe's financial decline will only fuel China's global domination as we deplete the world's limited supply of lithium and other rare minerals and cause more environmental harm. Instead, we should pursue limitless fusion and hydrogen power for our power grid and transportation needs.

Innovation is blooming for clean and abundant water and energy, but it is not getting the funding and priority it deserves. Redirecting political pork barrel spending, flawed electric vehicle strategy, and undependable wind and solar power frees up annual spending of $73 billion. Some of that can be used to provide an abundant supply of clean water for the US, optimize green hydrogen production for all our transportation needs, and optimize the production of limitless fusion power for our energy grid.

This will never happen with a D-S administration focused on pleasing its big-money campaign donors and not on the US being the global leader and beneficiary of next-generation technologies. Remember the warnings about Biden from Obama and Obama's Secretary of Defense in Chapter 2. Biden is once again on the right side of big campaign donations but on the wrong side of the best interests of the US and the world. The leadership and disasters of the Biden-Harris administration were soundly rejected in 2024, providing hope for more intelligent approaches to critical resources.

Water

Reversing the accelerated depletion of groundwater basins and reservoirs will occur with more vigorous conservation efforts, prioritizing as #1 our water infrastructure spending to repair or replace aging systems and fast-tracking investment in promising water tech research. We can implement plans to capture, treat, and store or safely discharge the 19.3 trillion gallons of US annual stormwater. Over time, this will refill our aquifers and reservoirs, eliminate periodic drastic water shortages, and prevent water from being cut off for small farms.

We can copy hydroponic and vertical farming techniques from the Netherlands and Dubai to cut agricultural water usage by up to 98% and process sewage and 19 billion lbs. of annual food waste to produce minimally fertilized crops, compost, animal feed, clean water, energy, and ammonia that can be processed into hydrogen fuel.

We can have a national, convenient collection and safe disposal system for toxins. New technology will allow plastic to be recycled into clean hydrogen without washing or sorting it. The wide use of infinitely recyclable plastic will eliminate plastic piling up in landfills. A strategy to address the hundreds of thousands of undocumented wells from fouling the ground will curb this environmental issue. Fracking will have sound plans for decontaminating and reusing the water required without causing soil subsistence or exploding wells that foul the ground.

We will invest in uniform testing and current innovations and processes to markedly reduce any more PFAS (forever chemicals), PPCPs, microplastics, and other toxins from entering our waters and our bodies and remediate those currently in our landfills and waters. Other innovations (including simple substitutions) can reduce, replace, and recycle other plastics. We will play a more impactful role in global technology for drinking water systems to replace the need for plastic water bottles and bring the world's waters back to their natural state and all the life within. This creates a healthier ecosystem that all can enjoy.

Energy for the Power Grid

Like the oil industry, the solar and wind industries will have plans to show minimal adverse environmental impacts. Reducing the killing of birds and whales from solar panels and windmills is needed to make them responsible supplements to fossil fuels today and the coming clean hydrogen and fusion energy booms in the next few years. Windmills generally fail before their fifth birthday, and the wind industry is financially struggling, so that may not be much of an issue. We can stop the proliferation of environmentally damaging massive solar farms and perhaps repurpose some existing ones to reclaim our landscape and heal the land they occupy.

Completing US pipelines (which should be able to be used in the future with ammonia or hydrogen) and simplifying the oil lease permitting process (with sensible environmental protections) will help countries (especially in Europe) that can use our LNG as we work with them to regain their trust and support their needs. That will be the single best way to dramatically lower the inflation burden as we transition to dependable, renewable energy while the tech and costs for hydrogen and fusion improve.

We have patented energy innovation and must guard it and stop giving it and other tech innovations to countries like China. Our zinc bromide battery storage system can be an excellent way to store and distribute grid power. CO_2 capture for closed-loop energy production is an excellent way to combine clean energy needs with CO_2 removal.

The concern over our 194 million lb. stockpiles of radioactive nuclear fission waste should be addressed with the Curio process that recycles spent fuel rods that still have 97% of their energy remaining. In about 100 years, these dangerous stockpiles can be used up.

Nuclear fusion tech is expanding rapidly. A new facility now takes only 2.5% of its prior design due to stronger magnets, and the process optimization is progressing swiftly due to AI. Fusion creates 4 million times more energy than fossil fuels with no CO_2, methane emissions, or radioactive waste. Its high heat can decarbonize industries like glass, cement steel, ammonia, and hydrogen.

Restoring our energy independence while we fervently innovate our energy future with hydrogen and fusion is more sensible than the climate hysteria that has been consistently, incorrectly, and fraudulently scaring us. Picture a world where the power grids are primarily powered by fusion with no radioactivity, creating a byproduct of needed helium. Water and space-based solar may also contribute significantly to our power grid capability.

Energy for Transportation Needs

Ridding ourselves of the frenetic bias for BEVs (despite their numerous problems) and opening our minds, investment, and strategy towards HFCs and solar-powered vehicles will stop us from rushing expensively into technology that will not be the best when tomorrow's tech is within reach. Despite all the bribing rebates and subsidies, BEVs only account for about 1% of registered US cars because most Americans want to avoid the many significant BEV issues. Green hydrogen fuel cell vehicles create no pollution and will require no power grid enhancements and just some retrofitting of the existing gas station infrastructure.

Ford loses $66,000 on every BEV it sells. A cynical comic would say that by selling hundreds of thousands of them, they are making it up in volume. Let's not continue to raid taxpayer funds and create deficits to fund King Joseph's folly. Without this bribery of car makers and consumers, the prices of these problematic cars would be ridiculous, and the market would crash.

Toyota's common sense approach balances the environment with most car buyers' common sense and needs. Their research shows that the amount of lithium and other minerals needed to make 1 EV could be used to build 90 hybrids and that the carbon reduction of those 90 hybrids over their lifetime is 37 times as much as that of a single EV. It is time to end this destructive BEV love affair. We will also work with

Achates Power's opposed-piston engine to increase the already excellent mileage of hydrogen cars.

Meanwhile, hydrogen transportation is happening. California has purchased ten hydrogen-powered trains from a Swiss company, and Toyota will supply Peterbilt and Kenworth with hydrogen-powered semi trucks. To meet all of our transportation needs, we will create greener hydrogen by optimizing some of the many discoveries that convert plastic, industrial, and other waste into hydrogen. We can even have a positive effect on eroding and flooding shorelines from rising sea levels by using excess seawater to convert it into hydrogen. Working with partners in South Korea, Germany, Japan, and the UK will accelerate this.

Imagine converting white hydrogen found in mines or creating green or blue hydrogen with carbon capture tech. Each of those would have zero or near-zero emissions. We can power our transportation (including planes, buses, trucks, and cars) and produce water as a byproduct of combustion.

Opposition to These Solutions

Why are the elites not embracing these manageable changes that can yield substantial environmental, energy independence, and quality-of-life benefits? They have elevated climate change and other rallying cries that are part of their belief system into fake religions. Remember the phony "97% climate consensus" peddled by the zealots as "settled science" to shut down scientific research and discussion? We live in the "Inquisition Era" of this New Dark Ages, where powerful aligned elites of the RAGS (religion, academia, government, science) and their media co-conspirators are blind and deaf to proven ideas that contradict theirs. This current inquisition and persecution must give way to the rebirth of the scientific method of open-minded investigation and conclusions based on stringent analysis and testing to determine facts and causality.

A few hundred years ago, that was not the case during the original Dark Ages. Then, the same coalition of elite RAGS accepted on faith and their own bias that the earth was flat and later that the sun and other planets revolved around it. Today's RAGS zealots are joined with the media and bear the same defective genes of their "flat earth" ancestors.

We need the fresh air of curiosity to replace the fraud and bias surrounding us. Courageous scientists, doctors, environmentalists, archaeologists, investigative reporters, and others must be able to present their data without recriminations, cancelation, loss of jobs, and character assassination that are part of our current Dark Ages. Reducing that lust for power over our lives, personal prestige and greed, and mindlessly clinging to unproven or false doctrines of the new "religions" will make for a better US and a more peaceful world.

***

The next few pages recall from the chapters of this book important domestic and global markers along the dangerous path the US has been following to join the Alliance of Repressive Regimes that ushers in the New Dark Ages. We can avoid that and rewrite the script for a globally positive ending if we wake up and woke down now.

PART III

The Perilous Path We Followed

This book outlines the journey we have been following, especially in the 20th and 21st centuries. Many of the steps of this journey have fallen perfectly in place to redirect us from becoming the Shining City on a Hill to abandoning our freedoms in favor of an authoritarian construct. Chapter 3 has an interesting "Checklist to Build a Socialist Country." Below is a more expansive version of that, showing more of the markers that have been passed on our hideous transformation path to join the expanding Alliance of Repressive Regimes.

Domestic Authoritarian Markers

- Our country has well-designed Founding Principles that have been eroded, corrupted, or canceled in our 250-year journey.
- Our political processes have been one of the biggest villains in our corruption and decline. Many politicians are driven by power, prestige, and personal enrichment and are not accountable for solving problems. Corrupt Capitalism is mainly the result of that 3rd item, the obsession with money. The resistance of Congress to term limits has allowed this corruption to metastasize.

- That bad example has been embraced by many of our institutions and in our personal lives.
- Many of us are not the strong people (Founding Principle #9) we used to be. We reward criminals and the undocumenteds, many have lost the work ethic we were noted for (2 million have left the workforce under Biden-Harris), and we let a "participation trophy" philosophy guide our actions domestically and internationally. Our woke military branches are unable to meet their recruitment goals.
- The ruling class of legislators, judges, and the Executive Branch are well cared for with pensions, superb healthcare, and other perks and still not accountable for solving problems. Their focus is on staying in control for the power, prestige, and personal enrichment opportunities. They have been elevated to be "more equal" and entitled than everyone else—a good principle for authoritarian Socialism.
- In 1950, almost 1 of every 3 Americans lived in poverty. By 1967, more than half escaped poverty without any significant government programs, and that rate was reduced by 18% to 14.2%. In 1967, President Lyndon Johnson chose to ignore that fact and, using the strategy of costly big government programs, began enacting his War on Poverty to buy votes.

    As of 2020, that war cost $28 trillion (adjusted for inflation) and only reduced the poverty rate by 2.8% over those 53 years. The cost was 3 times that of all US military action since the American Revolution. It has increased welfare, single-parent families, violence, corruption, and out-of-wedlock births. By any measure, it was a Socialist failure, but one that bought lots of votes and propelled us solidly along the path of untamed exponential government growth in cost and control of our lives—good prerequisites for authoritarian Socialism.
- The assassinations of JFK, RFK, and MLK in the 1960s robbed our country of 3 powerful unifiers who displayed some of the Solutionism processes in their professional lives. Their deaths created a massive opening for frustration, chaos, and lawlessness.

- The inclination of the human spirit for individuals, their countries, and the world is to believe in something larger than itself. Many of those with comfortable lives have become self-absorbed, bored, fixated on being entertained, and looking for trendy philosophies like Socialism or elevating extreme versions of activism into replacements for traditional religion. They are joined by those feeling the effects of unsolved societal problems in their lives.
- The primary architects of US Socialism have been Saul Alinsky and Cloward-Piven, much beloved by the left and embraced by the Dems, including Presidents. The goals of Alinsky and C-P were to worsen problems by overwhelmingly increasing them, discrediting and destroying institutions, and eliminating the freedoms in our Constitution and Bill of Rights. That prepares us for Socialism to fill the void it created with chaos and destruction.
- These Marxists have captured the souls of the Dems and transformed them into the Democrat-Socialist Party with passionate foot soldiers and leaders of extreme policies designed to replace our Corrupt Capitalism with Socialism (which is also corrupt).

    They have built an impressive Uniparty that includes the media, entertainment, big business, educators, Deep Staters, globalists, oligarchs, elites, wokesters, squishy Republicans, and RINOs. It is housed within their Wokesphere ecosystem, an echo chamber for their groupthink. Anyone out of sync with that is canceled, persecuted, prosecuted, fired, unfriended, de-platformed, or otherwise not allowed to speak. Those unaligned ideas would disturb their groupthink ecosystem. That is Wokeism Gone Wild.
- The original Dark Ages were ruled by a similar echo chamber of false doctrines from the coalition of the RAGS (religion, academia, government, science). The current-day RAGS are more potent than that due to the involvement of the media, the faux religions of extreme environmentalism and other extremists, and the many other members of the Uniparty. They delight in their role in bringing about the Global Reset for the New World Order. Once that happens, most will

be thanked for their service to the cause, and then they and their misguided passions will be disposed of.

- Beginning with Bill Clinton's Presidency, the gradual march to Socialism increased its pace. Despite his accomplishments as President, Clinton incorporated one of the overwhelms laid out by C-P when he enacted the Motor Voting Bill (and invited C-P to the signing).
- Some expected Obama to be the 2nd coming of Martin Luther King Jr., but the unity they thought he would create never happened. He often quickly judged situations based on the skin color of those involved. Racial strife and lawlessness were gaslit. This was somewhat expected, as he was raised with a strong Marxist influence that continued with his collegiate influence from Saul Alinsky, his choice of church attendance, and his community organization efforts to pressure banks often to make loans for subpar credit situations.

  Globally, his Presidency demonstrated appeasement to Communist and terrorist adversaries and apologies to the rest of the world for the sins of the US. His approach was embraced and enforced by his Cabinet (which even had a Communist for a time), and many of those joined the Biden-Harris Cabinet and have been pulling the same strings for them.
- Trump put a temporary halt to the Socialist journey and headed the US in another direction. His Solutionist approach significantly solved many problems. His bombastic style appealed to the MAGA faithful, and his results appealed to those focused solely on what politicians do, not what they say. Unfortunately, too many other voters judge by the words and tone coming out of a politician's mouth. And the VLWC's massive coordinated efforts were able to deny him a 2020 re-election victory. But he returned victorious in 2024.
- Rudy Giuliani wanted to be Trump's Secretary of State, but Trump wanted him to be the Attorney General in 2021. Had Giuliani taken the AG position, all or most of the Trump-related persecutions and prosecutions would never have happened. Trump would likely have been re-elected in 2020; Iran's financial viability and internal dissension

would have imploded and ended their support of terrorism; there would have been no wars in the Middle East and Ukraine; and there would have been less saber rattling from China, who would not have the added strength of Iran and Russia as aggressive partners on the move against the West.

- Less than 2 weeks before Trump took office in 2017, Obama set in motion a "poison pill" for the Trump administration. He approved the lifting of the moratorium on federal funding for dangerous gain-of-function research on viruses. The National Institutes of Health made it official in December 2017. In 2020, China presented the world with COVID. That produced a huge negative economic impact on Trump's last year in office, which negated the record-setting pre-COVID economy he had engineered.
- The COVID-19 gift from China allowed the successful use of the Basement Biden strategy to limit his campaigning, debates, and answering tough questions that would have placed him under more intense scrutiny. In 2020, voters ignored the warnings about Joe from Obama himself and Obama's Secretary of Defense, Robert Gates. That resulted in Joe's Trojan Horse Presidency, embracing the leftist positions he campaigned against in his Primary. He has also been accommodating to all the world's bullies, especially China, Russia, and Iran and its many terrorist proxies, just like his mentor Obama.
- That viral present from China also achieved another goal for an authoritarian lurch to the left. It acclimated us to following government mandates or suffering the consequences of firing, fining, intimidation, imprisonment, character assassination, and minimizing their free speech rights. Those mandates have often been wrong or detrimental, especially the ones related to COVID-19 (natural immunity, effective therapeutics, side effects of vaccines, wrong info about transmission), electric cars, and renewable energy. The idea is to get us used to following government mandates, just like in Russia, Iran, and China.

- As a valuable by-product of mandates, we are jeopardizing our financial stability as we and many Western democracies chase costly and unworkable energy foolishness—$5.6 trillion is the annual global cost to pursue but never realize "net zero" carbon emissions by 2050 (for 27 years that is a staggering $151.2 trillion). Much of this wealth transfer is going to China, using a deluge of coal factories to produce our woke, undependable, and problematic wind and solar power, and lithium battery electric vehicles.
- We prefer governing by Executive Orders, activist courts, and legislative trickery rather than three co-equal and effective branches of government. This is a throwback to the days of King George and a prelude to the coming permanent Uniparty authoritarian control.
- Propaganda is an authoritarian cousin of mandates. Much of it has occurred, including exaggerated job totals that made our 2023 economy look better than it was by some 443,000 jobs. Many job number additions are in red states, low-paying hospitality jobs, and government or part-time jobs. Families struggle to survive financially under Bidenomic inflation by taking multiple jobs and using their credit cards for daily living needs. Credit card debt now exceeds $1 trillion.
- Propaganda also takes the form of collusion between the government and Social Media. The security arm of DHS determined in 2020 that in-person voting posed no significant COVID risk and that mail-in ballots are less secure. When others began repeating that position, the collusion ring minimized or eliminated their voices.
- In Russia and other repressive countries that go through the charade of elections, strong political opponents are often persecuted and prosecuted and wind up either assassinated, jailed, or ruled invalid to run. Meanwhile, the leader is free to participate in corruption for his benefit and act like a king, with Executive Orders and mandates to do as he pleases, regardless of the other branches of government. This seems eerily similar to the US, especially with the inadequate protection provided for Donald Trump, resulting in 2 failed assassination attempts.

- Our elections resemble third-world elections and use the wealth of oligarchs and elites to "buy" the election results they want, sometimes even receiving tax deductions, just like they do for controversial ideological programs. We also allow wealthy elites to anonymously contribute huge amounts to 501 (c) (4) non-taxed organizations to destroy people they think could threaten their Wokesphere. This dark money and the 501 (c) (3) money are the corrupt mother's milk of politics that powers the left's Wokesphere Death Star. Its mission is to destroy people, companies, and institutions that stand in the way of their relentless march to authoritarian control. It has been very effective.
- A clear sign we are losing our democratic republic is the way Biden's cognitive issues have been lied about by the D-S and the media. Even more detrimental is the way Biden has been forced off the ballot for 2024 and replaced by his VP. She was so unpopular in the 2020 primaries that she exited them before the voting began. Without her getting a single primary vote in 2020 or 2024 or winning a contested Democratic Party convention, she was installed on the ballot by the power-hungry D-S, and their media allies quickly rebranded as moderates the Socialist team of Harris and Walz. Could the D-S have concocted a more authoritarian process? Some believe the political genius, Obama, has his fingerprints on this.
- Other corrupt election practices include the lack of uniformity of voter ID requirements, the prevalence of massive mail-in voting, paid ballot harvesting into drop boxes, not all voting machine counts allowing validation to a paper ballot, and significant voting other than on election day. These have all been considered too ripe for fraud in the past, but the D-S know that destroying election integrity is the necessary step in the 2024 elections to gain permanent Uniparty control. They are enhancing their efforts by having others instruct undocumented how to get drivers licenses and register to vote.

- Homelessness, crime, and unemployment are not successfully addressed with programs and plant-based therapeutics because they are overwhelms the left embraces to destroy the country.
- Our immigration policy is based on the politics of legalizing 30 million undocumenteds to become citizens and vote Democratic for permanent D-S control. It will happen if they win the 2024 elections. It ignores the 2021–2024 effects of 12 million illegal immigrants, some of whom are terrorists, drug mules, criminals, sex slaves, and criminal gang and cartel members. They happily support the wide-open Southern border, regardless of its enrichment of Mexican drug cartels and the Chinese mafia and the toll it takes on the people being trafficked into the US and the US economy, institutions, and citizens.

  More than 300,000 lives have been lost from Fentanyl trafficking in four years of King Joseph's reign. They appear to be just collateral damage and largely ignored. It is seen as a small price to pay for the greater good of permanent Uniparty control. The D-S are more focused on the comforts and needs of the millions of undocumenteds than the safety of our own citizens. A D-S Senator admitted to that in a February 2024 interview.
- Elimination of choices are fundamental for authoritarian countries. Instead of increasing health insurance choices, we are expanding governmental healthcare. School choice opportunities are plateaued, as the lobby for government indoctrinating schools is overpowering. These are disturbing signposts.
- The rights to protect one's life and property, freedom of speech, and gun ownership have diminished, while the federal administrative bureaucracies have become militarized and enjoy using that muscle. This positions those agencies for the coming new authoritarian Uniparty that will not tolerate any challenges. That Police State has been on display with the phony January 6 setup, proceedings, and treatment of trespassers; FBI tracking concerned parents at School Board meetings; and Trump-related prosecutions and persecutions, often unnecessarily battering down doors and using full assault

military protection and weaponry. Many of us have become fearful of rampant unpunished crime. This fear and punishing political opponents is right out of the Socialist-Communist playbook as necessary pre-conditions to make the Uniparty's Police State more acceptable.

- All Socialist and Communist countries promote the influence of the government and minimize the role and influence of traditional families in their children's lives. The US is right in line with that precept with extreme transgenderism, discouraging parental input on education, and school choice that threatens poor performing indoctrinating public schools.
- A number of our schools have succeeded in making our children dumber by dismissing the value of testing to measure success and using other "participation trophy" approaches. This is exemplified in our global ranking for math proficiency at 26th place.
- Education and the media have manipulated our thinking with their Pravda-like indoctrination. This was exposed during the COVID-19 remote education at home and the interference in the 2020 elections by the collusion of government and media disclosed by Twitter. The letter signed by 50 US intelligence leaders that incorrectly discredited the authenticity of Hunter Biden's laptop was a chilling example of Deep State corruption to win an election.
- Our government has become corrupt and bloated, spending extravagantly without solving problems. That spending has made the US the world's largest debtor at $35 trillion.
- Some say our "real" national debt is actually computed to be $200 trillion more than the reported $35 trillion. This is because of obligations other countries count in their debt, and we do not. Ignoring exploding national debt and creating a growing dependence on government are hallmarks of Socialist regimes.
- The annual cost of our bloated regulations has been reported as $2 trillion. If that regulation were a country, that amount would rank it as the 8th largest country in the world.

- Successful innovative results to stop the leftist-driven overwhelms are treated with disdain. Utah's success with transitioning more people from welfare to work is legislatively forbidden for any other state to implement. Texas's use of barriers to stop the illegal immigration invasion is being fought in the courts by the Uniparty, which wants the overwhelm to continue to complete their permanent government takeover after the 2024 elections.
- Republicans counter the leftists by discussing too much of their upcoming strategy instead of sticking to clear winning issues like border security, stopping massive inflation-causing budget deficits, and safety and crime reduction. Too much information passed on to leftists allows them to distort and create backlashes.
- We are not taking enough action to reverse the decline of our clean and abundant sources of water and energy, which are necessary for any country, especially a superpower. There are many technologies we can use to clean up our landfills and water supply and remove environmental toxins, but the passions of the D-S lie elsewhere.

If the extreme climate zealots were genuinely concerned, they would create a powerful global movement to pressure China and India to stop building coal plants and drastically reduce their pollution. They are the world's biggest polluters and contributors to climate change. That one change would have a massive positive impact on the global climate. These zealots could also strongly champion hydrogen power for transportation and nuclear fusion for grid power.

But that would not help to promote their climate religion dogmas of unreliable solar, wind, and lithium battery electric vehicles (with all of their problems). It would also lessen their exhilarating feeling of power over our lives from all the mandates, rebates, and choice eliminations they take pride in. Lastly, it would not satisfy the massive appetite for subsidies for the wind, solar, and electric vehicle behemoths that can be more willing to corruptly repay that with generous campaign donations.

- In the latest annual survey of countries with the most economic freedom, the US ranking is 25th. That pairs nicely with the latest annual survey of the happiest countries to live in. The US dropped from 15th globally to 23rd. These are not surprising when you look at how negatively things have progressed, especially in the last few years.
- The Biden-Harris "all of government" approach for the expansion of DEI, CRT, and ESG was designed to replace merit, results, culture, and tradition with quotas and flawed ideologies. The 1619 Project, in combination with tearing down statues and renaming buildings, streets, highways, and ships, is trying to rewrite history. This has been a US re-enactment of the 1966 Chinese Red Guard youth destroying similar cultural elements in China as we follow their lead to Socialism.
- All that needed to happen to complete our Socialist transformation was for the D-S to win the 2024 elections for President, the House, and the Senate. They continued their verbal assaults on Trump and his supporters, including lawsuits and lies from the Deep State and media. They unethically forced Biden off the ticket because they could no longer hide his mental decline, and he would lose the election for them. He was replaced with the extreme Socialist ticket of Harris-Walz. They received zero Primary votes and did not have to win a contested D-S convention.

With the help of the US Pravda media, they just had to falsely rebrand themselves as moderates and minimize any unscripted news conferences for 60 days. This selfish gift was given to them by the D-S and they only had to play dodgeball for this short period. If successful, they could skate into the White House and begin Obama's 4th term to complete his "fundamental transformation of the US."

Trump's re-election in 2024 has put a halt to that dystopian progress. If he is successful in implementing legislation and reporting measurable progress on issues, that halt can become a permanent stop.

Global Authoritarian Markers

- Socialism, Communism, and terrorist governments are currently trending, even though they have cost the lives of 100 to 200 million and produce poor results for most except the elites and oligarchs. These trends are built from deceitful and false visions of their dystopia, heavy doses of propaganda, and the mandates of a Police State to stay in power and squelch freedoms. They try to fill the hearts of their citizens with fear and hatred of imperfect democracies that provide a better level of freedom to their citizenry.
- Starting in the 1970s with President Nixon, the US (supported by much of the world) has paternalistically engaged with Communist China with more than $6 trillion transferred to them from accumulated US trade deficits. This has allowed their spies to steal tech and bribe politicians, businesses, and universities; they have monopolistic control and pricing of strategic materials and ingredients for pharmaceuticals, wind and solar power components, and many other needed products. They have hacked into our critical infrastructure systems for at least 5 years to neutralize our military and create havoc for citizens in the event of a conflict between the US and China.
- Bill Clinton was responsible for supercharging China's growth and global threat by getting them into the World Trade Organization. They have become the world's factory and use their monopoly positions at strategic times. Curiously, other US presidents have also enabled China to become the military, economic, and political powerhouse they are today. President Xi's expressed vision for China is to reach its goal to rule "all under heaven."
- China's media and leader have made strong statements recently about the desire to replace the US as the #1 superpower, but that has not been taken seriously. A few months after one of those statements, COVID-19 escaped from China. It circulated the globe, destroying thousands of businesses and killing 1 million Americans and 6 million

in other countries without any apology or transparent and realistic explanation.
- China has created a phony vision of its benevolence, victimization by the US and allies, and it being the savior of the world. The reality is they practice slavery, genocide, intellectual property theft, cultural erasing, ruthless control, discrimination, and support wars and terrorism they or their allies are involved in.
- China controls our pork production, owns 400,000 acres of US agricultural land, and is on our stock markets with companies that do not follow US accounting rules. China and other repressive regimes have learned to blend Corrupt Capitalism into their democracy and freedom-hating cocktail and supply it wherever and whenever needed to foolish individuals and country leaders. Along with partners like Qatar, they have given millions in donations to US universities to buy influence and for propaganda on TikTok and at US colleges to influence youth to be supportive of whatever they want to promote, like the butchery by Hamas that killed 1,200 Jews on October 7, 2023.
- The current size of the Chinese empire is 3 times its historical norm, and they are still focused on expansion. Hong Kong was 1st, and Taiwan and others in the South China Sea are in their crosshairs.
- Meanwhile, Europe has put itself on a path to self-destruct and become Eurabia. This is due to its nonsensical "unlimited" immigration policy that has spread across the continent hundreds of thousands of mainly young Muslim men from terrorist or theocratic countries. Anti-West and antisemitic violence and unrest are happening more frequently due to the lack of a strong assimilation process and sensible limits on immigration.
- Russia and Iran have instigated wars in Ukraine and Israel because they still must periodically distract their citizens from their poor regimes' results by harnessing anger and fear. Curiously, peace in the Middle East was budding with a nearly bankrupt Iran until Biden allowed them sanctions relief, which gave them over $70 billion in reserves. This allowed them to supersize their provision of weapons

and arms to Hamas, Hezbollah, and the Houthis for terrorist use against Israel and US bases and ships in the area. Iran was also able to provide weapons to Russia. The US has stupidly funded both sides of these two wars and only mounted mild responses, even though several Americans have been injured or killed.

- Before the Russian invasion, Ukraine had asked for planes they needed to protect their country and its citizens from death and devastation. Instead, the US waited and implemented financial sanctions against Russia after the invasion. That resulted in building a solid alliance between China and Russia. China is now more strongly aligned with the other repressive regimes of North Korea, Iran, Cuba, Venezuela, and many others. There is an exchange of military equipment, oil, and other trade to support the terrorism unleashed on Ukraine and Israel.
- While the US and Europe are distracted and depleting their weaponry and finances to help Ukraine, Iran will become a nuclear power and a more threatening country to deal with.
- Our "participation trophy" foreign policy shows appeasement to Russia, Iran, and China. The D-S are determined not to allow Ukraine to defeat Russia or Israel to defeat the Hamas terrorists, and our criticism and supply of weapons are done in a measured way to facilitate that. World Wars I and II would have ended in disaster for freedom if we had adopted that philosophy. Wars without winners and losers create instability, and they eventually re-erupt.
- The European NATO countries belatedly realize the Russian threat on their doorstep. They should have been better prepared with increased military spending. That could have supported Ukraine better and still provided for their security.
- China's impact has been enlarged by the alliances it has created with its colonialist Belt and Road Initiative, which burdens many impoverished countries with debt they cannot repay. Their influence has been expanded with the creation of the BRICS alliance, which is growing significantly in its efforts to dethrone the US and its USD as the global reserve currency and supplant that with an upcoming

BRICS digital currency. They have other alliances that are not only political and economic but also military. They are supporting repressive regimes in wars in Ukraine and Israel, and North Korea's and their own bullying in the South China Sea. Their actions directly contrast the phony vision they trumpet worldwide while they seek a global takeover.
- There are several ways to take down the US, including its internal decay (which China and the Middle East bullies spend heavily on with propaganda in the US and other tools). Losing our reserve currency status is the simplest way without firing a shot. The US will be unable to fund its huge budget deficits as the world divests its holdings of USD and US Treasuries.
- We have refused to loudly expose China's weaknesses while doing nothing to fix our own.

***

Could the script be written any better for the transformation of the US and its entry into the Alliance of Repressive Regimes? We must get off this path and choose the "Shining City on a Hill" path to change that ending. The first step in that re-direction has been the 2024 election of Donald Trump and majorities in the House and Senate. We must not backslide from lack of success that could produce election losses to the D-S and put us back on the Road to Perdition.

Conclusion

While you may have known some of the information in these 11 chapters, you now have a more complete understanding of our sense of urgency for change. You know how close we are to ushering in the New Dark Ages. This is similar to the original Dark Ages, which were held together by the coalition of the RAGS (religion, academia, government, science). Today's coalition is much stronger with the addition of media, entertainment, wokesters, phony Republicans, and extreme activist zealots substituting for religions.

The journey through this book began with Chapters 1 and 2. There, you saw how we are following in the footsteps of earlier world powers that decayed and declined. We have corrupted our Founding Principles with the leading role played by political institutions.

The Democrats have been a party consumed with a lust for power and will use any tactics and join with any force that can help achieve their goal of permanent control, so they never have to worry about elections again. The Dems have traded their party of the working class label to the GOP in exchange for its big money label. Big money is needed to fund their rebranding as the party of the extremist cults of the left. They are now the Democrat-Socialist (D-S) Party and welcome wealthy wokesters, squishy Republicans, and RINOs into their Uniparty. They vigorously promote the doctrines of their cults while trampling on our Constitutional rights that stand in their way.

Besides being the party of power, big money, and cults, their brand has other labels. They are also the party of lies, double standards, lack of transparency, open borders, military incompetence, mediocre and brainwashing education, disinformation and propaganda, intolerance and racial division, participation trophy strategy, and keeping as many as possible dependent on a bureaucratic, corrupt, and financially unsound government, They have built a Wokesphere echo chamber, which is they safely inhabit and viciously attack from.

The GOP has an unclear identity due to its mixture of globalists, RINOs, Never-Trumpers, MAGA, Conservatives, squishy get-alongers, and some Solutionists. They need to purify themselves as the D-S have done. Their unifying principle should be to accountably solve the nation's problems in contrast to the D-S principle of permanent Uniparty power.

The disasters wreaked by Socialism, Communism, and terrorism are responsible for the deaths of 100 to 200 million. They are exposed in Chapters 3 to 5, along with China's role in dethroning the US as the #1 superpower, the triggers that could result in the US losing its position in the world, and China's weaknesses that we have been unwilling to loudly expose. There have also been predictions beginning in 1978 by noted author-historians of the US downfall agreeing on the occurrence within this decade of the 2020s.

The Solutionist process for major internal national security problems runs through Chapters 6 to 8 and for major external national security problems in Chapters 9 to 11. Election integrity (Chapter 6) can be significantly improved and is the most critical issue of all due to the D-S goal of legalizing all 30 million illegal immigrants as a horde of new D-S voters for a permanent majority of the D-S Uniparty. Changing our authoritarian future can only happen with solid election integrity.

Our government processes (Chapter 7) are filled with legislative gamesmanship, trickery, and massive spending to feed an ever-growing and inefficient bureaucracy that lures more people into dependence on it. The Judiciary is not impartial and prosecutes and persecutes political opponents. The Executive Branch governs like a king, setting up a

Police State by militarizing administrative departments and spewing out Executive Orders to impose its will on the country and neutering Congress's role.

All three branches are very well taken care of, although they have not solved major problems for their citizens. Many are motivated by their quest for the 3Ps of power, prestige, and personal enrichment. Our tax deduction and political donation systems have allowed the wealthy to unduly "buy" elections or impose controversial policies and often get large charitable deductions for their efforts. There are solutions for minimizing all of this corruption.

Crime (Chapter 8) has purposely been allowed to run rampant while common-sense solutions for crime, homelessness, and unemployment are ignored.

Chapter 9 shows how we have intentionally flung open the floodgates during 2021–2024 to add more than 12 million illegal immigrants to accomplish the left's goals of legalizing what now totals 30 million undocumenteds and capturing their votes. That will produce a power grab to punch our ticket to our new permanent authoritarian destination unless we implement remedies.

Chapter 10 shows how we have foolishly nurtured Communist China with over $6 trillion in trade deficits to produce a military giant that intimidates its citizens and neighbors, funds wars and terrorism, produces a phony vision of its benevolence, and is amassing significant alliances to dethrone the US. The left's participation trophy philosophy, which is domestically destructive, is even more so internationally. That philosophy has led to an embarrassing and tragic pullout in Afghanistan and devastating wars in Ukraine and Israel, where we have funded both sides of these wars. We are ill-prepared to demonstrate strength to China with our woke military.

We allow the Chinese government and companies to not follow US financial standards and still be included on our stock exchanges; have their youth educated in our colleges and universities; bribe our money-hungry high schools and colleges with significant donations to spread propaganda and discord there; buy US businesses and agricultural land and control our pork processing and distribution; spy on our military and critical systems; steal US technology; and have hacked our critical US infrastructure systems for over five years.

We and the rest of the world have allowed China to become a monopoly supplier and use that monopoly pricing power over critical materials, including pharmaceuticals, solar and wind power components, and lithium and other rare minerals for batteries of electric vehicles and other needs. Their colonialist One Belt One Road strategy has ensnared many of its 154 beneficiary countries to essentially act as colonies for them, providing bases, ports, and precious mineral supplies. At the same time, many of these loans from China cannot be repaid. China is positioned well to win at Global Domination Monopoly, while we seem oblivious to their strategy or even the game being played.

Our abundant clean water supply (Chapter 11) from our lakes, rivers, and underground aquifers is seriously jeopardized by aging water infrastructure and the allowance of toxic materials, pharmaceuticals, and plastics to pollute our landfills and waters. There are things we can do now and discoveries we need to scale up to change that, but the attention is elsewhere.

Hydrogen discoveries (for more effective and less costly fuel cell vehicles) have identified several ways to efficiently produce green and blue hydrogen. This is the workable new tech we need to make more widespread, looking to South Korea, Japan, and parts of Europe for inspiration. Trains, cars, trucks, and jets have successfully used this tech, which requires no grid upgrades or building a glut of expensive charging stations. We must retrofit this into our existing gas station network (as has been done in Japan) to make for a simpler, cleaner, and cheaper solution.

A point worth repeating is that in 2021, an HFC Toyota Mirai set a Guinness record when it averaged 152 MPG and traveled 845 miles on one tank of hydrogen. Imagine that being boosted even further by using solar cells embedded in the body and an opposed-piston engine under the hood.

The alternative is to continue wasting taxpayer money on more wind and solar, as well as 500,000 new battery charging stations for problematic and expensive EVs with serious charging and grid concerns. Remember that Ford claims they lose $66,000 on every EV they sell. Do we really want to force ourselves into that losing proposition? And those "investments" will still fail to reach our 2030 and 2050 climate targets. That is despite annual global spending of $5.6 trillion (totaling $151 trillion through 2050), with much of that wealth transfer going to China.

Corrupt US pork barrel spending and the bribing rebates, subsidies, grants, and loans provided for undependable wind and solar power and problematic electric cars amount to $73 billion annually. Redirecting that can produce several positive outcomes. It can detoxify our land and waters, provide a clean and abundant water supply, and avoid drastic conservation mandates. Our power grid can become dependable with space and water-based solar power and limitless fusion power with no toxic waste. It can also clean up and reuse our dangerous stockpiles of radioactive nuclear fission waste.

Lastly, we can focus part of that $73 billion on partnering with other countries to lead the charge into clean, abundant, and cheap hydrogen-powered transportation. HFC vehicles get significantly better mileage with zero pollution. Also, hydrogen as the most plentiful element in the world is better than the rare earth minerals like lithium that are often not responsibly mined and are in shorter supply.

Every few days, there are reports of new advancements in fusion grid power and clean hydrogen to meet all our transportation needs. The lobbies for wind, solar, and EVs work with politicians to ignore those better alternatives.

Here's How You Can Make a Big Difference Now

MAKE YOUR VOICE HEARD WITH YOUR SENATORS AND OTHERS OF INFLUENCE TO SUPPORT ENDING THE SENATE FILIBUSTER PROCESS. This practice is outdated and allows senators to not be transparent and accountable for their votes. Thankfully this was not in place when the D-S had the Senate majority, but they vowed to do it if they were in the majority again. The Senate has to stop being a good old boys club where the minority can play god and kill legislation from the majority that was elected. The D-S should not complain, as this is what they wanted.

RESIST BIPARTISANSHIP CRIES FROM THE D-S. We must remind them how they did not practice it when the Senate was tied at 50-50 and they had a very slim margin in the House. We must return the favor in order to get our sensible Solutionist legislation passed, just like how they acted to pass their inflationary wish list.

STAY VIGILANT WITH YOUR ELECTION REGISTRATION AND VOTING, AND SUPPORT ELECTION INTEGRITY. Be sure to keep your registration up to date and continue to vote and elect Solutionist leaders to drown out the Socialist voices. Support the kind of reforms in Chapter 6 to ensure our elections are not hijacked and won by illegitimate votes, corrupt practices, or outrageous sums of money. You can support election integrity through one of the 3 organizations listed at the beginning of Chapter 6— www.whoscounting.us, www.earlyvoteaction.com, and the RNC website www.protectthe vote.com.

Next, hold your local, state, and national candidates and elected officials to be Solutionists. That means embracing the steps of Solutionism: problem prioritization, identification of the key issues and solution frameworks for those major problems, filling in all the details for those frameworks, and regular metric progress measurement and reporting to hold themselves accountable for solution progress.

Biden's protégé, Kamala and her fellow Socialist VP candidate, Walz were ready to complete Obama's desired "fundamental transformation" to make the US "unrecognizable." Patriotic Americans saw the unethical and illegal tactics of the D-S and where they were leading us and rejected it. We must continue that campaign.

If a candidate is a member of the D-S or a shill to get them elected, they should never deserve your vote. They will destroy our financial integrity and lose our precious reserve currency status, ruin our country, and roll out the red carpet for the leaders of the major global tyrants of Russia, Iran, and China. These new BFF comrades would welcome us into the New World Order and Alliance of Repressive Regimes.

No D-S will anytime soon become a Solutionist, and many Republicans may not be one now (that's what primaries are for). If an election has a Republican who is not a Solutionist (they may later become one) or has a style or rhetoric you do not like, consider again our democracy and dire freedom-ending consequences of a D-S Uniparty victory, hold your nose, and give that person your support.

Which Path We Follow Is Up to Us

We will soon either be Socialists (the easy first path) or Solutionists (the more challenging second path), and there is no peaceful co-existence between the two. The Democrat-Socialists (D-S) will use any means and anyone to their advantage and are incredibly hateful towards Solutionists since they block the path of the US to Socialism. That path will usher in the New World Order with President Xi of China realizing his dream and becoming the Godfather of Repressive Regimes, as freedoms and democracies are eliminated.

Any other identities individuals choose to adopt will not last. You only need to reflect on how polarized we are now. There is the remarkably unified D-S vs. everyone else. That "everyone else" will be more powerful and successful if we stop being splintered and unify, just like the D-S have done. We need to adopt the identity of Solutionists and purge rampant corruption from our government, institutions, and our lives.

As a significant part of that, we must re-embrace and stop corrupting our Founding Principles, especially Principle #9, and stay or become strong. That principle embodies the core beliefs of the 3 Rs that are not as universal as they once—the need to accept the personal risk they are taking with their actions, the need to respect others' lives and property, and the need for restitution for harm and damages caused. Returning to our Founding Principles will support the Solutionist methodology to become the Shining City on a Hill.

That is critical for revitalizing the US to stop the growing Alliance of Repressive Regimes from devouring democracies. China and its allied regimes in other Socialist, Communist, and terrorist nations are supported by brutal authoritarian control. Hong Kong was the first victim without hardly a shot being fired. Ukraine, Israel, and Taiwan are the current targets of focus.

Republican and Conservative are good terms, but they are missing a process for problem solving. Everyone should be able to embrace the Solutionism process that is designed to solve problems and not just talk about them. Fortunately, we have recent examples of Solutionism at work: Trump's 2017–2020 accomplishments; Ukraine's brave fight for survival; the new Argentinian President who is boldly trying to remake his country from a 100-year history of failed Socialism into a Solutionist one; the new Italian Prime Minister who is also abandoning her country's unproductive Socialist history; and several Republican governors who have taken a Solutionist approach to their states' problems.

Discovery and innovation are visibly flourishing (especially noticeable in Chapter 11). We must use the 2024 election results to redirect our path and make progress to become the Shining City on a Hill. Then those innovations will accelerate and benefit us and the world. But, if we lose focus and complete our authoritarian transformation, the pace of those discoveries and innovations will slow as economies become less free. Tight control of economies produces less reward for merit, resulting in fewer innovations, and those more limited benefits will generally be available only to the ruling class, oligarchs, and a few elites, who will be treated as "more equal" than everyone else. If you are not in those groups, the equality promised by Socialism will be apportioned to everyone else in the form of equal misery or equal mediocrity.

The Socialist path has just a few steps left to reach its destination. But the 2024 election result have halted that progress. It has also put us on a more difficult path that leads to a more rewarding destination. Our ungodly transformation clock has been put back several minutes, and we have a unique opportunity to permanently stop the completion of its journey to strike midnight. We changed history in a positive direction with the American Revolution and our involvement in winning WW I and II. **Let's wake up, woke down,** and do it one more time.

The US (including those who previously lived in authoritarian nations and see that happening here) has been sending out an SOS. We responded overwhelming in 2024 to be a part of the solution and stop the authoritarian lurch. We need to make the Solutionism process a routine part of government accountability. Trump is a unicorn President and instinctively acts like a Solutionist. We only have him for four years. So getting this process institutionalized will mean all future Presidents will have to focus on solutions and reporting progress whether they want to or not. We must transform our country in a positive direction into the Shining City on a Hill? If you want world peace, authoritarianism is not the path to follow.

This book must be more than an informative, shocking, and entertaining read. Your participation as a Solutionist is critical to freeing us from being pulled into that dystopian Black Hole that has no escape pod. It is up to each of us to "wake up and woke down" to get off this disastrous path. The coalition of the RAGS has paved that path, and some of the RAGS are showing signs of unraveling. Let's complete that unraveling and be the authors who rewrite that script for a better ending for the world. **2024 will be remembered as the year we responded to that SOS and began building our Shining City.**

For more information, visit https://www.ronmitori.com.

Notes

Dedication
1. Peter Lumaj, "Meet Peter Lumaj," *Lumaj Radio*, accessed June 18, 2024, https://lumajradio.com/?page_id=8.
2. "Drago Dzieran." Drago Dzieran. Accessed June 18, 2024. https://dragodzieran.com.
3. ChinaAid, "Pray for those who persecute you: Chinese pastor on CBN," ChinaAid, August 30, 2023, https://www.chinaaid.org/pray-for-those-who-persecute-you.
4. Yeonmi Park. *While Time Remains: A North Korean Defector's Search for Freedom in America.* Threshold Editions, 2023.
5. Rebekah Koffler, *Putin's Playbook: Russia's Secret Plan to Defeat America* (Washington, DC: Regnery Gateway, 2021).

Chapter 1
1. Reboot Foundation, 2023. "The TikTok Challenge," May. Accessed June 18, 2024. https://reboot-foundation.org/research/the-tiktok-challenge-curbing-social-medias-influence-on-young-minds/.
2. "Red Guards." *Encyclopaedia Britannica Online.* Accessed June 18, 2024. https://www.britannica.com/topic/Red-Guards.
3. Heritage Foundation, *2023 Index of Economic Freedom* (Washington, D.C.: Heritage Foundation, 2023), accessed June 18, 2024, https://www.heritage.org/index/ranking.

4. Centers for Disease Control and Prevention, "Overweight & Obesity Statistics," National Center for Health Statistics, last modified February 27, 2023, accessed June 19, 2024, https://www.cdc.gov/nchs/fastats/obesity-overweight.htm.
5. Heilpern, Layah. *Undressing Bitcoin*. London: Hachette UK, 2020.

Chapter 2

1. Green, Alexander. "Meet the World's Worst Economist." *Investment U*, December 18, 2019. Accessed June 19, 2024. https://investmentu.com/paul-krugman-meet-worlds-worst-economist/
2. Krugman, Paul. "Paul Krugman Says Don't Worry About Dollar Despite Recent Challenges." *Markets Insider*, February 6, 2023. https://markets.businessinsider.com/news/currencies/paul-krugman-dollar-dominance-weakening-currencies-china-yuan-russia-ruble-2023-2.
3. Bernanke, Ben S. "The dollar's international role: An 'exorbitant privilege'?" *Brookings Institution*, January 7, 2016. https://www.brookings.edu/blog/ben-bernanke/2016/01/07/the-dollars-international-role-an-exorbitant-privilege.
4. "Remarks by President Biden on the End of the War in Afghanistan." *The White House*, August 31, 2021. https://www.whitehouse.gov/briefing-room/speeches-remarks/2021/08/31/remarks-by-president-biden-on-the-end-of-the-war-in-afghanistan/.
5. Orwell, George. *1984*. New York: Harcourt, Brace & World, 1949.
6. Greenberg, Jon. "Tara Reade Has Accused Joe Biden of Sexual Assault. Here's What We Know." *PolitiFact*. Last modified April 2020. https://www.politifact.com/article/2020/apr/29/tara-reade-has-accused-joe-biden-sexual-assault-he/.
7. Wikipedia contributors. "Douglass Mackey." *Wikipedia, The Free Encyclopedia*. Last modified June 19, 2024. https://en.wikipedia.org/wiki/Douglass_Mackey.
8. Durkin Richer, Alanna. "Court Tosses Jan. 6 Sentence in Ruling That Could Impact Other Low-Level Capitol Riot Cases." *Yahoo News*, August 18, 2023. https://www.yahoo.com/news/court-tosses-jan-6-sentence-193648821.html.
9. No Labels. "Five Facts on Reforming the Electoral Count Act of 1887." *RealClearPolicy*, January 21, 2022. https://www.realclearpolicy.com/

articles/2022/01/21/five_facts_on_reforming_the_electoral_count_act_of_1887_812956.html.
10. Wikipedia contributors. "Joe Biden classified documents incident." *Wikipedia, The Free Encyclopedia.* https://en.wikipedia.org/wiki/Joe_Biden_classified_documents_incident.
11. Hur, Robert. "Special Counsel Report on Biden's Handling of Classified Documents." *CBS News*, February 8, 2024. https://www.cbsnews.com/news/biden-special-counsel-report-handling-classified-documents/.
12. Sprunt, Barbara. "Pelosi Rejects 2 GOP Nominees For The Jan. 6 Panel, Citing 'Integrity' Of The Probe." NPR, July 21, 2021. https://www.npr.org/2021/07/21/1018850848/pelosi-rejects-2-gop-nominees-for-the-jan-6-panel-citing-integrity-of-the-probe.
13. "How Trump's Alleged Hush Money Payments Led to His Charges in New York." *PBS NewsHour*, April 5, 2023. https://www.pbs.org/newshour/show/how-trumps-alleged-hush-money-payments-led-to-his-charges-in-new-york.
14. Levin, Mark. "Clinton and Obama Campaigns Committed Egregious FEC Violations, But Just Fines Imposed, No Prosecution." *Western Journal*, March 2022. https://www.westernjournal.com/levin-clinton-obama-campaigns-committed-egregious-fec-violations-just-fines-imposed-no-prosecution/.
15. Levin, Mark R. *The Democrat Party Hates America.* New York: Threshold Editions, 2023. https://www.pbs.org/newshour/show/how-trumps-alleged-hush-money-payments-led-to-his-charges-in-new-york.
16. Matalucci, Sergio. "The Hydrogen Stream: Germany, Italy Plan Hydrogen Pipeline to North Africa." *pv magazine International*, November 24, 2023. Accessed June 21, 2024. https://www.pv-magazine.com/2023/11/24/the-hydrogen-stream-germany-italy-plan-hydrogen-pipeline-to-north-africa.
17. "Argentina's Milei Announces 50% Currency Devaluation and Large Cuts to Public Spending." *EL PAÍS*, December 13, 2023. Accessed June 21, 2024. https://english.elpais.com/international/2023-12-13/argentinas-milei-announces-50-currency-devaluation-and-large-cuts-to-public-spending.html.
18. MacKinnon, Joseph. "Javier Milei Eliminates Half of Argentina's Government Ministries on First Day as President." *Blaze Media*, December 11, 2023. Accessed June 21, 2024. https://www.theblaze.

com/news/javier-milei-eliminates-half-of-argentinas-government-ministries-on-first-day-as-president.
19. Olivera Doll, Ignacio. "How Javier Milei would cut Argentina spending by 14% of GDP." *Buenos Aires Times*. Accessed June 21, 2024. https://www.batimes.com.ar/news/economy/how-javier-milei-would-cut-argentina-spending-by-14-of-gdp.phtml.
20. Sanchez, Sandy. "How President-elect Javier Milei can have a shot at fixing Argentina's chronic economic crisis." *Christensen Institute*, November 28, 2023. Accessed June 21, 2024. https://www.christenseninstitute.org/blog/how-president-elect-javier-milei-can-have-a-shot-at-fixing-argentinas-chronic-economic-crisis.
21. "Presidency of Bill Clinton." *Wikipedia*. Accessed June 21, 2024. https://en.wikipedia.org/wiki/Presidency_of_Bill_Clinton.
22. "Middle Eastern Foreign Policy of the Barack Obama Administration." *Wikipedia*. Accessed June 21, 2024. https://en.wikipedia.org/wiki/Middle_Eastern_foreign_policy_of_the_Barack_Obama_administration.
23. "Obama Fumbles 'JV Team' Question." *FactCheck.org*. September 7, 2014. Accessed June 21, 2024. https://www.factcheck.org/2014/09/obama-fumbles-jv-team-question/
24. Brian Hughes, "President Obama Faces Third Crisis with Justice Department Monitoring of Journalists," *Washington Examiner*, May 13, 2013. Accessed June 21, 2024. https://www.washingtonexaminer.com/president-obama-faces-third-crisis-with-justice-department-monitoring-of-journalists.
25. "NIH Lifts Funding Pause on Gain-of-Function Research." *National Institutes of Health*, December 19, 2017. Accessed June 21, 2024. https://www.nih.gov/about-nih/who-we-are/nih-director/statements/nih-lifts-funding-pause-gain-function-research.
26. Johnson, Ron. "Obamacare's Costs Are Soaring." Ron Johnson, Senator from Wisconsin. March 2012. Accessed June 21, 2024. https://www.ronjohnson.senate.gov/2012/3/obamacare-s-costs-are-soaring.
27. "Obama Donor Gained Nearly $1 Billion in Tax Credits in Solyndra Bankruptcy." Fox News. Accessed June 21, 2024. https://www.foxnews.com/politics/obama-donor-gained-nearly-1-billion-in-tax-credits-in-solyndra-bankruptcy.
28. Peter Morici. "Reagan's Economy vs. Obama's." RealClearPolicy. January 4, 2016. Accessed June 21, 2024. https://www.realclearpolicy.com/blog/2016/01/05/reagans_economy_vs_obamas_1508.html.

29. Roberts, Lance. "Economic Growth: Obama Vs. Reagan." Investing.com. Published September 9, 2014. Updated February 15, 2024. Accessed June 21, 2024. https://www.investing.com/analysis/economic-growth-obama-vs.-reagan-225151.
30. Mast, David. "How Barack Obama Fundamentally Transformed the United States." National Catholic Register. Accessed June 21, 2024. https://www.ncregister.com/news/how-barack-obama-fundamentally-transformed-the-united-states.
31. "Trump Administration Accomplishments." The White House. Accessed June 21, 2024. https://trumpwhitehouse.archives.gov/trump-administration-accomplishments/.
32. Bowyer, Jerry. "Trump Has More in Common with Lincoln than You Might Think." The Hill. Published September 29, 2020. Accessed June 21, 2024. https://thehill.com/opinion/white-house/518966-trump-has-more-in-common-with-lincoln-than-you-might-think/.
33. "Consumer prices up 9.1 percent over the year ended June 2022, largest increase in 40 years." The Economics Daily, U.S. Bureau of Labor Statistics. July 18, 2022. Accessed June 21, 2024. https://www.bls.gov/opub/ted/2022/consumer-prices-up-9-1-percent-over-the-year-ended-june-2022-largest-increase-in-40-years.htm.
34. "U.S. Economy Shrank for a Second Quarter in a Row, Raising Recession Fear." NPR. Published July 28, 2022. Accessed June 21, 2024. https://www.npr.org/2022/07/28/1113649843/gdp-2q-economy-2022-recession-two-quarters.
35. Stanek, Becca. "When Will Inflation End? Forecasts for 2023." The Week. Accessed June 21, 2024. https://theweek.com/inflation/1019344/personal-finance-when-will-inflation-end-forecasts-for-2023.
36. Rosenberg, David [@EconguyRosie]. "The downward revisions in 2023 totaled an epic 443,000. More than 40 percent of payroll growth in 2023 didn't even come from the survey but from the fairy-tale 'Birth-Death' model." Twitter, June 14, 2023. Accessed June 21, 2024. https://x.com/EconguyRosie/status/1743305794840408348?lang=en.
37. Valinsky, Jordan. "Consumer Sentiment Hits Record Low in June as Inflation Soars." CNN. Published June 10, 2022. Accessed June 21, 2024. https://www.cnn.com/2022/06/10/business/consumer-sentiment-preliminary-june-inflation/index.html.

38. "Congressional Record – House." 118th Cong., 2nd sess., March 12, 2024. Vol. 170, no. 44. Accessed June 21, 2024. https://www.congress.gov/118/crec/2024/03/12/170/44/CREC-2024-03-12.pdf.
39. "Fact Check: Biden Brags About Deficit Reduction While Adding Nearly $10 Trillion in New Spending." House Budget Committee. Accessed June 21, 2024. https://budget.house.gov/press-release/fact-check-biden-brags-about-deficit-reduction-while-adding-nearly-10-trillion-in-new-spending/.
40. Dunleavy, Jerry. *Kabul.* New York: Center Street, 2023.
41. Sullivan, Eileen. "Iran and U.S. Agree on Prisoner Swap, Opening the Way to Broader Talks." *The New York Times*, August 10, 2023. Accessed June 21, 2024. https://www.nytimes.com/2023/08/10/us/politics/iran-us-prisoner-swap.html.
42. Schweizer, Peter. *Blood Money.* New York: Harper, 2024.
43. Erickson, Peter, and Eric Eggers. "Will the Real Robert Peters Please Stand Up?" *The Drill Down with Peter and Eric.* Podcast audio, September 13, 2023. Accessed June 21, 2024. https://thedrilldown.com/podcast-episodes/will-the-real-robert-peters-please-stand-up/
44. Moore, Steven Nelson and Samuel Chamberlain. "Biden Exchanged 82,000 Pages of Private Emails as Vice President: Lawsuit." *New York Post*, October 31, 2023. Accessed June 21, 2024. https://nypost.com/2023/10/31/news/biden-exchanged-82000-pages-of-private-emails-as-vice-president-lawsuit/.
45. "IRS Whistleblowers Expose How Bidens Were Treated Differently." Committee on Oversight and Accountability. Accessed June 21, 2024. https://oversight.house.gov/release/hearing-wrap-up-irs-whistleblowers-expose-how-bidens-were-treated-differently%EF%BF%BC/.
46. Schweizer, Peter. *Secret Empires: How the American Political Class Hides Corruption and Enriches Family and Friends.* New York: Harper, 2018.
47. Cercone, Jeff. "Checking Robert Gates' Criticism of Vice President Joe Biden's Foreign Policy Record." *PolitiFact.* Published January 16, 2014. Accessed June 21, 2024. https://www.politifact.com/factchecks/2014/jan/16/robert-gates/robert-gates-criticism-vice-president-joe-biden/.
48. Gates, Robert M. Duty: Memoirs of a Secretary at War. New York: Alfred A. Knopf, 2014.
49. "Supreme Court's Affirmative Action Ruling Approved by Most Voters." *Rasmussen Reports.* Accessed June 21, 2024. https://www.

rasmussenreports.com/public_content/politics/biden_administration/supreme_court_s_affirmative_action_ruling_approved_by_most_voters.

Chapter 3

1. D'Souza, Dinesh, director. *2000 Mules*. Salem Media Group, 2022.
2. "Poll: Majority of Young Adults Have Positive View of Socialism." *Breitbart*, June 28, 2021. Accessed June 21, 2024. https://www.breitbart.com/social-justice/2021/06/28/majority-young-adults-positive-socialism/.
3. Blackbook of Communism. "100 Years of Communism—and 100 Million Dead." *The Wall Street Journal*, November 6, 2017. Accessed June 21, 2024. https://www.wsj.com/articles/100-years-of-communismand-100-million-dead-1510011810.
4. Cloward, Richard A., and Frances Fox Piven. "The Weight of the Poor: A Strategy to End Poverty." *The Nation*, May 2, 1966.
5. Orwell, George. *Animal Farm*. London: Secker and Warburg, 1945.
6. Orwell, George. *1984*. London: Secker and Warburg, 1949.
7. "Playboy Interview with Saul Alinsky." *New English Review*. Accessed June 21, 2024. https://www.newenglishreview.org/articles/playboy-interview-with-saul-alinsky/.
8. Haberman, Maggie, and Eileen Sullivan. "Trump Blames Media for Inciting 'Anger' After Bombs Are Sent to His Critics." *The New York Times*, October 25, 2018. Accessed June 21, 2024. https://www.nytimes.com/2018/10/25/us/politics/trump-attacks-media-bombs.html.
9. Perry, Mark J. "World Poverty Rate Plummets." *American Enterprise Institute*, July 13, 2015. Accessed June 21, 2024. https://www.aei.org/economics/aging/world-poverty-rate-plummets/.
10. Tiwari, Sailesh. "Stepping Up the Fight Against Extreme Poverty." *World Bank Blogs*, April 21, 2021. Accessed June 21, 2024. https://blogs.worldbank.org/en/developmenttalk/stepping-fight-against-extreme-poverty#:~:text=The%20COVID%2D19%20pandemic%20marked,one%20billion%20people%20escaping%20poverty.
11. "2022 Index of Economic Freedom." *The Heritage Foundation*. Accessed June 21, 2024. https://www.heritage.org/index/pages/report#:~:text=Economies%20rated%20%E2%80%9Cfree%E2%80%9D%20or%20%E2%80%9C,incomes%20of%20%E2%80%9Crepressed%E2%80%9D%20economies.

12. "Commentary." *The Heritage Foundation*. Accessed June 21, 2024. http://www.heritage.org/conservatism/commentary.

Chapter 4

1. National Association of Scholars. "Press Release: Confucius Institutes Rebrand to Circumvent US Policy, Report Finds." *National Association of Scholars*, June 21, 2023. https://www.nas.org/blogs/press_release/press-release-confucius-institutes-rebrand-to-circumvent-us-policy-report-finds.
2. "Russian General's Announcement Raises Alarm Bells." *MSN News*, September 2023. https://www.msn.com/en-gb/news/world/russian-generals-announcement-raises-alarm-bells/ar-AA1guZpL.
3. Singh, G. Parthasarathy. "Requiem for Democracy." *The Pioneer*, August 28, 2018. https://www.dailypioneer.com/2018/columnists/requiem-for-democracy.html.
4. Moffit, Rachel Greszler. "Heritage Explains: Biden's Recession." *The Heritage Foundation*, June 14, 2022. https://www.heritage.org/markets-and-finance/heritage-explains/bidens-recession.
5. Wu, Meng-Jie, and Nizar R. "Chinese Hackers Target Military in Preparation for Taiwan Invasion." *Politico*, April 16, 2023. https://www.politico.com/news/2023/04/16/chinese-hackers-military-taiwan-invasion-00092189.

Chapter 5

1. Kazianis, Harry. "China's Economy Past the Point of No Return." *The National Interest*, October 4, 2016. https://nationalinterest.org/blog/the-buzz/chinas-economy-past-the-point-no-return-18858?nopaging=1.
2. Williams, Anthony. "China's Debt Bomb Is Going Off under Xi Jinping." *Newsweek*, February 14, 2022. https://www.newsweek.com/chinas-debt-bomb-going-off-under-xi-jinping-opinion-1676918.
3. Chang, Gordon. "The Chinese Economy Is in a Death Spiral." *19FortyFive*, May 21, 2022. https://www.19fortyfive.com/2022/05/the-chinese-economy-is-in-a-death-spiral/.
4. Chang, Gordon G. "Time to Declare a 'People's War' on the CCP: All of China Is One Military Machine." *The Epoch Times*, September 12, 2023. https://www.theepochtimes.com/opinion/time-to-declare-a-peoples-war-on-the-ccp-all-of-china-is-one-military-machine-5490197.

5. Lombardi, Vince. "When you've got the momentum in a football game, that is a time to keep going and get it into the end zone." *Parade*. Accessed June 21, 2024. https://parade.com/1334566/rose-maura-lorre/vince-lombardi-quotes/.
6. Hanson, Victor Davis. "Imperialism: Lessons From History." *Imprimis*, July/August 2023. https://imprimis.hillsdale.edu/imperialism-lessons-from-history/.

Chapter 6

1. Mordock, Jeff. "Voter Fraud Convictions Challenge Narrative of Secure Elections." *The Epoch Times*, October 23, 2023. https://www.theepochtimes.com/article/voter-fraud-convictions-challenge-narrative-of-secure-elections-5556968.
2. Spakovsky, Hans von. "A Sampling of Recent Election Fraud Cases from Across the United States." *The Heritage Foundation*. Accessed June 21, 2024. https://www.heritage.org/voterfraud.
3. Bongino, Dan. "The Cold Civil War Is Getting Warmer." *The Dan Bongino Show*, January 25, 2024. https://bongino.com/ep-2173-the-cold-civil-war-is-getting-warmer.
4. D'Souza, Dinesh, director. *2,000 Mules*. Salem Media Group, 2022.
5. Bossie, David N. "Mark Zuckerberg's 'Donations' Rigged the 2020 Election." *The Washington Times*, April 13, 2022. https://www.presidentialcoalition.com/washington-times-david-bossie-mark-zuckerbergs-donations-rigged-the-2020-election/.
6. Bloomberg Philanthropies. "Michael R. Bloomberg Doubles Down with Additional $500M to Help End Fossil Fuels and Usher in a New Era of Clean Energy in the United States." September 20, 2023. Accessed July 9, 2024. https://www.bloomberg.org/press/michael-r-bloomberg-doubles-down-with-additional-500m-to-help-end-fossil-fuels-and-usher-in-a-new-era-of-clean-energy-in-the-united-states/

Chapter 7

1. Siconolfi, Michael. "Government Officials Invest in Companies Their Agencies Oversee." *Wall Street Journal*, October 11, 2022. Accessed July 9, 2024. https://www.wsj.com/articles/government-officials-invest-in-companies-their-agencies-oversee-11665489653.

2. National Association of Manufacturers. "The Cost of Federal Regulation to the U.S. Economy, Manufacturing and Small Business." Accessed July 9, 2024. https://www.nam.org/wp-content/uploads/2023/11/NAM-3731-Crains-Study-R3-V2-FIN.pdf.
3. Thorington, C. B. "Why Did the Great Depression Last So Long?" *A Divided World*, June 20, 2019. Accessed July 9, 2024. https://www.adividedworld.com/economic-ideas/why-did-the-great-depression-last-so-long/.
4. Bongino, Dan. "Dinesh D'Souza Releases Trailer for Can't-Miss New Film 'Police State'." *Bongino.com*, September 11, 2023. Accessed July 9, 2024. https://bongino.com/dinesh-dsouza-police-state-teaser.

Chapter 8

1. Schnell, Mychael. "Group Trying to Disbar Lawyers Who Worked on Trump's Post-Election Efforts." *The Hill*, March 5, 2022. Accessed July 9, 2024. https://thehill.com/homenews/administration/597163-group-trying-to-disbar-lawyers-who-worked-on-trumps-post-election/.
2. Gandhi, Mahatma. "Among the many misdeeds of British rule in India, history will look upon the Act depriving a whole nation of arms as the blackest." In *The Story of My Experiments with Truth*. Accessed July 9, 2024. https://libquotes.com/gandhi/quote/lbx1u8f.
3. Pollan, Michael. *How to Change Your Mind*. Netflix, 2022. Accessed July 9, 2024. https://michaelpollan.com/films/how-to-change-your-mind/.

Chapter 9

1. "All In with Chris Hayes." Episode 21, aired February 7, 2024, on MSNBC. Accessed July 9, 2024. https://www.nbc.com/all-in-with-chris-hayes/video/all-in-2724/9000375413.
2. Caddle, Peter. "Radical Islam, Not 'White Supremacism', Is the Biggest Terrorism Threat in Europe, French Minister Declares." *Breitbart*, May 21, 2023. Accessed July 9, 2024. https://www.breitbart.com/europe/2023/05/21/radical-islam-not-white-supremacism-is-the-biggest-terrorism-threat-in-europe-french-minister-declares/.
3. Goswami, Gopal. "As Europe is Fast Becoming Eurabia, The West Must Reassess Its Refugee Policy." *Firstpost*, April 2, 2023. Accessed July 9, 2024. https://www.firstpost.com/opinion/as-europe-is-fast-becoming-eurabia-west-must-reassess-its-refugee-policy-12345678.html.

4. Dinan, Stephen. "Cartels' Human Smuggling Fees Produce Estimated $XX." *Washington Times*, September 27, 2022. Accessed July 9, 2024. https://www.washingtontimes.com.
5. Schweizer, Peter. *Blood Money: Why the Powerful Turn a Blind Eye While China Kills Americans*. New York: HarperCollins, 2022.

Chapter 10

1. Baudelaire, Charles. *Le Spleen de Paris*. 1869. Accessed July 9, 2024. https://www.goodreads.com/quotes/8784723-the-greatest-trick-the-devil-ever-pulled-was-convincing-the.
2. State Council Information Office of the People's Republic of China. "A Global Community of Shared Future: China's Proposals and Actions." September 26, 2023. Accessed July 9, 2024. https://english.www.gov.cn/news/202309/26/content_WS6512703dc6d0868f4e8dfc37.html.
3. "The world according to Xi." *Support4Partnership*, May 31, 2023. Accessed July 9, 2024. http://support4partnership.org/en/news/the-world-according-to-xi.
4. Marc Morano, *The Great Reset: Global Elites and the Permanent Lockdown* (Washington, DC: Regnery Publishing, 2021).
5. Jeff Schogol, "Navy Reading List Becomes Latest Battle in the 'Woke Military' War," *Task and Purpose*, May 6, 2022, accessed July 9, 2024, https://taskandpurpose.com/news/navy-reading-list-how-to-be-an-antiracist/.
6. "Remarks by President Biden and Chancellor Scholz of the Federal Republic of Germany at Press Conference," *The White House*, February 7, 2022, accessed July 9, 2024, https://www.whitehouse.gov/briefing-room/statements-releases/2022/02/07/remarks-by-president-biden-and-chancellor-scholz-of-the-federal-republic-of-germany-at-press-conference/.
7. "Opinion: The U.S. is dangerously dependent on China trade, weakening America in any conflict over Taiwan," *MarketWatch*, March 22, 2023, accessed July 9, 2024, https://www.marketwatch.com/story/the-u-s-is-dangerously-dependent-on-china-trade-weakening-america-in-any-conflict-over-taiwan-9b8dfd96.
8. Michelle Makori, "Petrodollar Deal Expires; Why this Could Trigger 'Collapse of Everything' – Andy Schectman part 1/2," *YouTube*, August 10, 2023, accessed July 9, 2024, https://www.youtube.com/watch?v=pjtKeewv7pY.

Chapter 11

1. Loganathan, Paripurnanda, Saravanamuthu Vigneswaran, Jaya Kandasamy, Agnieszka Katarzyna Cuprys, Zakhar Maletskyi, and Harsha Ratnaweera. "Treatment Trends and Combined Methods in Removing Pharmaceuticals and Personal Care Products from Wastewater—A Review." *Membranes* 13, no. 2 (2023): 158. https://doi.org/10.3390/membranes13020158.
2. Pulliam, Susan, Shalini Ramachandran, John West, Coulter Jones, and Thomas Gryta. "America Is Wrapped in Miles of Toxic Lead Cables." *Wall Street Journal*, July 9, 2023. https://www.wsj.com/articles/lead-cables-telecoms-att-toxic-5b34408b.
3. Mehalko, Julia. "Abandoned Water and Oil Wells Are Exploding in Texas, Destroying Land Owners' Properties." *Savvy Dime*, March 8, 2024. https://www.savvydime.com/abandoned-water-and-oil-wells-are-exploding-in-texas-destroying-land-owners-properties.
4. U.S. Geological Survey. "Plugging the Gaps: How the USGS is Working to Fill Data Gaps for Orphaned Oil and Gas Wells." Last modified July 27, 2023. https://www.usgs.gov/news/featured-story/plugging-gaps-how-usgs-working-fill-data-gaps-orphaned-oil-and-gas-wells.
5. James, Ian. "As the Colorado River Shrinks, Federal Officials Consider Overhauling Glen Canyon Dam." *Los Angeles Times*, February 18, 2023. https://www.latimes.com/environment/story/2023-02-18/federal-officials-consider-overhauling-glen-canyon-dam.
6. Phenix, Duncan. "In Nevada, Lakes Mead and Powell Water Levels Rise, but the Runoff Is Slowing." *News Nation*, April 25, 2023. https://www.newsnationnow.com/us-news/west/in-nevada-lakes-mead-powell-water-levels-rise-but-the-runoff-is-slowing/.
7. Stillman, Dan. "The Great Salt Lake Seemed Like It Was Dying. But There's Been a 'Miraculous' Shift." *Washington Post*, April 9, 2023. https://www.washingtonpost.com/weather/2023/04/09/great-salt-lake-snowpack-water-level/.
8. "Emergency Measures Needed to Rescue Great Salt Lake from Ongoing Collapse." *Brigham Young University*, February 2023. https://pws.byu.edu/great-salt-lake.
9. Howell, Elizabeth. "Earth's Groundwater Basins Are Running Out of Water." *Live Science*, July 8, 2015. https://www.livescience.com/51483-groundwater-basins-running-out-of-water.html.

10. The Guardian. "How Vast Solar Farms Are Transforming the Mojave Desert." *The Guardian*, May 21, 2023. https://www.theguardian.com/us-news/2023/may/21/solar-farms-energy-power-california-mojave-desert.
11. Copper Courier. "Corporation's Drilling Could Sink Arizona Towns." *Copper Courier*, December 14, 2023. https://coppercourier.com/2023/12/14/corporation-drilling-sink-arizona-towns/.
12. U.S. Geological Survey. "Groundwater Decline and Depletion." *U.S. Geological Survey Water Science School.* Accessed July 10, 2024. https://www.usgs.gov/special-topics/water-science-school/science/groundwater-decline-and-depletion.
13. U.S. Environmental Protection Agency. "Residential Toilets." *EPA WaterSense.* Accessed July 10, 2024. https://www.epa.gov/watersense/residential-toilets.
14. Grace Communications Foundation. "Home." *Water Calculator.* Accessed July 10, 2024. https://www.watercalculator.org.
15. Kottasová, Ivana. "Dubai's Gigafarm: The Biggest Vertical Farm in the World." *CNN*, July 10, 2024. https://www.cnn.com/world/dubai-gigafarm-biggest-vertical-farm-climate-hnk-spc-int/index.html.
16. Earth.com. "New Hydrogel Can Extract Unlimited Amounts of Water from the Air, Even in Deserts." *Earth.com*, July 10, 2024. https://www.earth.com/news/new-hydrogel-can-extract-unlimited-amounts-of-water-from-the-air-even-in-deserts/.
17. Ocean Conservancy. "U.S. Plastics Pact's List of Problematic Items to be Eliminated." *Ocean Conservancy*, January 2022. https://www.oceanconservancy.org.
18. End Plastic Waste. "Recycling, Processing, and Collecting Plastics." *End Plastic Waste.* https://www.endplasticwaste.org.
19. Pew Charitable Trusts. "Preventing Ocean Plastics" and "Breaking the Plastic Wave." *Pew Charitable Trusts.* https://www.pewtrusts.org.
20. TWI Ltd. "What are the Pros and Cons of Hydrogen Fuel Cells?" *TWI*, accessed July 10, 2024. https://www.twi-global.com/technical-knowledge/faqs/what-are-the-pros-and-cons-of-hydrogen-fuel-cells.
21. Lloyd, Christy. "Toyota Hydrogen Fuel Cell Technology: Everything to Know." *Top Speed*, accessed July 10, 2024. https://www.topspeed.com/toyota-hydrogen-fuel-cell-technology-everything-to-know/.

22. Revell, Eric. "EVs May Make Air Dirtier than Gas-Powered Cars as California Pushes New Mandates: Study." *Fox Business*, March 5, 2024. https://www.foxbusiness.com/technology/evs-make-air-dirtier-gas-powered-cars-california-pushes-new-mandates.
23. Hardman, Scott, and Gil Tal. "Why Some Electric Car Owners Return to Gas." *Nature Energy*, 2021. https://www.nature.com/articles/s41560-021-00814-9.
24. Reedy, Jake. "Toyota's New Lithium-Ion EV Batteries Could Be a Game Changer." *MotorBiscuit*, accessed July 10, 2024. https://www.motorbiscuit.com/toyota-lithium-evs/.
25. Lloyd, Christy. "10 Ways Solid-State Batteries Will Change EVs Forever." *Top Speed*, accessed July 10, 2024. https://www.topspeed.com/10-ways-solid-state-batteries-will-change-evs-forever/.
26. Seymour, Nicole. "Toyota Study Shows We Don't Need EVs to Dramatically Lower Carbon Emissions." *CarBuzz*, accessed July 10, 2024. https://carbuzz.com/news/toyota-study-shows-we-dont-need-evs-to-dramatically-lower-carbon-emissions/.
27. Martenson, Chris. *The Crash Course: An Honest Approach to Facing the Future of Our Economy, Energy, and Environment.* Revised Edition. Hoboken: Wiley, 2023.
28. Puplava, James J. "The Beginning of the End Part III: Green Energy Realities." *Financial Sense*, October 5, 2023. https://www.financialsense.com/blog/20704/beginning-end-part-iii-green-energy-realities.
29. "Daniel Turner." *Power the Future*. Accessed July 12, 2024. https://powerthefuture.com/directors/daniel-turner/.
30. Cheang, Ming. "China and India Can't Wean Themselves Off Coal Anytime Soon." *CNBC*, January 11, 2024. https://www.cnbc.com/2024/01/11/china-and-india-cant-wean-themselves-off-coal-anytime-soon.html#:~:text=While%20China%20is%20the%20world's,strive%20to%20fuel%20economic%20growth.
31. Singer, S. Fred. *Hot Talk, Cold Science: Global Warming's Unfinished Debate.* 3rd ed. Oakland: Independent Institute, 2021.
32. Lomborg, Bjorn. "Point: No Need to Panic on Climate Change." *DC Journal*, September 14, 2023. https://dcjournal.com/point-no-need-to-panic-on-climate-change/.
33. Athrappully, Naveen. "Over 1,600 Scientists and Professionals Sign 'No Climate Emergency' Declaration." *The Epoch Times*, August 29, 2023.

https://www.theepochtimes.com/science/over-1600-scientists-sign-no-climate-emergency-declaration-5482554.

34. Biden, Joe, and Olaf Scholz. "Remarks by President Biden and Chancellor Scholz of the Federal Republic of Germany at Press Conference." The White House, February 7, 2022. https://www.whitehouse.gov/briefing-room/statements-releases/2022/02/07/remarks-by-president-biden-and-chancellor-scholz-of-the-federal-republic-of-germany-at-press-conference/.

35. "Scientists Just Discovered an Astonishing Way to Solve a Major Environmental Problem." *Yahoo! Tech*, July 12, 2024. https://www.yahoo.com/tech/scientists-just-discovered-astonishing-way-103000591.html.

36. "Zero Carbon Dioxide Emissions from Successful Production of Ammonia-Based Clean Hydrogen." *Energy Central*, accessed July 12, 2024. https://energycentral.com/c/cp/zero-carbon-dioxide-emissions-successful-production-ammonia-based-clean-hydrogen.

37. "Floating Solar Reduces Water Evaporation in Brazilian Reservoir by 60%." *pv magazine International*, February 6, 2023. https://www.pv-magazine.com/2023/02/06/floating-solar-reduces-water-evaporation-in-brazilian-reservoir-by-60/.

38. Domonoske, Camila. "New Battery Technology That Could Help Store Energy for the Grid is Struggling to Scale Up in China." *NPR*, August 3, 2022. https://www.npr.org/2022/08/03/1114964240/new-battery-technology-china-vanadium.

39. Stefan, Dana. "Half of Germany's Electricity Needed for Lufthansa to Use 100% SAF, Says CEO." *Travel Tomorrow*, September 29, 2023. https://traveltomorrow.com/half-of-germanys-electricity-needed-for-lufthansa-to-use-100-saf-says-ceo/.

40. Cox, Simon. "Nuclear Fusion Energy Could Be on Britain's Grid Sooner Than You Think." *The Telegraph*, March 13, 2024. https://www.telegraph.co.uk/business/2024/03/13/nuclear-fusion-energy-britain-grid-sooner-than-you-think/.

41. Chandler, David L. "Tests Show High-Temperature Superconducting Magnets Are Ready for Fusion." *MIT News*, March 4, 2024. https://news.mit.edu/2024/tests-show-high-temperature-superconducting-magnets-fusion-ready-0304.

42. Chandler, David L. "MIT-designed Project Achieves Major Advance Toward Fusion Energy." *MIT News*, September 8, 2021. https://news.mit.edu/2021/MIT-CFS-major-advance-toward-fusion-energy-0908.

43. Rubinkam, Michael. "Biden Administration Announces Plans for Hydrogen Hubs in Pennsylvania and West Virginia." *AP News*, October 13, 2023. https://apnews.com/article/hydrogen-hubs-energy-biden-climate-pennsylvania-west-virginia-d609a455a6dd018fca5af785f245c6fd.
44. Schmidt, Rachael. "Wisconsin Energy Storage Project Receives $9 Million to Help Store Carbon Dioxide." *The Cool Down*, March 8, 2023. https://www.thecooldown.com/green-tech/columbia-energy-storage-project-wisconsin-carbon-dioxide-grant/.
45. Vyas, Kashyap. "This Technology Turns CO_2 Into Useful Chemicals and Fuels." *Interesting Engineering*, May 1, 2023. https://interestingengineering.com/innovation/tech-turns-CO2-into-chemicals.
46. Kaufman, Alexander C. "The U.S. Bets Big on Small Nuclear Reactors as Energy Future." *HuffPost*, January 9, 2024. https://www.huffpost.com/entry/small-nuclear-reactors-energy_n_649f055be4b0c7e9d8e723e8.